CHARLOTTESVILLE

ALSO BY DEBORAH BAKER

CHARLOTTESVILLE

AN AMERICAN STORY

DEBORAH BAKER

Graywolf Press

Published by Graywolf Press
212 Third Avenue North, Suite 485
Minneapolis, Minnesota 55401

www.graywolfpress.org

Published in the United States of America
Printed in Canada

ISBN 978-1-64445-341-4 (cloth)
ISBN 978-1-64445-342-1 (ebook)

2 4 6 8 9 7 5 3 1
First Graywolf Printing, 2025

Library of Congress Cataloging-in-Publication Data

Names: Baker, Deborah, 1959– author.
Title: Charlottesville : an American story / Deborah Baker.
Description: Minneapolis, Minnesota : Graywolf Press, [2025] | Includes
    bibliographical references and index.
Identifiers: LCCN 2024048137 (print) | LCCN 2024048138 (ebook) |
    ISBN 9781644453414 (cloth) | ISBN 9781644453421 (ebook)
Subjects: LCSH: Unite the Right Rally, Charlottesville, Va., 2017. |
    Riots—Virginia—Charlottesville—History—21st century. | Protest
    movements—Virginia—Charlottesville. | White supremacy movements—
    Virginia—Charlottesville. | Soldiers' monuments—Social aspects—
    Virginia—Charlottesville. | Charlottesville (Va.)—History—21st century. |
    United States—History—Civil War, 1861–1865—Monuments—Social aspects.
Classification: LCC F234.C47 B35 2025 (print) | LCC F234.C47 (ebook) |
    DDC 975.5/481—dc23/eng/20250124
LC record available at https://lccn.loc.gov/2024048137
LC ebook record available at https://lccn.loc.gov/2024048138

Jacket design: Kyle G. Hunter

Jacket art: vintage postcard (top); photo courtesy of Ézé Amos (bottom)

Maps: Jeffrey L. Ward

For Nayan

We have to do with the past only as we can make it useful to the present and to the future.

Frederick Douglass, "What to the Slave Is the Fourth of July?"

CONTENTS

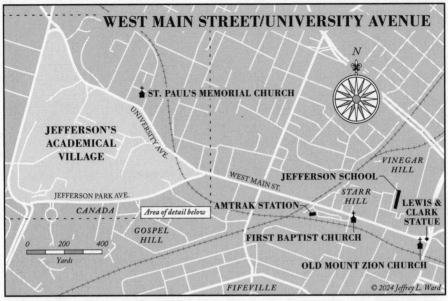

WEST MAIN STREET/UNIVERSITY AVENUE

N

✝ ST. PAUL'S MEMORIAL CHURCH

JEFFERSON'S ACADEMICAL VILLAGE

UNIVERSITY AVE.

VINEGAR HILL

WEST MAIN ST. **JEFFERSON SCHOOL**

STARR HILL

JEFFERSON PARK AVE.

CANADA **AMTRAK STATION**

LEWIS & CLARK STATUE

Area of detail below

GOSPEL HILL **FIRST BAPTIST CHURCH**

0 200 400
Yards

OLD MOUNT ZION CHURCH

FIFEVILLE © 2024 Jeffrey L. Ward

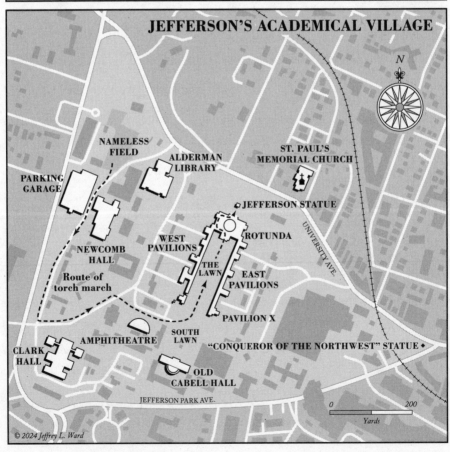

JEFFERSON'S ACADEMICAL VILLAGE

N

NAMELESS FIELD

ALDERMAN LIBRARY

ST. PAUL'S MEMORIAL CHURCH

PARKING GARAGE

🏛 **JEFFERSON STATUE**

UNIVERSITY AVE.

WEST PAVILIONS **ROTUNDA**

NEWCOMB HALL

THE LAWN

EAST PAVILIONS

Route of torch march

PAVILION X

AMPHITHEATRE **SOUTH LAWN**

CLARK HALL

"CONQUEROR OF THE NORTHWEST" STATUE ◆

OLD CABELL HALL

JEFFERSON PARK AVE.

0 200
Yards

© 2024 Jeffrey L. Ward

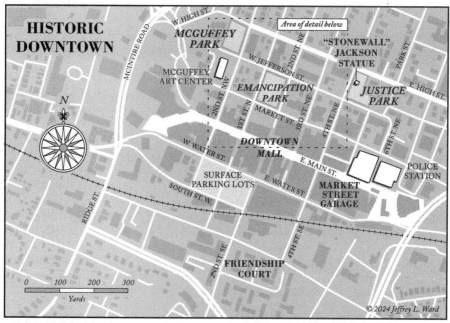

HISTORIC DOWNTOWN

Area of detail below

N

McINTIRE ROAD

W. HIGH ST.

MCGUFFEY PARK

MCGUFFEY ART CENTER

W. JEFFERSON ST.

2ND ST. NW

2ND ST. NE

PARK ST.

"STONEWALL" JACKSON STATUE

EMANCIPATION PARK

1ST ST. N

MARKET ST. N

3RD ST. NE

JUSTICE PARK

E. HIGH ST.

W. WATER ST.

DOWNTOWN MALL

4TH ST. NE

6TH ST. NE

SURFACE PARKING LOTS

E. WATER ST.

E. MAIN ST.

MARKET STREET GARAGE

POLICE STATION

SOUTH ST. W.

RIDGE ST.

2ND ST. SE

4TH ST. SE

FRIENDSHIP COURT

0   100   200   300

Yards

© 2024 Jeffrey L. Ward

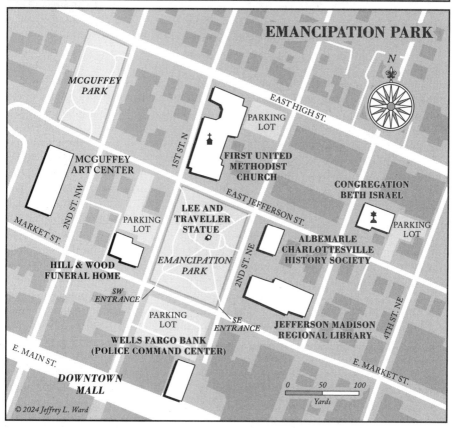

EMANCIPATION PARK

N

MCGUFFEY PARK

MCGUFFEY ART CENTER

EAST HIGH ST.

PARKING LOT

1ST ST. N

FIRST UNITED METHODIST CHURCH

CONGREGATION BETH ISRAEL

PARKING LOT

2ND ST. NW

MARKET ST.

PARKING LOT

EAST JEFFERSON ST.

LEE AND TRAVELLER STATUE

2ND ST. NE

ALBEMARLE CHARLOTTESVILLE HISTORY SOCIETY

4TH ST. NE

EMANCIPATION PARK

HILL & WOOD FUNERAL HOME

SW ENTRANCE

PARKING LOT

SE ENTRANCE

JEFFERSON MADISON REGIONAL LIBRARY

E. MAIN ST.

WELLS FARGO BANK (POLICE COMMAND CENTER)

E. MARKET ST.

DOWNTOWN MALL

0   50   100

Yards

© 2024 Jeffrey L. Ward

CAST OF CHARACTERS

Blue Ribbon Commission on Race, Memorials, and Public Spaces

Dr. Andrea Douglas, "the Art Historian," founding executive director of the Jefferson School African American Heritage Center, commissioner, cofounder of Swords into Plowshares

Don Gathers, "the Deacon," chair of the Blue Ribbon Commission, cofounder of Charlottesville chapter of Black Lives Matter

Lewis Martin III, lawyer, statues Defender, member of the Deplorables, plus Jane

Prof. John Edwin Mason, "the Professor," vice-chair of the Blue Ribbon Commission

Margaret O'Bryant, "Old Virginia," director of the Albemarle Charlottesville Historical Society, commissioner

Jalane Schmidt, leader of the 52 percent faction calling for the statues' removal, cofounder of Charlottesville chapter of Black Lives Matter, professor of religious studies, later cofounder of Swords into Plowshares

Activists

Grace Aheron, founder of Charis intentional community, later leader of Showing Up for Racial Justice, Puppetistas

Niya Bates, mentor to middle schooler Zyahna Bryant, public historian, member of NAACP

Wendy Baucom, founding member of Showing Up for Racial Justice and member of Congregate

Marissa Blair, friend of Heather Heyer, fiancée of Marcus Martin, plaintiff in *Sines v. Kessler* case

Zyahna Bryant, initiated petition to remove the statues of Lee and Jackson from their respective parks, great-granddaughter of desegregationist Thelma Townsend

Courtney Commander, activist, friend of Heather Heyer

Tony Crider, activist, Facebook livestreamer, photographer, physicist, husband to Megan Squire

Lisa Draine, activist and arts administrator, mother of Sophie and Rebecca

Emily Gorcenski, data scientist and anti-fascist

Heather Heyer, friend and coworker of Marissa Blair and Courtney Commander

DeAndre Harris, hip-hop artist, special education teacher's aide, victim of Market Street garage attack

Vizena Howard, president of 10th and Page neighborhood association, anti-gentrification activist, grandmother to Zyahna Bryant

Daryle Lamont Jenkins, anti-fascist founder of One People's Project

Will Jones III, barber, unofficial security to Wes Bellamy

Corey Long, activist with flamethrower

Marcus Martin, fiancé of Marissa Blair, plaintiff in *Sines v. Kessler*

Bekah Menning, cofounder of Showing Up for Racial Justice, member of Congregate Cville and clergy line

Rosia Parker, member of Charlottesville chapter of Black Lives Matter

Star Peterson, teacher, member of Showing Up for Racial Justice, medic at Jefferson statue, victim of car attack

Clare Ruday, ally of Richmond chapter of Black Lives Matter, nurse

Megan Squire, computer scientist and activist out of Graham, North Carolina

Andy Stepanian, media liaison for Congregate Cville

Katrina Turner, member of Charlottesville chapter of Black Lives Matter

Clergy and Members of the Clergy Line

Rev. Lehman Bates, member of Charlottesville Clergy Collective and minister at Ebenezer Baptist Church

Rev. Dr. Traci Blackmon, gave sermon at St. Paul's Memorial Church on the night of August 11th, Senior Pastor of Christ the King United Church of Christ in Florissant, Missouri

Rev. Brenda Brown-Grooms, member of Charlottesville Clergy Collective, copastor of New Beginnings Christian Community, friend of Holly Edwards

Rev. Brittainy Caine-Conley, aka "Smash," cofounder of Congregate Cville, member of Sojourners United Church of Christ

Brandy Daniels, UVA postdoc in theology

Rev. Alvin Edwards, founder of the Charlottesville Clergy Collective, minister at Mount Zion Baptist Church

Beth Foster, anti-racist from Chattanooga, ally of Daryle Lamont Jenkins

Rabbi Tom Gutherz, rabbi of Congregation Beth Israel

Apostle Sarah Kelley, member of Charlottesville Clergy Collective and founder of Faith, Hope, and Love Church of Deliverance

Bee Lambert, atheist, former member of Student Non-Violent Coordinating Committee

Eric Martin, member of Congregate Cville, Catholic Worker

Rev. Dr. Jeff Pugh, member of Congregate, professor of religious studies, Elon University, minister

Rev. Osagyefo Uhuru Sekou, author, musician, led nonviolent direct action workshops for Congregate Cville

Ann Marie Smith, Buddhist, member of Congregate Cville and Charis

Rev. Elaine Ellis Thomas, member of the Charlottesville Clergy Collective, Congregate Cville, associate pastor of St. Paul's Memorial Church

Rev. Seth Wispelwey, cofounder of Congregate Cville, member of Sojourners United Church of Christ

Rev. Tracy Howe Wispelwey, musician, member of Congregate Cville and Sojourners United Church of Christ

Rev. Phil Woodson, member of Charlottesville Clergy Collective, Congregate Cville, associate pastor of First United Methodist Church

At the Jefferson Statue

Anonymous students, anti-fascists, members of Black Lives Matter, professors

Caroline Bray, activist, fourth-year UVA student, Charlottesville native
Kristopher Goad, Richmond anti-fascist
Tyler Magill, DJ at WTJU
Natalie Romero, activist, second-year UVA student, plaintiff in *Sines v. Kessler*
Sophie, activist, fourth-year UVA student, native of Charlottesville
Elizabeth Sines, UVA law student, lead plaintiff in *Sines v. Kessler*
Devin Willis, second-year UVA student, member of Black Student Union, plaintiff in *Sines v. Kessler*

City of Charlottesville and Commonwealth of Virginia
Dr. Wes Bellamy, vice-mayor, professor
Dr. Holly Edwards, former vice-mayor, parish nurse of low-income housing estate
Bob Fenwick, city councillor
Kathy Galvin, city councillor
Maurice Jones, Charlottesville city manager
Terry McAuliffe, governor of Virginia
Mike Signer, mayor of Charlottesville
Kristin Szakos, former vice-mayor, first to propose Charlottesville consider removal of Confederate statues
Al Thomas, chief, Charlottesville Police Department
Nikuyah Walker, protégée of Holly Edwards, later first Black woman mayor of Charlottesville

University of Virginia
Mike Gibson, chief, University Police Department
Bonnie Gordon, music professor and viola player
Teresa Sullivan, president

Journalists
Sandi Bachom, livestreamer from New York
Katie Couric, Nat Geo documentary filmmaker, former TV journalist, UVA alumna
Ford Fischer, News2Share

Blake Montgomery, Buzzfeed News

Vegas Tenold, journalist and author of *Everything You Love Will Burn*, an account of the years he spent shadowing the far right

Jon Ziegler, Rebelutionary Live TV

White supremacists, white nationalists, neo-Nazis, neo-Confederates, Ku Klux Klan members

Andrew Anglin, defendant in *Sines v. Kessler*, editor of Daily Stormer

Christopher and Amanda Barker, Loyal White Knights of the Ku Klux Klan

Christopher Cantwell, defendant in *Sines v. Kessler*, *Radical Agenda* podcast host

Nathan Damigo, defendant in *Sines v. Kessler*, founder of Identity Evropa

James Alex Fields Jr., defendant in *Sines v. Kessler*, convicted murderer, perpetrator of car attack

Brad Griffin, Southern nationalist, owner of the blog *Occidental Dissent*

Michael Heimbach, defendant in *Sines v. Kessler*, founder of Traditionalist Worker Party

Dr. Michael Hill, defendant in *Sines v. Kessler*, founder of the League of the South

Dillon Hopper, defendant in *Sines v. Kessler*, founder of Vanguard America

Augustus Sol Invictus, defendant in *Sines v. Kessler*, coauthor of Spencer's "Charlottesville Statement," member of Proud Boys' Fraternal Order of the Alt-Knights. Real name, Austin Mitchel Gillespie

Jason Kessler, defendant in *Sines v. Kessler*, principal organizer of the Unite the Right rally

Elliott Kline, aka "Eli Mosley," defendant in *Sines v. Kessler*, organizer of August 11 torch march

Mike "Enoch" Peinovich, proprietor of TheRightStuff website, host of *The Daily Shoah* podcast

Richard Wilson Preston, Confederate White Knight, a Maryland Klavern

Robert Ray, aka "Azzmador," defendant in *Sines v. Kessler*, host of the podcast *The Krypto Report*, Daily Stormer

Thomas Rousseau, defendant in *Sines v. Kessler*, usurped Dillon Hopper's leadership of Vanguard America, later rebranded as Patriot Front

Jeff Schoep, defendant in *Sines v. Kessler*, National Socialist Movement, founder of Nationalist Front

Richard Spencer, defendant in *Sines v. Kessler*, founder of National Policy Institute

Michael Tubbs, defendant in *Sines v. Kessler*, national chairman of League of the South

Sacco Vandal, author of "In Defense of White Sharia," Mosley's lieutenant during August 11 torch march

Interludes

Sarah Patton Boyle, Charlottesville housewife, author of *The Desegregated Heart*

Harry F. Byrd, former governor of Virginia, US Senator

Colgate Darden, former governor, UVA president during era of Massive Resistance

John Kasper, Columbia University graduate, protégé of Ezra Pound, rabble rouser

T. S. Eliot, poet, author of *The Waste Land*, gave a series of lectures at UVA in 1933

Thurgood Marshall, chief counsel of the NAACP's Legal Defense and Educational Fund

Edward O. McCue Jr., Virginia state senator, member of the Defenders of State Sovereignty and Individual Liberties

Edward McCue III, son of McCue Jr.

Ezra Pound, poet, translator, and literary impresario. Author of *The Cantos* and *Jefferson and/or Mussolini: Fascism as I Have Seen It*

T. J. Sellers, founding editor of *Charlottesville Albemarle Tribune*, later managing editor of *Amsterdam News*

Gregory Swanson, first African American to attend UVA law school

CHARLOTTESVILLE

INTRODUCTION

It was Mother's Day weekend. The weather was gorgeous. The dog-woods dotting the streets of downtown were in their last blooms. Final exams at the University of Virginia were over and commencement was a week away. In a deconsecrated church on Market Street that Saturday, a spirited debate was taking place between two Democratic candidates for governor. Catty-corner to the church, in Lee Park, the annual, family-friendly Festival of Cultures was underway. Tables were filled with foods from the many immigrant communities that made Charlottesville their home. At 11:00 a.m. a group of 150 men, many dressed in white polo shirts and khaki pants, entered the park, along with ten women in white dresses. Their behavior was disconcerting in a way that only made sense later.

Around noon they set off again from a playground and park one block west and two blocks north of Lee Park, unfurling their various flags as they hit East High. Only the Confederate battle flags would have been readily identified. A man named Richard Spencer, shadowed by a security detail, led the procession to Court Square, a few minutes away. Word soon got out that something weird was happening near the courthouse. Spencer had just begun his speech when the news reached the reporters covering the candidates' debate.

"This is the beginning of a movement," Spencer shouted through a bullhorn. "This is the beginning of an awakening here in Charlottesville, an awakening that is going around the entire world."

Spencer may have planned to give his speech in Lee Park, but that was where the Festival of Cultures was taking place. Jackson Park in Court Square was an adequate substitute. Spencer, who had just turned thirty-nine, was a white nationalist, and Court Square enhanced his nationalist themes. Albemarle Country boasted three Founding Fathers and all of them—Thomas Jefferson, James Madison, and James Monroe—were said to have frequented a Court Square tavern on market days. Also, the focal point of the square and the half-acre park adjoining it, was a statue of another Confederate general: Thomas Jonathan "Stonewall" Jackson mounted on his horse, Little Sorrel.

Nonetheless, it was the statue of Robert E. Lee in Lee Park that provided the professed reason for Spencer's Charlottesville visit. Many of the men accompanying him carried posters featuring the Lee monument. After a recent and controversial city council vote to find the statue a new home, a circuit court judge had issued an injunction to delay its removal for six months. Into this local tempest rode Richard Spencer on his own high white horse.

For ten years, Richard Spencer had hawked his dream of a white America at conferences here and in Europe, backed in large part by a seventy-seven-year-old scion of the Regnery publishing empire named William Regnery II. Regnery had poured his considerable wealth into the institutes, societies, publishing arms, colloquia, speakers' fees, dinners, hotel rooms, and bar bills of a far-right brain trust, including Spencer's National Policy Institute, which he cofounded. "My support has produced a much greater bang for the buck," Regnery boasted in 2017, than anything produced by "the brothers Koch or Soros, Inc."

White nationalists and advocates for white civil rights like Richard Spencer had begun seeing their star rise in the summer of 2015, two years before, when Donald J. Trump began his hostile takeover of the Republican Party. As with Trump, the more the mainstream liberal media tried to lampoon their thought leaders of this brain trust, the more heads it grew. In an article on the rise of the far right, a veteran *New Yorker* journalist suggested that men like Spencer were living in an alternate reality where white Americans faced imminent extinction, the South was preparing to secede, and Donald Trump was going to be president.

With Trump's election the following year, this alternate reality abruptly replaced the one the *New Yorker* journalist and I lived in. Suddenly Richard Spencer had the answer to the question of the moment: What did we miss? He became the talking head everyone needed. Then, on the day of Trump's inauguration, while Spencer was explaining the significance of his Pepe the Frog lapel pin to a film crew, a masked man came up and clocked him. The resulting video went viral on Twitter, YouTube, Facebook, and broadcast media. The remixes, with background music from Joy Division ("Love Will Tear Us Apart"), Radiohead ("Just"), Wu Tang Clan ("Bring Da Ruckus"), and countless others, also went viral. Spencer came to Charlottesville to stage his revenge.

A 2001 graduate of the University of Virginia, Spencer knew the city well. I imagine his thinking went something like this: Charlottesville wasn't Chicago. It wasn't Baltimore. It was soft. The Black community, which had been divided over whether the Lee statue should be moved, was too beleaguered to pose much of a threat. But the city was overrun with his target audience—white progressives, left-leaning university faculty, and impressionable students who could be counted on to kick up a fuss. That fuss would, in turn, ruffle the complacent country club and horsey set, the church folk, and the Cavalier-mad UVA alumni who had never quite left behind their college days. There was the PR-conscious university administration, a Jewish mayor with high-flying political ambitions, and the publicity-hungry Black vice-mayor who had chosen the Lee statue as his signature issue. Finally, there was the picture-perfect city itself. Spencer clearly relished every incendiary word he dropped into the still pond of that spring afternoon.

To the men who accompanied him that day, he spoke of their need to find meaning and identity. Of their desire to be part of a movement, part of a story, a story of ideas. Those listening filled his chestnut exhortations with their unfocussed yearnings. "Our ideas have power." (We have power.) "Nothing can stop an idea whose time has come." (Nothing can stop us. Our time has come.) Spencer's inflection rose with each refrain.

"They are trying to take away our gods. They are trying to take away our ideals. They are trying to take away who we are," he declaimed.

"And in the stead of these monuments, god knows what they're going to erect: some monument to *death*, some monument to slavery and the Holocaust. . . . They want to memorialize *equality*."

He shifted to a more belligerent tone. "We will not be replaced from this world! Whites have a future! We have a future of power! Of beauty! Of expression! A greater civilization than what our ancestors were capable of! That is *our* future! That is *your* future!" With his voice rising in volume and quickening in cadence, he alluded to the city council vote to remove the Lee statue. "They want to put us in a museum!" he shouted.

He hit all the notes, many more than once. Everyone erupted in huzzahs. The rebel spirit of the Confederacy rose again. Or something like that. Channel 29 showed up in time to capture the crowd chanting, "They will not replace us, they will not replace us!"

Spencer had left by the time a dozen or so local activists showed up. They were met by men chanting "Hasta la vista, *antifascista*" and were soon surrounded. A man in a kippah was assailed with slurs. An altercation left one activist on the ground. The police arrived and ordered everyone to disperse. Activists trailed the rump procession out of the park shouting, "Racists get out of here!" in reply to persistent questions about where all their Black friends were. The route took the men past a synagogue where a bat mitzvah was underway. They strolled down Market Street toward their cars at the bottom of the hill. By 3:30 p.m. they were gone.

Around 10 p.m. that evening Alison Wrabel, a reporter from the *Daily Progress*, Charlottesville's local paper, was walking back from an evening out when she saw a long line of men with torches heading toward the now empty Lee Park. Perhaps the procession had something to do with UVA's upcoming commencement, a man standing nearby ventured. Chants of "Blood and soil" echoed in the night. Wrabel took a cell-phone video and posted it on Twitter with the caption "Lee Park right now."

After the torches were extinguished, her phone picked up the chants "No more brother wars" and "You will not replace us." A lone streetlight and the illuminated steeple of First United Methodist Church lit up the dark. Then the men launched into singing "Dixie" and "Tomorrow Belongs to Me," the song sung by Hitler Youth in *Cabaret*.

Wes Bellamy, Charlottesville's young vice-mayor, was just returning to town when his phone started going off. Wrabel's video clip had gone viral.

When I came across it the next day, I called my eighty-eight-year-old mother from my home in New York. "Happy Mother's Day," I said. "What on earth is going on down there?"

After "Charlottesville," which is how the Unite the Right rally that took place three months later came to be known (at least to those who don't live there), I couldn't stop thinking about it. A woman named Heather Heyer had been killed when a car sped down a narrow street and rammed into a crowd of counterprotesters. Watching the footage of the August 12 rally and the torch march that preceded it, I was spooked by how gleeful these men looked, and alarmed at how young they were. Were they, like the election of Donald Trump, a harbinger of some future I was too old or ill-equipped to grasp? Was "Charlottesville" simply their opening salvo? I wondered how the events of those days would be explained by the future. Though it would be years before I came upon the clip of Spencer speaking in Jackson Park, I was already asking myself what kind of awakening was underway.

Cataclysmic events may at first appear entirely unforeseen, but they don't come out of the blue. The ground has been prepared for them; the path clear only in retrospect. In this way, August 12, 2017, the day of the Unite the Right rally, reminded me of the September 11 attack on New York, a city I had called home since graduating from the University of Virginia in 1981. So I asked myself, what hadn't I understood about the city I was born in? Which chapters in history had I not truly reckoned with? Virginia had seen more Civil War battles than any other state and paid the steepest price in blood and treasure. But I was hard pressed to see the connection between Charlottesville's Confederate statues and Hitler Youth, between Southern white supremacy and European fascism. Which histories—*whose* histories—were in play? How far back did I need to go? It felt as though American and European national creeds were being remixed and weaponized in ways I couldn't wrap my mind around.

Trump's election, too, had left me stranded in the present, looking for the signs I had missed, and wondering what sort of future America was being taken to. For Civil War historians, Trump was reawakening the "giant sleeping dragon of American history." For historians of fascism, Trump was following a script they'd spent their lives studying. Attacks on the press, the judiciary, political opponents, foreigners, and foreign influence were familiar and distinct keynotes in Mussolini's rise to power. Trump's affinity for dictators and strongmen, the incendiary mass rallies promoting a cult of personality, and the explicit incitement of mob and state violence provided more substance to the charge. And when he came to power, he didn't hide his contempt for international institutions; he scrapped treaties, long-standing agreements, and time-honored democratic norms.

I wondered if fascism was limited to a distinct historical period, or if it was a part of human nature, rearing its ugly head when conditions warranted. Were its seeds to be found in the fateful contradictions of our founding documents and the Faustian bargain we struck over the institution of slavery? Or were they rooted in the flawed character of Thomas Jefferson himself? The nature of this awakening appeared to go to the core of who we are and the myths and folklore that have sustained us as a nation.

On the second anniversary of the Unite the Right rally, I traveled to Charlottesville and heard a woman give a sermon in First Baptist Church on West Main Street, a church founded in 1863 by freed African Americans. First Baptist hosted many ministers that evening, representing a wide array of religious traditions, but this sixty-four-year-old pastor seemed to stand apart, mounting the stairs with difficulty, wielding her cane like a queen with her scepter. She didn't speak of the rally. She described the future, not the past, and gave it a fearful shape and coherence. Listening to her, I had moments of recognition, but they were interrupted by panicked, involuntary denials, preventing me from seeing as far or as clearly as she did.

By the time I met Rev. Brenda Brown-Grooms a couple of months later, a wariness and weariness had set in around the entire subject of August 12. This was particularly true when it came to outsiders asking questions that elicited answers they weren't ready to hear. Outsiders who were often insensible to the pain they caused simply by asking. Back then I hoped this woman could put an end to my questions and that would be that. What had she taken away from the events of 2017? What did she think they meant? Not just for Charlottesville but for everyone.

Rev. Brown-Grooms didn't believe some forgotten chapter of history might throw light on why Charlottesville had been chosen. She didn't need to time travel to Hitler's Munich or Mussolini's Rome. Nobody was surprised by the appearance of these men, she said. And then she looked at me and paused, as if she realized she was talking to a child. "Nobody Black or brown was surprised. Why would we be? We live with that all the time. We kept hearing stuff like 'these people are outsiders.' No, they're not. They live here. Walmart is their headquarters. They are buying guns and toting them and pointing them. They have a lovely time."

Pastor Brenda didn't need to know the history; the present provided evidence enough. Richard Spencer and his brothers represented America's most indelible commitment. The *Daily Progress* might put "white supremacy" in quotation marks, as if its existence was purely theoretical, but for Rev. Brown-Grooms white supremacy was the lie America couldn't stop telling itself. White people knew it, she said, and so did people of color. Otherwise, why would they need to rig the game? "Why keep changing the goal posts, if we aren't already as good or better? Why the rage? Why the cheating. Why the lying?"

In those days, I had no intention of writing about Unite the Right. I work in archives and write about people, generally long dead, who lived in historical periods I believed I understood. Besides, I hadn't lived in Charlottesville since the 1990s. How well did I really know the city and its residents? I was also wary of giving far-right luminaries attention or nourishing their sense of self-importance. I worried about how my parents and siblings, who lived in Albemarle County, would respond. Lastly, I hadn't been there.

Later, I asked myself. Was this what Rev. Brown-Grooms expected of a white woman? I kept coming back to her words. When they dragged the Tallahatchie for Emmett Till, she said, they kept coming up with Black bodies. The difference now, she said, is phone cameras. Raw footage has made the ugliness and the lies inescapable. I began wondering what a Unite the Right archive would look like. Beyond phone footage, there would be tweets, livestreams, podcasts, time-stamped photographs, video blogs, emails, texts, and message boards. An independent media collective called Unicorn Riot had posted an enormous trove of Unite the Right chat logs. Using this trove, a massive court case, *Sines v. Kessler*, was being brought against the rally's principal organizers by those injured that weekend. More material would doubtless be unearthed in discovery. Could I portray these men without sensationalizing them? What did I owe the victims of that weekend beyond an honest effort? Whose stories would I focus on? I weighed these questions for a long time.

This I knew from the outset. There were not, as President Trump had said, "very fine people, on both sides." Among those on the street where Heather Heyer was killed were individuals who had known something awful was going to happen; people who had done their best to prepare themselves and the city. For their trouble, they were dismissed as alarmists and viewed with annoyance. They were given lectures on the First Amendment and dressed down on their language and behavior. Worst of all, like latter-day Cassandras, they were seen by the university, city officials, and law enforcement to constitute a threat, perhaps a violent threat, to civil order. And then, after it was all over, they were blamed for having been on the streets at all. They are still blamed, more quietly now, compounding the traumas they carry.

I wanted to know who they were, what they believed, and what lessons they learned. I wanted to understand why their warnings fell on deaf ears. So, this book ended up being more about these lonely prophets than the likes of Richard Spencer. They don't have made-up names, they don't carry flags or sport similar haircuts, and they don't speak in ways calculated to offend. I believed knowing something of them might better prepare the rest of us for a future in which the certainties of the past no longer apply.

There is a direct path from the Unite the Right rally of August 12, 2017, to the Stop the Steal insurrection of January 6, 2021. As I researched this book, many more towns and cities in America began seeing armed vigilantes staging rallies and protests, protecting their God-given right to this or that, including their right to threaten unarmed people. Much like school shootings, these clashes began to seem par for the course. The dark money seeding their efforts has found its way into our national politics. I watched the governor of Virginia declare war on "divisive history," while African American fiction and history and young adult books touching on queer sexuality were removed from library shelves. Entire curricula were outlawed. Many found themselves unprepared, struggling to ask themselves how well they knew the place where they have lived their lives, their neighbors, their own hearts.

The story Charlottesville tells about itself has long been central to the uplifting one America tells of its beginnings. The people who prepared for the arrival of these men knew a less flattering and far messier one. I asked myself, who might recast this story? Can we find a different path from the one we are traveling down, with our increasing civil unrest and ever widening political divisions? Would the city of Charlottesville play a role in this re-envisioning? Or would this bleak chapter be willfully forgotten, as so much of America's dark history has been.

Here is the story of Virginia I was taught as a schoolchild. In the mid-seventeenth century, a century after Virginia's first colonies were established, English settlers began traveling inland from the Chesapeake Bay and peninsular Tidewater regions. Those who traveled by way of Virginia's longest river, the 348-mile-long James, cut a path across central Virginia that ended at its headwaters in the Blue Ridge Mountains. The Rivanna, a forty-two-mile tributary of the James, traces the eastern edge of Charlottesville, delineating the city limits from the surrounding countryside. Thomas Jefferson considered Albemarle County, where he built his beloved Monticello on a mountain overlooking the city, to be America's true birthplace. It was here, on this mountain, that the animating ideas behind the Declaration of Independence took form. Like the settlers who had preceded him, including his father, Peter, Jefferson hungered to expand this Eden west across the continent. This holy land of liberty was "a garden of boundless fertility" that "belonged in white hands."

In my fourth-grade textbook, *Virginia: History, Government, and Geography* (1961), commissioned by Virginia politicians in the midfifties, with distinct editions tailored for elementary, middle school, and high school grade levels, the origins of Virginia were invariably framed as the origins of the nation. This was irrespective of any such claims made by the French, or the Spaniards who founded St. Augustine in 1565, and who likely considered these English colonizers squatters and bandits. But in this sharply Anglo-Saxon version of America's Genesis, the Virginia territory was named by the English invaders for their virgin queen. In doing so they betrayed their wishful belief that the land itself was innocent of man's touch. For me Virginia was the daughter Queen Elizabeth I never had with Sir Walter Raleigh, the courtier with the handy cloak, the writer, statesman, explorer, and royal favorite, until he wasn't.

Unlike the later settlers of the Massachusetts Bay Colony, the English invaders were not fugitives from religious persecution, not brooding and dour Dissenters, rabble-rousing evangelicals or, heaven forbid, Roman Catholics. They were stolid Anglicans. They were adventurers and disinherited second sons of English nobility. They had an unbridled hunger for the landed estates and social position the laws of primogeniture had denied them. And so, the name given to this land by the Powatan people, Tsenacommacah, was for a long time forgotten, along with the history, language, and memories of the native peoples who had lived here from unknown times. In its place arose an origin story born of a calculated forgetfulness.

In April 1619 a surgeon named John Woodson arrived from Dorsetshire, accompanied by his wife, Sarah, in the retinue of a new royally appointed governor. Luckily, he wasn't among those who first tried to settle the region. Three decades earlier, in 1590, Sir Walter Raleigh's toehold on Roanoke Island, the first English settlement in North America, was found abandoned three years after it had last been visited by supply ships. All that remained was an empty fort and an inscription carved into a tree. Had the English settlers, which included women and children, all been massacred by Indians? Kidnapped? No one knew. In the nineteenth century, feverish scribblers would tell the story of the "lost colony of Roanoke Island" and the tragic fate of Virginia Dare, the first child of Anglo-Saxon heritage born on American soil. By the early twentieth century her birthdate provided an occasion to celebrate "Anglo-American" power. But the sixteenth century had no time for such fancies. Sir Walter cut his losses, turned his cold eye toward El Dorado, and gave Virginia no further thought.

The turn of the seventeenth century brought another wave of Englishmen. Dr. John Woodson wasn't among this second lot, either. In 1607 the Virginia Company of London, a trading outfit with a Royal Charter and a slate of investors eager to cash in on the New World, sponsored a new settlement on the James River. As every schoolchild in Virginia knows, Jamestown became Virginia's first capital. This settlement, too, had trouble sustaining itself, prey as it was to starvation, disease, and raiding parties. Only shards and broken artifacts remain today. English aristocrats were not well suited to the frontier life, it appeared, particularly when it came to forging lasting accommodations with its native residents. Indeed, Virginians pioneered the practice of their forcible removal.

The discovery that the Tidewater area around the Chesapeake Bay and its catchment was ideal for the cultivation of tobacco soon set off a crazed land rush. Dr. John Woodson, part of this third wave, arrived in 1619, the same year a Portuguese galleon en route to Vera Cruz was intercepted by two English privateers. Sixty of the ship's hundreds of African captives were taken and, of those, twenty or so were brought to the shores of Virginia in late August and sold for supplies. As the writers of the 1619 Project might say, this was where the Snake entered the Garden. As scholars have since noted, the Atlantic slave trade had been underway for a century by then, and earlier Spanish settlements in Florida had made copious use of enslaved Africans. Yet the English colonies of Virginia have maintained their grip on the way we were told the story of our beginnings.

In 1625, six years after Woodson's arrival, and eight years before he himself was killed in an Indian raid, the colony undertook its second census of residents. This is where Dr. John Woodson's place in America and Virginia's origin story is finally established. Of the twenty-three Africans recorded in the colony, six were listed as living in the Woodson household, making John Woodson among the first English enslavers in colonial Virginia. In future censuses indentured servants, wherever they came from, carried names; kidnapped and trafficked Africans were relieved of theirs and lost to history by design.

It was this weighty family heritage that Rev. Phil Woodson, the associate pastor of First United Methodist Church, carried with him when he approached the pulpit on Mother's Day, the morning after Richard Spencer's torch rally in Lee Park. Woodson was a young family man, only recently ordained. That morning the front pages of both the *Daily Progress* and the *Washington Post* showed the lighted spire they all now sat beneath, towering above the torches in Lee Park. Born and raised in Charlottesville, Rev. Woodson understood the stubborn allegiance to the Lee statue in the pews. A Woodson ancestor had sacrificed a foot for the Confederacy, and his family still had the wooden leg to prove it. But he felt the dispute over the Lee statue had been a distraction from addressing the city's current problems with race.

Not long before, Woodson had invited a facilitator to moderate a church discussion of Ta-Nehisi Coates's *Between the World and Me*. This was not a book addressed to white people looking to atone for the sin of racism. Nor was it a manual on how to confront the legacies of slavery and segregation. It was a book-length letter from a Black father to his fourteen-year-old son that gave its white readers a raw and unvarnished account of what it is like to grow up as a Black man in America without the belief that the arc of the moral universe bends toward justice. The book's 2015 release coincided with a massacre of Black churchgoers in Charleston, South Carolina. Coates challenged Governor Nikki Haley to remove the Confederate flag from the Columbia statehouse. His views on white people didn't change when she did.

As part of his personal response to this book, Rev. Woodson had tried to take himself apart as a white man, itemize the advantages that had accrued to him over the course of four centuries, purge the untruths that had warped his understandings, and then gingerly reassemble himself into a more race-conscious man. Like many white Americans, he was asking himself what a true reckoning with white supremacy, within oneself, within one's community and country, entailed. This included asking why it had taken him so long to do so. This included asking if such a reckoning was even possible. With the arrival of these torch-bearing men, Rev. Woodson had decided their community had run out of time for reflection. "Silence and inaction are the tools of sin," he began.

"I don't know how you feel about this statue and its removal, but I do want you to pick a side," he told his congregation. "And I need you to ask yourself: is it the side with those who are hurting—those who are afraid, those who are being intimidated . . . or are you on the same side as those people carrying torches?" He gently reminded them of those who sometimes slept in Lee Park, in the shadow cast by the general who waged a war to keep men like them in bondage. Rev. Woodson concluded his sermon by inviting everyone to hear Christ's call.

Perhaps some of those listening shared their young pastor's sense of urgency. Others may have resented the implication that they were somehow to blame for the arrival of these men in their city. Still others might have asked where this was heading and whether they wanted any part of it.

Less than a year later, I was in Charlottesville trying to find my own way forward, beginning by going backward.

PROLOGUE

The Unveiling

Charlottesville, in the foothills of the Blue Ridge mountains, is a small southern city of ten square miles and just under 50,000 people. The city is bisected by two railway lines. The Norfolk Southern runs freight north south, and what was once known as the Chesapeake & Ohio runs freight east west. At the intersection of these two lines, midway down the mile-long stretch of West Main Street, sits the former Union Station (now Amtrak), offering passages north to New York, west to Chicago, and south to New Orleans.

West Main turns into University Avenue at a freight train overpass, west of the Amtrak station. Just before that overpass, Paul Goodloe McIntire, a wealthy financier and local benefactor, erected a statue titled *Conqueror of the Northwest*. This statue is one of a collection of monumental bronzes McIntire scattered around his beloved home city. Raised a century ago, the statue depicted the military officer George Rogers Clark on his mount heading westward, trailed by armed soldiers on foot. Clark was shown subduing a native chieftain; his horse close to trampling a woman holding an infant in a cradleboard. From this statue, it is only a five-minute walk to a statue of Thomas Jefferson at the foot of the neoclassical dome of the Rotunda on the Grounds of the University of Virginia. The Rotunda crowns the northern end of the Lawn, a wide grassy esplanade defined by ten pavilions, five on each side, linked by covered brick walkways. This "Academical Village" was the original footprint of "Mr. Jefferson's University" and was built by enslaved workmen following Thomas Jefferson's drawings. Once you arrive here, you have left the city; the university is in Albemarle County.

For a long time, West Main Street was a service corridor connecting the university on one end with the city's old downtown business district on the other. If West Main is Charlottesville's central artery, the Black neighborhoods that wind around it are its heart. This part of the city had been their world since the days of slavery, when a freedman could buy land. After the Civil War, the newly emancipated migrated to the city from the countryside, looking for places to live and work. As the cheapest land ran along the railway tracks, some of the most careworn homes in these neighborhoods date to Reconstruction.

Part of the ethos of that time, one articulated by the Virginian Booker T. Washington, was that economic advancement and social standing would come through owning property. Virginia once boasted many Black landowners; Albemarle County and its city seat was no exception. The hardworking home-owning residents of Charlottesville's Black neighborhoods—Fifeville, Canada, and Gospel Hill on the south side of West Main; 10th and Page, Venable, Starr Hill, Rose Hill, and Vinegar Hill on the north—congregated on Sundays. There was First Baptist Church, next to Union Station, Ebenezer Baptist on Sixth Street NW, Zion Union Baptist on Fourth NW, and Mount Zion First African Baptist next to the Trailways bus depot, where West Main became East Main.

A child can't readily conceive of time as a succession of generations; there is only the vivid present and the sepia-tinged and shadowy olden times of grandparents. During my childhood the people who lived in these neighborhoods were only one or two generations removed from the long night of slavery. The oldest of them would have had parents forced to labor on a nearby plantation. They might have been owned by a professor or the university itself. They may even have had an ancestor who slaved for one of the three founding fathers who called Albemarle their home. Descendants of the extended families of Jefferson, Madison, or Monroe were likely among them. The realization of how close my lifetime is to this history still astonishes me.

At the point where West Main became East Main, Paul Goodloe McIntire planted another statue. This one dominated a small traffic circle and depicted the explorers Meriwether Lewis and William Clark of the 1803–1805 "Voyage of Discovery." Sacajawea, the Lemhi Shoshone guide who led Lewis and Clark from the Dakotas across the Rockies to the Pacific, was crouched at their bootheels. William Clark was brother to the Conqueror of the Northwest down the road; all three men were "great and heroic sons of the soil of Albemarle County, sent forth on their high missions and fateful destinies," according to one of the speakers at their installation, "by the prophetic wisdom of Thomas Jefferson."

In the mid-1970s, the white downtown business owners on East Main found they were rapidly losing customers to more easily accessible suburban malls. The grid of narrow streets that comprised downtown had been designed to accommodate the carts and carriages of the eighteenth century, not the automobiles of the twentieth. In a Hail Mary pass, the city hired a gifted urban planner to turn East Main Street into a bricked-over pedestrian mall with a tree canopy of willow oak. Woolworths with its luncheonette, Tilly's Shoes, an Army Navy outlet, Standard Drug, and Leggett's department store eventually gave way to pricy restaurants, boutiques, high-end gift shops, and antique stores. For some, "the Downtown Mall" displaced Lee Park, one block north, as the city's civic center.

The acre on which Lee Park sat once bore the home of Col. Charles S. Venable, who had served as Gen. Robert E. Lee's aide-de-camp during the war. In 1918, the land was bought by Paul Goodloe McIntire and gifted to the city. Six years later he planted another bronze, the statue of Robert E. Lee. The commander of the Army of Northern Virginia was depicted hatless, mounted on his white horse, Traveller, and installed as the park's centerpiece. Back then the square was adjacent to the central post office, county courthouse, and prominent houses of worship; one of the oldest synagogues in the South was a block away. Lee Park became a place for white people to gather and genuflect to Virginia's most famous general since George Washington.

Given that Lee never once visited the city, the choice of a Confederate general over the nation's first president was telling. By 1924, the year the statue was unveiled, surviving Confederate veterans were dwindling, enabling the myths surrounding Lee to allay more painful thoughts of an ignoble and devastating war. In anticipation of the statue's arrival, there had been a cross burning on a mountain near Thomas Jefferson's Monticello, just then preparing to open to the public. The Klan staged a celebratory parade accompanied by a marching band up and down Main Street, beginning at the C&O station on its eastern end and ending at the Black enclave of Vinegar Hill. Thousands of spectators lined the streets. A Black barber standing outside his home watched the robes go by and identified every single one of them by their shoes.

On the much-awaited day of the statue's unveiling, speeches by clergy, civic leaders, and university presidents extolled Lee, "that stainless leader of a stainless cause," without let or hindrance. It was left to the Grand Commander of the Sons of Confederate Veterans, a prominent Klansman, to narrate for the crowd that charged moment, near two o'clock on a July afternoon in 1863, when the tides of war turned against them and their way of life.

"See [Lee] as he struggles up the bloody heights of Gettysburg . . .

"Under the piercing and admiring eye of his Commander"—that would be God—"the decisive hour has come, and the fate of the Confederacy is hanging in the balance."

William Faulkner, who was a writer in residence at UVA in the 1950s, contemplated this same moment in his novel *Intruder in the Dust*. Faulkner conjured it as a fourteen-year-old white boy might—Pickett in his long oiled ringlets waiting for Longstreet to give the word—by comparing it to Christopher Columbus's epic gamble, "that moment in 1492 when somebody thought *This is it*: the absolute edge of no return, to turn back now and make for home or sail irrevocably on and either find land or plunge over the world's roaring rim." This captures the knot Southern military historians and battlefield aficionados have sought again and again to retie; if not for this twist in personality, that turn in the weather, had but the mighty Stonewall Jackson lived to see Gettysburg, first Cemetery Hill and then the world would have fallen at the feet of Lee's Army of Northern Virginia. This moment is a touchstone of countless memorials, ceremonials, and reenactments. It captures something of the fatalism that still grips the imagination of parts of the white South.

"The battle is joined."

I imagine the Grand Commander paused here, letting the crowd fill the silence with their thoughts, while preparing himself to summon General Lee's last battle cry, one that would ring in the ears of his soldiers for the rest of their lives. For many that may be mere moments; for the luckier ones, some of them standing there in Lee Park for the 1924 ceremony, years.

"Come on, men, *come on*. My God! *Would you live forever?*"

Every member in the crowd is now gripped by that familiar thrall, contemplating once again that fatal plunge over the world's roaring rim.

"And they expire in a perfect halo of glory."

The word *slavery* occurred twice in all the speeches given that day; once in passing reference to the "slavery question," and lastly to insist that Lee "abhorred it." There is one reference to "negro" in the form of an anecdote about a "cotton-headed" loyal retainer. There was a lot of florid talk about the beauty of Virginia, affectionately referred to as the Old Dominion. The word *cause* appears twenty-nine times, and in each instance the speaker affirms its righteousness and pledges his eternal allegiance. There was a hint of sourness in the suggestion that one day an unbiased historian would grant their sacred cause an honorable verdict. This was a backhanded way of acknowledging that such a verdict still eluded them. (It eludes them still.) In the finale, Lee's great-granddaughter Miss Mary Walker Lee, standing on top of the speaker's lectern, waved to the assembled and pulled the rope that unveiled the general atop his mount. The master of ceremonies felt the celebrations had gone off splendidly, but confessed to his diary that he did not like the statue *at all*.

Two weeks after the statue's unveiling, a spate of cross burnings around the county ended with the bombing of a Black church west of town, close by the birthplace of Meriwether Lewis, and less than a mile from where I grew up. A flaming cross was planted in its ruins. According to the *Daily Progress*, this cross burning, like those that preceded it, caused considerable excitement.

This was how Charlottesville's Black citizens were made to understand what the arrival of Lee's statue meant for them. It was an easily grasped lesson.

PART I

A Beautiful Ugly City

March 2016–January 2017

CHAPTER 1

Lee Park

Wes Bellamy arrived in Charlottesville in 2009, a recent college graduate. Five years later, working as a computer science teacher, he ran for a seat on city council. The Black community was skeptical. Some called him "Fresh Prince." Some saw him as a privileged, down-South college boy who, having only lived in the city a short while, understood little of their struggles. Others believed he was out for attention or using them as a stepping stone to bigger things. One or more of these assessments may have been true, as they will be for most up-and-coming politicians.

On Saturday, June 4, 2013, the final weekend before the polls closed, Bellamy hosted a cookout in Lee Park. Disappointed by the turnout, he made the rounds of the Black churches the next morning to make his final pitch and encourage everyone to vote. Instead, he got a schooling. How could he possibly represent the Black community if he didn't understand a cookout in Lee Park was a slap in the face? Could he not see the centerpiece of this park was a statue of the man who had fought to keep them all enslaved? Did he not know brother so-and-so had had his face slashed in that park and others had been spat upon?

He lost the election by five votes.

Three years after his defeat at the polls, on March 20, 2016, Wes Bellamy was back at Lee Park. He was there as the city's new vice-mayor and, at twenty-nine, the youngest city council member ever elected. The week before, Bellamy had received a call from a Charlottesville High School freshman. She asked him: Was he going to "*be* about it, or just *talk* about it"? He was caught flatfooted; he had no idea what she was referring to. Furiously Googling while she went on, he figured it out. She wanted him to get rid of the city's Confederate statues.

In 1904 Virginia passed a law that made it illegal for any county to "disturb or interfere with any monuments or memorials." This law was part of a widespread backlash against Reconstruction, a period when the newly emancipated made profound political, economic, and social gains. Civil War monuments became one way to repudiate Reconstruction and to tell a more sanitized story of the war. Since then, the law had been revised twice. Then, in October 2015, a judge in Danville, Virginia, ruled that the 1904 law did not apply to cities, only to *localities*. Virginia legislators leapt to close the Danville loophole. Bill 287 was written to strengthen the protections of the 1904 law by prohibiting local communities, counties, localities, *or cities*, from removing or modifying any monument or war memorial.

The most iconic of Virginia's Confederate statues was a colossal, mounted Lee, erected in 1890 and sited at the head of Monument Avenue in Richmond, the state capital and second capital of the Confederacy. Virginia's Democratic governor, Terry McAuliffe, hadn't been eager to open that Pandora's box, but in the wake of the 2015 Charleston massacre, a nationwide debate over Confederate statues and flags had begun and he was obliged to take a stand. When Bill 287 arrived on his desk, he vetoed it. This was what prompted Zyahna Bryant, the Charlottesville High School freshman, to pick up her phone and call Wes Bellamy.

Bellamy devised a plan. The weekend following the governor's veto, Bryan Stevenson, of the Equal Justice Initiative out of Montgomery, Alabama, was coming to town for Charlottesville's annual book festival to promote his book *Just Mercy*. At a private party before his talk, Bellamy asked Stevenson to call on him during the Q & A so that he could ask Stevenson what he thought should be done about Charlottesville's Lee and Jackson statues. Getting the answer he needed, Bellamy would then formally call for their removal at Monday night's city council meeting. On Tuesday morning he would hold a press conference in Lee Park.

Almost as soon as he put the question to Stevenson, Bellamy's phone began vibrating with death threats.

Zyahna Bryant was a Charlottesville native, a good, hardworking student, and the eldest daughter of a loving mother. She was often told she was too loud, too big, and too bossy, and outside of the spaces where she felt most at home she sometimes felt like a spectacle. Sustained by her church, Mount Zion First African Baptist, and a close circle of grandparents, mother, and aunts, she found her voice at a far younger age than Wes Bellamy had, holding her first protest when she was in middle school. Sixteen-year-old Trayvon Martin had been to her generation what Emmett Till had been to her great-grandmother's. Standing on the corner outside her grandmother's home in the 10th and Page neighborhood, she held up a sign protesting his killing by a self-appointed security guard named George Zimmerman. She planted "Justice for Trayvon" and "Honk for Justice" signs in her grandmother's front yard. While the jury deliberated on Zimmerman's fate, Zyahna moved her protest to the federal courthouse: a twelve-year-old girl corralling ten-year-olds with popsicle stains on their shirts. Fifty people showed up in support.

As a UVA undergraduate, Niya Bates had been Zyahna's tutor and mentor. She remembers a middle school student fired with a revolutionary spirit who, in homework sessions with her closest friends, talked constantly of organizing. But Zimmerman's acquittal marked the end of Zyahna's childhood. It was now legal to kill Black people, she concluded. All you had to do was say you were scared of them. She organized another protest regardless.

In ninth grade, Zyahna wrote a school paper responding to the prompt "What one thing would you like to see change in Charlottesville?" She decided she would get rid of the Lee statue. She wanted to reclaim the park for those in her community who had stayed in Charlottesville when so many had left. Among those who stayed were her great-grandmother Thelma Townsend, who had fought to desegregate the city's schools, and her grandmother Vizena. In early spring of 2016, her paper became a Change.org petition. "I am reminded over and over again of the pain of my ancestors and all of the fighting they had to go through to get to where they are now," she wrote. By the time of Bellamy's press conference in Lee Park she had over five hundred signatures. She was the first to speak.

Zyahna began by saying a public park ought to be a place where everyone felt comfortable, and Lee Park was not a welcoming space for people like her. Times had changed, she said, and the city should keep pace, not be stuck in the past. She spoke of her love for Charlottesville and her community. She hoped everyone could see their way to doing the right thing.

Will Jones III, Wes Bellamy's barber, confidant, and unofficial security, stood at the back of the crowd in a red baseball cap with speaker wires coming from his ears, as if he were listening to music rather than eavesdropping on the twenty or so flag-bearing men standing next to him. These were the Virginia Flaggers. They were accompanied by an allied group who called themselves the Army of Northern Virginia-Mechanized Cavalry, known for their fondness for high-end pickups with custom license plates. In 2013 the Flaggers had raised their first Confederate flag on I-95 outside Richmond. Since then they had been responsible for dozens of "memorial" Confederate battle flags, ranging from 20 by 20 feet to an enormous 31 by 51 feet, seen alongside major highways. Installation ceremonies were accompanied by a color guard and renditions of "Dixie." Alluding to their slogan of "Heritage not hate," Zyahna observed, "We need to find a separation between heritage and hate."

Despite its prominent location next to the Jefferson Madison Regional Library, for most locals, Black and white, the presence of the Lee statue barely registered. Yet the moment Zyahna had stepped up to the podium, any perception of the Lee statue as a sentimental relic of a bygone era changed. The proximity of the Flaggers to this young girl's plainspoken appeal switched a low current of unease into a high-tension wire.

Bonnie Gordon, a local musician and music professor, knew Zyahna from an after-school arts program. "I went to support a kid who I thought was doing a cool project in school, not a kid who I thought was taking on Flaggers," she said. "The things they were yelling at her! I think they might have called her a bitch." That these people could be so nasty to a child made her wonder what else they were capable of. Ann Marie Smith,

another middle-aged white woman, was also there that day. Zyahna had
been a classmate of her eldest since kindergarten. Smith was completely
flummoxed by what Zyahna had to say. "I was, like, dang. Not everyone
was having the same experience of Charlottesville I was."

The Black community's unspoken agreement to stick to their own
parks had kept the peace. But now Zyahna was asking why they should
cede this ground. Even to ask this question required her to ignore all
those telling her that no good would come of it. Some would say this
was where the trouble began. For Zyahna it began eleven days later
when a UVA student wrote a snarky story about her on the far-right
news site Breitbart. Her petition used only her first name; he included
her surname. Threatening letters, texts, and phone calls soon followed,
letting her know that they knew where she lived and went to school.

Zyahna maintained her composure in the face of the Flaggers' animosity. The next speaker, an organizer of the Charlottesville Pride festival that took place in Lee Park every year, struggled with hers. "What
does that have to do with Lee," a woman shouted at her, "Robert Lee
wasn't gay." The LBGTQ speaker's words were lost amid the heckling. A city councillor named Kristin Szakos moved forward to shield
her. Szakos wasn't surprised by the hostility. She'd been raised in
Mississippi.

A Black minister, then two white women, joined her. With each
successive speaker the protective circle got larger and the jeering louder.
"Wake up and smell the coffee!" "Carpetbagger!" Those who had come
out in support of the vice-mayor or the young girl appeared subdued by
the growing venom. The heckling became so obnoxious that a diffident
white-haired woman approached one of the loudest men. She had to
look up to talk to him. "The man that's speaking is a pastor," she said.
"Please, please let him speak and show some respect." "I'm a minister
too," he replied, sarcastically, and continued unabated. I asked her if she
had ever given the statues much thought. "No, no, I had never thought
about it. So many things, I never thought about."

Despite the ruckus, Wes Bellamy, the final speaker, appeared re-
laxed. "Are you gonna let anyone else talk?" the Flaggers demanded before he could begin. "What about white slavery?" At one point he turned

his back, to address the crowd behind him. "You will hear in the months coming, that there may be no legal ground to do this, that this is about heritage, not hate, and that this is stirring up 'trouble,' that this is making our community divided. But when I see the people here, of different races, of different ages, here to battle for what is right, I am encouraged."

Since Zyahna's call, Bellamy had been canvassing his community. His elders told him to leave it alone, that white people would never allow their statues to be taken down. He decided they were afraid, that they were conditioned to be afraid. Because that was safe. He thought, as ambitious young men often do, screw being safe. Vizena Howard, Zyahna's grandmother, put it differently. "Sometimes it takes someone to come here from outside to get things going, you know, because everybody gets comfortable with where things are. Nobody speaks up on anything. That's Charlottesville. And so, they come in and do this and do that. It wasn't always what we needed. Right? But that's because nobody would speak out about what it was we *did* need. So, you know, people would say, 'Wes is coming here, starting trouble,' you know, stirring up things. But I didn't look at it that way. I thought, *maybe it's a good thing*. Like John Lewis says, 'good trouble.'"

Phil Woodson, then an elementary school music teacher, happened to be driving down Market Street when the press conference was in progress. All he could see from his car were white men and women holding Confederate flags. His immediate thought was, "Man, where's the church in the midst of this?" meaning the church whose front steps and columned portico looked out on the statue of Robert E. Lee. That was the moment Phil Woodson received God's call. Not simply a call to ministry, but a call to be a pastor at First United Methodist.

The journalist covering the press conference gave the Flaggers as many column inches as those who had shown up in support of the vice-mayor. The next morning residents would read in the *Daily Progress* about how Wes Bellamy was promoting "open strife," creating "division and hatred, not unity." White readers who hadn't given the statues much thought, but who were inclined to suspect Bellamy's motives, might have conceded the Flaggers had a point. Others, I imagine, would have considered them colorful curiosities or harmless cranks and rushed on with their day.

And therein lay the crux of the dilemma that would be faced by all those who decided to follow fifteen-year-old Zyahna Bryant's lead, but perhaps no one as much as Charlottesville's young vice-mayor. By using his position as city councillor to call for the statues' removal, Wes Bellamy would be labeled a troublemaker. By white people who could not for the life of them see what the fuss was about. And by ordinary citizens, white and Black, who couldn't understand why he had decided to go there. Even by white people who claimed to be sympathetic to the aspirations of gifted young people like Zyahna Bryant. And precisely because Zyahna was so young, it would be Wes Bellamy they would settle on to blame for all that followed. Not that Zyahna or her family were spared, but in Bellamy they found a choice target: a big Black man with a little power. "The more you stir the pot, the worse it stinks," one Flagger warned. "It's getting a lot of people upset."

The following month, on the day of a public hearing on the Lee statue, a Scottsville area group calling itself "The Ladies of the Confederacy" had their own rally in Lee Park. The ladies arrived in hoop skirts. Their menfolk dressed up as Confederate soldiers. There was a Robert E. Lee look-alike. After an opening prayer, they brandished a petition defending Lee's worthiness to maintain his pride of place.

To the first of their petition's two claims, that Robert E. Lee had freed his slaves, a weary historian would explain, once again, they were not Lee's slaves but his late father-in-law's. And he freed them only when a court compelled him to honor the terms of his father-in-law's will. The second claim was that no one worked harder to heal the nation after the Civil War than Lee did. This was what I'd been taught. But this was more dissembling. In victory, Grant had bent over backward to accommodate the pride of his esteemed adversary, hoping he would accept defeat like a true soldier. But in the years after Appomattox, Grant became increasingly disturbed by Lee's defiant comportment. While forfeiting any political ambitions, Lee held the North hostage to veiled threats to renew hostilities and denigrated the Union victory, in the words of one historian, as a "triumph of might over right." If war is waged with guns, peace is fought with stories, and Lee's framing of the Union victory has long prevailed in the South.

Regarding war monuments, however, Lee was forthright. When the prospect of a Gettysburg monument arose, he wrote, "I think it wiser . . . not to keep open the sores of war but to follow the examples of those nations who endeavored to obliterate the marks of civil strife, to commit to oblivion the feelings engendered." Unlike almost every other Confederate general, Lee did not spend his final years writing his memoirs. Indeed, Lee went to fantastic lengths, one writer noted, "to prevent [his] celebrity from becoming a source of income." Was this an act of penance? Or an attempt to commit to oblivion his own feelings about the war? Regardless, from the moment of his death, five years after the end of the Civil War, Lee, the soldier and Virginia gentleman, became central to how white Virginians thought of themselves, how they remembered the Civil War, and how they memorialized the sacrifices made for the Confederacy.

There was a fan club vibe to the Ladies of the Confederacy Facebook chatter about Robert E. Lee. It was as if a boy they had all gone to school with had ended up in Hollywood and they were now competing over who had known him best. One Scottsville woman indulged a fantasy of the Lee statue coming to life. "If [our] opponents could actually hear Lee speak for himself, it might knock some sense into them." Until that happened, armed lookouts stood guard at each corner of Lee Park while the Ladies of the Confederacy rallied to keep Robert E. Lee on his pedestal. A white woman with a stroller flipped them the bird before disappearing into the library across the street.

"The vice-mayor himself made a brief appearance," one woman posted on Facebook. "When he jogged into the park, SPAT on the statue (multiple witnesses saw this and said he has done it before), then jogged off. . . . He clearly thinks he is above the law."

In the spring of 2016, Jason Kessler, a Charlottesville resident, blogger, and self-published pundit, was thirty-three years old. He knew little of the Virginia Flaggers or the Army of Northern Virginia-Mechanized Cavalry. He hadn't attended the Lee Park press conference. Still, he registered the attention the controversy was generating, and the hostility Wes Bellamy was attracting.

Somewhere along his life's wayward path, Kessler had learned that

attention can be monetized. Kessler was eager to be famous and con-
fident he deserved to be. He had tried his hand at writing fiction and
poetry and self-help texts, but that hadn't gotten much traction. Now
he embarked on a deep dive into Bellamy's Twitter feed in search of
tweets that wouldn't sit well with his newfound allies and constituents.
He found them. Bellamy was in Atlanta with his wife when the anonymous calls began. "You Black nigger, we're gonna show them who you
really are. We're gonna take everything from you. We're gonna break
you down."

Kessler released the old tweets on his blog on Thanksgiving Day
and made sure the press got wind of them. The tweets described sex
acts with vulgarities for genitalia. White women were rape accusations
waiting to happen. One retweet described white women as smelling
like deli meat. Bellamy retweeted: "Eat it while she asleep if she moan
it aint rape," with the acclamation, "Word." He expressed contempt for
Black people who acted white. Kessler highlighted a tweet in which
Bellamy said he often tuned out white people when they spoke at community meetings. Bellamy was a "blatant Black Supremacist," Kessler
wrote. His efforts to remove the Lee statue from Lee Park were part of
an "Afrocentric racial agenda."

Kessler's discoveries landed in Wes Bellamy's strenuously ordered
life like a high explosive. News of his tweets was carried in the *Daily
Progress* and the *Richmond Times-Dispatch*. He was placed on administrative leave from his job at Albemarle High School while an investigation was launched. On December 1, he was forced to resign from a
seat on Virginia's Board of Education that he'd only held since March.
Through his spokesman, Governor Terry McAuliffe said he was hor-
rified. Finally, Charlottesville's mayor, Mike Signer, told a *Washington
Post* reporter that, in the interests of the common good, Bellamy should
consider resigning his city council seat. The tweets had inflicted "real
harm to our community."

UVA's student newspaper, the *Cavalier Daily*, looked at how Bellamy's
tweets had evolved. In the earliest tweets "faggot" was a staple; later
ones expressed solidarity with the victims of the Pulse nightclub massacre. The most recent tweets called out rape culture and provided links

to an organization helping sexual assault victims and another helping young Black women succeed.

So, who was Wes Bellamy, really?

In his early years in Charlottesville, he was a restless young man with ambitions and dreams that seemed to drive him in so many directions at once that he sometimes got lost along the way. By his own lights, he was trying to find his voice as a young Black man. He'd outrun a childhood where domineering men seemed to hold all the cards. He learned a different manhood from the barbers who did his weekly cut while he was in college. He ran workshops for young men who reminded him of his younger self. He participated in the 2012 protests and vigils surrounding the death of Trayvon Martin. He organized winter coat drives and hosted an annual giveaway of Thanksgiving turkeys. He played hoop, hung out with Will Jones III at the barbershop, and pursued a doctorate in education. Wearing a suit and bowtie, he'd courted the fatherly church elders and the motherly community organizers. Finally, he'd become a father and a husband. He had come so far and so fast that, upon first reading the tweets, unable to recognize the man who wrote them, he refused to admit they were his.

Councillor Kristin Szakos, who had stepped up to shield the LBGTQ speaker at the Lee Park press conference, remembers the day Bellamy first appeared at city council. There had been months of debate over a fifty-year water plan for the city, she said, which involved thinking about whether the city was going to grow or stay the way it was. They heard from all the usual suspects. The developers. The historic preservationists. The neighborhood associations. Bellamy had waited until the end of one long meeting to stand up and ask the assembled: When were they going to start talking about issues that affected his people? Education. Housing. A living wage. Szakos had been waiting for someone to come along and interrupt a conversation dominated by white people and their interests. Someone to bring the concerns of the Black community before the dais. "I'm so glad you're here," she said after he sat down.

Szakos couldn't square the tweets with the young man who attended Pride events and defended the rights of women. Most of the tweets were, she noted, retweets, not things he said. Still, it was a gut punch.

She told him he couldn't bluff his way out of it. By Sunday night, after consulting with his wife, Bellamy posted an apology on Facebook, owning everything. He admitted his comments were disrespectful and ignorant. "In the course of trying to mature and find my way . . . I came up short of the man I aspire to be."

At the first city council meeting after Thanksgiving, he spoke as if he had undergone a crash course in self-awareness. "This city helped me grow from an angry young man with limited experience with others outside of my comfort zone, to the leader who's willing to stand up and fight for the rights and civil liberties of my brothers and sisters from the LGBTQ community, and anyone whose rights are in jeopardy." This was what Charlottesville's progressive white community wanted to hear. But I wondered if it was Bellamy's more pugnacious self, absent in the video recording of his public apology at city council, that spurred him to take on the statues.

Bob Fenwick, who had defeated Bellamy in his first run for council, was the first councillor to respond. A Vietnam vet who prided himself on his independence, Fenwick began by castigating those supposed white allies who had abandoned Bellamy as gutless. "If anyone thinks this is not about racism, I will remind them of a few years ago when a DNA test proved beyond a reasonable doubt that Thomas Jefferson had a relationship with Sally Hemings. Then as now, the town exploded." Kathy Galvin, another councillor, signaled her support. The mayor backpedaled his *Washington Post* comments. He now believed in second chances. Bellamy wouldn't forget who stood by him and who had bailed.

While the white community equivocated or waited to be placated, the Black community closed ranks. A soft-spoken and tenacious community organizer named Nikuyah Walker called out the mayor for giving Jason Kessler cover. "When you're talking about Wes's comments, the comments he made? He is a man who grew up in the South who has suffered from the legacy of slavery. And for people, including you, Mike Signer, to call his comments troubling? Like you were never a man and never twenty-three and never insulted anybody. . . . Wes doesn't owe any of us an apology. . . . You all want him to come forward and keep begging for forgiveness. And to allow somebody like Jason Kessler? To influence how you all responded to Wes? You all should be ashamed."

After her comments, a short, stocky man approached the mic with a speaker blaring Tom Petty's "I Won't Back Down." He turned to face the audience with his arms outstretched like a prize fighter and introduced himself to those who didn't yet know who he was. "My name is Jason Kessler," he shouted, "and I am here on behalf of over nine hundred petitioners to demand that Wes Bellamy be removed from his office as councillor for the City of Charlottesville." The council's support of the disgraced Bellamy, Kessler said, betrayed the liberal and progressive values they claimed to stand for. When he accused Bellamy of being a rape fetishist, the crowd exploded, and whatever else he had to say was lost in the pandemonium.

Turning to face Bellamy, Kessler pointed his rolled-up speech at him and told him his days were numbered.

CHAPTER 2

The Blue Ribbon Commission

Three months after Wes Bellamy's press conference in Lee Park, the Charlottesville city council passed a motion calling for the establishment of the Blue Ribbon Commission on Race, Memorials, and Public Spaces. The commission's charge was to find ways to broaden a historical narrative that for too long had been dominated by wealthy planters and enslavers, be they founding fathers and presidents, Confederate generals, wealthy benefactors, or UVA administrators. The disposition of the Confederate statues was but one item in a list that would give more public visibility to the story of Black Charlottesville. From the middle of June through the end of November 2016, the commission would explore a range of options for the parks where the statues sat, the mayor explained, including the possible addition of new memorials or new signage providing "context to reflect current values." A final report would be drawn up by year's end so the city council could debate and vote on the commission's recommendations.

When I first listened to the audio recordings of the commission's fifteen meetings, including three public forums across six months, I formed an impression of the nine commissioners based on their range of references, their accents, their way of expressing themselves, and their marshaling of arguments. I gave the ones who most interested me nicknames. The elected chair of the commission was a deacon at First Baptist. He became "the Deacon." The Deacon kept the meetings humming along with color-ful turns of speech that gave nothing away as to what he was truly think-ing. "The Professor," named as vice-chair, taught history at UVA. He spoke in perfect paragraphs even when he was thinking out loud, which he did quite often. Until he mentioned he was descended from both en-slavers and enslaved, I imagined him as a white man in a bow tie. In him I heard the commission's divided soul and historical conscience.

"The Listener," a former piano tuner, spoke less often, but none-theless conveyed that he heard every voice, read every email, and kept them suspended in scrupulous fair-mindedness. "The Art Historian" was the founding executive director of the Jefferson School African American Heritage Center. She spoke with scholarly precision and cool detachment. Then there was the longtime director of the Albemarle Charlottesville Historical Society. I hadn't heard that strangled Virginia drawl since my childhood, so I named her "Old Virginia." Of all the commissioners, I identified most closely with "the Archivist," the timid, white-haired local historian who had braved confronting the Flagger at Bellamy's press conference. I shared her enthusiasm for deep dives into old newspapers and obscure discoveries.

But the voices I really focused on were those of Charlottesville's con-cerned citizens. While the commissioners voted on who would be chair and vice-chair, decided who would serve on what subcommittee, and how public engagement would be handled, they sat in patient silence. When the first Community Forum opened on July 27, 2016, at the Jefferson School African American Heritage Center, I finally got to hear from them. Most sounded white and retired or close to it. Those arguing that the Lee and Jackson statues should remain where they were overwhelmed those in favor of moving them by a large margin. Even those who felt uncomfortable with the statues' presence in pub-lic spaces treated the entire subject of what should be done about them gingerly. "What good can come of it?" the first person who rose to speak asked. "If we remove something or take it away . . . it will create greater conflict." He sounded white too.

Broadly speaking, those calling for the statues to be removed were more recent arrivals in Charlottesville. The first person to advocate for

removal, however, was the exception. Garnett Mellen traced his ancestry back to the earliest Virginia settlers and claimed many Confederate
veterans among his ancestors. The most notorious of these, he admitted reluctantly, was the Virginia planter Edmund Ruffin, the Virginia
Flaggers' mascot. Ruffin was a Fire-Eater and had long believed a war
over slavery was inevitable. He was said to have fired the first shot at
Fort Sumter. It was this shot that pushed Virginia into seceding, with
disastrous consequences. When news of Lee's surrender reached Ruffin,
he wrapped himself in a Confederate flag and shot himself. His distant descendant wasn't so melodramatic. Mellen pointed out that Civil
War memorials and statues are by their very nature divisive and that he,
for one, would be happy to visit Lee Park without tiptoeing around the
white elephant at its center.

Seventy-year-old Mary Carey came closest to drawing a direct line
between the Lee statue and a childhood of segregated movie theaters
and whites-only drinking fountains. Her mother had warned her never
to venture into Lee Park, she said. After story time at the library, Black
children had to sit on the sidewalk while the white children played in
the park. She didn't need a historian to tell her what purpose the statues served in the Jim Crow social order. If Mary Carey had an opinion
about what should be done about the Lee and Jackson statues, however,
she kept it to herself.

Among the concerned citizens who spoke in favor of keeping the
statues in place were historic preservationists, a former mayor, Civil
War buffs, the descendants of Confederate soldiers, and small business
owners focused on local tourism. In a handwritten, hand-delivered letter to the commissioners, one Lee defender insisted she was not a racist,
a Virginia Flagger, or an ancestor worshipper. She was simply a person
who had grown up in Charlottesville who deeply appreciated the "ex-
quisitely rendered horses and riders in their frame of blooming flowers
and trees." She agreed that the story of slavery needed to be more ade-
quately addressed. However, unlike those "zealots," city councillors and
newcomers Wes Bellamy and Kristin Szakos, she did not believe the
story of slavery was the only story worth telling. Nor should the telling
of that story "necessitate the vengeful expunging of another." In other

words, the statues' white defenders were willing to allow Black people "their" history, so their own could remain untouched. They imagined these two histories might peacefully coexist, one ugly and painful, the other framed by flowers.

Though no one was calling for the statues to be destroyed, a former curator of the Oriental Institute Museum at the University of Chicago believed the movement to remove "our cultural heritage" from Lee Park was akin to the zeal of Islamic militants to destroy the remains of ancient civilizations. He cited the Taliban's destruction of the Bamiyan Buddhas, and the demolition of ancient Palmyra by ISIS. "I did not expect to be facing the same situation here," he concluded, as if his decision to retire to Charlottesville now needed to be revisited.

There was a general feeling among the statue defenders that moving a public monument amounted to an erasure of history, an unprecedented travesty, if not the barbarism the retired curator spoke of. One man likened removing Lee and Jackson to book burnings and went on to ask if the fact that the White House had been built by enslaved labor meant that it, too, had to be torn down. Would Monticello or the University of Virginia be next? And if so, where would it end?

Zyahna Bryant, the high school student who had started it all, was impatient with such arguments. Did people sincerely think, she asked, that the history of the Civil War and slavery and Robert E. Lee would be erased if a statue honoring Lee was moved someplace else? Textbooks would still be written; teachers would still teach. And there was always Google. "The statue is not going to make a difference in how the history is told. It is just going to be a question of whether we honor that history."

There seemed to be a sincere anxiety at play here. The national debate over Confederate statues and flags was taking place during an unusually fraught presidential election year. The Lee statue appeared to be swept up in this, pitting longtime white residents of Charlottesville against more recent, younger arrivals. The phrase "radical empathy" was frequently summoned by the latter, as if these comfortably settled white people concerned about the cultural heritage of the Confederacy were suffering from an illness that, in the interest of neighborliness, required sensitive handling. Clearly, the statue defenders wanted the city to continue paying tribute to Lee. But what were people meant to honor if not the cause for which the war was fought? Lee the Virginia gentleman? Somebody's Confederate ancestor? History with a capital *H*? A "touchstone" of someone's childhood? A "priceless and irreplaceable" work of art?

Historically, the state of Virginia has been better known for its clergy, statesmen, and military leaders than for its appreciation of the arts. Famous Virginia artists were scarce as hen's teeth. So whenever anyone began opining that the Lee and Jackson statues should be preserved as works of art, my attention wandered. Writers were also in short supply. When Charles Dickens visited, one observer noted that Virginia couldn't offer their distinguished guest much in the way of a literary circle. "The forte of the Old Dominion is to be found in the masculine production of her statesmen, her Washington, her Jefferson, and her Madison, who had never indulged in works of imagination, in the charms of romance, or in the mere beauties of the *belles lettres*." Yet somehow the statue defenders managed to concoct Civil War romances from thin air. One man held that Robert E. Lee had saved Charlottesville from suffering Atlanta's fate as depicted in *Gone with the Wind*.

Henry Shrady, the sculptor behind the monumental Ulysses S. Grant Memorial in DC, had the original commission for the Lee statue. Unfortunately, he died before his rendering of Lee could be cast. By the time a successor was found, Shrady's clay model was unusable. Still, many clung to Shrady's imprimatur. The new sculptor represented the general not as a man in the flesh but one of rough-hewn rock. The Stonewall Jackson statue, installed in 1921, showed more technical skill, but all anyone really wanted to talk about was the statue of Robert E. Lee.

The equestrian statue offers a kind of visual shorthand for the story of the man mounted astride a horse, or at least of how he died. Little Sorrel's leg is lifted high on the Jackson statue because Jackson died of battle-related wounds (friendly fire). Since all of Traveller's feet are on the ground, Lee is understood to have died, as so many Confederate generals did, in his four-poster. A horse also conveys superiority, a belonging by birth to an equestrian, or high-born, class. Since the genre of equestrian statue was first conceived, in sixth-century Greece, the toppling of empires had always targeted horse-and-rider monuments. When news of the signing of the Declaration of Independence reached New York, a statue of a mounted King George III, America's first bronze, was melted down and made into bullets for the Continental Army.

By the 1920s, equestrian statues were as anachronistic as the cavalry charge, making them little more than expensive kitsch. At the time of the Lee and Jackson unveilings, modernism was well underway, challenging not simply the nature of form but the choice of subject matter and the visual language used to convey it. In the late nineteenth century Auguste Rodin's *The Burghers of Calais* portrayed the anguished surrender of power rather than its heroic triumph; no horses, no elevating plinth. In 1916 Russians erected a monument to Lenin in St. Petersburg; his mount was an armored car. The Art Historian tried to convey the art historical context of the statues, but she might as well have been speaking a foreign language.

Instead, attendees offered up a range of suggestions that would enable the Lee and Jackson statues to remain undisturbed. This was referred to as "adding to, not subtracting, from history" and "more history rather than less." One man suggested a Peace Pole. Such an installation could be done cheaply and quickly, he argued, and was available in three sizes, inscribed with up to eight languages expressing the wishful sentiment "May Peace Prevail on Earth." Another said he could design an app that would provide all the missing historical context. This too had the advantage of economy. Others wanted to add a new statue or two, generally legendary and long-dead African Americans.

What struck me most about such suggestions was not that the white people offering them were comfortable with the prospect of, say, Harriet Tubman or a Peace Pole sharing a small park with a Confederate general. Rather, it was that in their eagerness to accommodate the feelings of their Black neighbors, they had clearly given the subject little thought. It was as if the specter of what might be unleashed if the statues were moved created an uneasy consensus: move fast.

By the close of this first community forum, two public-minded city residents on opposing sides stood out for me. One was a forty-nine-year-old biracial UVA professor, and the other was a sixty-four-year-old lawyer. The latter, Lewis Martin III, spoke first. He was one of a group of older, white Republican men speaking out in defense of the statues and calling for them to remain where they were. They called themselves the Deplorables, plus Jane, with Jane being the author of the hand-delivered letter and the lone Democrat. Martin was only three generations removed from the Civil War; his great-grandfather had been a Confederate soldier. As a boy his father had taken him to visit battle-fields (60 percent of Civil War battles took place on Virginia soil). He did the same for his son. Save for two years in the Army Reserve, Martin had lived his entire life in Charlottesville.

As a young boy Martin had discovered a series of biographies published by Bobbs-Merrill in his church library. From *Tom Jefferson, Boy of Colonial Days* and *George Washington, Boy Leader*, he moved on to books on Virginia's military history. Douglas Southall Freeman's four-volume *R. E. Lee*, published in 1934 and 1935, had pride of place on his bookshelf. My father, a Civil War history buff, had the same unabridged editions, along with Freeman's three-volume *Lee's Lieutenants: A Study in Command* (*Manassas to Malvern Hill, Cedar Mountain to Chancellorsville,* and *Gettysburg to Appomattox*). Freeman portrayed Lee as "one of the small company of great men in whom there is no inconsistency to be explained, no enigma to be solved." Lewis Martin's reverence for Lee was as much a part of him as his Christian beliefs.

Martin held forth in a folksy conversational style, beginning with a meandering description of car trips up north to see his former UVA classmates, "courtesy of Mr. Henry Ford." Passing through little counties and towns, he noticed that Billy Yank, a statue of the common Union soldier often used as a war memorial, was nearly identical to the Johnny Reb statue that stood in front of the Charlottesville city courthouse in Court Square. When he asked a Civil War historian why, he learned both had been struck in the same Massachusetts foundry. He relayed their back-and-forth in the manner of a country lawyer leading a witness to a self-evident conclusion.

"I thought, well, isn't that interesting! About what time did these statues go up?

"Well, they went up about the same time as the statues went up here in Charlottesville."

"Well, why was that . . . how old were these [Union and Confederate] veterans?"

"Well, those men were in their sixties and probably seventies if they were even still alive."

"And who were the people who put these statues up?"

"It was their children and grandchildren."

Martin's point was that the South's desire to commemorate the sacrifices of their soldiers was no different from similar efforts up north. This was why he didn't buy the idea that there was any connection between the Lee and Jackson statues and Jim Crow. By eliding the difference between life-size memorials to the common soldier and monumental ones of Confederate generals, Martin made them appear interchangeable.

The other, less airtight reason Martin rejected the Lee statue's association with Jim Crow was that he found it difficult to believe Charlottesville's greatest benefactor was a racist. Paul Goodloe McIntire's name was inscribed all over the city and the university. He had gifted not only these statues but also the land for the whites-only McIntire Park and the Blacks-only Washington Park. "By the way," Martin said, "when you talk about separate but equal, when I was a little boy, I went to the wading pool at McIntire Park. If you go up and look at the swimming pool in Washington Park"—here his genial tone turned sharp—"you tell me who got the better end of the deal."

Ten minutes after Lewis Martin III sat down, Dr. Jalane Schmidt, the last member of the public to weigh in, stood up. Schmidt had been at Charlottesville's Pride celebration in Lee Park the previous year when someone wove a rainbow-colored feather boa through Traveller's bridle in a playful effort to include Lee in the festivities. After selfies posted on social media showed people posing with Lee's mount, someone called in a complaint that the Lee statue was being vandalized. The police arrived and unceremoniously stripped Traveller of his accessory. Schmidt had been struck by the fact that on the one day set aside for queer visibility, everyone was obliged to maintain a reverent posture toward the statue. When she read about the Blue Ribbon Commission being seated, she made it her business to attend.

As a professor of religious studies, Schmidt knew next to nothing about the Civil War and the Confederacy, and even less about local history. At the time Ta-Nehisi Coates was tweeting about his own deep dive into the Civil War, so she began reading everything he was reading. The hashtag #twitterhistorians was another resource. From the first public forum in July to the last one in November, it was clear she had drafted her remarks in advance, stuck to her talking points, and never went over her time. Jalane Schmidt became the nemesis of the Deplorables, plus Jane, and Lewis Martin III, in particular.

She introduced herself simply as a local. She acknowledged that she hadn't lived in the city long, but she had come to love it enough to learn some of its history. Then she got to her point. At the time of the Civil War, she said, the population of Albemarle County and Charlottesville together was around 26,000. Of that number nearly 14,000 were enslaved. She paused to let the figures sink in and then underlined their significance. "So. The majority." To hear people talking about how their Confederate ancestors had defended the city and so on gave her cause to wonder, *Defend from whom? And to what end?*

"For the majority of citizens here," she said, speaking of March 3, 1865, the day Union troops arrived, "this was Liberation Day." Then she took aim at those who had spoken at length about their Confederate heritage. "There is no moral equivalency between the struggle for freedom, which is the greatest American struggle there is, and those who fought to impede the freedom of these people. That is, Confederate soldiers." She ended on a conciliatory note. She would prefer to relocate the statues to a nice park "so that we can reflect about citizenship and freedom with everybody's history being accounted for." After that, the Deacon quietly told her to keep showing up. The Professor did too. Some of those calling for Lee's removal exchanged contact information.

In the months to come, Schmidt's overlooked enslaved majority, the 52 percent—the percentage of the city and county's total population—would provide the wedge around which a more focused call for the removal of the Lee and Jackson statues would cohere.

Four meetings later, on September 1, the Blue Ribbon Commission hosted a fast-talking Civil War historian. Gary Gallagher, a retired UVA

professor and civil rights activist, spent his allotted fifteen minutes pars-
ing four distinct narratives of the Civil War and how they shaped the
myths and histories we had all imbibed. It was a subtle presentation, and
listening to him I got the feeling that Professor Gallagher had already
decided it would be lost on most. In my experience few people spend
much time thinking about *how* they know what they think they know
about the Civil War and Robert E. Lee. We just know it and are disinclined to revisit the subject, except to confirm what we already know.
Still, he charged boldly ahead. He called these four distinct narratives
"memory traditions."

In the war's immediate aftermath, he began, there arose the Reunion
memory tradition. For those who had remained loyal to the United States
(i.e., the majority), Union victory was defined by the expectation that
now that the nation had been reunited, it was time to move on.

The second was the Emancipation memory tradition. Here, the Union
victory was defined not by reunion but by the end of slavery. This tradition also arose amid the war's aftershocks and was embraced by the
newly emancipated, freedmen, abolitionists, and Radical Republicans
for whom the Civil War was a war to free the slaves, full stop.

By the end of the nineteenth century, as Confederate and Union soldiers began dying off, a third narrative began to take hold. Gallagher
called this one the Reconciliation memory tradition. This was the one I
was steeped in as a child. In the Reconciliation account of the war, slavery and emancipation began to be airbrushed out, replaced by a storyline that described the Civil War as a tragic conflict of "brother against
brother." Statues of Billy Yank and Johnny Reb were not just identical
in appearance but represented equals in courage and sacrifice and worthiness of honor. This new narrative led to a widening divide between
how whites and Blacks recalled the war. During this period the mold-
ering, long-dead Robert E. Lee was resurrected. He went from being a
regional figure of interest largely to Virginians to a venerable hero and
national symbol of reconciliation.

Of relevance to Charlottesville's Confederate statues, Gallagher then
spoke of the fourth and final memory tradition, commonly known as
the Lost Cause. Like the Emancipation and Reunion narratives, the

Lost Cause arose in the immediate aftermath of the war. Unlike them, the Lost Cause emerged from a defeated, grieving, and defensive South, mired in maudlin nostalgia for the graces and wealth of its antebellum past. The first major tenet of this narrative, Gallagher held, was that neither secession nor the war was about slavery. The second tenet was that the Confederacy fought a war it was fated to lose, but its sacrifice was for the highest, most cherished constitutional principles. The deification of Robert E. Lee was another feature. Lastly, the Lost Cause nearly always included accounts of loyal slaves who had fought alongside their masters.

"I've seen figures as high as one hundred thousand Black Confederate soldiers," Gallagher said. "That's a hallucination. There were thousands of Black men with the Confederate armies. They were not soldiers. Underline. *Were not soldiers*. Underline. *Were not soldiers*." Gallagher spoke with the exasperation of a man who had heard sufficient Lost Cause nonsense to write a book about it.

Gallagher's outline of the four memory traditions was drawn from the work of David W. Blight. Blight, the author of the masterful *Race and Reunion*, has written that the Lost Cause expanded its narrative hold on the South through an assortment of arguments, organizations, rituals, and holidays. Lost Cause diehards, often former Confederate officers, were particularly evident in Virginia in the decades following the war, shaping people's memories by writing memoirs and giving speeches like the flowery ones that accompanied the unveiling of the Lee statue. One such officer, speaking to the Southern Historical Society in 1877, referred to Reconstruction as a second civil war, one in which the South had finally triumphed. This win erased any need to talk about the causes of the first one. "This was never easy for Union veterans to swallow," Blight writes, but that was "how white supremacy became an integral part of the process of national reconciliation."

Professor Gallagher viewed the Lee (1924) and Jackson (1921) statues as Jim Crow monuments, demanding deference, rather than true Confederate memorials honoring the fallen. He also produced a packet showing how Lee's reputation evolved in the decades following the Civil War. By 1965, the war's centennial, Lee and Lincoln were considered the two great figures of the Civil War, evidence of the long life of the Reconciliation narrative. Combined with the legacy of the Lost Cause, this narrative succeeded in expunging any acknowledgment of the shame of slavery, or the jubilant news of emancipation. White Southerners' quick-tempered sensitivities on these subjects were indulged and placated at the expense of the emancipated and their descendants. One might say they were treated with radical empathy.

Gallagher went on to demonstrate how slavery was written out of the Lost Cause rationale for the war. In his packet were four quotations from Confederate leadership, two from President Jefferson Davis, and two from Vice President Alexander Stephens. The first quotes predated the outset of the war and included Alexander Stephens's March 21, 1861, Cornerstone speech identifying slavery as the decisive factor in the decision to secede, and white supremacy the "great physical, philosophical, and moral truth" underlying the Confederate cause. The second set of quotations came after the war when the dissembling began. With the clock ticking, Gallagher galloped on.

I was familiar with the Cornerstone speech, but I'd never heard of Stephens's postwar 1868 treatise *A Constitutional View of the Late War Between the States*. As Stephens identified himself as a protégé of Thomas Jefferson, I took a detour to read it. Professor Gallagher characterized the treatise as unreadable, but I found it rather mesmerizing. It appeared that once Stephens was released from prison for treason, friends from the North came to visit him. Consequently, he decided to structure his treatise as an interminable debate between himself and imaginary Yankee interlocutors, one in which he would roundly correct their mistaken view that the South went to war to preserve the institution of slavery and spread it to other states. In the opening pages of *A Constitutional View of the Late War Between the States*, Stephens scoffs at such a simplistic notion. Slavery was but a minor consideration!

Stephens begins by taking his prewar "great physical, philosophical and moral truth" of white supremacy, and deftly substituting it with the "great principle of Independence and Sovereignty," better known as states' rights. For added legitimacy, he credited Thomas Jefferson as the "Great Apostle" of states' rights. It was a bold move, and Jefferson Davis joined him in vigorously peddling this new line. To elude moral censure over the South's backward fight to keep human beings in chains, a practice long abandoned by civilized nations, Stephens turned the Civil War into a moral crusade in defense of the highest Jeffersonian constitutional principles. People were still parroting the rationale of "states' rights" as the cause of the Civil War to the Blue Ribbon Commission.

Yet the more Stephens fulminated, the more he seemed a haunted man. He compulsively repeated his points. "This whole subject of slavery, so-called, [was] but a drop in the ocean compared with those other considerations." The $2 billion vested in the bodies of the enslaved? A sum of money representing more wealth than all the nation's railroads and industries combined? This was "but dust in the balance, compared with the rights of Independence and Sovereignty."

Eight hundred pages of passionate madness followed.

By the time the second community forum took place on September 22 at Buford Middle School, the idea that the statues might be utilized as educational tools "to understand our past to benefit our present and our future," as one white woman put it, had gained ground. The Art Historian pointed out that even if the plaques were rewritten to make it clear that Lee and Jackson had fought and lost a war in defense of slavery, on their plinths or off, the statues would still exact deference. Words could not compete with larger-than-life-size men with mythical backstories. Even so, the idea that leaving the statues in place would facilitate a dialogue on race was spoken about with great earnestness. In fact, it was the public hearings of the BRC that were providing the classroom they envisioned Lee Park becoming.

At this second forum, more Black residents began to weigh in. Alongside a belief that the money involved would be better spent elsewhere, a few found something fishy about this sudden desire to remove the statues from their parks. If Lee and Jackson were taken away, there would be nothing, apart from a few tiny plaques, one obscured by a trash can, to document their history. "Everything that is Black history in this town is a plaque," seventy-year-old Mary Carey noted in her second appearance. "You got to get on your knees to read them." When she was a little girl, she said, the actual slave auction block was still in Court Square. At some point, it was replaced by a tiny plaque set in the sidewalk. Her fear seemed to be that their history would once more be erased or diminished, as the auction block was, if the statues were removed. While clearly no one in the Black community was consulted about the installation of these Confederate statues, their presence nonetheless provided vivid reminders of the ugliness they and their ancestors had suffered and survived.

The comments of a Black veteran and longtime resident named Lee Porter also stood out at this second forum. Porter's great-great-grandfather, a man "who wasn't known for being a slave," worked in the local wool factory. Upon seeing a group of Confederate soldiers approach, he had sent his son into a barn to hide. To their request for water, he pointed at a bucket, then at the well, and told them to help themselves. Whereupon one soldier leveled his musket at him and blew his chest right out. "So, history. I got history," Porter noted laconically. "I know more about Charlottesville history than most people will ever know. But nobody wants to hear it from me because I see it from a different standpoint."

It was true. The most impassioned statue defenders believed that four generations in Virginia, or a Confederate ancestor who was by Lee's side at Appomattox, or simply their childhood memories should give special weight to their testimony. Not once in the three community forums did they give any indication that they heard or absorbed the testimony of the city's longtime Black residents. They could hardly call such people "outside agitators" or "carpetbaggers." While they often disdained the white 'guilt and shame liberals' who came from somewhere else, they still engaged with them, if only to dismiss their opinions as mere faddishness or "presentism." But they never seemed to acknowledge there might be local people with even deeper investment in the city and the ideals it so vigorously declaimed. It was as if the defenders had some congenital condition that made them incapable of processing a story like Porter's or giving it equal weight to the stories they told.

I imagine that was why many Black residents were disinclined to weigh in. What was the point? I learned later that some commissioners had noted the defenders' tone deafness. And perhaps some of their fellow citizens had too; by the second community forum the number of people calling for the statues' removal now equaled those calling for the statues to remain in place.

As if to provide evidence of the defenders' hardness of hearing, Prof. Gallagher's account of the Lost Cause and Reconciliation narratives' role in exalting Robert E. Lee had not penetrated the cast-iron mindset of Lewis Martin III even a little. All that mattered to Martin was Prof. Gallagher's opinion that the Lee statue should remain in place, not to be worshipped as a graven image, but as a historical artifact. Martin had been on a mission since the first public forum. When it was his turn to speak, he returned to trial mode to recount his conversations with Lee's detractors.

"Typically, I'll say, have you ever read a biography of Robert E. Lee? And they'll say no. And I'll say, Well, why not? And they'll say, well, because Lee's a traitor. And I'll say, Well, that's very interesting. If Lee's a traitor, then I wonder why the United States has a fort about eighty miles southeast of here, a major army installation, named after Robert E. Lee. If Robert E. Lee is a traitor, I wonder why it is that his statue stands in the Statuary Hall in the Capitol Building of the United States of America in Washington, DC. If Robert E. Lee is a traitor, I wonder why it is that his portrait hangs in the superintendent's office at the United States Military Academy at West Point." Martin continued in this vein until his time was up and he was obliged to rest his case.

If Lewis Martin III's views embodied the lock the Reconciliation and Lost Cause narratives had on the defenders' understanding of the Civil War, by continuing to speak on behalf of the 52 percent, Jalane Schmidt gave voice to the lost Emancipationist legacy. Her arguments had shifted since the first community forum. It was as if she realized that finding common ground with Lee's defenders was another Lost Cause. Now she addressed the commissioners directly.

The history of the 52 percent had been swept under the rug by the white masters of the Jim Crow era, she began, and some of them were

still at it. She begged the Blue Ribbon Commission to take the opportunity to clean house. "Don't punt. Don't kick the can down the road.
Don't shy away. Be a leader on this issue locally. And nationally." She
warned against a "Kumbaya compromise": keeping the statues where
they were, with face-saving additions. "The 52 percent deserve more than
just crumbs from the master's table." She suggested renaming Lee Park
Liberty Park and throwing a party to celebrate March 3, 1865, the day
Charlottesville surrendered and the 52 percent were liberated.

Jalane Schmidt's position that there was a right side and a wrong
side to the war had the virtue of moral clarity. Her take-no-prisoners
tone granted all those reluctant to disavow their Confederate ancestors
or their admiration for Lee no further standing. It was inconceivable
to me that Lee's defenders would ever attend a party celebrating the
Confederacy's defeat. Their idolization of Lee was bred in the bone. It
was why Lee was up there and not George Washington.

By November 1, ten days before the last of the three community
forums, the voices of the public calling for removal may have multiplied,
but there was now disarray among the commissioners. After studiously
avoiding voicing any opinion for six months, they began to nervously
discuss where they stood on the matter. There wasn't much enthusiasm
for adding new signage along with a vague instruction to "transform"
the statues where they stood. Only a commissioner who was also a landscape designer saw possibilities in what might be done to the statue to
render it less toxic. Take the general off the horse. Cover him in kudzu.
Bury him. The Professor wanted the statues to stay in the city; he just
wasn't sure where to put them.

The Deacon and the Art Historian appeared to be the only staunch
proponents of the "Relocate option" for Lee. The Art Historian believed recontextualization was impossible. As it stood, when a visitor
approaches the Lee statue, from whatever direction, the eye is forced to
look up. Paul Goodloe McIntire was a cosmopolitan man, she said, well
versed in art's visual language; he knew what he was doing. She was
content to leave Jackson in place in a nod to its reputation as a superior
work of art but proposed moving Lee to McIntire Park, where there was
already a Vietnam veterans memorial. She argued that for those who

consider Lee's statue a tribute to the fallen or an icon of their heritage, a veterans park was a more appropriate place to venerate him. Lee Park was where the city's various festivals took place, including those celebrating diversity. The Archivist was won over, and the Listener was intrigued, but the question as to which way the vote would go remained wide open.

After hours of back-and-forth, someone suggested both options be forwarded to the city council. The Art Historian pointed out that if it was too hard for them to choose one or the other, city councillors would find it even harder. Then one commissioner, an older white woman with a giggly and girlish voice, made a motion to call for a straw vote. I hadn't given her a nickname because her comments had always struck me as wishy-washy, and most of the time they were passed over in silence. Her motion was immediately seconded by the strangled voice of Old Virginia, the grand dame of the Albemarle Charlottesville Historical Society. This time, something about Old Virginia's voice reminded me of all the reasons I had left Virginia. It wasn't so much what she said that got under my skin as the way she spoke, with a clubwoman's overbearing air of condescension, disguised in halting speech.

It was late. I heard weariness and resignation in the voices of those who realized they didn't have the votes to remove Lee. Before the vote was taken, the language characterizing the nature of "transform in place" was watered down. Old Virginia suggested "based on historical fact" be changed to "based on historical analysis." No one objected. The Deacon sighed and revised the wording. The woman who had made the motion wanted to avoid "angry words" like "challenge and confront" to avoid unpleasantness, so once again language was watered down. Lee would remain a hero to some and a traitor to others.

"Where common memory is lacking, where people do not share in the same past, there can be no real community," I once read. The residents of Charlottesville were eager to return to sleeping in separate beds. The final vote was 7–2 in favor of "transform in place." The Deacon said that in his humble opinion the result amounted to "a cold cup of chitlin soup." Yet, unlike a certain unnamed presidential candidate, he said he would accept the results of the vote.

A week later, Donald Trump was elected president of the United States, and suddenly the statues provided the impetus for a proxy insurrection on Charlottesville Twitter. Three days after the election, on November 10, the final community forum of the Blue Ribbon Commission was called to order in the auditorium of Walker Upper Elementary. The Professor opened with an emotional twelve-minute speech answering those who interpreted their straw vote as a simple vote to keep the statues in the park. He struggled to make their decision to transform the Lee statue sound as radical as he felt it needed to be. Yet no matter how long he spoke, no matter how forcefully he revisited Charlottesville's history of white supremacy, in the end Lee remained exactly where he was, in the city's central historic square.

Listening to the distraught Professor, I couldn't help but think of little Mary Carey watching the white children play in the park her mother had forbidden her to enter. She hadn't really cared about the statue. She had just wanted to play with the other children. But Robert E. Lee had held the Blue Ribbon Commission in thrall, like the brilliant battle commander he once was, silently directing the terms of their discussion on his fate. Notwithstanding the need for some kind of memorial recognizing Black Charlottesville's history, sometimes a park is a park. Not an art museum or a classroom, but a shady place where anyone can sit on a bench and read a book from the Jefferson Madison Central Library across the street.

Jalane Schmidt had arrived that evening with a group of activists from a recently formed chapter of a national organization called Showing Up for Racial Justice. Many of them were wearing white T-shirts with "52%" printed on the front. The tables were now turned. Those members of the public calling for the removal of the statues overwhelmed the statues' defenders, 38–13. Jalane Schmidt called on the commissioners to reconsider their votes, move both statues, and raise a monument to the 52 percent, commensurate with the magnitude and heroism of their struggle.

She ended her speech by reading the 1866 testimony of an enslaved man named Wesley Norris. During the Civil War, Norris had been captured attempting to flee for freedom. As punishment, his owner,

Gen. Robert E. Lee, ordered his overseer to tie him to a post and give him fifty lashes. While the overseer went to work, Lee enjoined him to "lay it on well." "Not satisfied with simply lacerating our naked flesh," Norris recounted, "Gen. Lee then ordered the overseer to thoroughly wash our backs with brine. Which was done."

"Put that on a plaque," she said and sat down.

A member of Showing Up for Racial Justice pointed out they were already seeing Confederate symbols being used by "dangerous people in dangerous ways." Those who had voted to keep the Lee statue in place had expressed optimism that the transformation would succeed even though it had never been done anywhere else. "What are the stakes if you are wrong?" she asked. Another said that their decision would embolden the neo-Confederates. She compared the present moment to the white backlash against Reconstruction and the racial terror that followed. Zyahna Bryant said that fence-sitting amounted to siding with white supremacists. In an email to the commission, Jalane Schmidt warned them they were playing with fire.

Four days after Thanksgiving, the commissioners had their final meeting at CitySpace, a conference room overlooking the Downtown Mall. They decided to vote again. They voted unanimously to rename the parks in which the statues stood. Following Jalane Schmidt's proposal, they called for the city to recognize March 3, 1865, the day General Philip Sheridan arrived in Charlottesville with his troops, as Liberation Day. Then, as the Art Historian had proposed, they separated the fate of the Lee statue from Jackson's and decided to vote on both options and to send the results of both votes to city council. The Relocate option for Lee now went seven in favor, two opposed. The vote on Transform in Place was five in favor and four opposed.

For Stonewall Jackson and Little Sorrel, the Deacon was the lone holdout against Transform in Place and the lone vote for Relocate. The Professor asked him if he might change his vote so, at least on one statue, they could be unanimous. The chair of the Blue Ribbon Commission thought for a bit. If the commissioners agreed to implement his proposal for the transformation of the Jackson statue, he would change his vote to keep it where it was. They agreed to consider it.

"Erect a thirty-five-foot statue of Nat Turner standing behind Jackson with a hatchet in his hand."

With the delivery of their final report on December 19, 2016, the work of the Blue Ribbon Commission on Race, Memorials, and Public Spaces was done. In the New Year, the five members of Charlottesville's city council would have to make sense of it all and render their verdict.

CHAPTER 3

The Art of Trolling

In the weeks after Trump's election an up-and-comer on the far right named Richard Spencer appeared on NBC, NPR, and CNN. Profiles of him appeared in the *Washington Post* and the *Los Angeles Times*. More were in the works. Showtime was putting out feelers for a documentary. Then, just before Thanksgiving, Spencer gave a speech at the annual conference of his think tank, the National Policy Institute. NPI was dedicated to the "preservation of the heritage, identity, and future of European people in the US and elsewhere." Spencer might have ended his speech declaring that America belonged to Europeans. But he knew his moment. America belonged to white people.

"America was, until this past generation, a white country designed for ourselves and our posterity. It is our creation; it is our inheritance, and it belongs to us."

This was met with a roar of approval from the hundred or so men assembled, culminating in scattered, stiff-armed Nazi salutes, like a mini-Nuremberg rally. He acknowledged these with a sloppy salute, not bothering to put down his drink. A clip of this went viral. I watched it while tracing the arc of Spencer's journey from obscurity to Charlottesville. And when I did, something about the world I had known abruptly shifted. Two twentieth-century sources of national pride, providing decades of patriotic uplift, collapsed in a heap. That we had fought a "Good War" against the horrors of Nazism and fascism. That our country's civil rights leaders had scored a moral triumph over racist Southerners and politics as usual. I knew these were national mythologies that historians did their best to complicate; by pointing out the Red Army's role in breaking the back of the Wehrmacht, for example, or the communist and nationalist forces of China doing the same to Japan. Still, it hadn't occurred to me that the American creed they embodied could be dispensed with altogether, replaced by something called the "alt-right."

This was a term coined by Spencer in 2008, on the eve of Obama's election and the collapse of the US economy. The alt-right was a reaction to mainstream Republican politics, to the Christian right, libertarianism, paleo-conservatism, and the "war on terror." It was the online edgelord's response to what was once called political correctness or multiculturalism and is now called woke. It was old-fashioned white nationalism and white supremacy, with its grab bag of bigotries, wrapped in contrarian, countercultural, and hypermasculine cool. Like the hip alt-weeklies of yore, it had its own outlets where an ironic sense of style and subversive humor had been shaped and fashioned in the company of those with like-minded dispositions.

Kicked off traditional social media, the figureheads of this new movement created a replacement "alt-tech" with their own browsers, plug-ins, payment processors, web hosting, domain registrations, and VPN services. "They are just building a copy-cat version of the internet playground," data scientist Megan Squire has said, describing how the rise of these new platforms allowed men like Spencer to say the formerly unsayable in the name of edginess. In so doing, the "alt-right" stole the glamour of the rebel, the revolutionary, the outlaw, the punk, and the perennial stance of *épater les bourgeois* from the boomer left. They used it to skewer the moral pretensions and ideological conformity of progressives, and the square, self-serving Republicans in Name Only, War on Terror–supporting dads. For many, it had a dark, naughty allure. I got it.

With a knowing nod to Steve Bannon, with whom he keenly aspired to ally himself, Richard Spencer used the media attention to openly audition for the role of Trump's brain. He offered a political language for the incoming administration. No more foreign wars, a proud embrace of white heritage, the cultivation of white grievance, a flirty fascism, and a renunciation of "globalism."

The latter was a newish euphemism, replacing *cosmopolitan*, for Jews. But it was also an abstraction that needed a face. The Jewish financier and funder of democracy initiatives George Soros provided it. Similarly, the woke liberal elite driving the conversation in media, business, and culture, were either Jews or in the pay of Jews, and thus hostile to a political order in which Christian white men claimed ascendancy. In place of the founders' notion of religious freedom, one that, on paper, protected not just Jews and Muslims, but also atheists and infidels, the alt-right proposed a Christian nation, if Christianity is understood to be an aspect of white heritage, stripped of long-standing ethical notions of right and wrong. Some foresaw an indivisible, sea-to-shining-sea, white nation; others, a confederacy of single-race, single-religion "ethnostates."

Spencer even called himself a Christian Zionist; Israel, which quarantined and policed Christian and Muslim Palestinians in the townships of the West Bank and the Gaza Strip, exemplified his idea of an ethnostate. The two movements had a shared history. In 1941 a right-wing Zionist proposed to a German diplomat the solution to the Jewish "problem" lay in Jewish resettlement in Palestine. By then of course Nazi Germany had other plans. And when, in a debate with Spencer, a rabbi at Texas A&M Hillel insisted that the Torah taught "radical inclusion and love," Spencer pointed out that, on the contrary, blood and soil white nationalists shared not only the Zionist's vision of a single-race ethnostate but a virulent hostility to assimilation. The rabbi had no answer to that.

Spencer was far happier debating who would or wouldn't be admitted to his Klan than getting to the nitty-gritty of how to make one hundred million Americans disappear. In a bold step beyond Mitt Romney's "self-deportation," Spencer called for "a peaceful ethnic cleansing." He was joking. There would be nothing peaceful about it. In 2012 Spencer had published a piece on the AltRight.com website titled "Is Black Genocide Right?" "Instead of asking how we can make reparations for slavery . . . we should instead be asking questions like 'Does human civilization actually need the black race?' [and] 'What would be the best and easiest way to dispose of them?'" This went overboard and was taken down, like a product release before the market was ready. Spencer's cavalier pose over the prospect of genocide was calculated to throw a normal person off, stuck in "he can't be serious" mode. One journalist wrote that Spencer's ideas didn't arise from deep conviction. It was an intellectual exercise, "performed for his own amusement." The ferocity of his vendettas argued otherwise. Spencer isn't amused. That's an affectation. He is enraged.

Amid the media furor he'd stoked by summoning Adolf Hitler, Richard Spencer decided just then to appear on the podcast of Andrew Anglin, the balding, squirrelly-eyed editor of the neo-Nazi website the Daily Stormer. Why, I wondered, with the mainstream media at his feet? Because he was embarked on a vendetta. Spencer divided his time between a loft above a chocolate shop in Alexandria, Virginia, and the picturesque mountain ski resort of Whitefish, Montana (pop. 8,000), where his Dallas-based parents had a vacation home. In the latest chapter of a long-running feud, the Whitefish city council had recently declared Spencer persona non grata. This was where Andrew Anglin came in.

"Never back down" was Spencer's personal credo. He had started with the local paper. His wife wrote a letter accusing the city council of orchestrating a Stalinist witch hunt against her husband. A social death sentence, perhaps, but a henchman's bullet at the back of the head? A midnight transport to the gulag? Overstating the harm, then playing the victim, was part of the white nationalist toolbox. Rand and Sherry Spencer, Richard's parents, wrote another letter. A downtown commercial property his mother had developed was being unfairly targeted by protesters. Her Realtor made the mild suggestion: sell it. For Spencer this amounted to backing down. Time for the big guns.

Andrew Anglin and Richard Spencer scarcely knew each other, but they understood each other. Learning of Spencer's feud with the Whitefish city council, Anglin activated his cyber mob. When Sherry Spencer's Jewish Realtor picked up her phone, she heard gunshots. Then slurs: "You fucking wicked kike whore." She was doxed. One of Anglin's boys made a meme featuring a photo of her twelve-year-old son at the Auschwitz gate. The campaign spread to local rabbis, and then anyone with a vaguely Jewish name. Local businesses that exhibited "Love Lives Here" window signs had their phone lines tied up. The governor met with the mayor, but there was little anyone could do.

Though the practice of choreographed mega harassment has since become ubiquitous, the experience felt unprecedented to Whitefish residents hoping to spend their retirement in vigorous exercise. Two people involved in preparing Charlottesville for the Unite the Right rally told me the saga known as Gamergate was an important inflection point in the development of the weapon Andrew Anglin unleashed on Whitefish after Richard Spencer's appearance on his podcast. Even gaming journalists struggled to describe what was underway when, between August and October 2014, over two million posts attached to the Gamergate hashtag went out on various social media, but largely on Twitter and Reddit.

Most of these posts targeted Zoë Quinn, a game developer who uses the pronoun *they*. Bomb threats were called in to Quinn's public appearances. Quinn was menaced by pornographic descriptions of how they'd be raped and graphic fantasies of how they'd be killed. Quinn was then doxed: their address and phone number were published, forcing Quinn to move to safe houses in case someone decided to hunt them down and carry out their threats. Anyone who spoke up in Quinn's support was dogpiled.

Why? Quinn had designed a game conveying a day in the life of a person suffering from depression. Some gamers didn't take kindly to the editorial space Quinn was given for trying something arty. A writer named Leigh Alexander suggested that creators like Quinn were challenging the cultural mores of traditional gaming. After years of guns, coins, flash-bangs, and sexy damsels, Alexander predicted hard-core gamers would soon lose access to their fantasy fix of "high octane masculinity." Not because of PC culture but because they were no longer gaming's primary demographic.

The threats multiplied exponentially in mid-August, when Quinn's ex-boyfriend posted a jeremiad falsely accusing Quinn of sleeping with

a reviewer for positive review coverage. Now Gamergate was about journalistic ethics. While couch surfing to elude the trolls, Quinn infiltrated
a chatroom on 4chan, an anonymous imageboard forum. Imageboards
were online bulletin boards for picture posts and commentary, often
taken from other online sources. Quinn discovered that the entire
Gamergate saga was the product of a handful of 4chan users colluding
via multiple "sock puppets" (phony online identities) to weaponize the
amorphous grievances of young men. Here were boasts about getting
Gamergate to go viral. The coordinated gaslighting of journalists. The
tracking of who was getting the most traction. The chat logs began on
August 18 and ended just over two weeks later, the day Quinn posted excerpts of their machinations. In response, 4chan removed Gamergaters
from the platform for doxing. This led to the founding of 8chan, which
would soon become the Wild West of imageboard platforms.

If journalistic ethics was a cover, what was it a cover for? For gamers
to be spared having to think about their mental health? For gamers to
be allowed to forget that women were flesh-and-blood gamers, not just
pixilated avatars? For Zoë Quinn to suffer, preferably a grisly and painful death by their own hand or someone else's? Maybe the trolls wanted
all these things. Maybe it was just "fun and games." But for many who
glommed on for the ride, it was, in the words of one Charlottesville activist, "come for the misogyny and stay for the fascism."

This was a new kind of gaming, one that involved flipping the script
of who was really being bullied, who was the real sexist, racist, or fascist.
On 8chan the Gamergate troll swarm became the new, turbocharged,
and versatile propaganda weapon. Here, whoever could manipulate the
AI algorithms that drove social media behavior could amass followers
and direct vengeance; a school for aspiring vigilantes. Meanwhile, the
media was ill-equipped; the rules under which it operated had been reverse engineered to trap it into broadcasting the Gamergate message
further afield. To push back, to take bad faith arguments seriously, to
express outrage in any form, was to become a pawn in their game.

By 2016 Andrew Anglin had figured out how to use the Daily Stormer
to mobilize the dark energies of extremely online 8chan men like those
behind Gamergate. In 2017 Steve Bannon explained what he had learned

THE ART OF TROLLING

from Gamergate to a Breitbart reporter. Coordinated online gender and racial harrassment, he realized, could be a useful political tactic, simultaneously terrorizing adversaries, coercing Republican allies and hijacking media coverage. Subsequently, the playbook would be taken up by normies, Trumpers, and foreign powers. Covid and QAnon conspiracies would metastasize online, culminating in the Big Lie and the attack on the Capitol.

But Anglin got there long before Bannon did, organizing his troll army into small and localized crews called Stormer Book Clubs. Their tasks might involve doxing people, hacking their accounts, or targeting them with obscene and threatening flyers. They also engaged in meme wars, which is best described as a digital version of psyops. Stormers and 4chan adepts create memes to spread disinformation, hijack narratives, or inject insurgent ideas onto the battlefield of social media. A reporter for *Vice* called memes the "IEDs of information warfare." Meme warfare enthusiasts believe memes can reprogram or disrupt entire societies, upend elections, and create new realities. At Spencer's behest, Anglin brought this arsenal to Whitefish.

Responding to Whitefish's alarm, Spencer gave a statement. Everyone was overreacting. It was all a joke to trigger people. After his *Sieg heil* moment, he said the same thing. "Everyone is blowing it completely out of proportion. . . . It wasn't a political statement. It was a joke. Trolling even." Six days after the harassment of Whitefish began, Anglin raised the stakes. He was sending his Stormer Book Clubs into this idyllic Rocky Mountain town, filled with million-dollar log cabins, overpriced boutiques, and shops selling custom-made athletic gear, to stage a Clockwork Orange–style spree of murder and mayhem. Two hundred "skinheads" would be bused in, arriving on Martin Luther King Day, armed with high-power rifles. Whitefish went on full terror alert. Six hundred counterprotesters showed up in subzero weather.

Anglin's army never showed.

Was Andrew Anglin showing Richard Spencer, the far-right's new media star, that his pretty boy life in this picture-perfect ski resort could be upended on his whim? Possibly. Far-right alliances were notoriously treacherous. Anglin's loyalties, if he had any, lay with the "throwaway men" of his troll army and his paymasters, whoever they might be. It was also possible that Spencer was using Anglin to show his Whitefish neighbors that, in this moment of his ascendancy, he wielded powers beyond their understanding. Left unable to judge the level of threat, Whitefish was incapable of responding to it.

Eight months later, Charlottesville would find itself in similar waters.

So, if "Love Lives Here" white people weren't welcome in Richard Spencer's America, who was? Whiteness isn't a simple category, a checkmark in the Caucasian box. For sophisticated trolls like Spencer, "our people" was a semimystical if not genetic bond with the Anglo-Saxons; or, given his part-German ancestry, a generic and ahistorical idea of Northern Europe, including those Nordic countries Hitler so fancied. Never Asia or Africa. Despite Latin America's colonial ties with Spain and Portugal and the waves of German and Italian immigrants (including Nazis and fascists) who enriched its culture and its gene pool, Spencer felt no kinship there. He associated Latin America with migrants who crossed the border to become part of the American underclass.

Sometimes a Christian faith and devotion to family was upheld, sometimes a pre-Christian, folkish, and pagan past. For others, invocations of faith were derived from some fetishized Crusader past drawn from hours of playing *Assassin's Creed*. For Richard Spencer Christianity was a "spirit" he deployed to vanquish his enemies on the godless and depraved left. Christian nationalists were not evident at Unite the Right; but the weaponization of Christianity in the service of white nationalism, white supremacy, and the patriarchy would have its moment.

Queers weren't white, unless you were the dandy Milo Yiannopoulos, or were keen to reclaim the homoerotic warrior banner of the Spartans. Spencer denounced deviancy and porn culture, but when it came to gay men he equivocated. Queer women and trans people of whatever stripe were beyond the pale. A driving hatred of communists, Jews, and feminists was characteristic of "our people." For Spencer the left, including the progressive "Love Lives Here" white people, were to be defeated on every front.

In some instances, intellectual affinity with a particular historical moment was a stand-in for hereditary descent. Spencer was partial to the Roman Empire, but also Napoleonic France and 1930s Germany. In America, he claimed, a "coherent" European and Christian national culture emerged after the Great War. High art enhanced these period sympathies, as evidenced by Spencer's love of Wagner. He often poses as an intellectual with a taste for bold ideas, experimental theater, and operatic spectacle. "I think of myself as a poet at times," Spencer has said, claiming a poet's interest in language and rhetorical device. The "great battle for the soul of the west" was a spiritual battle, he insisted, not an actual military campaign. It operated at the level of culture.

To appeal to upper-middle-class and professional white men who feared competing or having to answer to women and minorities, "our people" were educated, even highly educated. Spencer himself studied English and music at UVA, received a master's in humanities at the University of Chicago, and pursued a doctorate at Duke, before abandoning all that to become a so-called public intellectual. Spencer believed that higher education should be limited to "a cognitive elite, dedicated to truth." For everyone else there was trade school.

The cultivation of hatred and the hunger for domination were both sterling qualities of "our people." As was a reverence for "Western civilization." In the 1860s, Western civilization had little to do with whiteness and everything to do with the life or death contest between the eastern "barbarism" of tzarist Russia and the British Empire. In the United States, Christianity was the justification settlers of European descent brought to bear for forcefully depriving "savage" indigenous peoples of their lands. It was only in the late nineteenth and early twentieth centuries, the golden age of US imperialism and Reconstruction, that "Western civilization" became the jewel in the crown of white supremacy.

"It was as if the wounds of the Civil War were being healed by uniting the former white adversaries through their whiteness," the classicist Rebecca Kennedy has written, "a whiteness explicitly defined through the Classical as the root of their shared identity." By the 1940s, she notes, Spanish, Greek, Italian, and Eastern European immigrants were granted an honor that had been reserved for the "Anglo-European" immigrants of Northern Europe. They became white. As race is a legal as well as a social construct, the understanding of who is or is not white is rarely stated explicitly; it involves cultural and behavioral shifts, often accompanied by a change in class status. The self-identification as "white" is cemented by identifying an Other. Among Christian nationalists, Muslims and "illegals" have replaced Jews and Catholics, at least for now. After World War II, Jews were considered white, albeit conditionally.

Here an age-old superstition reared its hydra head, cloaked in the facile language of the seminar room. The phrase *Judeo-Christian*, Spencer insisted, was a political slogan that distorted both the "metaphysical and historical nature" (Spencer had a weakness for hollow abstractions) of Jews and Europeans. Conquest was a signature trait of white Europeans. Despite the violent expulsion of Palestinians from their land in 1948, Spencer felt Jews had shown insufficient appetite for empire building. Spencer's patron, William Regnery, distinguished Ashkenazic Jews of France, Germany, and Eastern Europe from the Sephardic Jews of Spain, Portugal, North Africa, and the Middle East. Based on God knows what, Regnery believed Ashkenazic Jews might be half-white.

In an essay on Marcus Aurelius, the Russian Jewish poet Joseph Brodsky once observed that the past and the future are united only in our imaginations. And our imaginations are fired by the dread of being without precedent in history and the equal dread that we are inconsequential in its glare. The stronger this dread, Brodsky seems to say, the more grandiose our notions of antiquity and of the utopian futures we conceive for ourselves from the histories available to us. This was the lens through which I tried to understand how men like Spencer chose their identities and curated their histories, hatreds, and visions of the future. Did the white ethnostate begin with their fear of inconsequence? Which then exploded into a preemptive and hysterical dread of immanent extinction? Or was this just an elaborate justification for indulging their predilection for violence?

The chant "You will not replace us," heard at the May 13 torch rally in Lee Park, is imported from European fascism. In the twenties and thirties

Jews, Romany, and homosexuals were spoken of as existential threats to native populations, much as migrants are spoken of today in the United States (an absurdity in a country made up of migrants). This created the mandate for the camps and crematoria. Damon T. Berry defined white nationalism as the belief that "the white race is imperiled and that it is the duty of every white man and woman to do what they must to protect it from biological extinction." *Genocidaires* have always claimed that it is *their* existence that is under threat, even as they go about the business of extermination.

Spencer's Big Idea was that the establishment of a white ethnostate would usher in a period of cultural renewal, a renaissance that would rescue whiteness from "fat goofballs in Dockers." This read to me like a backhanded admission that the trouble facing whiteness was of its own making. Spencer has never undertaken a systemic critique of progressive pieties. On the rare occasion he engages with contemporary culture, he is dismissive. Though his National Policy Institute has a publishing arm, he has never written a book or made any creative contribution to the Western canon he so heralds. The parry and thrust offered by journalists, the peacocking on various online platforms, constitute his entire oeuvre.

Spencer did, however, produce a "meta-political manifesto." He worked on it for over a year and would release it on the eve of the Unite the Right rally. He titled it "The Charlottesville Statement" and hoped it would be as accessible to "normies" as the Port Huron Statement was. The Port Huron Statement, the 1962 manifesto of Students for a Democratic Society, was a far-ranging critique of the politics of the Cold War, the arms race, income inequality, big labor, and race discrimination. "The Charlottesville Statement" offered nothing of the sort. The first of its twenty points read: "Race is real. Race Matters. Race is the foundation of identity." Then, helpless to resist, Spencer donned academic drag. "Whiteness is shorthand for a worldwide constellation of peoples, each of which is derived from the Indo-European race, often called Aryan." So much for normies.

There is no such thing as an Indo-European or Aryan race. The terms are derived from a mid-nineteenth-century linguistic theory that traced syntactical similarities between European and Asian languages, including languages spoken in Iran, Afghanistan, and the northern reaches of the Indian subcontinent. Outmoded cant, recycled as cutting-edge theory, is the enduring tic of the perpetual grad student trying to come across as smart and sophisticated.

To the degree that previously stifled or marginalized voices are now being sought out, critically discussed, and celebrated, white men are losing their spot in the cultural limelight. While they maintain their hold on power and money, they can no longer count on our undivided attention. Their storylines no longer resonate. Too often, they terrorize. The white nationalists and white supremacists among them have concluded that if we will not love them, respect them, admire them, then perhaps we will fear them. Young men now engineer spectacles of shock and awe, but where they embrace the triumph of the antihero, we reap tragedy. Each grim and deadly performance shows us how defenseless we are. Eric Harris and Dylan Klebold. Elliot Rodger and Dylann Roof. Robert Bowers and Payton Gendron. Though there are no tickets to purchase, no national tours, we are their captive audience.

Hence their embrace of the dark side of American history. Hence the proliferating militias, the vigilante normies bringing guns to the Capitol and children's story hours. The new white nationalists can, as Hitler did, cherry-pick the illiberal precedents of American history to model a means to achieve their dreams of an ethnostate. The 1830 Indian Removal Act provides a ready template for genocide and ethnic cleansing; Jim Crow and racial terror provide a means to police the borders of non-white ghettoes, townships, and reservations. And there were ample analogues for expropriation of wealth and property under the rubrics of "Manifest Destiny," evangelizing "Christianity," "urban renewal," or "democracy and freedom." These models, templates, and policies were as American as apple pie. While I searched for appropriate historical precedents, these ideas resurfaced and reclaimed the American political imagination. The white nationalist revolution had arrived.

It was tempting for me to believe Spencer's white nationalism was a grift aimed at rich white men like William Regnery who were used to leveraging money to protect money. It was always more than that.

Spencer is a skilled manipulator. He subscribed to the Nietzschean notion that great men shape history and power creates its own reality. As perilous climate conditions, extreme income inequality, and algorithm-driven radicalism foment more and more instability, Spencer will be recognized as a catalytic agent. We don't have to imagine what it would be like to live in a country with indoctrinated trolls armed with AR-15s waiting on orders from their cult leader. We are living it. Like Trump, Spencer led his followers to expect all their vanities and desires and fears deserved to be catered to, their grievances and bigotries indulged, just by virtue of being white American men.

Also like Trump, he scorned them all. He reeked of contempt for those who hadn't been born to his class, with his trust fund and his level of education. He belittled those who looked up to him and embraced his empty promise of brotherhood. Most of all, he resented his need for them. For someone who had started life with everything America had to offer, but for whom that wasn't enough? I couldn't imagine a more forsaken existence. Nor a more American one.

The "alt-right," like Br'er Fox's Tar Baby, trapped a rabbity media desperate to parse the secret of Donald Trump's appeal. But it also engaged impressionable young men and women intent on finding meaning in their lives. The more they engaged with it, the more difficult and dangerous it became to extricate themselves. For some, Spencer's pseudo-intellectualism, with its seminar room trimmings, was the hook. For Andrew Anglin's troll army, it was a shared taste for twisted and vulgar humor, an interest in weapons, weight training, meme creation, and street warfare. For a twenty-six-year-old woman named Samantha Froelich, it was listening to Nathan Damigo talk searchingly about alienation. Damigo, who founded a group called Identity Evropa in March 2016, joined Spencer's circle of courtiers later that year. He brought with him an IE member named Eli Mosley.

During these same months, Samantha Froelich also found her way into this circle. Twenty sixteen had been a hard year for her. Left by the boyfriend she imagined she would one day marry, she had rebuilt her life on her own, only to have him suddenly return. In the interim, he had become a fascist. If she wanted to be with him, he told her, she had to join him in his newfound beliefs. Though she scarcely recognized him as the man she once loved, toward the end of 2016, she went online and found Identity Evropa.

Identity Evropa was bespoke. It was classy and clean cut, not evil and coarse, like Nazis. Froelich would never become a Nazi. That was a line she would not cross. Unlike the flags and banners festooned with swastikas, the Identity Evropa flag was minimalist white or teal blue with a triangular dragon's eye floating at its center. Damigo prided himself on his classical aesthetic, hence the spelling of Europa with a Roman *v*. A photograph of Michelangelo's *David* often featured on Identity Evropa's posters, conveying a bleached marble whiteness, a homoerotic manliness, and peak "Western civilization" (forgetting the fact that the biblical King David was a Jew). The posters were inscribed with enigmatic slogans: "Our Future Belongs to Us" or "Protect Your Heritage." Though its propaganda was tailored to recruit college-educated men, women were welcomed.

In an interview segment of "The Young Turks," a progressive YouTube news program, Froelich watched over Christmas, Nathan Damigo came across as polite and respectful, a square-jawed, smiling, and intense young man in a suit and tie. Damigo questioned the cult of diversity but said that if people wanted to live in a more heterodox society, they should be free to. As for himself, he believed pluralism was a failed social experiment, begun in 1965 when President Lyndon Johnson revised immigration policies and opened the country to Asians, Africans, and Latin Americans. This turned the demographic tide against white people. Though Damigo was twenty-nine, he looked and spoke like an undergrad who hadn't done the assigned reading but believed he could talk his way around it.

The coming presidency of Donald Trump, Damigo continued, offered an opportunity for a more open dialogue between those who embraced diversity and those who questioned it. "If that is really how they feel, then they need to come to us earnestly and we need to come to them earnestly." In the meantime—and here Damigo's brow furrowed—the attacks needed to stop. Though "Identitarians" were doggedly racist, they pretended to be offended by the charge. This was a snare, designed to flip the script of racial grievance. It was a quick turn from "We have a right to exist" and "Don't *all* lives matter?" to portraying white people as under siege or as victims of anti-white prejudice. Nathan Damigo and Richard Spencer danced this dance all the time. For Froelich, a young woman adrift, Damigo's apparent eagerness to engage with anyone who shared his desire to talk openly about what it meant to belong, was deeply appealing.

Damigo had dropped out of high school to join the Marines. After two years at Camp Pendleton, he served two tours in Al-Anbar Province at the height of the Iraq counterinsurgency. Returning stateside between his first and second tours, he drank to keep his nightmares at bay. On one of his leaves, he mixed muscle relaxants and a bottle of Jack Daniels in the expectation he would fall asleep and not wake up. Back in Iraq, his nerves calmed, but the PTSD returned when he came home. A few days after the anniversary of a friend's death from an IED explosion, he got plastered, confused a cab driver for an Iraqi, and pulled a gun on him. He was surprised to hear him respond in English. He took the man's wallet, was apprehended, and later convicted of armed robbery.

"It's like they took him when he was eighteen, and put him through a paper shredder, and then sent him back to us," his mother said on the eve of his sentencing and dishonorable discharge. "We get to try and put all the pieces back together. Sometimes it's like Humpty Dumpty, they don't go back together. There's going to be pieces missing."

In a similar manner, the War on Terror started out with a splash but then went so far off script that it called into question the story we'd been telling ourselves: America as the world's watchdog, bringing the good news of democracy to the benighted and backward. Alternatively, America facing down and triumphing over an existential threat. First Nazis and fascists, then communism, and then, overnight, militant Islam. But now, like Nathan Damigo, the story had pieces missing.

Hollywood told a version of Damigo's life: in the clear-eyed years after an attack on America, an American patriot signs up to serve as soon as he comes of age. Yet in the process of becoming a more effective assassin, his mind is destroyed. The result is a killing machine with just enough glitches to make the audience believe he is still a human being. That is what white male American mass culture now amounted to. You can call it white supremacy or white nationalism, American imperialism or Western Civilization, except that any nation can replicate it. *Rambo*, *Predator*, *Top Gun*, and *The Bourne Trilogy* have a global audience.

Richard Spencer would never have been suckered into enlisting. His father, a "country club Republican" out of Dallas, had been a supporter of the Texan who launched the War on Terror. His son referred to that Texan as "W." On his YouTube videos, Spencer's patricidal scorn toward the former president is palpable. He scoffed at the idea that America ever went to war to safeguard democracy, as W's fellow boomers learned from World War II histories, war memoirs, and Steven Spielberg. Nor did he believe our wars were about spreading democracy. The idea that Saddam or Osama was our generation's Adolf Hitler and "W" a latter-day Winston Churchill was nothing but lies and boomer propaganda: overcompensation for a waning empire.

The failure of both parties to address the disaster that arose from Bush and Cheney's lies gave Donald Trump his opening. Coming off his primary win in New Hampshire, Trump called out W's lies—to his brother's face—from a debate stage in South Carolina. Spencer could hardly believe it. Met by a chorus of boos from the representatives of the Republican establishment, Trump ended up sweeping the state. Tracking the Trump power surge on his blog, Spencer had marveled at that. I had too. Had I served tours in Iraq or Afghanistan, had I children or a husband who did, I would have offered Trump my rage on a platter. No one else asked for it. Trump understood this. Richard Spencer understood this. Damigo and Anglin did too.

If there is a memory tradition to console us for the meaningless sacrifice of better men than Nathan Damigo, it has yet to arise. It is easier to pretend these wars had never happened than to reflect even for a moment on what *had* happened. Even those who left off paying attention before the credits rolled understood, at some level, they'd been conned. By the media, the military, and the entire political establishment. And no one had paid the price. America had taken an entire country apart in a vengeful rage and then forgot about it. In prison Damigo bulked up his slight frame and, under the mentorship of another Iraq War vet, immersed himself in a library of white nationalist and neo-Nazi literature. Even after we tire of them, our overseas wars continue. And then they come home. How many souls are out there waiting, like IEDs, primed to explode?

Damigo was a true believer and a subtle recruiter. After serving his sentence he slimmed down, slicked back his hair, and hid his prison tattoos and his fascism under a button-down dress shirt to affect a more collegiate appearance. Identity Evropa's project was to get ordinary people like Samantha Froelich past their moral inhibitions to transgress the social norms they'd been raised with. Damigo and Spencer were figuring out what worked and what didn't. They were seeing how far they could go. Every recruit was tested.

New members were instructed to refrain from using racial slurs or Jew baiting in public. They were trained to be articulate and well dressed. Whenever somebody said something vile or posted an over-the-top meme in the Identity Evropa chatroom, new recruits were told by their handlers to ignore them. Whoever said there would be statues of St. Dylann Roof in the ethnostate, for example, was just being "edgy." No one could possibly mean that. Leadership tolerated these crazy extremists, but no one took them seriously.

This and similar deceptions were all in accordance with Identity Evropa's playbook, articulated in a Daily Stormer style sheet. Humor, shopworn metaphor, and playing devil's advocate provided plausible deniability. They were joking. They were speaking metaphorically. They were simply asking questions. "The unindoctrinated should not be able to tell if we are joking or not." The idea was to make fun of your own racism or, as Damigo played it, be self-deprecating and earnest. A humorless racist was a killjoy for new recruits like Samantha. You should be playful, mischievous, even flirtatious. *Keep her guessing.*

At the same time, new recruits were subject to a process of desensitization. Soon Samantha was scrolling past the most heinous remarks without blinking. Her ability to stomach offensive humor became a measure of her proximity to the inner circle and her distance from the uncool "cucks" and "normies." The idea was to cultivate a sense of superiority over those who weren't yet ready for the big reveal. Secret code words or numbers, freshly coined ethnic slurs, and furtive, cheeky *Sieg heils* cemented the new recruit's bond with other IE members. When elaborate jokes about gassing the kikes began to seem normal, they were getting closer to becoming fully fledged members.

The final kick, withheld until indoctrination was complete, was learning that humor was a ploy. It isn't simply that you don't see the jokes anymore. You are in on them. Once the norms had been breached, Damigo could start whetting your appetite for violence. Now you really do want to gas the kikes. Now you are dead serious about the coming RaHoWa—Racial Holy War. And yes, there absolutely would be a St. Dylann statue in the white ethnostate. Saying you were only joking was a cover, the ever-ready recourse whenever there was unexpected blowback. Richard Spencer would be the first to agree that their "fun and games" were something of an acquired taste. And of course, there was no telling who out there didn't get the joke, who was simply waiting for the "unironic" marching order. Someone like Eli Mosley.

His real name was Elliott Kline, but he'd taken to referring to himself as Eli Mosley after Oswald Mosley, an English fascist. Like Nathan Damigo, he had a backstory. He was a burned-out Iraq War veteran. He had spent six years in the army being trained to kill "mud people." He called himself the "unironic exterminationist" because irony and satire were lost on him. He was just crude. His crudeness was so contrived, so practiced, there was a kind of pathos to it. At the same time, he was just the sort of dogsbody Richard Spencer needed to have around, if only to be the butt of his mockery. Mosley didn't appear to be fazed by such treatment; he would later tell Samantha he was biding his time. After the revolution he would take over and Richard Spencer would be the first one "against the wall."

As Mosley told it, after leaving the army he became a Twitter troll. Every so often he'd get kicked off and then he would have to open a new account and rebuild his audience. Before he joined Identity

Evropa in 2016, he'd been a member of the Proud Boys, a violent neofascist street gang. Gavin McInnes, the Canadian cofounder of Vice Media, started the Proud Boys in June 2016, a few months after Nathan Damigo founded Identity Evropa. The Proud Boys had a ranking system that got them talked about. Proclaiming yourself a Western chauvinist was the first degree, with successive degrees, like Boy Scout merit badges, granted after that. Being made to recite a list of breakfast cereals while undergoing a beating, forswearing masturbation and pornography, and pledging allegiance to guns were among their rites of passage. McInnes described the Proud Boys as alt-right but without the hate, or alt-lite. Though they often showcased non-white members like Enrique Tarrio, later to play a seditious role in the January 6 insurrection at the Capitol, they were as racist and misogynist as they come.

Mosley, for one, couldn't resist needling a fellow Proud Boy for being a Jew. He had a bee in his bonnet about Jews. This led to his being doxed by another Proud Boy, so in September 2016 he migrated to Identity Evropa. He took on public-facing duties and commandeered leadership whenever Nathan Damigo went AWOL. Mosley met Richard Spencer on Inauguration Day, after Spencer had been sucker punched. Had Mosley been there, he told him, that would not have happened. When he wasn't booking Spencer's flights, or fixing his computer, Mosley worked as an exterminator, fantasizing that every cockroach he killed was a Jew. Soon he began referencing himself in the third person, telling his girlfriend to call him *Judenjäger*, the Jew hunter. He worshipped Dylann Roof.

In the last week of December Samantha Froelich was being vetted for Identity Evropa membership. By New Year's Day 2017, she was in. By the end of that year, she would begin to deconstruct how her life had been upended by her involvement with Identity Evropa, Nathan Damigo, Richard Spencer, and Eli Mosley. She would describe this journey in a deposition for the *Sines v. Kessler* court case, the one brought against the organizers of the Unite the Right rally on behalf of those who were terrorized or injured in Charlottesville on the weekend

of August 11 & 12, 2017. The documents that came to light in the discovery process were important to my research, but it was Samantha
Froelich's deposition that showed me that what Richard Spencer and
his confederates were doing to their recruits echoed what Trump was
doing to the rest of us.

CHAPTER 4

Holy Works

Some might begin the story of those who came together to defend Charlottesville with Zyahna Bryant's petition to remove Charlottesville's Confederate statues. Zyahna would have begun it earlier, on July 13, 2013, with George Zimmerman's acquittal for the murder of Trayvon Martin. For others, the epiphany arrived on November 24, 2014, when a grand jury declined to press charges against Officer Darren Wilson in the killing of Michael Brown in Ferguson, Missouri. For Rev. Phil Woodson of First United Methodist, it was Wes Bellamy's March 2016 press conference in Lee Park. Jalane Schmidt and her brigade of "52%" T-shirts might have said it was the 2016 Blue Ribbon Commission hearings that brought them together. For Rev. Dr. Alvin Edwards, the pastor of the historic Mount Zion First African Baptist Church, the story of the city's defenders began the night after Donald Trump declared he was running for president. That night, June 17, 2015, Dylann Roof entered Mother Emanuel AME Church in Charleston, South Carolina, and massacred nine congregants.

In the three decades Rev. Edwards had lived in Charlottesville, his Baptist faith, biblically fundamentalist and socially liberal, had served him well. He'd been chairman of the school board. He'd served as mayor. He could get the police chief, the mayor, even the president of the University of Virginia, on the phone if he had to. He bore the weight of his senior position in the Black community with dignity but he off-set his formal manner with a stock of humorous stories designed to put people, often white people, at ease. But when the Mother Emanuel massacre took place, none of that seemed to matter.

Mother Emanuel wasn't just any church. One of its founders, Denmark Vesey, was tried and hanged for leading the largest slave revolt in US history. Vesey planned the revolt in Mother Emanuel. The church's spiritual ethos was rooted in Black liberation theology, as articulated by its founding intellect, James H. Cone. Cone held that the individual must be liberated before the community can be and that the act of prayer provides the means of liberation. Radical prayer of the truly faithful was the vessel by which social justice was made visible and liberation achieved, both inside and outside the church.

Dylann S. Roof knew none of this when he joined a dozen parishioners for their weekly hour of Bible study. He chose the church because he knew it was "historic" and, unlike "the ghetto," a soft target. He took the precaution of waiting until everyone's eyes were closed in prayer before pulling out his gun. In six minutes, he reloaded it five times. After leading the police in a car chase, Roof was arrested. Because he hadn't eaten, they sent out an officer to fetch him a hamburger from Burger King.

Black people can readily imagine how such an arrest would have played out had a Black man shot up a church filled with white people, executing them on their knees. Every Black person killed by a police officer gives them practice. White people may be new to this exercise, but young people who have grown up with school lockdowns and mass shootings can readily compare the efficiency with which Black men are dispatched with how white men who kill their high school classmates are treated. Nothing can be done to stop them. White men composing manifestos filled with other men's ideas, documenting their descent into hell with selfies, are simply the bug in the system now. A useful bug for someone, this generation must eventually conclude. This has been a formative if unspoken lesson for the activists and clergy who found one another in Charlottesville. The officer who brought Dylann Roof that burger did his part to bring the point home.

Rev. Edwards was not alone in seeing that Roof's actions, with his twenty-five-hundred-word manifesto calling for a race war, illustrated with selfies taken at Confederate heritage sites and museums, posed a specific threat to his community. Cities and towns all over the South had suddenly realized that Confederate statuary and battle flags flying above statehouses now amounted to unexploded mortar shells planted in public squares and on courthouse lawns. The establishment of the Blue Ribbon Commission, like the governor of South Carolina's decision to remove the Confederate flag from the state capitol building, showed how frantic they were to defuse them.

Rev. Edwards held a prayer vigil for the families of the murdered parishioners. He'd held similar vigils when guns took the lives of residents in Charlottesville's low-income housing estates. The city's white Christian clergy never participated. But after this vigil, an older "Caucasian" woman approached him. What else was he going to do? she asked. He might have taken offense but instead her question haunted him. What else *was* there to do? Was there a way to prepare a community for a threat that didn't involve more men with guns? He invited his fellow Christian ministers, the "Caucasian" ones, to join him and his fellow Black ministers, for breakfast in a nondescript conference room at Mount Zion. He directed his first question at them.

"If this shooting had happened at Mount Zion, do you think I would have called you to ask for help?" He let the question linger. "Because what have you done? You have shown no interest in the work of civil rights. No interest in making sure there was a level playing field for our children. No interest in doing anything with any Black churches that I know of." When there was trouble, he wanted to be with people he knew would be there for him. Rev. Edwards held an annual Back to School Bash, providing free supplies and backpacks to underserved children. Only the local synagogue regularly contributed. If they could establish trust among themselves, he suggested, maybe their congregations would follow. In the meantime, should Charlottesville face a similar crisis he would know where to turn.

Asking white pastors to reflect on their indifference, while asking them for fellowship, captured something of what it had taken for Rev.

Edwards to enlarge the space allotted to a Black man in Charlottesville. If that meant listening to them relieve themselves of their guilt, confess what they had failed to understand, he was patient. He had learned to work through the unnecessary stuff to get to the question of justice. Out of Rev. Edwards's aspirations, and his breakfasts, the Charlottesville Clergy Collective was born.

Rev. Elaine Ellis Thomas, an associate pastor at St. Paul's Memorial Church, joined soon after the breakfasts began. A slight and elegant woman with a halo of curly silvery blond hair, Thomas was a recent arrival and still finding her feet. During a sermon she gave in the wake of the Ferguson verdict, a prominent St. Paul's parishioner had walked out. Located in the heart of the university grounds, St. Paul's was an Episcopal church that had long catered to the city's social and political elite.

Her first impression was that the Clergy Collective was off to a rocky start. There was a lot of talking past each other. Everyone seemed to have a different view of what was needed and what purpose the collective should serve. Part of Rev. Thomas's adjustment to Charlottesville was relearning the social codes of her North Carolina youth. Voices of women like herself often went unheard by senior male clergy with evangelical temperaments. Rev. Edwards, of an older, more patriarchal generation, sometimes called women whose names escaped him "Little Miss."

Some of the Black clergy present wanted to use the Charleston tragedy to seek some form of reparation, Rev. Thomas recalled. Others were openly aloof to the white clergy who had shunned them for so long. So there were wounds. But where there were wounds, she felt, there was holy work. Some ministers felt the point of the monthly breakfasts was too nebulous and stopped coming. She stayed on. During her first year no more than eight people showed up and, for most of that time, she was the only white person. Among the regulars were Rev. Brenda Brown-Grooms and Apostle Sarah Kelley, both Black women and Charlottesville natives. Sarah Kelley had founded her own nondenominational church. Brenda Brown-Grooms was copastor at another. Both grew up poor and fatherless, and little escaped them.

When she was a young girl, Pastor Brenda had an invisible friend whose presence was as vivid to her as one of her sisters. They held long conversations. Then she read the biblical story of Samuel. Samuel had heard the voice of God three times before he realized just who was talking. She realized then that God didn't speak to just anyone. He only came around when He wanted something. It took her a while to figure out what that was, since she hadn't ever seen a woman preach. What she had seen was that women ran the churches, and their money supported the work churches did. When church leaders said women couldn't be ministers, she knew this was a lie. She had learned to watch who was lying and to ask herself, *Why this lie? Who benefits from it?* Well, clearly, men preachers benefited. This was the first of two lies that marked her childhood.

The second lie came from the same fourth-grade illustrated textbook on the history of Virginia I had as a child. The illustration opening chapter 29, "How the Negroes Lived Under Slavery," showed an enslaved family standing on the deck of the ship that has brought them to America. All of them are dressed in colonial-era clothing, the husband in a wide-brimmed hat shaking the ship captain's hand next to his wife in a bonnet with their children. The young Brenda read this illustration as an attempt to portray captured and trafficked Africans as hopeful immigrants to "a land of dreams and opportunity."

I studied that illustration while living away from Virginia for a year in what amounted to a foreign country. I read the drawing as a scene of parting, depicting a white master who, having freed his "servants" and arranged for their passage to Liberia, was now wishing them bon voyage. The newly freed woman holds a handkerchief to her face, as distraught at being torn away from Virginia as I was. The chapter began with a statement: "Life among the Negroes of Virginia in slavery times was generally happy." Then came some waffling: "They were not so unhappy as some Northerners thought they were, nor were they so happy as some Southerners claimed." Happy or unhappy, the chapter continued, Negroes paid no mind to the debate over slavery. Enslaved or free, the text suggested, it was all the same to them.

"Who benefited from this lie?" Pastor Brenda asked. "Clearly I don't."

Her studies at Union Theological Seminary in New York, with eminent theologian James H. Cone and others, had deepened her understanding of God. When she listened to white evangelicals talk, she didn't hear the voice she knew. Their ceaseless moralizing was foreign to her. "Whether I like your lifestyle or understand it has nothing to do with it," she told me, referencing their homophobia. "We're *all* God's people." Cone expressed a corollary sentiment when he wrote, "Being black in America has very little to do with skin color. To be black means that your heart, your soul, your mind, and your body are where the dispossessed are." Pastor Brenda was with the dispossessed.

While she pastored elsewhere in Virginia, she received a yearly call from a white pastor inviting her to join her at the church she had founded in Charlottesville. She invariably replied, "Bless your heart, oh no, thank you." She'd had a stroke at forty-two and no power on earth could challenge what her lived experience had taught her about white people. Then one day she picked up the phone and when she heard the weariness in this woman's voice her heart turned over. That was the power of God. In 2011 she returned to Charlottesville to copastor at New Beginnings Christian Community.

Sometimes, she says, they hear from other church leaders, "We have this person who we think would fit very nicely in your congregation." She takes that to mean they don't want them. "We say, 'Send them on.' Cuz you're an idiot." New Beginnings is not a social club. It welcomes addicts trying to keep clean, alcoholics trying to keep sober, or just blue- or white-collar criminals seeking redemption. There are regular people, too, she says. White or Black, Latino or Asian, brokenness is a human condition.

For Pastor Brenda evil is a fact of life. "The first one at church is the devil, he is never late, and he never misses a Sunday." When you have all that evil in the room, she says, it tries to break you. It pulls and pulls at whatever virtue, whatever God you have in you. Her work was to reclaim people from the dark side. Because she sometimes lost this battle, she never lost sight that life itself is at stake. Pastor Brenda's voice was like a river with tricky currents, working in many registers at once. It was almost as if she was really talking to God, and I, like everyone else, was eavesdropping on a conversation in midstream. Under her frank and telepathic gaze, I felt stripped, humbled, and entirely out of my depth.

From the beginning, Rev. Elaine Thomas of St. Paul's Memorial,

Pastor Brenda of New Beginnings Christian Community, and Apostle Sarah Kelley of the Faith, Hope, and Love Church of Deliverance, were stalwart attendees of Rev. Edwards's Clergy Collective breakfasts. Upon his ordination, Rev. Phil Woodson of First United Methodist overlooking Lee Park joined them. As a matter of course, when Rev. Edwards was away, Rev. Lehman Bates of Ebenezer Baptist would step in, offering the opening and closing prayer as Edwards always did. This reflected their standing as prominent Black pastors and elders of the community. And as men.

What started as informal monthly breakfasts after the massacre at Mother Emanuel would begin to change after Trump's election, the unrest over the statues, and the publication of Wes Bellamy's old tweets. The Sunday following Thanksgiving, they invited their congregations to join them for a prayer walk on the Downtown Mall. This was the Clergy Collective's first public demonstration. The idea was to hold a vigil for those who felt threatened by the new ugliness. Over a hundred people joined, but even Rev. Edwards and Rev. Bates couldn't help but notice that few Black congregants had chosen to attend.

Pastor Brenda remembered catching Apostle Sarah Kelley's eye that day. A prayer walk would not be enough to counter what a Trump presidency would mean for the Black community. Democracy is a delicate thing, she told me. If you lose your vigilance, if you don't tend it, the world can turn on you. Just like that.

If the Clergy Collective represented the older, historically encumbered Christian establishment of Charlottesville, in the latter half of 2016 a younger cohort began finding one another. If this group shared a common core of belief, it was liberation theology. Where Pastor Brenda labored to strengthen the Holy Spirit in drug addicts and former felons, these individuals sought Jesus in the "drag queen, the young Syrian, the tattooed bartender and every other face that has ever been on the margins of the Christian Empire." They understood racism, sexism, homophobia, and the domination and exploitation of weaker nations by more powerful ones as a heresy against God that demanded they bear witness. In the coming year they would work together to figure out what

that meant, sometimes alongside and sometimes apart from members of
Rev. Edwards's Clergy Collective.

When one of these younger ministers, Rev. Seth Wispelwey, reflected on his halting path to ordination in his late thirties, it was the
path of a man often at odds with himself. There was the divide between
the scientific ethos of his childhood home and the certainties his education at a conservative Christian school was meant to instill in him.
There was the divide between his awareness of the privileges granted
him as a straight white man and his hesitation to use his privilege for
fear of upstaging those less likely to be heard. Finally, there was the divide between the man who wanted to be all things to everyone and the
man who wanted to understand who he really was. Even to ask this
question betrayed his privilege. "You don't have to figure out why you
are here," America has told men like him, he says. "We made all this for
you. You can be whatever you want to be."

Wispelwey overlapped with Richard Spencer for two years at UVA,
graduating in 2003 without a plan. He took odd jobs as a ranch hand, a
lifeguard, a film extra. He traveled to Texas to organize young Christians
at U2 concerts on behalf of the global AIDS crisis. There he met Tracy
Howe, his future wife, a singer-songwriter who traveled throughout
Latin America and America's borderlands, singing in colleges, music
festivals, churches, and prisons. Tracy once thought of herself as an
artist and culture worker. Music was how she served people. The violence visited upon Ferguson's Black community in the wake of Michael
Brown's death changed that. Moved by the spirit of the young activists
she found there, she experienced a moment of kairos. In Christian theology this Greek term conveys an idea whose time has come, compelling a person to make an existential commitment. Her dedication to the
cause of racial justice soon became her husband's.

They both enrolled at Harvard Theological Seminary, where the work
of Father Gustavo Gutiérrez, the godfather of liberation theology, as well
as other Jesuit teachers, left a powerful impression. The couple returned
to Charlottesville in 2013 so that Seth could work remotely at a nonprofit. They bought a house in the city and found a home at Sojourners,
a United Church of Christ house of worship. The United Church of

Christ was congregationalist. Congregationalism was a Protestant form of church governance in which each church is independent and autonomous, with administrative duties covered by Members in Discernment rather than a strict church hierarchy. Members in Discernment like the Wispelweys had finished seminary. Upon the completion of their ordination papers, which in 2016 they were still working on, they would become ordained ministers.

Joining them at Sojourners was another Member in Discernment. Under a baseball cap emblazoned with the word *Love*, Brittany Caine-Conley's nut-brown hair was half-shorn and half-long, like a trendy tonsure. Everyone called her Smash, as in "Smash the Patriarchy," but her affect was less iconoclastic than levelheaded and reflective. Growing up in Harrisonburg, a half hour north of Charlottesville, church was something Smash sought out for herself without knowing what she wanted from it. After attending a conservative Christian church her senior year in high school, she heard about a Methodist church called Rise. Rise created a sacred space for those who had been raised in conservative Christian churches and suffered harm from them. Smash found in Rise a foundation for her growing faith and was soon enrolled in seminary.

After graduation, she moved to Charlottesville, arriving in 2014, a year after the Wispelweys. She chose Sojourners because it was affirming of queer people like herself, both as congregants and in positions of leadership. While writing her ordination paper, she took odd jobs to support herself. Among her Sojourners duties was staffing its outreach table during the annual Pride festivities in Lee Park. One year she walked over to introduce herself to the young woman at the table for Episcopal youth. Her name was Grace.

Grace Aheron had wanted to be an Episcopal minister her whole life. Yet when she arrived at UVA, she veered from skipping church altogether to attending services at a conservative evangelical church. Her readings for a course in liberation theology finally joined her understanding of God with her understanding of herself, a multiracial and queer daughter of the South. After a year of service, she returned to Charlottesville to live in the vicarage adjoining the Good Shepherd Church just south of town.

Though she was neither a seminary student nor an ordained minister, Grace had been invited by the minister at Grace Church Red Hill to take over the eight-acre plot that adjoined the vicarage and, in exchange for a nominal rent, make something of it. Good Shepherd, like Grace Church Red Hill, was one of a string of twenty parish churches established around the turn of the century. Ministers would travel among them, offering services to poor and isolated mountain people in the hollers of the Blue Ridge. Some years before, Good Shepherd's congregation had been absorbed into Grace Church Red Hill down the road, leaving empty the 1905 cobblestone church with its red door.

Grace decided to start an intentional community. Typically, such experiments in communal living share a common faith, whether political or spiritual. As a UVA student, Grace had visited Casa Alma, a local Catholic Worker homesite run by a couple with young children. Casa Alma provided her a model. She named her community Charis.

While her partner looked after the chickens and did carpentry repairs, Grace worked as a program manager and youth minister for a small nonprofit arts organization run by the Wispelweys. People of all ages dropped in for Charis's monthly potluck. Smash joined them. Part of the Charis ethos was welcoming the stranger, so housing-insecure guests and asylum seekers were hosted. Idealistic young people of similar sensibilities moved in and out, taking jobs in town, and growing food based on permaculture practices. They read Jacques Ellul on Christian anarchism, the poet Audre Lorde, and books on environmental justice. They sang songs. They shared living expenses and their favorite music. A list of chores was posted on the refrigerator. There was a garden to tend and honey to harvest. Surrounded by books and houseplants, Charis became a place for young people to live in accordance with Jesus's teachings. Here they fine-tuned their commitments to one another, to God, and to the world.

The Charis mission took on imperialism, capitalism, and environmental destruction. Inspired by the writings of Ched Myers, Grace advocated for "radical discipleship." For evangelicals, the life of Jesus as it is portrayed in the Gospels provides the answer to the question What would Jesus do? In his exegesis of the Gospel of Mark, Myers provided the missing historical context: the Roman occupation of Palestine. In Myers's reading, Jesus was an organizer who fought for the liberation of those oppressed by Roman imperial rule and their settler colonial practices. So, the Romans crucified him. It was a short leap from there to connect the fate of Trayvon Martin and Michael Brown to that of Jesus. Wasn't Jesus an unarmed youth of color killed by the police? These were the kinds of conversations heard at Charis.

If Grace had to pick a moment when her focus shifted from sustainable living to anti-racist activism, it was either Zyahna's appearance at Wes Bellamy's press conference, or the call she got from Bekah Menning, a church leader at Grace Church Red Hill. A Michigan native, daughter of ministers, and the mother of a young child, Menning was interested in starting a local chapter of Showing Up for Racial Justice (SURJ), an organization founded in response to the Southern backlash that greeted Barack Obama's election. Grace put Bekah in touch with another woman, a forceful, no-nonsense lawyer who had set up a Showing Up for Racial Justice page on Facebook soliciting interest.

Of the twenty-three who attended the initial planning meeting on July 12, 2016, in Bekah Menning's living room, eighteen were women. Five clergy attended, including Smash and Tracy Wispelwey, along with three UVA professors (two in religious studies, including Bekah's husband). Among the rest were the wife of a UVA dean, a social worker, a health care worker, a business consultant, and an architect. This deliberately leaderless organization would play a decisive role in the events leading up to August 12, as would the collective leadership of the Wispelweys, Smash, and Grace Aheron.

Though Grace made the initial introduction, she held off investing herself initially. She found white people came with a lot of hemming and hawing over what form their activism should take. There were paralyzing discussions about process and consensus building. It was always: Should we take up this space? Should we start a book club? Such questions had their place, but it was possible to sit around too long asking them. Like Rev. Edwards of the Clergy Collective, Grace had limited patience for breast-beating. She was action oriented and pragmatic. Or at least as much as an anarchist living out a Gospel-driven faith in the woods could be. Still, when meetings opened to the public in August 2016, Grace began to attend.

The first challenge for Showing Up for Racial Justice was finding Black allies. "White people always want to come in and do something for us," Bekah Menning heard one Black woman say, adding to her hesitancy. Though the organization had grown in tandem with the Movement for Black Lives, there was as yet no local chapter of Black Lives Matter. The Charlottesville chapter of the NAACP was battling generational divisions between its older leadership and younger, more restive members like Niya Bates, the former tutor to Zyahna Bryant. As more people joined SURJ, some of them coming straight from the Blue Ribbon Commission hearings, a program began to take shape. Guided discussions with the Catholic Workers at Casa Alma touched on the fate of the Lee and Jackson statues. Sightings of Flaggers or Jason Kessler around town intensified questions about how to respond. The threat posed by the incoming Trump administration added a sense of urgency.

Grace kept people coming to meetings, even the jumpy anti-fascist types who showed up later. This was due partly to her rapport with students and partly to her friendships with Smash and Bekah. The ethos of Showing Up for Racial Justice also mandated it. People new to the work of social justice were often intolerant of ideological differences, prone to calling people out like the apparatchiks of old. Grace personified the SURJ practice of "lifting people up and calling them in." Bekah Menning, slightly older than Grace, gave the young people at Charis credit for moving her to a more radical place.

Out of the breakfasts at Mount Zion First African Baptist, the potlucks at Charis, kitchen dinners at the Wispelweys', and gatherings in living rooms and church basements, friendships were made and alliances were forged across race, faith, ideological, and generational divides. Other organizations and individuals, both secular and religious, would arise and have a part to play. But these souls formed the holy core of the city's response to what would soon become known as the Summer of Hate.

CHAPTER 5

A Beautiful Ugly City

All five city councillors had spent the holidays poring over the final report of the Blue Ribbon Commission, trying to make sense of the commission's decision to separate the fate of the Jackson statue from the Lee. The split votes on Relocate vs. Transform in Place were also hard to parse. Some councillors' minds had long been made up on the subject. Others may have done some soul-searching. Either way, when the January 17, 2017, city council meeting was called to order, the time for equivocation had come to an end.

Council chambers were unusually packed. Tensions ran high on whatever emotion righteousness uses for fuel. One woman had driven down from Maryland, arriving in a hoop skirt and bonnet. Some carried "Save the Statue" signs while others wore white "52%" T-shirts under winter jackets. A sizable contingent of the Black community, including those who wouldn't be caught dead at a city council meeting or a Blue Ribbon Commission hearing, had cast aside their doubts and answered Vice-Mayor Wes Bellamy's Facebook call to attend and make their presence felt.

First, however, everyone would have to sit through the State of the City mayoral address. Mayor Mike Signer couldn't resist a soapbox and, once he had mounted it, was loath to leave. He had only just begun when Wes Bellamy asked for a moment of silence to mark the recent passing of former vice-mayor Dr. Holly Edwards, a parish nurse for low-income housing residents and a community activist beloved and mourned by many.

Signer painted a rosy portrait. Charlottesville ranked third among Virginia cities for quality of life and fourth in the nation for entrepreneurs and startups. Expedia touted it as the number one place to visit, and Travelocity ranked it first among small cities for foodies. The city's fiscal soundness was attested to by its Triple A bond rating and $6 million budget surplus. The mayor was leading an initiative to bring more transparency and accessibility to local government by expanding online voter registration and instituting Robert's Rules of Order for council meetings. A makeover of West Main Street was in the offing. Following this fanfare, the mayor proposed to double the city's investment in affordable housing.

The city Mike Signer described was not the one the late Holly Edwards had known. At her funeral service at Mount Zion Baptist Church, filled to overflowing, her eulogist and close friend, Rev. Brenda Brown-Grooms, remembered her as a bespectacled thinker, a strategy artist, a poet, vegetarian, and behind-the-scenes peacemaker. She would size up people and then quietly suggest an idea they would later imagine had been their own. If a consensus emerged after contentious debate, it was because of her silent presence. Holly had left behind four young daughters and a grieving husband. Knowing she was dying, she cultivated a group of women who could speak for the underserved, amplify their needs in city forums, and one day take her place. She groomed Nikuyah Walker, the voice of the community's support for Wes Bellamy when Jason Kessler released his tweets, to succeed her in politics. For these women Charlottesville had always been two cities, one white and wealthy, one Black and perpetually striving to get out of the cul-de-sac of economic stalemate. Pastor Brenda spoke for them when she called Charlottesville a "beautiful ugly city."

Much like the mayor's boosterish portrait of Charlottesville that evening, the sunny celebration of American history has often required discounting its darker sides. For many white city residents, it was the invocation of Thomas Jefferson, not Robert E. Lee, that had long provided a reliable source of civic pride. Every schoolchild visited Monticello at least once. There, Jefferson's bookshelves provided proof of his wide-ranging intellect. Clocks and other inventions showed his engineering wizardry; gardens and vineyards showcased the fruits of his horticultural experiments. For most of my life, the story told in this house and its spectacular setting left little space to reflect on the lives of the 607 people he was said to have owned over his lifetime. We confined ourselves to the study of this carefully curated home and the carefully curated man who lived there.

I am old enough to recall the disdain that greeted Fawn Brodie's 1974 biography of Thomas Jefferson. Virginius Dabney, the longtime editor of the *Richmond Times-Dispatch*, a descendant of the Jefferson family and author of histories of Virginia, Richmond, and the University of Virginia, wrote an entire book debunking Brodie's outrageous suggestion that Jefferson had fathered children with his slave and dead wife's half-sister, Sally Hemings. Then, in 1998, an article in *Nature* confirmed what the public, and many in Charlottesville, had already concluded. Drawing on DNA collected from Jefferson's rumored Black descendants, it showed that, contrary to the conclusions of even his most recent biographer, Jefferson had "in high probability" fathered one if not all of Hemings's six children.

Thomas Jefferson and Sally Hemings: An American Controversy would soon appear in paperback. In it, Annette Gordon-Reed had taken apart the historical consensus, asking the pointed questions Jefferson's male biographers had avoided so as to keep Jefferson's hallowed legacy and moral standing from being tainted by intimate association with a Black woman. Jefferson left little in the written record that might suggest Sally Hemings and her children were anything other than house slaves. Gordon-Reed's methodical interrogation of the remaining sources demonstrated how his biographers chose to favor the testimony of Jefferson's white descendants over that of contemporary visitors to Monticello, his son Madison Hemings, and, it must be said, simple common sense. "It's all about the questions we ask," the historian Nell Irvin Painter once said. "The questions have changed. I mean, the questions always change. That's why we keep writing history."

Yet even science failed to convince holdouts. When Monticello finally accepted the DNA results, a newly formed Thomas Jefferson Heritage Society initiated a yearlong study in which twelve of thirteen eminent scholars labored to maintain a stance of skepticism. In 2011, they revised their report but not their conclusions.

After the DNA revelation, a new tack was taken. In an essay on Jefferson and "the problem of slavery," one historian summed up the many horns of the Jefferson dilemma: a Civil War in one man's mind. "Jefferson was a man of many dimensions," William Cohen began, "and any explanation of his behavior must contain a myriad of seeming contradictions. He was a sincere and dedicated foe of the slave trade who bought and sold men whenever he found it personally necessary. He believed that all men were entitled to life and liberty regardless of their abilities, yet he tracked down those slaves who had the courage to take their rights by running away. He believed that slavery was morally and politically wrong, but still he wrote a slave code for his state and opposed a national attempt in 1819 to limit the further expansion of the institution. He believed that one hour of slavery was worse than ages of British oppression, yet he was able to discuss the matter of slave breeding in much the same terms that one would use when speaking of the propagation of dogs and horses."

From such perorations we, humble lay readers, are left mired in the riddle of "seeming contradictions," thinking about Jefferson and his genius, remarking on the irony or the hypocrisy, toggling interminably between admiration and censure. Yet, rather than accept the plain truth that Jefferson made a premeditated devil's bargain over slavery, we are expected to give Jefferson's passionate declarations as much weight as his material actions. Fifteen-year-old Zyahna Bryant would have called him out: Was he going to "*be* about it, or just *talk* about it"?

Biographies of complicated male geniuses are an entire genre, as if being a prodigy enables the artfully phrased honorable intention or the haunted lament of the deathbed to forever forestall brute and tragic consequence. How would a biography of the complicated genius of America read if written by a runaway slave? A man unjustly imprisoned? A native chief of a massacred tribe? An inmate of an internment camp?

A concubine who lived alongside her enslaver, bearing his children, for thirty-some years? If we cannot imagine such a tome, what was all this ballyhoo about history for when, to Black Charlottesville and many others, it was clearly full of perversion, obfuscation, self-serving lies, and omissions?

When the controversy over the DNA results was at its peak, Richard Spencer was a student at UVA, taking it all in, and Niya Bates was a third grader with hazel eyes. She remembered it as a time when Sally Hemings was all over the local news or talked about in hushed tones in church and the grocery store. That year, her class visited Monticello and Bates raised her hand to ask the tour guide who this Sally Hemings was. "We don't talk about her," was the answer she got. She went home to ask her mother the same question and was thunderstruck. "Thomas Jefferson had children with *a Black woman*?!"

The muzzling of history was experienced by Black families as if the shame of enslavement, alongside the long-standing pain and horror of it, was theirs alone. Every praise song for Thomas Jefferson deepened the wound and extended the silence. Niya Bates remembers being surprised when her mother suddenly appeared for a school trip to a botanical garden. Later, she realized previous field trips had all been to plantations and Civil War battlefields. It was her grandmother who told her which city establishments refused to serve Black people, which made them wait outside. As the Blue Ribbon Commission hearings were getting underway, Monticello hired Bates to train a new generation of tour guides in how to break these silences. Drawing on material artefacts unearthed by archaeologists, she drew a picture of the daily lives of the enslaved and the stark choices they faced. In the course of this work she discovered her own ancestors among those Jefferson enslaved.

"You can't stand in any corner of this city," a local activist named Tanesha Hudson noted, "and not feel the master sitting on the top of Monticello. He looks down on us. He's been looking down on this city for God knows how long." Virginians would own and trade more people than any other state. Black hands cleared the land, drained the swamps, and built its cities, towns, and universities. While Jefferson entertained his lofty ideas about liberty and the pursuit of happiness, the labor of men in chains went on uninterrupted in the fields below. Tanesha made this history personal. What kind of man, she asked, has a baby with a fourteen-year-old? Who was also his wife's half sister? "He never freed her, but he gave her all those babies. He never once thought I should free this lady and make her life better."

I'd never truly faced how methodical the erasure of Black history had been. Nor had I asked what purpose a whitewashed history served, though I had considered similar questions when it came to the lost histories of (white) women. Clearly, the first aim was to obscure the irrevocable fact that slavery had entailed the destruction of millions of lives. The second was to spare the descendants of those who had materially profited, the discomfort of thinking about that, being called to account, or even repenting of it. My ancestors were not slaveholders, but the immensity of the slave economy, and the role penal labor played in the economy that replaced it, implicated them regardless. Jim Crow brought these profits into my lifetime and compounded them.

"We figured out how to get social power, we figured out how to get political power," the late Holly Edwards said, "but within this community, we are not stakeholders in wealth and economic power. That is the bottom line." Edwards traced the loss of stakeholder wealth and economic autonomy back to the razing of Vinegar Hill, the Black neighborhood closest to the white businesses of downtown East Main Street. As part of a HUD-sponsored, nationwide "urban renewal" program, twenty acres of Black homes, businesses, and prominent gathering spaces were reduced to memories. Like the City Beautiful movement of the 1920s, urban renewal of the 1960s was the polite word for land appropriation. James Baldwin called it "Negro removal."

Prevented from patronizing white establishments after Reconstruction, Black residents had created their own business economy in Vinegar Hill. At its peak, the Hill boasted two churches, restaurants, antique shops, a clothing store, two grocery stores, a pharmacy, laundry, cobbler, tailor, seamstress, hat cleaner, and an elementary school. There was a barber for white men and another, Pollards next to Inge's corner store, for Black. In the forties, Pollards was the meeting place for the town's Black intellectuals. Carver's Inn hosted Black travelers.

But the Depression brought loan defaults. White speculators became slumlords for those who couldn't afford housing elsewhere. By the 1950s, the all-white downtown business association began to lobby city council to raze the Hill and redevelop the well-placed land on which it stood. A referendum was held, but the poll tax meant not everyone had the means to vote. The demolition took five years. By 1965, one hundred years after the Civil War, Vinegar Hill was a wasteland.

Eugene Williams had worked in insurance on the Hill. A leader of the Charlottesville chapter of the NAACP during the struggle to desegregate the city's schools, he is now in his nineties. He and his fellow business owners were encouraged to think they might buy a plot on the razed land just like everyone else. But when the land came up for sale, it was so expensive not even white businesses could afford it. Williams concluded the real reason the Hill was razed was that downtown white businesses were losing customers to Black ones. The land stayed vacant for twenty years, an eyesore and a source of bitterness for those who had been forced to leave. Even now most of this area includes acres of empty parking lots.

Families living in dilapidated shacks may have welcomed the move to public housing. For those living in gracious homes, with children who took piano lessons and attended dance recitals, the sense of belonging proved impossible to recover. Brenda Brown-Grooms turned ten the year Vinegar Hill was demolished. She and her six younger brothers and sisters lost not just their home but their church, Zion Union. Only her school, now the Jefferson School African American Heritage Center, remains standing. In 2011 Holly Edwards negotiated an apology from the city to the six hundred residents and thirty-nine business owners whose lives were uprooted and livelihoods destroyed. Most were long gone by the time the apology arrived.

A generation after Vinegar Hill's razing, I witnessed a similar unraveling. In 1991, after ten years in New York, newly married and pregnant, I moved with my husband to Fifeville, just south of West Main, across the C&O tracks from what had once been Vinegar Hill. Fifeville reminded me of my childhood, a little bit of the country in the city. Services in the county were negligible and poverty commonplace. White classmates lived in unpainted clapboard houses with no plumbing. Others were so deep in the backwoods cars couldn't make it down their roads. Elderly Black couples sat on sagging front porches just like my Fifeville neighbors did.

Such a view fails to account for the calculations of municipal neglect. Black neighborhoods were always the last to receive city services such as water, sewer, or storm drainage lines. In the 1970s some neighborhoods still didn't have mail delivery or garbage removal, no matter how many times residents applied to the city to remedy it. While white neighborhoods had tree-lined streets wide enough for cars to pass abreast, the streets of Black neighborhoods were narrow and bare, with few sidewalks. Houses were often so close together you could talk to your neighbor at her window from yours without raising your voice.

In the years I lived in Fifeville, the university had just completed a $230 million hospital expansion. Fifeville was the blight in its gleaming path. Half its houses were rentals, with over 70 percent in poor condition. There were nip joints and gambling houses. Elderly drunks and younger drug dealers frequented Tonsler Park. Weekly candlelit processions, led by Rev. Alvin Edwards of Mount Zion First African Baptist, tried to disrupt the drug traffic. His tires were slashed, and his phone was tapped. Speculators and medical professionals snatched up property, including ours, when we left. The university turned a blind eye to the new hospital's impact on Fifeville. Like the city and the white community, it was happy to cultivate an underclass until the property value of the land their homes sat on outweighed the value of a captive source of cheap labor. When the crack epidemic abated, gentrification followed. Higher property taxes and rents displaced working people from neighborhoods they'd lived in for generations. It was all foreseeable.

Holly Edwards was prescient, Pastor Brenda said. She knew something was coming. Against powerful resistance from both the city council and the Black community, she secured $60,000 to launch a city-funded "Dialogue on Race." The idea wasn't to flush out "white supremacy," Frank Dukes, the man I called "the Listener" on the Blue Ribbon Commission, told me. That was still a shocking term back then. Nor was it about racial reconciliation. How do you reconcile, he asked, when there was never a history of friendship? The idea was to find a bridge across the chasm. While a great many white people showed up at Charlottesville High School ready to talk, only a handful of Black residents did. This led to an outpouring of frustration.

Rev. Lehman Bates, later of the Clergy Collective, worked with Holly Edwards on the Dialogue on Race. Yet his efforts to get the elders of his church to participate failed. The prospect of answering white people's questions was too unsettling. He paraphrased what they would have said: "You have been the cause of so much pain. You have made it impossible for me to explore my dreams, to attend UVA, and *you don't even know*. We have the stories of our grandmothers, our great-grandmothers and mothers. They told us what it was like to work for a rich white family. How they were disrespected and ill-treated." The struggle to be educated rankled the most. "You didn't teach me, right? And when it came to history, in a book of five hundred volumes, you gave us two pages.

"And so that understanding was never gained by the white community," Bates continued. "They would say, 'But hey, I want to hear, I want to understand, I want to empathize.' And, you know, it's not that simple. It's not an intellectual exercise. My parishioners didn't want to be part of it. Silence was the only power my elders had."

For Rev. Bates's elderly parishioners, the Dialogue on Race came too late to heal the pain of a lifetime of social ostracism. The Blue Ribbon Commission hearings saw more participation, but I wondered if the effort expended on unearthing Black Charlottesville's history was being engineered to deflect a weightier discussion. Without a material reckoning, did this amount to anything more than an exercise in rebranding and self-congratulation? Wherever the statue ended up, whatever the text on his plaque said, Robert E. Lee would remain in his saddle. I was beginning to understand the Black community's resistance to taking part in civic life outside their churches. I was beginning to appreciate what it took for them to show up in city council chambers the evening the statues were to be voted on, three days before Trump's inauguration.

It was Councillor Bob Fenwick who finally raised the subject that had filled council chambers. Fenwick was something of a maverick. He worked in construction and home renovation and considered himself an expert negotiator. Despite having attended every session of the Blue Ribbon Commission, he claimed he was unable to see a path forward. He'd had enough of symbols and political theater. Was it possible to move the statues *and* invest in Black communities? The statues could wait, but the people couldn't. "It's time to show me the money," he said.

Wes Bellamy spoke next, his first words since calling for a moment of silence to mark Holly Edwards's passing. Holly had been one of the first people he called when Jason Kessler released his old tweets. She advised him to forget the statues, to choose domestic violence as his issue. When Mary Carey, the seventy-year-old who had yearned to play in Lee Park, warned him that the city was not what he thought, he didn't listen. He had believed it when white people said they wanted to empower those who had long felt excluded. Until the Flaggers showed up at Lee Park, he hadn't really understood.

Bellamy described the death threats he'd received. They knew his daughters' names. Bananas and a stuffed monkey were thrown on his property. "You will die next week," one note read, and a week later the wheel lug nuts on the family car were found loosened. Just that day, he said, he'd been bum-rushed by a stalker on his way to city hall. He reminded the assembled of the man who had attacked his character, tried to break his will, and destroy his livelihood. He quoted Martin Luther King's definition of the white moderate as a person who "prefers a negative peace which is the absence of tension to a positive peace which is the presence of justice." It was the white moderate, he said, who told him the city didn't have any problems with race until he arrived.

Then, as if answering Fenwick's demand to show him the money, Bellamy provided a list of proposals for a $4 million "equity package" for the Black community. He introduced a motion that the details be discussed and voted on that night. Kristin Szakos promptly seconded.

Szakos had her own history with the statues. When she moved to Charlottesville from eastern Kentucky, it struck her as odd that such a cosmopolitan place flaunted these Confederate icons. In 2012, on the 150th anniversary of the Civil War, and the 250th anniversary of Charlottesville's founding, a local historian gave a talk. During the Q&A, Szakos, then in her second year on city council, asked if the time had come for the city to ask whether these statues still represented its values. The room let out a collective gasp.

Her travails began. She was approached at the grocery store. Why open that can of worms? She got an earful on the campaign trail. There were the good ole boy, Robert E. Lee worshippers, she said, and then there were the outright racists. But when her name and address appeared on the Aryan Nation website, the tenor changed. One caller told the child who answered the phone to tell his mother she was a "fucking whore." Someone plastered her car with Confederate flag stickers. Another caller told her what time she had turned off her bedroom lights the night before. So Kristin Szakos knew as well as anyone the statues would continue to attract unwanted attention. That the threats would not stop coming. She made a motion to remove Lee and rename both parks. Bellamy seconded.

Kathy Galvin voted no on removing Lee but yes on renaming the parks. She proposed that an amount equal to the cost of moving the statue be allotted to a HUD-sponsored program aimed at helping public housing residents get on the road to self-sufficiency. This was a transparent attempt to buy off the Black community by using their own concerns about the cost of removing the statues. No one seconded.

Until Bellamy brought up King's definition of the white moderate from his "Letter from Birmingham Jail," Mayor Mike Signer felt certain he had persuaded him to keep the Lee statue in Lee Park. This was a measure of the high value he placed on his own thinking and powers of persuasion. Signer prided himself on his results-oriented approach to the statue question. He arrived that evening prepared to expound on this at great length. In his prefatory remarks, he took pains to express his own "abhorrence of slavery" and his desire "to create bridges rather than divisions." But what was the practical effect of moving the Lee statue he asked, vis-à-vis advancing the cause of racial justice? Not seeing any material benefit, he concluded it was an empty political gesture. He voted no on removal, yes on contextualizing it and renaming the parks.

Three hours into the January 17, 2017, city council meeting the vote was two for Lee's removal, two to keep him where he was. All eyes turned to Bob Fenwick.

He abstained.

After a long moment of shocked silence, cries of "Shame!" and "Coward!" exploded. Signer gaveled through the uproar. Nikuyah Walker, Holly Edwards's protégée, tried to say something, but Signer talked over her. Kristin Szakos said Fenwick's abstention was basically a no. Walker again tried to say something, but Signer threatened to have her removed. When she continued, he vowed to suspend the meeting. Chaos reigned. Only when Wes Bellamy spoke did the room quiet. He asked for clarification on what Robert's Rules of Order allowed and disallowed. He probed Fenwick's thinking, looking for an opening. When he ran out of the allotted time, Szakos moved for more and Bellamy seconded. After a few rounds of this, Signer called for a break and retreated to the bathroom behind the dais to throw up. More time was allotted, and again Fenwick abstained. It was after midnight when Kathy Galvin spoke.

"Mr. Fenwick, would you entertain a motion that would keep the statue in Lee Park, but contextualize it in accordance with the Blue Ribbon Commission's guiding principle[s]?"

"No."

They moved on, exasperated. Bellamy got his $4 million equity package through, with a 5 to 0 vote. Both parks would be renamed. Fenwick restated his feeling that the statue issue was giving them an opening to do things for the Black community.

I couldn't follow Fenwick's thinking. Was he forcing Bellamy to acknowledge that he owed him something for his vote? Was $4 million insufficient? Whatever it was, it amounted to a horse trade over an issue that, for the Black community, was now about more than money. At the same time, the ugliness in the air had white residents over a barrel, anxious to prove that the armed men parading around Lee Park had nothing to do with their beautiful Charlottesville. Bellamy might never have succeeded in getting his equity package through without the emotions stirred up by the unspoken white fears about what had been unleashed.

Black residents who'd put aside their skepticism and answered

Bellamy's call were furious when the meeting closed with the statue issue unresolved. "Y'all don't want to hear us, y'all want this town to be the same old shit that's it's always been," one man fumed. Kristin Szakos told the *Daily Progress*, "The people planning to vote against this were going to vote against it no matter what the Commission said." The chair of the Blue Ribbon Commission, Don Gathers, called Fenwick's abstention cowardly. "That was six months of work that's amounted to absolutely nothing."

Two days later, Fenwick called a press conference to announce that he would vote to remove the Lee statue and rename the park. But it was too late. He would never be forgiven.

INTERLUDE

Heart of Whiteness

After the president of the United States declared there had been very fine people on both sides in Charlottesville, I believed a Rubicon had been crossed. *He's gone too far*, I thought. *People won't stand for that.* I waited for the penny to drop, but life continued as before. To correct my blind spots, I began reading. Perhaps finding the germ of the present in the past is just something writers tell themselves to exert control over events that are effectively beyond their control. But it was what I knew. I didn't know how far back I'd have to go, but as Charlottesville felt too close and too raw, Alabama seemed as good a place as any to start. The road from Alabama back to Charlottesville was convoluted, filled with unexpected twists and turns before a sudden drop into a rather large hole.

In the early winter of 2017, I put Taylor Branch's three-volume account of the civil rights movement and John Dollard's 1937 *Caste and Class in a Southern Town* in my bag and flew to Birmingham. I drove to Selma and Montgomery, then farther south down the long piney roads of the black belt. I visited churches, museums, and preserved-in-amber antebellum mansions built from cotton fortunes. On the outskirts of Eufaula, near the Georgia border, I visited the spot where a Black man was lynched. I traveled there after meeting his youngest grandchild. Behind a tidy, backwoods Baptist church I visited the burial plots of her mother and grandmother. Her grandfather's body was never found, she said, but the leader of the lynching party had thrown his shoes on this church's front lawn. The white man who had led the two-day chase on horseback, the man who had lynched her grandfather, disposed of his body, and taken his shoes, was her other grandfather. This wasn't the germ of the present in the past but the past's haunting afterlife. A tragedy of Greek dimensions alive in the flesh of a woman younger than I was.

That night, lying abed in a Motel 6 in Eufaula, rereading Martin Luther King Jr.'s "Letter from Birmingham Jail," I came across his mention of six, mostly forgotten, white Southern writers. One of them was a Charlottesville housewife named Sarah Patton Boyle. From her I would learn that Richard Spencer wasn't the first to unleash the combustible mix of fascism, Nazism, white supremacy, anti-Semitism, homophobia, and Lost Cause defiance on the streets of Charlottesville. A man named John Kasper was.

This was the drop.

In the spring of 2018, I moved to Charlottesville for the first of three annual writer's residencies at the University of Virginia. Then I disappeared down the hole.

The stage was set for John Kasper's appearance when, on May 17, 1954, the US Supreme Court declared segregated schooling unconstitutional. The *Brown* decision was vague as to how and when desegregation was all going to happen, so a second decision followed a year later. *Brown 2* remanded desegregation cases to the lower courts, directing Southern schools to integrate "with all deliberate speed." In early 1956, the all-powerful US senator Harry F. Byrd (D-VA), chair of the Senate Finance Committee, urged a coalition of Southern politicians, nearly all Democrats, to sign a "Southern Manifesto" drafted by prominent members of the Southern caucus. From Rosemont, a colonnaded mansion set on a knoll overlooking the Shenandoah valley, Byrd vowed Virginia would defy federal authority.

Byrd, a former governor, was FFV, First Families of Virginia. His ancestor William Byrd I established a vast tobacco plantation on the north bank of the James River in 1674; his son William II founded the city of

Richmond. Thirteen generations of Byrds followed, including a captain in Washington's army and a colonel in Lee's. "Virginia breeds no Huey Longs or Talmadges," John Gunther wrote in his sprawling 1947 narrative, *Inside U.S.A.* "The Byrd machine [is] the most urbane and genteel dictatorship in America." By 1955 the "Southern Manifesto" had been undersigned by one hundred Southern politicians. The Commission on Public Education was seated to study school desegregation, providing Byrd's filibustering a bureaucratic veneer. In the meantime, the Charlottesville school board resolved that city schools would remain segregated for the 1955–56 year.

In February 1956, Byrd announced that any Virginia school pursuing desegregation in accordance with the Supreme Court's ruling would be denied state funding. Should public schools be shuttered as a result, the governor proposed state funds be appropriated for tuition grants so that white families might send their children to private academies. State lawmakers began drawing up legislation exhuming Civil War–era legal justifications of interposition and nullification. This movement became known as Massive Resistance. Other Southern states followed Virginia's lead.

In early July, John Kasper, a twenty-six-year-old graduate of Columbia University, arrived in Arlington, Virginia, from New York City. The *New York Herald Tribune* described him as a "Hollywood version of the All-American boy." Another outlet noted his smoldering charisma. Working alongside a UVA student, Kasper planted crosses on the lawns of Chief Justice Earl Warren and his fellow justice Felix Frankfurter. After setting them on fire, he sent photographs of the burning crosses to every member of the Virginia General Assembly to stiffen their spines as they convened in special session to strategize their response to a federal district court's expected ruling in favor of the NAACP. Charlottesville, meanwhile, was preparing its own response. On July 12 the Defenders of State Sovereignty and Individual Liberties, a statewide white citizens council, organized a mass meeting at Lane High School. Over twelve hundred people showed up. Every seat in the auditorium was taken. The lobby and hallways were packed. Loudspeakers broadcast to a jammed parking lot.

Three members of the General Assembly traveled from Richmond to speak out in support of Massive Resistance, arguing desegregation would be "the beginning of the end of Virginia." A prominent judge, both a member of UVA's governing Board of Visitors and St. Paul's Memorial Church, insisted it was a "sacred duty and the priceless natural right of parents to mold their children in accordance with their beliefs and customs." Over the next ten days, nearly 12,000 local citizens (Charlottesville's white population was then around 20,000) signed a petition calling on school administrators to ignore all court orders to desegregate. (I looked in state and local archives for that petition and the names of those who signed it, but, like so much of the history we are never taught, it was as if it had never happened.)

A week later John Kasper arrived in Charlottesville, intending to start a race war.

On Saturday, August 4, he managed to get a meeting with the mayor, police chief, and city manager in pursuit of a permit to hold a rally in McIntire Park. He gave them copies of his manifesto, "Virginians on Guard," a "Segregation Forever" flyer, and mentioned his plan to solicit residents for membership in his newly formed Seaboard White Citizens Council. They invited him to return on Monday, to meet with state senator Edward O. McCue Jr. McCue, a member of the Defenders of State Sovereignty and Individual Liberties, had been one of the speakers at the July 12 mass meeting at Lane High School. Under the plan he proposed that evening, the General Assembly would take over the city's schools and refuse to admit Negro students.

The following day, a Sunday, Sen. McCue Jr. met with the mayor, police chief, and city manager and decided that Kasper's rally would only stir up trouble. When Kasper returned on Monday, only the police chief was present. Kasper's permit was denied. Undeterred, he tracked the city fathers down. The city manager denounced his manifesto as "disgusting trash." Kasper found Mayor Sol Weinberg behind the counter of his drugstore. There was nothing to worry about, Weinberg assured him. Despite the court decision, announced that morning, ordering the local school board to admit Negro students the coming school year, they were exploring more legal avenues. Kasper then showed up at the state senator's Charlottesville office. Edward McCue Jr. had returned to Richmond, but his son, Ed McCue III, was there. Like his father, McCue III laid the entire mess at the feet of the city's Jewish mayor. Segregation and mongrelization were being aided and abetted by communists and Jews.

"That Jew has been in for twelve years and was just re-elected for more," the senator's son told Kasper. The "evil smelling crowd in City Hall is the gang responsible for Charlottesville being the first city in Virginia to put nigras in its schools." The city's silent majority was dead set against this. "They sit back quiet but if it really comes, they'll explode." He assured Kasper that his father had everything well in hand. Kasper didn't buy it. "Another politician," he wrote in disgust in an open letter to the city's white citizens, "willing even at this late hour to sell our children into slavery."

A week later Kasper was arrested and charged with handing out membership applications to his Seaboard White Citizens Council without a permit. His associate, a gas station attendant and chair of Kasper's council, was mocked by the plainclothes officer interrogating him. "You know you have no education," he said. "You aren't smart enough for a job with a Citizens Council." In 1924 Charlottesville's leading citizens made up the KKK; in 1956 politicians, judges, businessmen, bankers, Realtors, and members of UVA's Board of Visitors made up the Defenders of State Sovereignty and Individual Liberties. A UVA math professor was president of the local chapter.

After paying a hundred-dollar fine, Kasper was released. As he was leaving the jail, a group of police officers approached him to shake his hand. They apologized for how he'd been treated, grumbled about the police chief, and asked for membership applications. With or without a permit, Kasper planned to hold his rally in McIntire Park the following Saturday, August 18, 1956.

John Kasper had targeted Charlottesville in part because the NAACP had. Thurgood Marshall, the chief counsel of the NAACP's Legal Defense and Educational Fund, brought a suit against Charlottesville's school authorities because he imagined that if he couldn't integrate

Charlottesville, it couldn't be done elsewhere. On Marshall's side were seventy students whose families were willing to risk their livelihoods for their children's education. Thelma Townsend, Zyahna's grandmother, was among these parents. Under Eugene Williams's leadership, the Charlottesville chapter of the NAACP was the largest and fastest growing in all Virginia, boasting over fifteen hundred members. Arrayed against Marshall were the Byrd machine, the *Daily Progress*, the *Richmond Times-Dispatch*, the Defenders of State Sovereignty and Individual Liberties, and Governor Thomas B. Stanley. Marshall and his Richmond associate, Spottswood Robinson III, hoped the University of Virginia would provide a courtly, moderating influence.

At the turn of the century UVA had been the best public university the South had to offer, but as Governor Byrd had invested more in roads than education, it had been starved of funds. Though UVA maintained its air of gentility, by 1956 it was an intellectual backwater. The director of its School of Education, Dr. Henry Garrett, was the star witness for Virginia's defense of segregated education in the *Brown* case. Garrett was a keen promoter of "racial hygiene"; he was also a supporter of the neofascist UK-based Northern League. UVA's Board of Visitors had just awarded James J. Kilpatrick, a columnist for the *Richmond News Leader*, a gold medal for impassioned editorials defending segregation, employing the same arguments used to defend slavery a century before. Like McCue II and III, Kilpatrick believed Jewish agitators were behind integration efforts.

Against such a backdrop, UVA president Colgate Darden, a former governor, counted as a moderating influence. He lamented the unlawful defiance of Massive Resistance and entertained the hope that Virginia might find a sensible means to address the school crisis. If he imagined UVA's new Thomas Jefferson Center for Political Economy and Social Philosophy might provide a path forward, he was mistaken. The founding director of the center was a Nobel Prize–winning economist named James McGill Buchanan. Buchanan had chosen this innocuous-sounding name to cloak his profoundly radical mission.

Thomas Jefferson believed that only a system of broad, free, public education, supported at state expense, could ensure the survival of the

American experiment. The founding of the University of Virginia was among his proudest accomplishments. Reconstruction saw elected Black delegates and their white allies fulfill Jefferson's vision of widely available public education. But Buchanan now proposed dismantling Virginia's entire public education infrastructure, selling off school properties, and returning Virginia to the days of privately managed instruction, preferably overseen by clergy, as had been the case in the nineteenth century. At the outbreak of the Civil War this system had left over a third of the white population unable to read and write. In Buchanan's "Virginia Plan," public schools would be replaced by "private academies," charter schools paid for by taxpayers but reserved for white students. Buchanan's ideas soon found their way into legislation enacted by the state assembly.

Education was only the beginning. Like Senator Byrd, Buchanan had little sympathy for ordinary Virginians. The rich and powerful business interests that had long dominated Virginia politics were his constituents. Why should the federal government, he asked, have the power to force the wealthy to pay for any goods or programs that served only "ordinary citizens and the poor"? Beginning in the early 1970s until his death in 2013, Buchanan became the principal muse of Koch-funded think tanks and their legislative agenda of first starving, then privatizing public services. Buchanan's new "social order . . . built on individual liberty" was the old feudal banditry dressed in Jeffersonian language. As Nancy MacLean wrote in *Democracy in Chains*, Buchanan's "Virginia Plan" aimed to revolutionize the way people thought about government, until there was no government to think about at all.

John Kasper had no standing among Virginia's oligarchs. To them, he was a Yankee and a rabble-rouser. His way was not the "Virginia Way." The Virginia Way was a chivalric code among the political elite, Democrat or Republican, that enshrined inequality and paternalism. Kasper had no interest in such niceties. Integration posed an existential threat and rather than facing it squarely, the powers that be put him in jail. "What had the world come to," he asked a *Washington Post* reporter upon his release, "when white citizens are denied the right to save their own race from mongrelization?" Virginia's defiance of federal authority, alongside President Darden's pretense of moderation, gave Kasper an opening to aggravate the crisis.

Key to John Kasper's sense of himself was that he saw himself as part of a militant avant-garde, a flamethrower. Much like his doppelgänger Richard Spencer, he had contrarian reflexes. Growing up in conservative Camden, New Jersey, Kasper was known as a troublemaker with left-wing sympathies. At Columbia, where he majored in philosophy with a minor in English, he referred to himself as an "intellectual fascist" and professed an admiration for Machiavelli and Stalin. It was in an American literature class that he was introduced to the work of the poet, translator, and literary impresario Ezra Pound. And it was Pound, as much as the legal stratagems of the NAACP, that put Charlottesville in Kasper's sights.

Ezra Pound's wartime radio broadcasts out of Rome, fulminating against America's entrance into the war on behalf of the Allied powers, resulted in his indictment for treason in 1943. In 1945 he was captured and detained before being returned to America to face trial. Pound begged to be put on the stand to make the case that his broadcasts were constitutionally protected free speech. Instead, his lawyer negotiated a deal that he be hospitalized in lieu of execution. When Kasper first wrote him, Pound had been an inmate at St. Elizabeth's Hospital for the Insane in Washington, DC, for six years. On my return from Alabama, just before moving to Charlottesville, I took a train to New Haven to read Kasper's letters to Ezra Pound at Yale University's Beinecke Rare Book and Manuscript Library.

How a poet and champion of the work of Rabindranath Tagore, James Joyce, Henry James, W. B. Yeats, T. S. Eliot, Robert Frost, William Carlos Williams, Marianne Moore, H.D., Ernest Hemingway, and Langston Hughes became a follower of Mussolini and a raving anti-Semite is not a mystery I need to solve. While much has been written about Pound's fascism and anti-Semitism, the third strand in the braid of his obsessions, white supremacy, is less noted. From Kasper's letters to Pound, I learned that the five- and fifteen-minute speeches he brought to Charlottesville, addressing segregation, states' rights, and miscegenation, even the slogans he shouted, were all provided to him by Ezra Pound.

The linchpin of these speeches married European anti-Semitism to Dixie-flavored white supremacy; or what Kasper called, in shorthand, "the kike behind the nigger" speech. "Nothing highbrow," Kasper advised Pound when asking for more on this theme, "something to stick in the mass mind." For white supremacists, the idea that African Americans won their rights through their own agency was literally unthinkable, hence McCue II and III's conviction that Charlottesville's Jewish mayor, not Thurgood Marshall, was behind the push to desegregate. During this same period, the racial covenants that peppered Charlottesville's property deeds kept "negroes," but also Jews, from owning property in white neighborhoods. Learning of Kasper's association with Pound, I began to explore the continuities and links between Pound and his circle and the fever dreams of the white supremacists, eugenicists, and political economists of Virginia.

Pound's culture war against the "arthritic milieu" of London began upon his arrival from Pennsylvania in 1908, aged twenty-two. Wearing trousers tailored from billiard cloth, a pink jacket over a black shirt, and a sombrero, Pound was the American upstart, a cowboy, the orientalist artiste with the pointy red beard who couldn't stop talking. Shocking the gatekeepers of high culture invigorated him. Even before the 1914–18 Great War delivered the coup de grâce to what then passed for London's literary rule, Pound's edict to "make it new" freed his coterie of writers from all that was stultifying about the English language. He introduced non-British writers, mainly writing in English and often living in exile, to patrons and publishers. He bullied editors of little magazines into publishing their heterodox works. He reviewed their books and loaned them money. The shift in Pound's interests and ambitions began after he moved to Italy. By the mid-1930s he was publishing pro-Mussolini articles in the *Chicago Tribune*. He was convinced Il Duce was the man to bring about a new Renaissance.

To fully measure Pound's hold on the Anglo-American imagination, and on received notions of "Western civilization," I had to contend with T. S. Eliot, Pound's most influential protégé. Eliot is perhaps best known as the author of the book from which Andrew Lloyd Webber conceived the musical *Cats*. But Marlon Brando's recital of his poem

"The Hollow Men" in the final scenes of *Apocalypse Now* is a better measure of how deeply Eliot has wormed his way into our national psyche. Born in St. Louis, Eliot arrived at Harvard an unworldly youth self-conscious about his Southern drawl in the company of Boston Brahmins. Meeting Pound in London, he reconceived himself as a dour English banker. Begun as a disguise to protect his nerves, this became an ever more baroque performance. He became a protean fixture in the world of twentieth-century "English" letters while hidden behind a facade of chaste inscrutability. Anything "common" or "vulgar" left him squeamish. He was a man fruitfully at odds with himself.

I encountered my first T. S. Eliot poem, "The Love Song of J. Alfred Prufrock" (1915), in high school. I was struck by its peculiarity, unexpected metaphors, and tragicomic portrayal of a young man seized by social anxiety. Thereafter I read everything he wrote. On his say-so, I left the Romantics for the French Symbolists. I sought out dusty copies of the literary magazine he edited. I read the source texts named in the twenty-two notes appended to his 1922 masterwork, *The Waste Land*. I internalized Eliot's particular canon and his era and fell headlong for his idea of what it meant to be cultured. In his seminal 1919 essay, "Tradition and the Individual Talent," Eliot spoke of the imperative of maintaining an awareness of "the pastness of the past," alongside an awareness of the past in the present. Works of art from the past form a tradition that is unsettled and rearranged with the arrival of a new work of art. Thus, to be cultured, every "individual talent" had to be thoroughly versed in *all* literary history, not just the English canon but the entire "mind of Europe." He instructed: "If you want it, you must attain it by great labour."

I labored.

I won't attempt to summarize *The Waste Land* except to say that the near-final line, "these fragments I have shored against my ruins," was for me a shorthand for the lament that the Great War's suicidal frenzy had left Western civilization in shambles. When the long-lost original draft of *The Waste Land* was published in 1974, its facsimile showed the heavy hand of Ezra Pound. Pound cut entire sections, excised the epigraph ("The horror! The horror!" from Joseph Conrad's *Heart of Darkness*), and altered for tone. Where the poet expressed uncertainty, Pound rebuked him in the margins, "'Perhaps' be damned!" Pound seemed to have a sixth sense for the deeper disturbances in the culture and for the soul who channeled them. Eliot didn't just dedicate *The Waste Land* to him; for the rest of his life he believed he owed Pound everything. One man's nervous breakdown over an unhappy marriage became a masterpiece of twentieth-century apocalypse.

In his half-century project of writing *The Cantos*, Pound appeared to seek a similar triumph, employing many of the same strategies as in *The Waste Land*, but to far different effect. In his own creative quest for new poetic means and material, Pound pirated dead languages, medieval Chinese poetry, Japanese Noh plays, and the Anglo-Saxon dirge. In *The Cantos* he used fragments of untranslated dialogue in European languages as well as Provençal, ancient Greek, Latin, Chinese, Arabic, Egyptian hieroglyphs, and American and English vernacular. While *The Waste Land* is often obscure, its language is both mysterious and compelling, as if you'd gained telepathic access to a tortured and well-read soul's delirium. The obscurity of *The Cantos* offers no such access. At times even Pound found his work incomprehensible. "The secret of Mr. Pound's poetic character will only gradually emerge from a detailed analysis of every passage," a perplexed reviewer named Allen Tate wrote on the publication of Pound's first thirty cantos. Tate, a Southern poet known for his critical acumen and massive cranium, insisted that while *The Cantos* didn't say or add up to anything, they were *highly distinguished*.

What does it mean when a work of art is so opaque that nothing about it can be stated with any certainty except that it is a work of high distinction? It hardly matters now; the scramble to make sense of Pound's unfinished opus had begun. Returning to *The Cantos* after many years, I wondered if its opacity was by design, requiring a cultlike submission to the force of Pound's obsessions. Where his 1913 Imagist manifesto had called for everyday speech and no wasted words, *The Cantos* beckoned the reader down a dark and wordy labyrinth. Once you got too far in, like our latterday QAnon seekers, it was hard to find a way out. Depending on your resourcefulness and patience, there may be rewards beyond proving your culture cred. But life is short. Pound's art was autocratic. If you

didn't get it, he said, you could go back to reading Tennyson. Disdain vied
with defensiveness over his work's inscrutability.

In 1933, after three decades abroad, Pound embarked on a "valo-
rization of our national heritage." To claim an American ancestry for
the fascist fever overtaking Germany and Italy, he fixed his magpie eye
on our favorite eighteenth-century American philosophe. In the 1920s
T. S. Eliot had given Pound the complete works of Thomas Jefferson.
In 1933 Pound sent his wife to fetch the volumes from London. In the
first thirty cantos, Pound had skated between classical antiquity, the
Renaissance, and contemporary Europe. For subsequent cantos, Pound
abandoned the versified correspondence of Italian princes for the letters
of Thomas Jefferson. This brought America's revolutionary heritage into
the story of Italy as it began its second decade of fascism. That was one
result. His 1934 pamphlet, *Jefferson and/or Mussolini; Fascism as I Have
Seen It*, was another.

"If the reader will blow the fog off his brain and *think* for a few minutes," Pound argued in the scornful tone of the kingpin he believed himself to be, that reader would find Jefferson's "true heir" in Mussolini.
Pound rhapsodized on the *real* genius of "T.J." and Il Duce, extolling
their "completeness of knowledge, intelligence carried into a third or
fourth dimension." This summed up Pound's estimation of his own intellect and his sweeping claim to divine a historical moment and truth
that most people—lady golfers were often singled out for special abuse,
but he had a handbag full of cretins to deride—were utterly incapable of
grasping. Jefferson was a Renaissance *Übermensch*. Blessed with a many-
minded vision, T.J. could see beyond the limits of self-interest, particularly that of small-minded merchants, bankers, and industrialists whose
only allegiance was to whatever made them money. Jefferson's attachment to Monticello provided a metaphor and a model for Pound's herald-
ing of a new Renaissance; Jefferson had created an entire civilization in
revolutionary-era Virginia, a model nation for a mutinous age. Jefferson's
adage, "The tree of liberty must be refreshed from time to time with the
blood of patriots and tyrants," is now a far right meme.

Pound had a habit of changing the meaning of words, sometimes
simply by spelling them differently. This enabled him to insist that such

and such a word or phrase meant what he wanted it to mean, even if that meant turning its more commonly understood meaning on its head. As for T.J.'s famous declaration "all men are created equal," Pound could explain. Jefferson had a reputation for making excessive statements. Such a statement needed to be given its proper context. Jefferson didn't mean that men remained equal or were genetically equal. "All men are created equal" was just another way of saying "all men are sons of Zeus."

Pound didn't limit his analysis to "what Tom Jefferson *said*;" that, he maintained, was the mistake of "the left." For Jefferson, words were tools. "I am concerned with what he actually did, with the way his mind worked [. . .] when faced with a particular problem in a particular geography." Was slavery a "particular problem"? Jefferson was too shrewd to "jeopardize his power with untimely fights" on behalf of the abolition of slavery, Pound argued. Jefferson's Louisiana Purchase, on the other hand, was the "greatest single territorial conquest" in history. Unlike Clive's conquest of India, Jefferson hadn't had to cheat or bribe indigenous traitors on the field of battle. He simply went over their heads. Finally, Jefferson had governed with "limited suffrage," "by means of conversation with his more intelligent friends." In conclusion, Jefferson and the nation he willed into existence, first with his presidency and then through his "deputies" Madison and Monroe, was fascist, avant la lettre. Pound's final point was that the left was "completely, absolutely, utterly, and possibly incurably ignorant of Jefferson and nearly ignorant of the structure of American government, both *de jure* and *de facto*."

Twenty years later, confined to St. Elizabeth's, Pound remained intent on using "Kulchur" and Kasper to give fascism an all-American face. If he once required others to divine the meaning of his *Cantos*, he now wanted an army of disciples to—as he put it—"press the word to the action." Hugh Kenner, Pound's most devoted reader and decipherer, was not alone in worrying about the sort of people finding their way to St. Elizabeth's. To truly appreciate Pound's thought, Kenner believed, required both an excellent formal education and an openness to having that education "modified" by Pound. Without such grounding, Pound's "crankish notions" would rattle around in the "fervent void" of empty heads. This was charitable. Pound set great store by his crankish notions.

John Kasper proved an avid lieutenant. At Columbia most of his friends were Jews; he soon began aping Pound's anti-Semitism. His letters mimicked Pound's contrived misspellings, and he took to writing in dialect, à la *Uncle Remus*, much as T. S. Eliot once did in *his* letters to Pound. Kasper gossiped and backstabbed and competed with Pound's other protégés for favor. In 1953 he opened the Make It New bookshop on Bleecker St. in Greenwich Village. In those years, the Village was packed with Beat poets, abstract expressionists, jazz artists, and bebop musicians. Kasper displayed Pound's books in the front window. He stocked copies of *Mein Kampf* and *Hitler's Secret Conversations, 1941–1944*. Pound suggested books on Italian fascism and anti-Semitic periodicals. Yet most of the store's habitués, like most of Kasper's friends, were Black writers, artists, and musicians, among them LeRoi Jones. This was because Kasper's Black girlfriend was busy stocking the store with works by Black writers.

Kasper also published a line of cheap paperback offsets under the imprint "Square Dollar Books." Pound had been talking about a line of books aimed at college students for years. "Textbooks for students who want first things first," he wrote in the promotional copy. Among the works Pound aspired to introduce to course syllabi was *Mullins on the Federal Reserve*, a pamphlet of excerpts from *Secrets of the Federal Reserve Bank*, by Eustace Mullins. In 1947 Pound commissioned Mullins to write an in-depth account of how the nation's banking reserves had been placed in the hands of Jewish international bankers "for the purpose of carrying out their nearly fulfilled world dictatorship plan." Mullins was Kasper's sometime roommate. He was also a Virginian, a Holocaust denier, and a proud son of the Confederacy.

Pound's hostility to the Federal Reserve and to bankers echoed Jefferson's fierce opposition to the Bank of the United States, proposed by the first secretary of the treasury, Alexander Hamilton. Jefferson feared a national bank would be used as a tool for Northern monied interests, granting them an upper hand over Southern planters, who were nearly always their debtors. That didn't forestall him from weaponizing debt when it came to the project of separating indigenous peoples from their land. In an 1803 letter to William Henry Harrison, which doubtless caught Pound's eye, Jefferson had pushed for the establishment of trading houses to lure native tribes into debt until they were forced to cede "lands which they have to spare & we want" for necessities "which we have to spare, and they want."

The subsistence life and agrarian values of the humble freeholder that Jefferson celebrated as an American ideal were a far cry from his own lavish lifestyle. Yeoman farmers grew their own food and lived without the regrets that ruffled Jefferson's conscience as a slaveholder, and therefore weren't morally compromised. So, he made a romance of them. In 1827 Jefferson's debts amounted to $1 million in current exchange. Unable or unwilling to live within his means, he blamed banks for enabling him to indulge his taste for French wines and quixotic building projects. After his death Jefferson's debts were paid with the lives of those he enslaved. For Pound the extent to which a society curbed usury was a measure of how civilized it was, but he too had a taste for the finer things. He also had the foresight to marry a rich woman.

Another Square Dollar book packaged excerpts from the work of Louis Agassiz, a Swiss-born American biologist and opponent of Darwin. Agassiz believed that only the white race was descended from Adam and Eve, and only the white man was formed in the image of God. Any blessings accruing to white men in the way of wealth and power amounted to proof of God's favor. The destitution and degradation of Black people were proof of divine displeasure. Twenty years after calling for justice for the Scottsboro Boys, Pound propagated the claim that white people were not just racially superior but God's anointed. Pound himself had no religious beliefs, but he saw that Christianity could be utilized to further his racist agenda. Richard Spencer felt similarly.

Jefferson's *Notes on the State of Virginia* made an eighteenth-century version of the same argument. "Race science," later known as eugenics, was the attempt to provide a scientific basis to white supremacy. At the turn of the twentieth century, UVA's president, Edwin Alderman, began recruiting white-robed men of science to create a center for the study of eugenics at the medical school. They arrived eager to prove theories about the "negro's" criminal proclivities, susceptibility to disease, and limited educational potential. One of Alderman's recruits, Dr. Ivey Lewis, a geneticist, dean of Arts and Sciences, and member of the Defenders of State Sovereignty and Individual Liberties, helped sustain the "scientific rationale" for the state's burgeoning racial integrity movement. This effort culminated in the passage of the Racial Integrity Act in 1924. (Lewis's half sister, a columnist with the *Raleigh News and Observer*, would become the South's leading female opponent of integration.)

"Virginia Again Leading Nation," the *Daily Progress* crowed when Ivey Lewis gave a lecture on the Racial Integrity Act, declaring that the mixing of Blacks and whites had led to the fall of the Roman, Greek, Egyptian, and Indian empires. "The purity of the white race in America we regard as a basal necessity," Lewis said, "for the maintenance of the heritage which we have received." The law instituted the "one drop rule" whereby a person with any documented African ancestry, whatever their skin color, was designated Negro and subjected to Jim Crow. Interracial marriage was outlawed and criminalized. The director of the Bureau of Vital Statistics believed native people of "pure Indian descent unmixed with negro blood" no longer existed. This was ethnic cleansing by idée fixe.

Virginia's use of state policy to preserve "racial integrity" was of abiding interest to European fascists. Drawing on the work of UVA eugenicists, in 1924 the US government passed the Johnson-Reed Act. This law revised immigration laws to encourage immigrants from Northern and Western Europe and restrict those from Southern Europe. Hitler made note of it in *Mein Kampf.* In a May 1942 war broadcast out of Rome, Ezra Pound held that Hitler's eugenics program was central to his plans for Germany and had his wholehearted support. "[T]he breedin' of human beings deserves MORE care and attention than the breedin' of horses. . . . That is point ONE of the NAZI program."

For over half a century the teaching of eugenics shaped the thinking of Virginia's political elite and informed how medicine and medical research were practiced in UVA's hospitals and clinics. Three UVA medical school graduates went on to devise the infamous longitudinal Tuskegee Syphilis Study (1932–72) in which hundreds of Black men, infected with syphilis, were left untreated for the purpose of study. Hospital buildings were named after eugenicists, and the library was named for the man who brought them to UVA. Eugenics remained part of the biology department's core curriculum until Ivey's retirement in 1953. While the National Science Foundation was pouring federal funds into hard science, Ivey Lewis and his UVA colleagues were still practicing "natural science." Natural scientists believed that once the laws of nature had been clarified, a divinely inspired moral and political order, rife with notions of racial hierarchies, would be revealed.

At the height of Ivey Lewis's hold on the university, in May 1933, T. S. Eliot was invited to give a series of lectures. In the pained voice of a physician delivering news of a terminal illness, Eliot's second and third lectures laid out the ills evident in contemporary letters: the loss of belief in original sin and the proliferation of blasphemies. His introductory lecture, however, "The Meaning of Tradition," began on a different note. Though it was his first visit to Virginia, he addressed Virginians directly, suggesting that he composed it soon after he arrived.

On the cross-Atlantic journey, Eliot began, he'd had little expectation of finding a sense of tradition surviving anywhere in America. Crossing the Potomac into Virginia in early May, however, was like arriving in another country. The countryside was captivating. To a friend he wrote of the riot of brilliant birds—cardinals, tanagers, bluebirds— and of trees in wanton bloom; "like a sub-tropical Devonshire." To Ezra Pound's wife, Eliot wrote that the university itself was "rather backward," but happily so. He admired the Palladian architecture of the university's founder architect, and believed it "would please Ez." And its economy appeared to be just the right mix of rural and industrial. Even its soil was "more opulent" than any other.

His stay in Charlottesville reminded him of the 1930 book *I'll Take My Stand* and rekindled his feeling of kinship with the twelve young Southern writers out of Vanderbilt whose essays were collected there. He found something affecting in their quixotic "stand for a cause which was lost long before they were born." Eliot, who identified himself to his UVA audience as a New Englander, rather than an Englishman or fellow Southerner, made the case that Virginia had a greater potential for the reestablishment of "a native culture" than even New England did. Unlike New England, with its sordid and "half dead mill towns," Virginia had been spared an invasion by "foreign races." It was a healthy distance from New York. His brief time in Charlottesville had compelled him to emend his seminal 1919 essay "Tradition and the Individual Talent."

He explained: "[A nation's] population should be homogeneous." When two or more cultures, races, or faiths exist in the same place, they are likely "to become adulterate." The presence of freethinking Jews was particularly injurious, leaving those in his audience to imagine New York was overrun. In Charlottesville he found a pleasing native culture defined by agrarian values, the white race, Christianity, and the absence of Jews and other foreign influences. In fact, Jews had lived in Charlottesville since the colonial era. They were landowners and storekeepers, provisioning plantation owners like Thomas Jefferson. It was a Jew named Jefferson Monroe Levy who would save Monticello from ruin. But Eliot wasn't entirely wrong. Until the 1950s, when there was an influx of émigrés from Europe, only three Jews were known to have served on UVA's faculty.

Such high praise was undoubtedly well received; Eliot had beautiful manners. In a letter to a friend from his Harvard days, Eliot described what this last outpost of homogeneity, steeped in "native culture," amounted to. His dynamic conception of tradition and talent had been replaced by a dying order. Charlottesville was immured in a narcotic past, he said, as stagnant and moribund as the Land of the Lotus-Eaters. Observing "poor whites creeping about, immobile negroes sitting on kegs or poised at street corners," he marked them as a "people waiting for nothing to happen. A somber, sad country; as alien in its way as California, but almost wholly without vulgarity." Eliot's Charlottesville stay coincided with an orgy of book burning at thirty-four universities across Germany to "purify" German culture of Jewish authors and "corrupting foreign influences." Radical Nazis had just released the "Prussian Memorandum" demanding the prevention of "any further penetration of Jewish blood into the body of the German *Volk*."

Eliot never allowed these lectures, published as *After Strange Gods*, to be reprinted.

Both Eliot and Pound entertained the idea that America, heir to what was left in the rubble of European civilization, might rebuild where they supposed America itself began, in the pure and beautiful land of Virginia. The provocations underlying the Square Dollar series were similar. Who better represented Jefferson's true beliefs? The descendants of the master or of the slave? Who better represented America? The Anglo-Saxons who arrived in Virginia bearing land grants from the British Crown or its indigenous inhabitants and polyglot immigrants? And, finally, who better represented the American ideal: the Christian freeholder, Jefferson's heralded but still subjugated small farmer, or the New York Jewish banker and Northern industrialist? By extending his battle lines as much around Jefferson as around Confederate statues, Richard Spencer forcefully recentered America's beginnings in English settler colonialism, in Enlightenment grandees, Southern heritage, white supremacy, and anti-Semitism. Eliot and Pound, with their more erudite talk of native culture and revolutionary Renaissance, had laid the groundwork.

When asked for his thoughts on Western civilization, Gandhi famously responded that it was a good idea. The fear that barbarians are at the gates, that civilization faces a looming collapse comparable to the fall of Rome, was a twentieth-century invention of the European empires. For Gandhi, it was the British Empire that claimed ownership of Western civilization, not white people. Western civilization uses pomp and circumstance to distract the world from its crimes against humanity. Western civilization is the flag of those who realize that the signifiers of culture, education, and high status they inherited or worked hard to achieve, no longer compel deference, but indifference.

Notions like Western civilization are resuscitated in times of cultural crisis accompanying the threat posed by both the rise of new powers and new ways of seeing. For many, this has proved profoundly disorienting and politically destabilizing. If Western civilization ever existed, it has destroyed nearly everything it ever touched, including the idea of Western civilization. Richard Spencer hoped to breathe new life into assumptions that remain deeply etched in our cultural fabric, perhaps nowhere more so than in Charlottesville. Eliot and Pound were more sophisticated (and more obfuscating) in their critical appraisals, broader in their historical and cultural references, but as another devastating European war approached, no less reactionary in their instincts.

Contemporary white nationalism produces flags, patches, crests, armorial emblems, heraldic symbols, logos, and crude homemade shields. They recruit followers not with works of art and imagination but with memes, livestreamed displays of dominance, and hackneyed performances on YouTube. Just as Pound assembled oddments of texts and untranslated dialogue for his *Cantos*, they appropriate and recombine ancient Norse emblems, Celtic runes, even the Buddhist and Hindu "swastik." Though ill-disposed to Christian ethics, their crusader uniforms feature iron, Celtic, Christian, and St. Andrew's crosses. Their symbols often reference European ethnic, nationalist, linguistic, and religious identities specific to historic conflicts and empires about which they, and Pound before them, knew little.

None of these symbols have much to do with whiteness, per se. The notion of whiteness has evolved since first codified by Enlightenment race science. Indeed, the most American aspect of Richard Spencer's representation of white nationalist thought is his insistence that whiteness, like anti-Semitism, is an ancient, transnational phenomenon rather than the self-serving and provincial invention of eighteenth-century Virginia planters, dependent on the labors of the enslaved to sustain their pretense of being civilized. Then, as now, it is a sign of backwardness and a portent of savagery.

On his trips to DC to see Ezra Pound, John Kasper often stayed at the Arlington, Virginia, home of another visitor to St. Elizabeth's. George Lincoln Rockwell has long been credited with Americanizing Hitler's National Socialism by combining white supremacy with Nazism. But Pound was there first. The membership list of Kasper's Seaboard White Citizens Council became the basis of Rockwell's soon-to-be-founded American Nazi Party. According to Rockwell, Kasper received near-daily instructions from Pound, acted on his orders, and parroted his opinions.

Also according to Rockwell, Pound planned to move to Monticello after his release from St. Elizabeth's.

One of Kasper's friends from Greenwich Village was the African American painter and musician Ted Joans. Joans couldn't recall Kasper ever expressing strong feelings about race. He did, however, remember him saying he was ready to go to any extreme to make himself known. That sooner or later his time would come.

PART II

The Ghost in the Machine

January 2017–August 2017

CHAPTER 6

Capital of the Resistance

In the song cycles of eleventh- and twelfth-century France, paladins were knights who left Charlemagne's court to protect Gaul from invading Saracens. Germany, Italy, and England developed variations of this legend, immortalizing the paladins' chivalric deeds in music, literature, and works of art. In *World of Warcraft*, a Paladin is depicted as a knight with a lion's head. There were any number of strategies to playing a Paladin, but Emily Gorcenski liked to get the big Angry Dragon to attack her. She would make herself the target, then members of her team would close in. While they distracted the Angry Dragon with their various weapons, the Healers would come in and see to her wounds so she could be kept alive. She worked her way up to being a raid leader. A demanding one.

"I would run my team like Bill Belichick runs his football team. Be kind of a dickhead about it. Lots of yelling and screaming, as was the norm for hardcore gaming. I mean, I didn't scream that much, but it happened once or twice. More swearing than screaming. I've taught more than one person's two-year-old child the word *fuck*. That's when they're like, 'Okay. We can't raid without headphones anymore.'"

When Emily was three, her father brought home a Commodore 64, one of the earliest personal computers. She eventually taught herself how to take it apart and play games on it. She was five when her parents divorced, and she hasn't seen her mother since. Later, her best friend got a Windows PC, and one day in 1995 they clicked on America Online and discovered the internet. At twelve she learned from her father that he wasn't her real father. That her mother had had an affair. This explained why she didn't look like anyone else in her Polish American family. Her skin was darker, she had an Asian cast to her eyes, and nearly black hair. Still, he had raised her as his own and they never spoke of it again.

A tall, slim adolescent, Emily was passionate about ice hockey, hunting, and computers. She played right wing or defense. Her team won state championships. There were hunting trips with her father and uncle. As for her studies, she tended to be a slacker. She was arrogant and thought she knew everything. She nurtured secret crushes on girls whom she was nonetheless mean to. If she thought about her future, it was with the certainty that she wasn't going to spend forty years at some boring job talking about specs. She wasn't going to carry a briefcase and drive a Ford Taurus. She was going to see the world. And if she couldn't be a fighter pilot because of her poor vision, she would design the greatest fighter plane *ever*.

Then, in 2004, during her senior year at Rensselaer Polytechnic Institute and just after a semester at Princeton doing nuclear physics, Emily was diagnosed with Graves' disease, a thyroid condition. Just before graduation, she had to leave school without her aeronautical engineering degree. Now her dream of designing fighter planes was gone too. She moved in with her grandmother in rural Connecticut and, once her condition had stabilized, worked as a stock clerk at Barnes & Noble. She watched her friends from high school descend into drugs and alcohol abuse, boredom and sexual frustration. She might have, too, but for *World of Warcraft*. This became her gateway to the world outside South Windsor. She still missed the comradery of her college friends and their intense nightlong conversations, but *WoW* helped her rediscover a sense of purpose and connected her to gamers all over the world.

In these years she wasn't yet fully Emily. Some might say she was a woman trapped in a man's body, but she didn't describe herself that way. She said that in college she began thinking she might be bisexual or gender fluid. She didn't have all the words for what she was feeling; few people did back then. And a large part of her remained a reactionary asshole heavily allergic to any kind of introspection. This attitude left her unable to question the gaming community's similar hostility. It was easier to stop thinking about it and just focus on the next raid. It took her three years to save up enough to finish her degree. By the time she moved to Charlottesville for a job in 2008, she had worked her way into the highest ranks of *World of Warcraft*.

She met C, the woman who would change her life, through a dating app. Soon after they married, C told her she should see a gender therapist. Somehow, C knew. As soon as Emily stepped into the therapist's office, she knew too. The therapist saved her life. *World of Warcraft* had suppressed a large part of who she was. She now needed to be out, to be herself. The moment she quit playing, the real world beckoned. She began to travel.

Over the years it would take her to fully transition, Emily began rethinking everything. She had learned how to be a boy. She had lived that life. Though that information was no longer applicable to her, it was valuable knowledge to have when it came to understanding people. In advance of Unite the Right, she gave a great deal of thought to the plight of young white men. Her life, like those of her friends from high school, had gone off the rails. Different people deal with this differently, she told me, but at no point did she consider becoming a Nazi.

Nor did she agree with my suggestion that perhaps these young men were filled with self-hatred. She thought it had more to do with mismanaged expectations. Boys (white boys) are groomed to believe they are destined for greatness, she said. They are raised with the idea that they are entitled to riches, renown, and due deference. When they haven't achieved the financial well-being or received the respect they consider their birthright, they can spiral into depression. Joining a hate group, she said, is easier than admitting you are afraid your life will end in failure. But it isn't the only option.

Emily's transition involved internalizing an entirely different operating code from the one she'd been raised with. This new code made her kinder, to others but also to herself. She began to reconsider the right-wing attitudes and assumptions of her conservative upbringing. The problem was not Black people demanding equal rights or queer people demanding labor protections. The problem was a very small number of very wealthy people controlling a disproportionate amount of the world's resources. She also began waking up to the harm her work could cause. In college she had worked on a government-funded project in which she used differential game theory to figure out how to make a drone chase a person. She modeled her approach on the "homicidal chauffeur problem" which pitted a car's speed against a pedestrian's ability to maneuver. She asked herself: *What if she began using her skills to do good?*

For eight years in Charlottesville, she wrote software for medical devices and aerospace control systems, both heavily regulated tech spaces and subject to a complex certification process. After Trump's election, online chatter suggested there had been Russian interference. Since she had the day after Thanksgiving off, she decided to spend it looking into the certification process for voting machines. The first thing she discovered was that some states required certification, and some didn't. She began reading every test report for every model of every machine from every manufacturer. Software quality requirements were basically nonexistent. She started live tweeting in her usual snarky way every time she came across some security hole. Her follower count began to climb.

That January, on her last big trip before her surgery, she attended the Women's March in Prague. Nearly everything she saw in Europe reminded her of what was happening at home. She mused on whether Trump could fairly be called a fascist. She tweeted about a North Dakota bill enabling drivers to commit vehicular manslaughter against protesters, and an incident in Buffalo in which a car *did* drive into a group of protesters. She posted a State Department Org Chart showing all the resignations that had taken place since Trump's election and the positions that remained unfilled. Assistant secretaries in the Office of Civilian Security, Democracy, and Human Rights were all gone. Arms Control and International Security were hollowed out. She predicted veteran civil servants would end up in think tanks where their institutional memories would be exploited by foreign interests.

The chart went viral. The Democratic Party tweeted it out, but that was all they did. It was like everyone was just waiting for the other shoe to fall.

Not one shoe but an entire rack. One executive order followed another, each punctuated by Trump's spiky Sharpie-thick signature. Capping the week after his inauguration came the Muslim ban, signed with a flourish on Friday, January 27. This suspended the entry of immigrants from Syria, Iran, Iraq, Libya, Sudan, Yemen, and Somalia for a period of ninety days, effective immediately. Travelers with valid visas and green cards arriving at immigration windows were held incommunicado, denied food and water, and compelled to sign papers agreeing to leave the country. Hundreds of lawyers and demonstrators mobbed the airports.

In Charlottesville, Mayor Mike Signer's hair was on fire. He called the senate offices of Tim Kaine and Mark Warner. He had back-to-back meetings with legal and social services to confirm Charlottesville's Muslim refugees would have a place to turn. He drank a lot of coffee. Visiting a local mosque, Signer heard from Syrian, Afghan, and Iranian families. They feared they had "escaped the frying pan only to fall into the fire."

There was no fire. The Muslim ban didn't affect residents with valid visas. Because of the delicacy of the situation, however, the director of the local chapter of the International Rescue Committee implored the mayor not to refer to Charlottesville as a sanctuary city. It might cost them HUD funds or incite some form of retribution from the Trump administration. But Mike Signer felt something had to be done and it was up to him, as mayor of a "world class city," to do it.

After graduating from Princeton, Mike Signer had pursued a doctorate in political science from Berkeley. Then he received a UVA law degree. He had a local law practice. He was also a published author. He had written a primer on political leadership in the form of a biography of James Madison. He referred to himself as a constitutional scholar and professor, citing a class titled "Race, Policy, and the Past" he taught at UVA's Batten School of Leadership and Public Policy.

All these achievements contributed to his political profile: a forward-looking, start-up-embracing, intellectual statesman.

Signer was also a fount of clichés. He often spoke about authenticity, as if he realized how little he had of it. He was deliberative and pedantic, in thrall to abstractions and rulebooks. After a failed run for lieutenant governor six years before, he had scaled back his political ambitions. He launched his campaign for city council, "One Charlottesville," flanked by seven former mayors, along with his wife and twin toddlers. After his election, he was the near-unanimous choice of his fellow councillors for mayor. As he had only been a Charlottesville resident for a relatively brief time, this was curious.

Charlottesville operates under a "weak mayor" form of government. The day-to-day running of the city, and all its fiscal business, is the responsibility of the city manager, a hired professional. In council chambers the mayor runs the agenda, but otherwise the role is ceremonial. For this reason, the position generally went to the person with the most seniority and the most community support. Despite raising four times as much money, Signer received far fewer votes than the other newly elected candidate, Wes Bellamy, and the incumbent Kathy Galvin. Kristin Szakos, who had already served as vice-mayor, was the natural choice.

But Signer wanted desperately to be mayor. He aspired "to lead where others had followed." Square-jawed, blond, and well over six feet tall, Signer's outsized ambitions seemed to hold everyone captive. Only Szakos, the city council member who first suggested the city might consider moving the Confederate statues, abstained from voting for him. That Wes Bellamy voted for him said a lot about his ambitions, which, like Signer's and unlike Szakos's, went beyond a seat on the city council. As mayor, Signer's constant displays of leadership, his unbridled hunger for the public eye, left the impression he had more power than he did. This exasperated the city manager. It also set Signer up for blame when things went south. He never seemed to grasp this simple fact.

In his January mayoral address on the state of the city, Signer portrayed himself rather differently from his campaign literature. People had the wrong idea about him, he said. He often felt like an outsider. His father had died in a car accident before he was born, in India, to an American. Consequently, he was stuck with the name of an obscure Hindu prophet until the age of seven, when his mother remarried into a New Jersey/New York Jewish family. So he was Jewish. This was news to at least one of his fellow council members. Charlottesville has a close-knit Jewish community; Signer would have been hard to miss at High Holidays. After Trump's election, Signer began to publicly claim his stepfather's Jewish ancestry as his own. Some saw political calculation in that.

In response to Trump's Muslim ban, Signer decided to make a "bracing rhetorical call" in defense of America's "deepest principles of religious toleration," so familiar to him from his work on James Madison. It was Madison who codified the writ of religious freedom: "Congress shall make no law respecting the establishment of religion." Signer planned to hold a rally at city hall until the city manager told him he couldn't. This filled him with consternation. He argued himself hoarse. When the city manager held fast, he instead staged a "press conference" in *front* of city hall.

Over seven hundred people showed up. A bluegrass band played "This Land Is Your Land." Khizr Khan, the Gold Star father and local who had electrified the Democratic Convention with his paean to the Constitution, opened the proceedings. Even when Jason Kessler arrived with a bullhorn and read out Wes Bellamy's old tweets, Khan continued undaunted. In his own speech, Signer referenced his paternal (step) grandfather, a Jew who had fought the Nazis in World War II, and quoted the words emblazoned on the pedestal of the Statue of Liberty by the Jewish poet Emma Lazarus. But the most noteworthy moment was his declaration that henceforth Charlottesville would be known as "the Capital of the Resistance."

Did this not violate Signer's oft-stated principle of "making progress not waves"? Hadn't he insisted that advocacy should not cast issues in absolute terms? How was this different from the moral grandstanding he accused Wes Bellamy of? When a constituent expressed surprise that Signer hadn't attended Bellamy's press conference in Lee Park, Signer told him he didn't feel it was appropriate for a mayor to advocate against a government he was a part of. What, then, was he doing in front of city hall with a rented sound system?

Whatever his intentions, Signer was seizing the spotlight, asserting mayoral control over the story he wanted to tell, and away from the one told by his vice-mayor. His story returned everyone to the fairy tale of America's founding fathers and the principles they enshrined in the Constitution. On such subjects Signer was the expert, and Charlottesville, as the veritable cradle of democracy, provided the perfect platform on which he could shine.

When the city council met on February 6 for the final vote on the statues, the tally was known but the mood in chambers was as volatile as ever. Even in this most local of spaces, those people President Trump had emboldened clashed with those who felt under siege. After the fireworks of public comment, Mayor Signer and Councillor Kathy Galvin restated their views for keeping the Lee statue where it was and voted accordingly. Bob Fenwick and Kristin Szakos cast their votes to remove it. The vote in favor of renaming Lee and Jackson Parks was unanimous.

Wes Bellamy spoke last. The rage directed at him was unceasing. At every interruption, Signer broke into Bellamy's remarks, threatening to stop the proceedings or have people escorted out. Bellamy's patience during Signer's stem-winders on Robert's Rules of Order was really something. After revisiting the terms of his $4 million equity package for the Black community, passed at the previous council meeting, Bellamy turned to address the accusation that his actions on the statues had created racial divisions.

I had heard something of Wes Bellamy on visits home. No one gave the statues a second thought until Wes Bellamy brought them up, people said. Many forgot that Zyahna Bryant was the immediate instigator. Even Bellamy forgot. But each time I heard him blamed for inciting racial divisions, I was flummoxed. It was like the riddle of which came first. The confusion of cause and effect felt calculated in a way I couldn't put my finger on. I found that if I reframed the question to "Why couldn't Wes Bellamy have let sleeping dogs lie?" it became easier to parse. This way it was clear that everyone knew the dog was there, but in the interest of civic harmony, everyone had learned to tread carefully. The man waking the dog was reminding them of a sore subject. And with the new president, this was no time to be making trouble.

I don't think I realized how circumscribed my own thinking was by a fear of this dog until I began talking to people in Charlottesville. I had instinctively understood why Black elders like Holly Edwards believed nothing good would come of fooling with the statues. It was why she had advised Bellamy to choose a different cause. I also understood why white people believed Charlottesville had no race problems until Bellamy started in with the statues. They suffered from a fear of this dog, too, even if they hadn't stopped to figure out its source. It was simpler to blame Wes Bellamy. This is the power of the dog. It keeps us quiet and conflict avoidant. All for fear of the dog. Yet the more we shrink from this fear, the more fearsome the dog becomes. And justice never gets served.

Thomas Jefferson was careful to tread lightly around "the passions, the prejudices, and the real difficulties" provoked by the mere mention of emancipation. Initially, he refrained from publishing his *Notes on the State of Virginia* because he knew that some of his views might inflame Southern planters' reactions beyond remedy. When legislative action on slavery in Virginia was proposed, he feared that if it failed, it would "rivet still closer the chains of bondage." (Of course you can also call this self-serving claptrap.) Abraham Lincoln, far from an abolitionist, was confounded by Southern intransigence.

Abolitionists called the sleeping dog "the Slave Power." This referred not simply to the planters or the slave states, but to the expansionist designs of proslavery money and influence in Washington and beyond. When Charles Dickens visited America in 1841 he upbraided the North not only for bowing down to Southern slaveowners over the institution of slavery, but also saw in their failure to address the plague of gun violence a similar deference. In 2012 Ta-Nehisi Coates posted an essay by Tony Horwitz on his blog that echoed Dickens's point. Horwitz, the author of *Confederates in the Attic*, wrote that just as Americans had once appeased and abetted the Slave Power, they were now appeasing and abetting the spread of guns. As with the Slave Power, the rhetoric of the Gun Power was framed as a defense of the Constitution. Just as the Slave Power portrayed slavery as a blessing, pushing for export to new territories, so Wayne LaPierre's NRA depicted guns as providing peace of mind in the face of threats posed by unseen enemies. George Soros, working in league with the UN, aimed to impose a global gun ban to undermine American power, LaPierre claimed, to erase "dominant traditional American values."

"The NRA has become a neo-Confederate movement that sees Federals as foes," Horwitz warned. It stokes paranoia by claiming that if Obama were to be reelected, that would mean "'the end of our freedom forever.' That's more or less what Fire-Eaters said about Lincoln in 1860." When Trump campaigned against Clinton, the NRA cry became "Charge the cockpit or you die." The NRA deputized patriots and pushed to place guns everywhere. Those of us, white, Black, or brown, who find the proliferation of guns unsettling, and who see our freedoms curtailed by the shadow guns cast over our lives, are given no means to respond to this display of menace.

The sleeping dog asserts its power in more subtle ways as well. For many white people, of whatever political stripe, being reminded of our whiteness is unsettling. It sounds like an insult. It sounds like an accusation. We don't think of ourselves as white. We are Americans. We are mothers or daughters, fathers or sons. We are Christians. We are sports fans or cat lovers. A president saying Trayvon Martin could have been his son exasperates us. Why did he have to mention that and thereby remind us he is Black, and we are white? Such things ruffle our awareness, disturb the way we think of the world and the affirmation we feel entitled to.

The white moderate has established certain rules, cultural codes, and behavioral strictures that often go unquestioned. The historian Steven Hahn has written that the transition from slavery was accompanied by the imposition of an assortment of coercive practices often viewed as the "proper, and needful remedy," not only for the newly emancipated but for Northern and Western wage laborers. These "Enlightened humanists" who saw "free labor and harsh vagrancy laws as two sides of the same social coin, detested enslavement but viewed convict labor as desirable, and celebrated contract freedom even when it could produce near servitude. . . ." He goes on to point out that "these were less contradictions in terms than part of a coherent package of thought and class sensibility in which liberal optimism was yoked to visions of the social order where power could be denied while being wielded." Toni Morrison would call this "the ghost in the machine."

When measured against these rules, both unspoken and legislated, those least likely to share the class sensibilities of the present-day white moderate, that is, poor whites or people of color, will of necessity be found wanting. The white moderate polices such "norms" unthinkingly, never expecting they might be policed or judged themselves, particularly for breaking some newfangled rule, some trendy social code they had no hand in writing. Called out, they can become confused, defensive, aggrieved, or vengeful.

Every new generation challenges members of an older one to rethink themselves, and the cast-iron judgments, hidden assumptions, and social codes they were raised with. This isn't always about racial reckoning; in the push to rethink the role of women in society, some men chose to liberate themselves from patriarchy's trap. What would it be like for white people to be sprung from the self-centered and disabling trap of whiteness? These younger, sundry voices can relieve us of the cussedness and blinkered vision that comes with age. This reorientation requires effort and is not without discomfort, but it does not put us in mortal peril.

In seminary, Pastor Brenda learned that the opposite of love isn't hate. It is fear. When people used to being in control begin to feel they are losing control of their story, their way of life, she said, they get frightened out of their wits. For those whose lives are now and always have been under threat from white people, the desire to tread softly so as not to awaken the dog in us, our delicate feelings or our dangerous fears, is reasonable.

Yet we cannot fail to note the presence of those who are looking for an opportunity to inflame these fears and fuel our grievances until they become unmanageable. They are the Fire-Eaters of our time. Their project is to quicken the journey from anxiety (at being called racist or being canceled) to resentment (at having to watch our words), to the conviction that our way of life, and possibly our lives, are in danger. Their propaganda gives those who are rattled, apprehensive, or actively spoiling for a fight permission to act with impunity. Ordinary Americans now show up at city council or school board meetings, hospitals, and private homes consumed by righteous fury. They terrorize doctors, nurses, judges, prosecutors, jury members, trial witnesses, the Capitol Police, elected legislators, election workers, journalists, schoolteachers, librarians, Asian Americans, Muslims, Jews, Hispanic Americans, and children figuring out who they are. This should not be happening.

It is easy to lose sight of the fact that this is calculated. There is money to be made and power to be seized. Hand in hand with the Gun Power, these forces are growing stronger every day. This is the nature of backlash. It is real and indomitable. Much depends on how we respond.

The debate over the Confederate statues had given the city of Charlottesville an opportunity to talk about race and to address the wounds left by slavery, Jim Crow, segregation, mass incarceration, and inequality. To keep this conversation going, Wes Bellamy's $4 million equity package included an allocation of $10,000 in one-time funding to underwrite a second Dialogue on Race. Would this establish racial harmony, redress the history of injustice? Bellamy asked. No, he said, it would not. But they had to keep talking to one another.

With the vote to remove the Lee statue and rename the parks now finalized, Wes Bellamy moved to settle the waters. He reminded people that righteousness, including that of his own supporters, had a civic cost. He called out the Lee statue defender, Lewis Martin III. Martin had participated in the first Dialogue on Race. Martin had been a guest at Bellamy's wedding. Lewis Martin was not his enemy, he said. Kathy Galvin or Mike Signer were not his enemies. He turned to those with the Save the Statue signs. "You are not my enemy, and I am not yours." The Maryland woman in the hoop skirt laughed scornfully.

He continued. They might disagree on the statues today, but tomorrow they might agree on something else. He asked that people listen to one another. Respectfully.

"However, I will be very clear, we will not be bullied. We will not be pushed away. And, for the last time, we are not going anywhere."

Almost despite Signer's effort to brand Charlottesville the Capital of the Resistance, by early spring something approaching a resistance had begun to take shape. Attendance at Rev. Alvin Edwards's Clergy Collective breakfasts was twice what it had been the previous year. Grace Aheron, Tracy Howe Wispelwey, and the activists of Showing Up for Racial Justice had graduated from planning meetings to hosting monthly public workshops. Name tags now included pronouns. Partnerships had been forged with the NAACP, the Legal Aid Justice Center, and the local public housing association. Together they called out the *Daily Progress*'s ongoing portrayal of Jason Kessler as a "blogger" or "alt-right" rather than a white supremacist or white nationalist.

On March 15 a newly ordained Rev. Tracy Howe Wispelwey organized Showing Up for Racial Justice's first public action, a vigil for a missing trans woman named Sage Smith. A police investigation into her disappearance had languished for years. Grace Aheron had reached out to Rev. Smash, also now ordained, to put the word out on her network of faith leaders. Among the many who attended the vigil were Rev. Phil Woodson from First United Methodist, Jalane Schmidt, and members of Sage Smith's family. A shrine in front of the police station asked, "Where is Sage Smith?" After the second vigil, on April 13, the Smith family secured a meeting with Chief Al Thomas.

Emily Gorcenski hadn't really followed the statue debate. She wasn't religious or particularly focused on issues of racial justice. A side effect of her transition, however, was a preternatural clairvoyance about what was happening in America. While recovering from surgery she spent a lot of time on Twitter. She tweeted an article about the infiltration of law enforcement by white nationalists. She retweeted a Free Speech petition featuring a photo of a school bus with the legend "Boys are boys . . . and always will be. Girls are girls . . . and always will be." "Freedom of Speech," she observed, was being used as a delivery system for a panoply of ideas that seemed benign but were, in fact, coded bigotry. In the real world, she said, people speaking Spanish in public were being assaulted. By mid-March, Emily was feeling fit enough to attend the first Sage Smith vigil. It was here that she was introduced to Charlottesville's activist community. As the only trans person present, she spoke briefly. Grace and her partner, Rowan, were amazed to find someone of her caliber living in Charlottesville.

Emily was one of the first people I interviewed. She answered personal questions simply and honestly. One evening I asked her how her wife had known about her gender dysphoria. Her answer captured what it was like to live as a stranger in one's own body: "According to her, I was spending a lot of time crying." But alongside the clairvoyance that had attended her transition was a newfound feeling of vulnerability. Before her surgery, she told me, she had seen her rights as a trans woman trampled. No one stepped up in her defense, not the city's Office of Human Rights, not her city councillors, not her friends. This didn't surprise me. What surprised me was that Emily hadn't anticipated this. Growing up male in a deeply conservative Polish American family, she was raised, I imagine, to expect her rights would always be respected. Girls learn otherwise. From this experience, she decided it was up to her to make the world she wanted to live in.

"My mentions are a trash fire, and my country is steaming at full power towards an unprecedented crisis, so I took a cute selfie to feel human," she wrote before leaving on another trip to Europe. Eleven days before Richard Spencer arrived in Charlottesville with a small army of khaki-clad men, Emily raised her regimental colors to flush out the trolls. "I'm trans, I'm cute, I'm at peace, and I'm at war," she wrote. "I love being trans."

Emily had stopped crying.

CHAPTER 7

We're Raising an Army, My Liege

In the far-right media ecosphere that spring, everyone was a pundit. If 2016 had been the year of the Meme Wars, where online troll swarms took over social media and found each other on Twitter, Richard Spencer forecast that 2017 would mark the beginning of the war In Real Life. Fifty years after the Summer of Love, Andrew Anglin was predicting a "Summer of Hate." On March 4, 2017, when two dozen "March 4 Trump" rallies devolved into clashes between pro- and anti-Trump forces, Nathan Damigo opined, "The line between violence and politics is blurring."

In mid-March Damigo told an Identity Evropa woman that in response to some statue being removed by the University of Virginia, Richard Spencer was planning to stage a protest in Charlottesville. Damigo was vague on the details. Sometime in May.

"Wherever Richard shows up the media follows lol," she replied. "Should be lit." Damigo sent her a link if she wanted to read about it. They were working with a few other alt-right groups and hoping they could rustle up about 150 people to join them.

"I don't identify much with Southern culture," she replied, "but I still think it's horrible they're trying to erase history."

Damigo corrected her. This wasn't about the South or history being erased. It was an attack on white people. It was ethnic cleansing. That's why they all had to go.

She was game. "I love Virginia."

Damigo had missed the "March 4 Trump" rallies, but he was ready for the April 15 Patriot Day Free Speech rally in Berkeley. He spent the week leading up to it in a Sacramento baseball field learning hand-to-hand combat and battle formation. His training was sponsored by an ultranationalist, racist neo-Nazi fight club called the Rise Above Movement. RAM members had been holding regular training sessions in boxing and martial arts as a way of preparing their members and allies for ostensibly "political" rallies in Huntington Beach, San Bernardino, and Berkeley.

Political violence is generally understood to mean the use of force to achieve political ends, but the "March 4 Trump" rallies had no discernible political agenda. The men who showed up for them had no demands. They had suffered no injustice. Though they were happy with Trump as president, they were hardly partisans. Their staged violence had more to do with a quest for infamy, fortune, and fun. They wanted to watch the world burn. They were chaos agents. Clips of their clashes with anti-Trump protesters, pulled from mainstream media or provided by members, would be turned into memes and posted on their website to drive up RAM membership. A dozen Rise Above Movement members wearing skull masks and goggles accompanied Nathan Damigo to Berkeley.

Though promoted as a free speech rally, after it was over no one would remember who spoke or what they said. After a morning of skirmishes in Martin Luther King Park, in the late afternoon leftist activists had reportedly thrown some kind of smoke bomb. When the wind blew it back in their faces, they retreated down Center Street, west of the UC Berkeley campus. Rallygoers took after them with a roar. The various militia members present, many of them ex-military and retired law enforcement, insisted they had come to Berkeley to do security. Yet they, too, pursued the retreating leftists with a spring in their step. There was no police presence. That was how the Patriot Day Free Speech Rally became the Battle of Berkeley.

Earlier that day Damigo had been filmed standing with his crew in skull masks, rolling up his sleeves, jutting his jaw, but not quite ready to launch himself into a hostile crowd. In the chase down Center Street, Damigo found his target, a nineteen-year-old woman standing alone with a red bandanna over her face. She grabbed his shirt just before his punch landed, square in her face, knocking her head back. As she fell, she dragged him into some shrubbery, but he righted himself and ran away. Six seconds later she was back on her feet.

The thirty-six-second video clip of Damigo's punch went viral. By the end of the day, Samantha Froelich, working as membership coordinator for Identity Evropa, would be swamped by new membership applications. "Nathan should punch women in the face more often," the IE member helping her with intake interviews texted.

"Hahahahaha," she texted back.

In the early hours of April 16, Richard Spencer uploaded a YouTube commentary titled like a think tank seminar: "What Berkeley Means." "We have entered a world of political violence, and I don't think anything will be the same," he began. Mike German, a former FBI agent who had once infiltrated white supremacist groups, agreed. The Battle of Berkeley wasn't a riot, he said. It was "low-level political warfare in the streets of an American city." Law enforcement disappeared in midafternoon, allowing the forces to battle it out. For hours. "The lack of policing," German said, "gives these violent groups the impression that their violence is sanctioned, and that makes them far more dangerous." A lesson Charlottesville might have learned from.

Before Spencer addressed Damigo's punch, he wanted to make something clear. The majority of the rallygoers at Berkeley—Trumpers, Rise Above Movement gangbangers, Patriot Prayer, and Oath Keepers militias—had likely never heard of the alt-right or of Richard Spencer, excepting perhaps the Proud Boys. But the Proud Boys had explicitly rejected his brand of white identity politics. Their loyalty was ostensibly reserved for Western civilization and the Constitution. Similarly, Stewart Rhodes, the Oath Keepers leader and one of the speakers at Berkeley, had traveled over a thousand miles, allegedly to protect the First Amendment. Spencer believed the obsession with the Constitution was a leftover of boomer liberalism. Constitutions were bougie. Trumpers like Rhodes were "boomer goobers." Spencer's message, rather "*our* message is not 'muh free speech.' Our message is WE WILL CRUSH YOU." Though the men who showed up at Berkeley might not yet realize it, *he* was their lodestar. His vision alone embodied the "truest, most intense version of Trumpian nationalism."

Trump, however, had recently veered from the Trumpian nationalism Spencer was trying so hard to affiliate himself with. The week before Berkeley, in response to a chemical weapons attack in Syria, Trump ordered fifty-nine Tomahawk cruise missiles to attack a Syrian air base. This broke Richard Spencer's cardinal rule. No foreign wars. Spencer staged an impromptu antiwar protest in front of the White House only to be glitter bombed by someone who *had* heard of him. The *Independent* reporter who recorded the glitter bombing reupped the Inauguration Day sucker punch to remind everyone who Richard Spencer was. Returning to his Alexandria loft, Spencer began his video commentary sitting on a black leather couch with a large plastic Pepe the Frog squatting next to him. "It has been an intense forty-eight hours, to say the least," he opened, vibrating with rage, his hair freshly washed of glitter, his face blotchy. "I have to be brutally honest. I am deeply disappointed in Donald Trump. I'm shocked. And I am angry."

Spencer's desire to be taken seriously contended with his fear of being taken for a shill. He relived the emotions of the previous day and struggled to come to terms with his dashed expectation that the full power of the American state would heed his dazzling and visionary intellect. He mocked UN Ambassador Nikki Haley's moral outrage over photographs of children foaming at the mouth. He railed at Trump's feckless channeling of "W." "I feel like I'm in a goddamn time warp when I see that Paul Wolfowitz is writing op-ed pieces for the *Wall St. Journal* again."

He was tempted to blame Jared Kushner for Syria because that would "get a bit of a Jewish narrative going," but after dropping hints of this, he shifted course. For Spencer, there were right reasons to go to war and wrong ones. Self-defense, of course. The desire to take territory, rape women, enslave people, or for the simple vainglory of it, were all defensible. Had America gone to war in Iraq to take its oil that would have been justified. It was wars cast in moral righteousness that he deplored. Americans were never innocent, never liberators or freedom fighters. That was the delusion of "goody goody Midwestern types who want to think of themselves as very moral." Such delusions served only to obscure America's unadulterated desire to dominate.

On this last point, many leftists might agree. But Spencer also lionized despots and dictators, much as Trump did. He treated the ruled, the raped women, the gassed children with amused contempt. He knew only histories of warring European states or imperial conquest and nothing of uprisings, insurgencies, strikes, boycotts, and marches for civil rights. But Spencer's grave demeanor signaled an announcement: the cavalry was not coming. Trump may have given visibility to his white supremacist, white nationalist, white "Identitarian" crusade. But such powerful ideas would have found an audience with or without "aging goofball politicians." Spencer concluded, "It's up to us."

But with the Battle of Berkeley now making national headlines, powerful ideas had suddenly taken a back seat to street warfare. It was almost as if the ideas had never really mattered, just the power grab. This new development, however, posed a predicament. Despite his conqueror-or-die speeches, Spencer was a coward. And because he treated his ego as an extension of his body, a delicate vessel. Spencer needed a middle ground between filming YouTube commentary from the cushiony safety of a black leather couch and leading a cavalry charge. This was where Charlottesville would come in. Not long after Berkeley, Nathan Damigo sent Spencer a Slack message with a link to a YouTube video of a torch march. They should try something like that, he suggested. Spencer was inspired.

Richard Spencer now turned his attention to the viral punch. Did Damigo even realize he had hit a woman? A ninety-five-pound white woman was not Spencer's idea of an existential foe. He wasn't convinced this was the right play. Or maybe he just wanted to take Damigo down a notch. "We don't punch women in the face," he told Eli Mosley. "We open hand slap them to demonstrate authority. Otherwise, we treat them well."

A seventy-eight-page affidavit submitted by Spencer's ex-wife documented her own treatment at his hands. Choking a woman, pulling her down the stairs by her arms, legs, or hair were apparently other acceptable means of demonstrating authority.

Before the sucker punch, Richard Spencer was known as the person who had roused a room full of young men to salute him with Heil Hitlers. If the Roman salute had been a question, the sucker punch was its answer. In the medium of the viral video, both were acts of trolling. In real life, it was rhetoric meeting reality. After the sucker punch, a debate unfolded online over whether it was okay to punch a Nazi. This suggested that the sucker punch was the exception that proved the rule that leftists were more focused on mutual aid, community defense, and peaceful protest than street fighting.

By the time of the Battle of Berkeley, however, a more militant faction of the left had shown up. West Coast anarchists had begun sporting black hoodies and black motorcycle helmets, and often carried gas masks. They obscured their identities with ski masks, balaclavas, and sunglasses. The media instantly began referring to such people as "black bloc" or "Antifa." Originating in Europe in the 1980s, black bloc had migrated to the United States during the WTO protests of 1999 and resurfaced during the Occupy movement. Back then, black bloc tactics were tailored for state adversaries and revolved around rock throwing and smashing store windows. This provided the police a rationale to crack down on more peaceful protesters, thereby enhancing black bloc's personae non gratae status. Antifa was a more recent coinage. More than the common ideology Spencer was trying to forcibly impose upon those who showed up at Berkeley, it was the prospect of hand-to-hand fighting with "Antifa" that unified the right. More than Black people or Jews, "Antifa" became the longed-for "existential foe."

So, who or what is "Antifa"? Because the anarchist journalist collective It's Going Down was a critical resource for anyone covering the far right, I asked them. IGD's spokesperson told me that "Antifa" was not the same thing as anti-fascist. Anti-fascists sit at their computers doing open-source intelligence (OSINT) work, listening to right-wing podcasts, and doing deep dives on social media. This often soul-crushing research is done to identify the fascists behind the monikers, and out their noxious beliefs to their employers, families, and the public. Anti-fascists pressure venues to cancel events. They educate the public. Anti-fascists are real, IGD said, whereas "Antifa," derived from Europe's "*antifascista*," originated as far-right cant. The media latched on to it as a useful counterweight to "alt-right," until it became a broad-brush term for (largely) young white people participating in street protests in the age of Trump, rather than the legions of internet sleuths working behind the scenes on laptops. "It sounds so much better when you put a name on it because then it becomes a conspiracy," the It's Going Down spokesperson continued. "A conspiracy directed by Soros. That is shadowy." Though *Antifa* is often used colloquially to refer to anti-fascists, I've tried to maintain the distinction.

There was one major difference between the punch Spencer received and the one Damigo delivered. The first punch humiliated a would-be fascist: the second valorized one. However many fascists were punched, only the act mattered; the aggressor remained anonymous. Where the far-right used violence as a means of self-aggrandizement and recruitment, leftists had no brand to maintain. They gave no speeches, charged no dues, sold no merch. Operational security was easier for them because leftists were more adept at building trust-based alliances than the far-right was. They fought in the service of protecting their communities and then disappeared. This made it easier for journalists to portray both sides as equally violent, a reflex that the far right is quick to exploit.

In the early 1960s, when George Lincoln Rockwell's American Nazi Party was looking for traction, Jewish organizations approached television executives and newspaper editors to ask that they not give Rockwell coverage. They feared media attention would swell his coffers and garner him new followers. As the memory of the camps was still fresh, the idea of a quarantine policy when it came to all things Nazi was adopted, though the tactics of the "Barnum of the Bigots" were often irresistible. Rockwell's "Hate Bus," covered with swastikas, dogged the Freedom Riders. Only the Jewish editor of Rockwell's local paper, the *Northern Virginia Sun*, consistently defied the ban.

Nowadays, the proliferation of media platforms has made the notion of a quarantine of far-right views seem quaint. Moderating the major platforms for hate speech is akin to cleaning the Augean stables. One of the first questions I was asked when I started talking to Charlottesville activists was, "Are you going to talk to them?" The correct answer was no.

In those days I hadn't listened to enough podcasts or watched enough YouTube videos to know the flavor combinations of racism and anti-Semitism and misogyny and homophobia each far-right leader favored. Group acronyms mutated like viruses throwing out variants. I could barely keep track of the aliases. This one dressed up his animosity in flamboyant speech and offensive humor. That one had an air of practiced affability. Another was adept at straight-up lying while projecting a wholesome all-American air. Some tricked conscientious journalists into following them down rabbit holes. Most just took over the mic and yakked them into submission. Finally, there were those in thrall to violent fantasies, yet who also obsessed over their weight and exchanged sour dough recipes and diet advice like fifties housewives. All knew how to exploit the journalistic practice of giving equal time to both sides. The obligation to deliver headlines and clicks worked in favor of attention seekers. They made good copy.

Mocking them, too, made it easier to overlook the fact that every single one of them nurtured a propensity for violence or an appetite for power, and very often both. Some journalists couldn't imagine they believed what they said they believed. They thought it was a game, not a calculated strategy to spread their message. As I wasn't a journalist, I felt no obligation to hear them out in person. I was used to writing about people with only an archive to work from. I also knew I'd be the hapless, tongue-tied sort to get stuck in their sticky web. I left the talking to them to Daryle Lamont Jenkins. When he approaches far-right figures, he is unflappable. However they try, they cannot get under his skin.

A legendary Black anti-fascist who has tracked hate groups since the late eighties without the cover of anonymity, Jenkins pioneered the strategy of internet sleuthing to dox racists. This was a tactic he lifted from right-wing activists who published the names and addresses of abortion providers. With his associate, Laura Sennett, he keeps tabs on the extremist groups for their nonprofit, the One People's Project. Every year Jenkins attends Jared Taylor's American Renaissance Conference and the Conservative Political Action Conference (CPAC), to hang out, chat, eavesdrop on conversations, and document. His capacious size gives him an air of punk indifference. He counsels those who infiltrate far-right groups and mentors internet sleuths. Fascists, Nazis, and Klan members go to him when they are looking to recant. As part of this work, Jenkins traveled to Charlottesville for Unite the Right.

So would a freelance journalist named Vegas Tenold. In the months leading up to Unite the Right, Tenold had been shadowing the leaders of the Nationalist Front, an umbrella alliance that would eventually include the four far-right organizations that would dominate the streets on August 12. Along with the documents that came to light at the *Sines v. Kessler* trial, and the trove of chat logs posted by Unicorn Riot in the immediate wake of the Unite the Right rally, Tenold's work helped me understand how Nazis, fascists, neo-Confederates, and alt-right groups like Identity Evropa and Vanguard America had put aside their differences and egos long enough to end up marching together in Charlottesville. Tenold also provided a cautionary tale about what can happen when a journalist spends too much time in the company of silver-tongued Nazi rogues.

Tenold began his foray in 2011 by hanging out with Jeff Schoep, a balding and burly neo-Nazi. At nineteen, Schoep had joined the National Socialist American Freedom Movement, a direct descendant of Rockwell's American Nazi Party. This made NSAFM the oldest neo-Nazi organization in America. In 1994 Schoep took it over and renamed it the National Socialist Movement. Then, by allowing members of smaller groups, such as skinhead gangs or klaverns, to join while retaining their regional associations, NSM became the largest neo-Nazi organization in America. Schoep pioneered a Youth Corps for teenage boys, and a Stormtrooper cadre for seasoned street fighters. He held regular rallies and made a decent living off the desire of young men to accessorize themselves in swastika-themed regalia.

Tenold then went into the woods, where the Klan, "the Original Boyz in the Hood" as their T-shirts and bumper stickers had it, were holed up. The first Klan rally he attended was a lackluster event made memorable by the arrival of a pickup full of skinheads. Kluxers considered skinheads godless Nazis, Tenold learned, whereas skinheads viewed Kluxers as hicks in silly costumes. In this pickup, however, was a young man who was neither a skinhead nor a Kluxer but someone who was eager to find common cause with both. A few years hence, the baby-faced and bespectacled Matthew Heimbach would provide Tenold his most eager subject. Heimbach was the link between neo-Confederate white supremacists in thrall to their hatred of Black people and the Jew-baiting neo-Nazis dressed up as storm troopers.

Back then Heimbach was a bristly headed junior studying history at Towson University, where he was already riding little waves of controversy and proving to be an agile networker. While still in college he began attending the annual conclaves of the neo-Confederate League of the South. In his senior year he invited Jared Taylor, publisher of a white nationalist magazine and website, to address his newly founded "White Student Union." Heimbach seemed to get along with nearly everybody, from the tweediest suits in right-wing media with thousands of followers to the anonymous boots of neo-Nazi brawlers. Unlike Richard Spencer, whom everyone loved to hate, Heimbach had a sunny, glad-handing disposition and wasn't too fancy for a street fight.

In October 2013 Heimbach was disinvited from the League of the South's annual conclave after he was photographed alongside robed Klansmen and neo-Nazis giving a *Sieg heil* under a burning swastika and flaming cross. All was soon forgiven. By the time the Southern Poverty Law Center identified him as the "new face of organized hate," Heimbach had founded the neo-Nazi Traditionalist Worker Party. His logo was a pitchfork inside a cog; his mantra was faith, family, folk. Members called themselves "Trad Workers."

In the summer of 2016, with Trump's campaign surging, Jeff Schoep approached Heimbach about forming an alliance. For Heimbach, the timing felt right. He understood intuitively that Hitler's National Socialist Party was the fountainhead of nationalist and supremacist ideologies gaining ground across Europe. He had spent his honeymoon networking with European fascists and learning about their struggles with the *antifascistas*. Marine Le Pen's National Front, once marginal, was now nearly mainstream. Austerity policies imposed by the EEU on Greece had made Golden Dawn the third-largest Greek party. Even centrist parties were being pulled to the right over the influx of refugees. Rome's Brothers of Italy or CasaPound Italia might be next. Heimbach liked to cite Ezra Pound's quip: "Democracy is now currently defined in Europe as a 'country run by Jews.'" There was no reason why America couldn't support a right-wing political party like those finding seats in European parliaments. Heimbach agreed to join forces on the condition that Schoep undertake some housekeeping.

Both George Lincoln Rockwell and David Duke discovered that flaunting swastikas was a dead-end game. Mimicking the Black Power movement, Rockwell began extolling a masculinist White Power instead. Heimbach would never renounce his allegiance to Hitler, but he was willing to revamp his rhetoric to obscure the extent of his neo-Nazi beliefs. Heimbach argued the white race wasn't any better than any other, but he reserved the right to take pride in it and advocate on its behalf. This was bosh, but to the uninformed it sounded almost like common sense. White power was now framed as white victimhood. White supremacy became white civil rights. Turning the language of left identity politics on its head made for a tidy and triggering bait and switch.

On November 5, 2016, three days before Trump's election, Schoep sent out an email to his listserv outlining Heimbach's strategy for mainstreaming neo-Nazi ideas. The swastika was the first to go. "The masses believe as we do," he continued, "but have steered clear of us due to our use of the swastika." In place of the swastika, the Odal rune would now appear on their flags and banners. The Odal rune was a less familiar Nazi symbol, used by the SS, so no less noxious. Second, NSM members who were also members of klaverns had to disrobe and desist from using racial slurs in public. In a final cosmetic touch, Heimbach wanted to change the name of Schoep's umbrella coalition from Aryan Nationalist Alliance to the less Nazi-sounding Nationalist Front. Their party platform remained unchanged.

Unlike Richard Spencer, Matthew Heimbach didn't sit on a black leather couch and hold forth. He wasn't invited to speak at colleges and universities. Instead, he drove his battered Toyota Corolla coast-to-coast addressing skinheads in the LA suburbs and League of the South chapters in Florida. By this point, Tenold was often in the passenger seat. Heimbach aspired to forge a political coalition by strip-mining the anger and despair of the disinherited and shattered white working class, much as Trump, the coal industry, and Purdue Pharma had.

Because the biggest concentration of Trad Workers hailed from West Virginia, East Tennessee, and East Kentucky, Heimbach concluded the motherlode of hate he sought would be found in Appalachia. Tenold suggested Pikeville, Kentucky, as a site for the first Nationalist Front rally. It was 98 percent white, and 80 percent of its voters had voted for Trump. And Kentucky was an open carry state. Where Tenold saw a region where you could "settle a bar bill with a half a tablet of Oxycontin," Heimbach saw the real America. His people. Whom he would lead out of the desert. Pikeville, where the Nationalist Front alliance between Heimbach and Schoep would have its debut alongside the League of the South, would be a May Day rally. "The left doesn't give two shits about the workers," Heimbach said. Neither did he.

The "Take a Stand for White Working Families" rally would take place on April 29, 2017.

Back in December, Richard Spencer had mulled running for an open congressional seat in Montana as an Independent. Not one to mingle with commoners, he invited Matthew Heimbach to DC for Trump's inauguration to discuss joining his campaign. Flattered, Heimbach dropped everything. "I guess he realized that I know how to talk to real people," Heimbach explained to Tenold. "It could be a big deal for us." After Heimbach drove ten hours from Indiana, Spencer never took his calls or responded to his texts. Heimbach returned to thinking Spencer was a douche and shared a laugh with his boys over the sucker punch.

After the Battle of Berkeley, Heimbach sent Spencer a valentine on Gab, a social networking site with a far-right user base. In it, he encouraged his Trad Workers to attend Spencer's upcoming speech at Auburn University. Seeing that, Spencer asked a new aide-de-camp to check if Heimbach might provide extra security. Again Heimbach jumped and again Spencer ghosted him. It was Tenold who ran into Spencer's new aide-de-camp snoozing at the New York departure gate of the Atlanta airport.

Mike Enoch ran TheRightStuff website, which hosted his popular alt-right podcast, *The Daily Shoah*. Internecine conflict had recently led to his doxing. Notwithstanding his seething anti-Semitism, Mike "Enoch" Peinovich was married to a Jew. In the ensuing troll storm Spencer stood by him. Tenold had followed the hubbub from a distance, but now, at the airport, he became Heimbach's envoy. Enoch was thinking of attending Pikeville, he reported to Heimbach. Spencer still hoped to work with him. Vegas Tenold knew nothing would please Heimbach more. As I said, a cautionary tale.

Pikeville's city officials quickly figured out who Jeff Schoep was and what his permit application for a "family reunion" in a local park amounted to. They couldn't stop his rally, but their event agreement required he carry liability insurance: $10,000 no one had. The Nationalist Front ended up at a campground. The town battened down its hatches: shops were closed; the university sent students home. Hashtags proliferated: #prayersforpikeville, #nohateinmyholler, #rednecksagainstracism. The day before the rally, residents put the word out on social media: "Pray. Stay safe. Show the world who we truly are."

Pikeville (pop. 7,000) is situated in a valley between two mountains; its wide and treeless Main Street enabled city residents and rallygoers to face off at a fifty-foot distance, with law enforcement in the middle and press walking back and forth. The consensus among city residents was that Pikeville was chosen on the assumption they were a bunch of ignorant and racist hillbillies. "We aren't what they think we are," one woman said. When the Klan came a few years back, a local newscaster recalled, Pikeville residents lined the streets with their backs to them.

On the day of the rally townspeople directed their remarks at the League of the South men lounging across the street. "How much does it suck to be you?" someone hollered. A red-haired woman carried a poster of Hitler with a gun to his head, captioned "Follow Your Leader." Others questioned the sincerity of the League's Christian faith. One man insisted Jesus wasn't white; the woman standing next to him asserted that the Garden of Eden was in Africa. Everyone was in high spirits. Daryle Lamont Jenkins stood with the locals, documenting who was there and with whom.

While the League of the South men awaited the thirty-two-car motorcade of Matthew Heimbach and Jeff Schoep, an ex-marine and sometime radio host named Sacco Vandal kept everyone entertained. Vandal's calling card, which started as an edgy take, was white sharia. Renouncing the Proud Boys tag of "Western chauvinist," Vandal argued that white people didn't conquer the world with civilization but with rape, pillage, and plunder. While anti-Muslim groups were sponsoring "March against Sharia" protests elsewhere, Vandal began calling for a white sharia, as a "living, breathing form of extreme, regimented patriarchy."

Evil things are always mere inches way from being laughable, C. S. Lewis once said. Only by being terrible do they avoid being comic. In Pikeville, Sacco Vandal jumped up and down, maligning those across the street as "clowns and patsies for a bunch of billionaire globalists," "lapdogs for rich Jews," and "pothead losers." Vandal's insults became harder to make out once a more organized group of protesters arrived with drums and noisemakers. They were about one hundred strong, with at least one flying the International Workers of the World flag. They shied away from on-camera interviews.

Heimbach and Schoep's caravan arrived an hour late, having belatedly discovered that GPS didn't work well in Appalachian hollers. "I thought fascists made the trains run on time," a joker in heart-shaped sunglasses shouted. On arrival, Heimbach realized they had forgotten a generator to run their sound system. They were, however, well equipped with flak jackets, Camel Baks, AR-15s, pistols, backpacks filled with spare ammo, gas masks, first aid kits, knives, ankle holsters fitted with pepper spray, and brass knuckles. Their speeches exhibited little awareness of having turned the town upside down. "Boring, boring, boring," the peanut gallery yelled as a spectral speaker droned on about child molesters, warmongers, and the Jewish lobby.

None of the speakers addressed the plague of opioid addiction, the closing of coal mines, or the struggles of working Appalachia. They had no grasp of how the citizens of Pikeville understood themselves. The people of East Kentucky had never been slave owners. They hadn't joined the Confederacy. Where Heimbach imagined he would find despair and anger, he encountered pride and cheek. At the end of the day the local police were credited for keeping order. But the most fulsome thanks were offered up to the Lord.

As the rallygoers retreated to their cars, someone's gun went off. Heimbach was served with a court summons related to his assault on a woman at a Trump rally. The highs of the day had been in posing with their weaponry for the media upon their arrival, then hanging out in the campground that night trading war stories. Though ostensibly Pikeville had been Jeff Schoep's show, just as the idea for the Nationalist Front had been, everyone knew he'd only brought a handful of men. Heimbach's Trad Worker Party paid for all the food. Even the few Vanguard America men who showed up paid tribute. Heimbach solicited Tenold's opinion as to what he should do about Schoep, drawing him in on his machinations. Heimbach soon usurped leadership of the Nationalist Front.

Overlooking Heimbach and Schoep's late arrival, Dr. Michael Hill, the graybeard and cofounder of the Alabama-based secessionist League of the South, was impressed by the level of organization. Hill hadn't flinched from posing for a picture alongside neo-Nazi Schoep and a few stray roman salutes and swastika patches. Not everyone had had time to sew on the new Odal runes. Jeff Schoep promised to show up for a League rally protesting a Lee statue removal in New Orleans the following weekend. Look for the black cross flags, Dr. Hill told him. Heimbach would appear for a joint action with the League of the South in Florida. The Florida chapter, led by a massive former Green Beret named Michael Tubbs, was one of the strongest. Heimbach would soon get the League of the South to join them under the Nationalist Front banner, a huge score. And Mike "Enoch" Peinovich would report to Richard Spencer that Heimbach had acquitted himself well.

A month after Berkeley and two weeks after Pikeville, Richard Spencer arrived in Charlottesville for his greatly anticipated daylong May 13 production. He and Nathan Damigo had quietly assembled some 150 men, marching under a variety of flags, for a daytime pop-up rally and an early evening supper under a tent in a park on the city's outskirts. Among those mustered were Matthew Heimbach, Mike Peinovich, Samantha Froelich, Eli Mosley, and Jason Kessler. The old gasbag David Duke even showed up. Jason Kessler was thrilled to be in such august company and networked furiously. Then came the pièce de résistance, the nighttime march with tiki torches to a rally at the Lee statue.

During the march, Heimbach was amazed to hear hoity-toity Identity Evropa men join in "Blood and soil" and "Hail victory!" chants. He was convinced they were building a real movement, one that before long would deliver a "Nationalist Socialist Revolution" to America. After the torches were extinguished, the Stormers took over, leading chants of "Gas the kikes!" and "Race war now!" By the time it turned rowdy, Spencer had left for the after-party. He liked to keep his optics clean. The Stormers answered to Andrew Anglin. Anglin didn't give a hoot about optics.

For Spencer, the evening was magical; the tiki torch march everything he hoped it would be. At the VIP after-party, boozed-up men and women stood in a tightly packed Airbnb kitchen, right arms extended toward him in Roman salutes, lustily chanting *Sieg heil Sieg heil Sieg heil Sieg heil* while he stood to one side smiling and looking directly at Samantha Froelich until she, too, crossed the line she once swore she never would. According to a Stormer present, after the festivities died down, the dozen or so women in attendance were paired up with leadership, "in a delightfully eugenic process of mate selection." Froelich ended up with Spencer that night, but thereafter became Eli Mosley's girlfriend. Dr. Michael Hill of the League of the South was soon kicking himself for having missed the fun.

Before the week was out, Kessler, whose petition to remove Wes Bellamy from the city council had come to nothing, was planning a far more ambitious affair, also to take place in Lee Park. He envisioned bringing together a vast array of far-right groups, from anti-government militias and motorcycle gangs to neo-Confederates, Proud Boys, blogger celebs, and "Identitarians." If he could get Spencer to attend, he could count on widespread press coverage. As a local, he'd reap the blowback, but he wasn't worried. It would be a mark of distinction in an otherwise undistinguished life. He called it Charlottesville 2.0.

As a young man Jason Kessler had had constant run-ins with law enforcement, mostly over minor traffic violations. When he wasn't living with his grandmother and father, he resided in a support facility for addicts and the mentally ill. Then, in 2007, he was accepted as a UVA transfer student from a local community college. Eight years after finishing high school, he received a BA in psychology and graduated into a hollowed-out economy. The only jobs he could find were menial ones he thought were beneath him, so he never stayed in them very long. He came close to being hired for a position at a local mental health non-profit, but they hired someone else.

In the fall of 2011, Kessler joined an Occupy protest camp in Lee Park. On November 9, 2008, the global order faced a financial collapse because of the trading practices of a few large financial institutions. In a matter of hours, almost a trillion dollars was marshaled to save the banks while ordinary Americans lost their homes, jobs, and life savings. An entire cohort graduated from college to work at Starbucks, Kessler among them. The level of legalized corruption the 2008 crash exposed was staggering.

Throughout their six weeks in Lee Park, Occupy organizers kept things clean, orderly, and peaceful. When Kessler joined them, he brought a tent and his own library. "He quickly went from talking about this and that," one Occupier recalled, "to 'we need to have Molotov cocktails' and 'we need to dig up rocks and throw them at police.'" This alarmed everyone. In the end, Kessler was forced out of the park, bellowing with rage and shouting incoherently.

One of Occupy's central demands was debt forgiveness for ordinary Americans. Instead, we got the Tea Party. For the Tea Party "populists" who arose in the aftermath of the 2008 crisis, it wasn't powerful banks and politicians who were to blame for the Great Recession but migrants and poor people. Kessler ascribed his political awakening not to the Tea Party but to a single revelatory tweet. Just before boarding a flight to South Africa, a woman named Justine Sacco had tweeted to her 170 followers: "Going to Africa, hope I don't get AIDS. Just kidding. I'm white!" Sacco was lampooning white obliviousness, but the internet rose up as one to damn her as racist. By the time she landed in Johannesburg she had lost her job, her reputation, and the life she'd known.

Jason Kessler saw in Sacco's public shaming over "a little racism" an echo of his own shaming at the hands of Occupy. He blamed affirmative action for his failure to land that mental health clinic job and social justice warriors for everything else. As the Tea Party had done, Kessler targeted the least powerful to take the blame for the dead-end life he faced. This is why it is a misnomer to cast white nationalists as right wing "populists"; ideologically they are fascists, seeking to remake the nation in their own image. Henceforth, Kessler's grievances were recast as rank injustice. Charlottesville 2.0 would provide him the means to even the score.

He set up a Charlottesville 2.0 server on Discord, a communication platform originally aimed at gamers but increasingly being used to host far-right chat rooms. Each group Kessler invited would have its own assigned channel. There would be separate channels for logistics, planning, and leadership. Early outreach went out via text to leaders like Dr. Michael Hill and Matthew Heimbach, but word of the rally would eventually spread through podcasts, Twitter, Gab, 4chan, and Facebook. The League of the South was first on board. Four days after the May 13 torch rally in Lee Park, Hill sent an email to the League of the South's listserv, announcing the call for resistance. Henceforth all communications were to be conducted on the League's Discord channel on the Charlottesville 2.0 server. Members should make every effort to attend, he said.

"If not you, then who?" Matthew Heimbach's flyers for Charlottesville 2.0 read, echoing the Jewish sage Hillel the Elder's question: "If not now, then when?" Heimbach was feeling the momentum a larger Charlottesville gathering could bring. "This is gonna be huge," he wrote on the Trad Workers' Discord channel. It was a full callout for his members. Heimbach had already received his first shipment of shields; one hundred helmets were on order. He turned to lodging.

The biography and profile pic of Dillon Hopper had recently been added to the Leaders section of the Nationalist Front website. Vanguard America, Hopper's white Identitarian group, was founded in 2015, a year before Identity Evropa and the Proud Boys. Hopper was a former

US marine from New Mexico. At Pikeville he had outfitted himself in a flak vest and carried a massive Franchi SPAS-12 combat shotgun. Informed of the upcoming rally, he immediately began thinking about shields.

In case Hopper didn't grasp the significance of what he was signing on to by joining the Nationalist Front, Heimbach underlined it. "We've got 90% of the real orgs in America. With the leadership being you, me, Jeff, and Dr. Hill. So that's a good table for us to sit at." Hopper got it.

"Now all we need is Spencer and Damigo," he said.

"Well, this is where Charlottesville comes in," Heimbach replied.

"We are raising an army, my liege," Jason Kessler texted Richard Spencer on June 5. "For free speech, but the cracking of skulls if it comes to it." Kessler had failed to register Spencer's yawning disinterest in the First Amendment or appreciate that language like this made him a "massive dork" in Spencer's eyes.

Charlottesville 2.0 now had a proper name: "Unite the Right: Battle of Charlottesville," and a date: August 12, 2017. Before agreeing to have his name added to the lineup, Spencer wanted assurance that "high quality" men, men like Mike Peinovich and Nathan Damigo, were coming. Eli Mosley was working on the Charlottesville 2.0 Discord channel and was in constant touch with Kessler, so Spencer doubtless knew who was coming. But the temptation to string Kessler along was irresistible.

Kessler didn't care about high-quality men. He might not showcase Nazis like Jeff Schoep or Robert "Azzmador" Ray, the new "Stormcommander" of the Daily Stormer troll army, but he wanted the cadres they would bring, preferably dressed in ways that wouldn't alienate normie patriots and neo-Confederates. To sweeten his invite to Schoep, Kessler promised him "a thousand or more Antifa or shitlibs eager to start violence."

Ten days after first approaching Spencer, Kessler sent him the finished design of the Unite the Right poster. Nathan Damigo hadn't answered his texts, but Mike Peinovich, Dr. Michael Hill, and Matthew Heimbach had committed to coming. The rabidly garrulous host of the *Radical Agenda* podcast, Christopher Cantwell, was another headliner.

Johnny Monoxide and Baked Alaska, two rabble-rousing alt-right pod-cast hosts, were in the lineup. It was quite a roster, put together in less than a month's time, likely with Mosley's help.

"We're ready to add your name when you give us the go ahead," Kessler wrote.

Spencer was still haunted by his Inauguration Day sucker punch. His first concern was personal safety, and he'd been told that putting his name on a poster was dangerous. With pop-up rallies he could make a swift getaway before "Antifa" realized he was there.

Kessler reassured him. "We have the full cooperation of the police . . ."

"I know that. It's a matter of discretion. Just give me an hour." Spencer made Kessler wait another day.

"I'm 100% in. Please put my name on the flyers for your event." Spencer gave Kessler a little head pat. "Thank you for your steadfastness. I really respect and appreciate it."

Megan Squire, a forty-five-year-old computer science professor at Elon University in North Carolina, tried to warn people, but with only three hundred Twitter followers, it was like shouting in the dark. Squire's area of expertise was a data-mining technique called social network analysis. That spring she wrote a code that enabled her to pull informa-tion off social media platforms to map the major nodes in far-right net-works. Eventually she built a database of names of those associated with right-wing extremist groups. What she saw in this data matched what she was seeing in Alamance County, where she lived with her family. Neo-Confederates, the Klan, and the "alt-right" were coming out from under every rock. Not unlike what her friends in Charlottesville were describing.

As in Charlottesville, in Alamance the past was preamble: after the Civil War, the Klan had hung Durham's first Black commissioner on the county courthouse lawn. During Jim Crow, a Confederate monu-ment was raised at the lynching site. Now the Freedom of Expression Tunnel Wall at North Carolina University in Chapel Hill had been taken over by Identity Evropa. A local group, founded by a member of the North Carolina chapter of League of the South, held a Confederate

Memorial Day Celebration. Identity Dixie, a militant street gang, joined the festivities. Ten days later a US marine did a banner drop featuring the acronym YWNRU, aka "You Will Not Replace Us," and a quote from George Orwell's *1984*: "He who controls the past, controls the future."

Meanwhile, a task force dedicated to countering far-right extremism had been gutted by the Trump administration. The Department of Homeland Security was focused on the threat of migrant caravans, and the FBI was redoubling its search for Islamic terrorists. The Justice Department kept no data on white supremacist and far-right violence and had no strategy to track, investigate, or prosecute acts of domestic terror. Squire and her husband, Tony Crider, a professor of physics at Elon and a seasoned livestreamer, did their best. Crider photographed faces, used Facebook Live to document alliances among various groups. But every time Squire heard of another rally, she had to ask herself where she would be most useful, out on the streets protesting, or home with her three monitors watching Tony's video stream and identifying who was there.

When Squire wasn't protesting or scanning livestreams, she was tracking 700,204 user accounts in two thousand different groups and categorizing them into ten different ideological associations. Anti-Muslim, anti-immigrant, anti-government militia, white nationalist, anti-communist, neo-Confederate, neo-Nazi, and alt-right orgs were among them. She watched them build power, watched as the interplay between the online world and the real world took shape. It didn't take long before she noticed that the Facebook event page for Unite the Right was connecting a broad range of groups. And the numbers kept going up.

Everybody is coming to this party, she thought. *This is going to be a big deal.*

CHAPTER 8

Fuck White Supremacy

The morning after Spencer's torch rally, word spread that a "Take Back the Park" vigil, organized by a group calling itself the Anarchist People of Color Collective, would take place in Emancipation Park that evening. While the fate of the Lee statue remained in limbo until the court case was resolved, Lee Park was now Emancipation Park. At 9:00 p.m., roughly five hundred city residents, including Don Gathers, the chair of the Blue Ribbon Commission, Vice-Mayor Wes Bellamy, with his wife and daughters, and numerous clergy, showed up at a candlelit vigil to "Outshine Their Torches with Love." Hymns and protest songs replaced the previous night's chants of "Blood and soil." Showing Up for Racial Justice, the city's public housing association, and a UVA student group calling for a living wage for university workers were among the organizations in attendance. Unaffiliated residents showed up too. Lisa Draine, a local arts administrator, came with her daughter Sophie, a UVA student about to leave town for the summer. Wes Bellamy told them, "It's great you're here, but don't let this be the end of the story."

Though various threads of civil society were beginning to work together, they sometimes struggled to find a common language. A bedsheet reading "Black Lives Matter, Fuck White Supremacy" was draped over Traveller's flank that evening. Not everyone was happy with the obscenity. And not everyone was clear on what was meant by "white supremacy," a phrase now on everyone's lips. Kessler said he wasn't a white supremacist but an advocate for white civil rights. Richard Spencer was a white nationalist. Was there a difference? More to the point, could anything be done? The activists of color who spoke at the vigil tried to provide answers, encouraging potential white allies to fight with them against white supremacy however and wherever it manifested itself.

In Alexander Stephens's Cornerstone speech, the Confederacy rested on the intertwined principles of "slavery and white supremacy." In the war's aftermath, Henry Grady, the editor of the *Atlanta Constitution* and apostle of the New South, told Southern politicians and business-men nothing had to change, that their economic future could still turn on the availability of cheap Black labor. "The supremacy of the white race of the South must be maintained forever, and the domination of the negro race resisted at all points." The fear that Black people would end up dominating white people found legal remedy in the form of Jim Crow and extralegal remedies in acts of racial terror. Though Jim Crow laws had been dismantled, the reflexes underlying those laws persisted, like an inherited gene sequence passed from one generation to the next.

As defined by Charlottesville's anti-racists, white supremacy wasn't just a historical wrong, limited to the South; it was an ongoing power dynamic, readily found in a penumbra of internal attitudes and sensi-bilities, institutional reflexes, and policy choices that, on casual perusal (or calculated dissembling), seemed to have little to do with race. Bred in the bone, white supremacy readily crashed the gates of policies and laws devised to contain it. As Ta-Nehisi Coates saw it, George Zimmerman's acquittal in the killing of Trayvon Martin wasn't a miscarriage of jus-tice, but American justice itself. "This is not our system malfunction-ing," he wrote. "It is our system working as intended."

At the vigil there was a lot of talk of "enemies" and what it would take to defeat them. Don Gathers spoke of taking back control of the city from those who had taken it over. He didn't name Jason Kessler, but with Richard Spencer's departure, Kessler now became white supremacy's local standard bearer. For such an unprepossessing individual, this was quite the promotion. Kessler, too, tended to inflate the power and stature of his adversaries, turning them all into violent "Antifa" cadres.

That night activists surrounded a Kessler associate who had shown up to film them. When he didn't answer their questions, his cell phone was knocked from his hand. Pam Starsia, a lawyer who had cohosted the first planning meeting of Showing Up for Racial Justice in Bekah Menning's living room, defended the action by saying videos were being used to identify and dox local activists. Then, as the park was about to close, Kessler himself appeared, bullhorn in hand, intent on rectifying the "vandalism" of the Lee statue by pulling down the Black Lives Matter, Fuck White Supremacy bedsheet. He then assaulted a woman of color in view of the police. When he refused to put down his megaphone, he was charged, not with assault, but with disorderly conduct and walked off in handcuffs.

Emily Gorcenski was in Berlin when Richard Spencer came to town. Suddenly, the crisis she'd seen her country steaming toward had arrived on her doorstep. "WHAT. THE. FUCK," she tweeted. "That's not like a small number of torch-bearing fascists." She tweeted a screenshot of the front page of the *Daily Progress* with the comment "Charlottesville is fucked." She followed this with a brief summary of the city's past, one rooted in the "best and worst of American history." Charlottesville, where Emily had now lived for nine years, was nothing like the gritty and depressed towns of rural Connecticut she had known growing up. Its aura of gentility, she said, made it an unlikely candidate for a hotbed of activism. "How the liberalist community in Cville responds," she tweeted, "will be a bellwether for how America responds to this growing issue." Then she returned to the real obscenity: Nazis bearing torches and shouting "Blood and soil" a half mile from her Fifeville home. From that moment, she began to mobilize her skills on the city's behalf.

Two weeks later, on May 31, to forestall another Flagger rally at the Lee statue, Solidarity Cville, a newly launched activist message board, announced that faith leaders planned to occupy Emancipation Park from 10:00 a.m. to 6:00 in the evening. Smash reached out directly to the faith community, asking them to bring their voices, bodies, and prayers. She asked that white people in particular not be scared into silence. Veronica Fitzhugh, a leader of Anarchist People of Color and a recent target of Jason Kessler, sent out an email inviting people to join in community defense and to put out the word "discreetly" to their friend circles. Local activists were increasingly cautious in their use of social media, preferring face-to-face communications or phone calls. Some had begun using Signal, an encrypted messaging app that enabled people to send text alerts, voice messages, files, and videos to trusted groups or individuals. After a set time, these communications would vanish automatically.

Rev. Phil Woodson and Rev. Elaine Thomas from the Clergy Collective joined activists Don Gathers and Jalane Schmidt that morning. Grace Aheron and her crew arrived from Charis. The Catholic Worker couple from Casa Alma came, as did Bekah Menning and members of Showing Up for Racial Justice. Having returned from Europe in time for her thirty-fifth birthday and the beginning of Pride, Emily was also there. She reconnected with the people she'd met at the Sage Smith vigil and was added to their Signal chat groups. More people showed than Smash had expected, with their numbers growing as the day wore on.

By the time the Flaggers arrived, there was no room for them. They unfurled their Confederate flags and glared from the sidewalk. One wound up holding hands in a circle of clergy, singing movement songs. It eventually dawned on him they weren't his fellow Flaggers. Coming two weeks after the "Take Back the Park" Mother's Day vigil, this gathering was, in Smash's view, transformative. Both she and Seth Wispelwey left the park that night feeling hopeful. By breaking down the misperceptions that had once kept them apart, the city's residents were coming together.

The following evening, Emily stumbled upon Jason Kessler and his entourage hanging out at Miller's, a modest beer and burger joint on the downtown pedestrian mall. In the wake of Richard Spencer's May 13 torch march, Kessler's public clashes with activists on the Downtown Mall had become more frequent. Despite his efforts to goad them into reacting, these encounters had yet to escalate beyond f-bombs and middle fingers. "They keep saying they're bringing guns and they're going to hit Nazis but they punk out," he complained on Facebook.

"Shit is happening in Charlottesville," Emily tweeted under an eight-second clip of "wannabe Richard Spencer, aka Jason Kessler" and his "band of shitheads." Emily identified Kessler for her seven thousand followers as one of the organizers of the May 13 torch mob. He wasn't, but he'd clearly briefed Spencer in advance. Emily's clip featured a quartet of young women from Showing Up for Racial Justice chanting "Fuck you, Kessler" while one filmed him with her phone. Local police officers with unreadable faces stood nearby.

In the spirit of community defense, activists had informed businesses on or near the Downtown Mall of their legal right to "refuse to employ, work with, serve or shop with Nazis." Similar advice was given to the public: "Refuse to sit next to them at a bar or restaurant. Refuse to let them sit peacefully in a public space." Flyers identifying Kessler and his friends were posted around town, warning residents to be on the alert and to "Know Your Local Nazi." Other establishments followed suit. A popular local brewery had banned Kessler for assaulting an employee for refusing to sign his Wes Bellamy petition.

That evening members of Showing Up for Racial Justice carried a cardboard sign addressed to those who hadn't been following what was going on. "This restaurant is serving those who did the torch march in Lee Park that terrorised people in this town. We will not allow this to continue." Another sign addressed the eight men (and a baby) at Kessler's table. "You do not get to terrorize communities of color with your torch rally and then hang out in peace."

Among those at Kessler's table was Jared Taylor. Daryle Lamont Jenkins considered Taylor the godfather of the alt-right. A Yale-educated Japan scholar, Taylor was the founder of *American Renaissance* magazine and host of the annual AmRen conference. Like Spencer's National Policy Institute, *American Renaissance* and AmRen had found a patron in William Regnery. Jenkins made a point to attend AmRen, featuring the tweedier end of the movement, every fall. That evening Taylor held forth before an audience of men in trucker hats at a table strewn with half-empty glasses of beer. For reasons best known to him, he had disguised himself as a French intellectual by donning a wig and Ray-Bans. A contributor to the anarchist media collective It's Going Down noted that both the wig and the French accent began to slip as the evening wore on and the alcohol took effect.

Joe Starsia, a former UVA lacrosse player and a member of Showing Up for Racial Justice, had responded to the Signal alert that evening. Starsia had been there on the afternoon of May 13 when Richard Spencer and his khaki pants crew appeared in Jackson Park. He emerged from that encounter bruised and shaken. At the next city council meeting, he confronted Mayor Signer and Councillor Kathy Galvin. Did they understand that whatever educational or historic value these Confederate statues may once have had was now outweighed by their power as symbols of hate? It wasn't too late for them to stand in solidarity with their Black neighbors, he said. Instead, Signer doubled down on his arguments to keep the statues where they were in an op-ed for the *Washington Post*.

Jason Kessler, wearing a badly fitting suit jacket, was livestreaming "Live from Charlottesville. Harassment by Antifa" in selfie mode while Starsia tried to block him from filming the chanting women behind him. Kessler's face shone with sweat in the light of his phone camera and, as the evening progressed, streetlamps. When Starsia brushed against him, Kessler called an officer over to arrest him on assault charges. Unlike the similarly spurious assault charge he'd lodged ten days earlier against Veronica Fitzhugh, a leader of Anarchist People of Color, this went nowhere.

"He's currently starting shit," Emily tweeted, "bumping into people then whining to cops." She didn't engage him directly but just before 9:00 p.m. she appeared in the background of his livestream. She did not go unrecognized. One of Kessler's followers wrote: "I want to smash that tranny faggot's face." Under his Facebook profile pic, this same person wrote, "the last thing . . . G[o]rcenski will ever see."

Jeff Fogel, a local civil rights lawyer, had been asked by local activists to come downtown to keep an eye on things. After having a hamburger and a beer with a candidate for city council at a nearby table, he spent an hour or so chatting with activists and police officers. Fogel, then campaigning for commonwealth's attorney, also engaged a man in a "Jones Heating and Oil" T-shirt who had been seated at Kessler's table. A campaign button, "Fogel for Commonwealth Attorney," was pinned to Fogel's neat plaid shirt.

Kessler then complained that Fogel had recently called him a cry-baby. A man sitting at Kessler's table chimed in with "Fogel is a communist piece of shit." Fogel headed toward him; the man got up from his chair.

"What did you say?" Fogel said. The man loomed over him.

Meanwhile, a young man with a pretty face tried to wind up Emily.

"I'm not a racist, dude," he called out.

"I'm not a dude," Emily said.

"You look like a dude. Do you even know what a Nazi is?" he asked. This was a trap.

During her travels in Europe, Emily often posted photographs of World War II landmarks. That was why she had a photo of the Monument to the Jewish People of Europe on her phone. This monument, between Potsdamer Platz and Brandenburger Tor, covers the square above Berlin's subterranean Holocaust Museum. Emily showed Kessler's friend the photo. This was also a trap.

He glanced at the photo. "Fuck Jews," he said.

Emily took a photograph of Fuck Jew's face and tweeted it. His hat carried the name of his employer, a local caterer. Emily accompanied the photo with the suggestion that next time he shouted "Fuck Jews" in a public place, it would be a good idea to wear a different hat.

Reading Kessler's posts on the Charlottesville 2.0 Discord channel, Dr. Michael Hill cited this Downtown Mall skirmish to gin up support for the Unite the Right rally on the League of the South's website. A "totalitarian Communist crackdown" was taking place in Charlottesville. "In response to the Alt-Right's peaceful demonstration in support of the Lee Monument on May 13th, the City of Charlottesville and roving mobs of Antifa have cracked down on the First Amendment rights of conservatives and right wing activists," Hill wrote. "They have threatened our families, harassed our employers [Fuck Jews employer had been alerted] and tried to drive us from public spaces with threats of intimidation. We are not afraid. You will not divide us."

By 9:30 p.m. Miller's manager had seen enough and asked Kessler to leave. He hung around the edges of the crowd for another twenty minutes, livestreaming, dogged by the handful of women who continued to chant "Nazis go home" at the holdouts. Emily stayed until midnight. When she got home, she discovered she'd been doxed. Before going to bed, she loaded her guns and moved her gun safe to her bedroom. At 1:00 a.m. she signed off: "Goodnight from the side that believes that carrying torches and chanting Nazi slogans is bad."

The charge officer on duty at the police station that night couldn't have said which side he was on. Is it unreasonable to expect a community police force to have a modicum of historical awareness? Most local officers couldn't find Congregation Beth Israel on a map. Some didn't know what a synagogue was. They did know Fogel as a frequent critic of law enforcement. Thus, after an evening spent watching Nazi-adjacent white supremacists, two weeks after a neo-Nazi torchlight rally, the seventy-two-year-old Jewish candidate for commonwealth's attorney was awakened in the middle of the night by six cops banging on his door with a warrant for his arrest on a misdemeanor assault charge. He wasn't even given time to change out of his pajamas.

This charge, like the one against Veronica Fitzhugh, was later dismissed.

Not every encounter with Kessler was documented: a Hispanic activist with Anarchist People of Color spoke at city council of being cornered by Kessler and his friends while they screamed "White lives matter" and "Go back to your country" in his face. Kessler disrupted activist trainings. He harassed establishments that refused to serve him. He targeted prominent activists of color. Some clashes unfolded in front of families eating in restaurants up and down the Downtown Mall on beautiful early summer evenings. Public reactions ranged from support of the activists to impatience, to furious complaints from patrons and business owners. The city's stakeholders could not obscure the grim reality: Kessler and his trolls were running amok. City leaders were ill-equipped.

Activists debated the best way to respond to Kessler's provocations. Emily had her steely composure and her Twitter following. Silent prayer slowed Smash's racing heart. Rev. Tracy Howe Wispelwey found it easier to sing than to shout. While some people could adjust the controls of their comfort levels, obscenity-laced clashes with Jason Kessler didn't accord with everyone's idea of racial justice work. Those for whom the phrase "fuck white supremacy" amounted to high ground sometimes alienated older or more faith-infused white activists. The Catholic Worker couple who led the listening circles at Casa Alma believed that the phrase was at odds with a message of peace and love. Wasn't this replicating the hate? they asked tentatively. If people wanted to turn away from hatred and racism, what were they were turning toward?

Younger, frontline activists were impatient with such talk, and nearly vitriolic at the idea that "our enemies are as much inside us as outside us." Such a stance showed a willed blindness to the violence these white supremacists were inflicting on the Black community. "These people are trying to kill my friends," the Casa Alma couple heard. "I'm not going to sit here and be civil towards them." Accusations of pearl-clutching, a put-down in heavy rotation those days, were common. Still, when asked to show up, Catholic Workers stood alongside those chanting "Fuck you, Kessler."

Bekah Menning had hosted the first Showing Up for Racial Justice meeting in her living room. For months she and others had led the planning meetings. Eventually, however, there were clashes over process within the leadership team. She eventually realized that for things to move forward someone had to step down. So, she did. Bekah would later ally herself with the more faith-aligned work of Smash and her neighbors, the Wispelweys. Still, she too showed up when she got word Kessler was making trouble.

Smash had once thought screaming obscenities was counterproductive. *Oh, don't yell at them, you are just giving them what they want,* she remembers thinking. But the more time she spent at protests, the more she realized that such reproaches carried the expectation that people of color would suppress whatever they thought or felt in the service of white comfort and some notion of "public order." "Instead of being empowered to draw on righteous anger and indignation," one Black activist complained, "we are told to be smaller, calmer, quieter."

Tactically, Smash said, screaming profanities at Jason Kessler was not a great idea. "But when people are wailing in the streets," she continued, paraphrasing Rev. Dr. William Barber of the Poor People's Campaign, "God is there and clergy should be there, too." So, she would offer the screamers water. For those inclined to shrink away, she would help them see why it was important to stand alongside those most likely to feel threatened by the gathering visibility, confidence, and aggression of men like Jason Kessler and Donald Trump. In these men people of color saw their worst fears about the world they struggled to live in confirmed. This was the essence of mutual aid and community defense.

Yet those who shouted the loudest, lasted the longest, and were least hesitant about being filmed were often young white women like Star Peterson. A longtime teacher with a background in special ed, Star was often among the first to show up on the Downtown Mall whenever Kessler appeared. For Star and her sister allies, the singsong chant "Fuck you, Kessler" served as a deflector shield to keep these men from taking up residence in their heads. For some white people, Smash said, stepping out in solidarity with Black community stalwarts like Rosia Parker and Katrina Turner, exploiting whatever protection their whiteness provided them, was transformative. So even if members of Charlottesville's activist community were working from different playbooks, they were all preparing themselves. They just didn't yet know for what.

Jason Kessler was not feeling exalted. Outwardly, he appeared to relish the attention, but on Charlottesville 2.0 he was seething. He was being disrespected; his rights were being interfered with. He wanted retribution. How could he best bring about a Berkeley level of violence to Charlottesville? "We should bring picket signs that can be used as sticks to bludgeon our enemies with." Most of the action at Berkeley was in the streets. What about a march through the city after the rally? What about burning an Antifa flag? Kessler wanted to publicize Unite the Right widely so that Antifa would show up with all they had. They would do the same. "Bring in the alt right, Proud Boys, [Kyle Chapman], Damigo, Spencer and fight this shit out."

"Assemble every motherfucker you can."

The night Kessler was banished from Miller's, Jalane Schmidt was sitting at a nearby table. If a Black passerby expressed curiosity about what the racket was all about, they were directed her way. She was taking down names and numbers for a Black Lives Matter chapter that she and Don Gathers were cofounding. Rosia Parker and Katrina Turner were among the first to sign on.

Jalane and Don had formed a quiet alliance during the Blue Ribbon Commission hearings. Jalane, like the man I nicknamed "the Deacon," had been frustrated by the silence of official Black Charlottesville on the fate of the statues. Rev. Alvin Edwards and Rev. Lehman Bates of the Clergy Collective, like the local NAACP leadership, did not weigh in publicly. Eugene Williams, the man who, with his wife, Lorraine, had filed suit with the NAACP to compel Charlottesville to integrate its schools, had wanted them left alone, citing more urgent needs. Jalane didn't tread lightly. She derided the NAACP leadership as "geriatric" and dismissed "old people like Eugene Williams living on the moral fumes of fifty years ago." It had taken the director of the NAACP four days to hold a press conference after the appearance of Richard Spencer's torch mob: "I'm not saying they were the Klan, but I think they wanted to intimidate," was her tentative takeaway.

The Clergy Collective, too, seemed to be lacking a sense of urgency. Their next breakfast wasn't due to take place until June 7, three weeks after Spencer and his men took over Emancipation Park. Even then, Rev. Edwards would be in Chicago visiting family. Jalane believed the overcautious approach of the city's senior Black leadership had given white moderates cover and opened the door for the Flaggers. By the time Richard Spencer and his crew of neo-Nazis and white supremacists arrived, the need for a local Black Lives Matter chapter became clear.

The Movement for Black Lives had its beginnings in the 2013 summer street protests that followed George Zimmerman's acquittal in the murder of Trayvon Martin. It had grown with the Ferguson uprising in the summer of 2014 and the protests surrounding Freddie Gray's death in the back of a Baltimore police van in the spring of 2015. But Trump's election caught the national leadership unprepared. Some thought the shift to electoral politics had come at the expense of grassroots work. It made BLM's leaders risk averse. The Charlottesville chapter was founded when Jalane Schmidt finally stopped waiting on them.

Even if the leaders of the Movement for Black Lives failed to see it, Charlottesville was staring at a crisis, the slow and unconcealed weaponizing of the city and its history on behalf of various strains of white nationalist and white supremacist ideologies. At forty-eight, Jalane Schmidt was older than the average BLM organizer. Raised in an intentional community in Newton, Kansas, she was the adopted biracial daughter of a Mennonite minister. When she was growing up, activists from all over the world brought news of their struggles to her family's dinner table. After receiving her doctorate at Harvard Divinity School, she did postdoc work at UNC and had arrived at UVA eight years before. She carried herself with athletic intensity and focus with a rhetorical style more pedagogical than ideological. When asked by a local reporter about the confrontations with Kessler, Jalane gave her a lesson on the evolution of racial justice tactics.

In response to the racial terrorism of lynching, church bombings, and laws that mandated where they could live, work, sit, and go to school, African Americans throughout the South put on their Sunday best and embraced the nonviolence preached to them by Dr. King. White people only began to take note when police beatings, water hoses, attack dogs, arrests, firebombings, and FBI surveillance brought out the press. Until then, African Americans endured the trials of Job in exchange for a modicum of white sympathy. But the respectability politics of the civil rights era, with Black preachers in gold cufflinks singing "We Shall Overcome," no longer carried the moral force it once had. King's tactics died with him. In the sixties and seventies, the Black Panthers organized armed militias and free health care clinics.

"The tactics always change with time," Jalane concluded, leaving open the question as to where on this spectrum Charlottesville's BLM chapter would fall. One thing was clear. Kessler and his crew were to be confronted at every turn. "The days when we bowed our heads and asked with trembling voices for our right to live comfortably in this country, without fear or intimidation," one member said, "are dead and gone."

On June 5, two days before the first Clergy Collective breakfast meeting after Spencer's torch mob, the *Daily Progress* broke the news that there were to be yet more rallies over the statues. Not only did the

Klan want its turn with a Charlottesville rally to "stop cultural genocide," so did Jason Kessler. Mayor Mike Signer called Rev. Lehman
Bates before the news became public. Both permit requests had met all
the requirements, he explained. Though their message was hateful, it was
protected speech.

One of the first things Rev. Bates was told when he arrived in Charlottesville
in 2006 was that he would do well provided he didn't rock the boat.
Wes Bellamy heard something similar, perhaps from the same people.
For a long time, Rev. Bates didn't fully grasp what that meant. He had
participated in Holly Edwards's Dialogue on Race and was proud of
the alliances he forged there. He was one of the founders of the African
American Clergy Police Partnership, where Black clergy met with police chiefs from the city, county, and university to discuss issues with
law enforcement. Finally, in concert with the local Unitarian church
and Frank Dukes, "the Listener" of the Blue Ribbon Commission, he
had worked to hold the University of Virginia accountable for its dismal
history with the Black community.

Bates's relationship with city officials was his means of keeping the
interests and welfare of the Black community at the forefront of the
city's attention. The police partnership protected Black people from
being treated with impunity. His voice was heard in rooms where he
was often the only Black person. Even so, his congregants would sometimes ask him to tone it down. They had known a precarious existence
and didn't want to lose what little purchase they had. So, in exchange
for a place at the table, he dialed it back. The specter of Uncle Tom hung
over him, he admitted, but what choice did he have?

When Signer told him of the upcoming rallies, Rev. Bates invited
him to address the Clergy Collective on June 7 when, in the absence of
Rev. Edwards, he would be presiding. Over thirty people showed, twice
the usual number. Among the new attendees were Seth Wispelwey and
Smash. They knew the July 8 Klan rally would be a practice run for
Jason Kessler's August 12 rally. They both hoped the collective could
provide a voice and a vehicle for spiritual witness.

Mayor Signer opened the meeting not by asking the Clergy Collective what they needed or how he could help, but by telling them what *he* needed and how *they* could help. First, they shouldn't "take the bait." If they showed up anywhere near the site of the Klan rally they would be giving the Klan the attention they craved. Second, they should organize uplifting events that would draw people away. The man who'd declared Charlottesville the "Capital of the Resistance" was telling everyone to stand down. City Manager Maurice Jones chimed in about the need to send a "positive message."

The police chief had already met with the NAACP, clergy members were told, and they had pledged to help with counterprogramming. The public historian Niya Bates had been at the NAACP meeting with the police chief. "When has ignoring the KKK ever worked?" she asked them. It was the last meeting she attended. To the chagrin of the newly formed BLM chapter, even Wes Bellamy had signed on to Signer's mandate.

Signer also hoped the *Washington Post* would see the wisdom of his approach and do their bit to peddle his message of uplift. In an email addressing the upcoming Klan rally, he wrote, "This rump, out-of-state chapter of a totally discredited organization will succeed in their aim of inciting controversy only if folks take their putrid bait, and that begins with the media. I encourage everyone to ignore this ridiculous sideshow and to focus instead on celebrating the values of diversity and tolerance that have made Charlottesville a world-class city." Predictably, this went nowhere, but the effects of the mayor's interference with the Clergy Collective's deliberations were profound and long-lasting.

Rev. Bates deputized Rev. Seth Wispelwey to plan the Clergy Collective's response to the Klan rally, but he soon regretted it. At their first planning meeting it was clear that Rev. Wispelwey was going to ignore the mayor's directive. Listening to this newly ordained white man with no real ministry talk about the need for the collective to bear "prophetic witness" on the streets, countering the Klan's race-baiting with love, alarmed him. Rev. Wispelwey and Rev. Caine-Conley needed to sit down and be quiet, he said, as the other white ministers had done. They should listen to those who had done the work and knew the community.

Bates considered Seth and Smash laypeople, not clergy. They had arrived at the collective with the familiar entitlement mindset of most white people. They might be well meaning, he said. But urban renewal had been well meaning, and his elders had lost their homes and livelihoods. It was hard for him to forget, too, those white Christian ministers who had left the collective because the idea of fellowship with a Jew or a Muslim, with woman ministers, let alone queer ones, was a bridge too far. Like most evangelicals, Rev. Edwards and Rev. Bates viewed homosexuality as a sin. Still, they welcomed Smash's presence at their breakfasts. Less so her voice.

Rev. Bates told me about a white pastor who had kept his membership in the Clergy Collective secret from his congregation. When it was discovered, his board called him on the carpet. Was he airing their dirty laundry? When he came back to say he could not continue to attend their breakfasts, he broke down in tears. Because he was feeling a little heat, Rev. Bates recalled, he was quitting.

"Okay, fine," Rev. Bates said. "That's well and good, but when the Klan comes, or when some extremist groups come, you still expect me to trust you? What happens when the bullets start flying? If you are walking with me, I know what I'm willing to sacrifice and I better be damn sure you feel the same way. You don't want that level of relationship? *Fine.*" This was Rev. Bates's long experience of white Christian ministers. Why would these two be any different?

It was true that Seth and Smash had no congregations to answer to, no elderly church ladies whose fears might temper their talk of prophetic witness. They were largely unknown to the nonactivist Black community. If Seth and Smash answered to anyone, it was to local activists of color who felt the threat posed by Kessler and the Klan most keenly. While Seth had hoped the Clergy Collective would take the lead, he didn't insist that everyone participate. He asked only that the collective act independently of the dictates of law enforcement and politicians. Everyone was free to decide where their presence was most needed. Finally, Seth had grown up in Charlottesville. He had some understanding of the pressures Black ministers like Lehman

Bates and Alvin Edwards faced. He was less sympathetic to his fellow white ministers.

Nonetheless, a rift was beginning to emerge. On Rev. Edwards's return from Chicago, Rev. Elaine Thomas of St. Paul's tried to explain to him the sense of obligation that compelled her to participate in what Rev. Wispelwey and Rev. Caine-Conley were proposing. Later, she would find historic parallels in the clashes between the Southern Christian Leadership Conference and the Student Nonviolent Coordinating Committee. This tension, she said, proved productive in those years, and she hoped it would prove so for the Clergy Collective. The words of Rev. Brenda Brown-Grooms strengthened her resolve: "No religious tradition I know of tells me to turn away when evil arrives."

A week or so after the news of the rallies was made public, the first community meeting was held at Mount Zion First African Baptist Church. "The people were fit to be tied," Pastor Brenda recalled. Racist leaflets had begun to appear on people's car windshields. Her community asked her: "What are you going to do for us? Something is going on." Smash and Seth shared with her the intel Emily Gorcenski had begun collecting from anti-fascist infiltrators of far-right message boards, some of whom had begun sending direct messages to her Twitter feed.

"The activists were telling us, and then we were telling the police," Pastor Brenda recalled. But when the police tried to reassure people, telling them not to worry, that everything would be fine, people turned to her and said, "But we *are* worried." After that, she said, her people only wanted to meet with clergy. "You are our faith leaders," she heard. "You have to get us ready for this." Even if the mayor or the police chief couldn't see it, she was fully prepared for the possibility that these men would end up killing someone. On the eve of the Klan rally, she gave the white clergy of the collective their marching orders: "Black folks will not be in the front of this—we are in the front of it every day. We have born the weight forever. If you don't stand up for me, I am dead."

Yet before Seth Wispelwey could present his detailed plans for July 8, the city sent out a press release announcing the Charlottesville Clergy Collective would "lead the City's effort to project a 'unified' re-

sponse to the KKK rally." In concert with the NAACP, under the rubric of "Unity Days," the collective would sponsor a slate of events at the
Jefferson School African American Heritage Center on the morning of
the rally. This would be followed by a picnic and family fun in a local
arts park. Finally, for the duration of the rally, there would be a "Unity
Day Concert" at the Pavilion on the Downtown Mall.

It was the wrong message at the wrong moment. Rev. Alvin Edwards
was never going to be on the streets. He would never put his congregants in harm's way. Nor would he stoop to dignify the Klan with
his presence. It went against everything he had worked hard to build
for his community. But neither did he want to be portrayed as Mayor
Signer's patsy. But that is what Signer made him.

For a man who prided himself on promoting unity, Mike Signer
succeeded in dividing the Clergy Collective just as it was beginning to
find its feet.

A week after news of his rally became public, Jason Kessler posted an
announcement on Facebook that Charlottesville's activists would be
sure to see. That coming Saturday he would be on the Downtown Mall
for a Proud Boys meetup. Kessler had recently been filmed undergoing
the Proud Boys initiation ceremony of being forced to recite a list of
breakfast cereals while being gently slapped around by his crew. "They
are going to be visiting here a lot more often," he wrote, "as we bring
solidarity and UNITE THE RIGHT." More privately, on Discord,
Kessler instructed those who planned on joining him to bring their
MAGA hats. "If Antifa fucks with us it'll look like average Trump supporters and Alt-light are under attack." On Saturday, June 17, he wrote
again on Discord: "There's a 'Proud Boys' meeting here tonight the left
is extremely triggered about." This was Kessler's way of saying the highest Proud Boys merit badge might be theirs.

At a "March 4 Trump rally," a Proud Boy in homemade armor,
later identified as Kyle Chapman, brought a stick down on a protester's head, launching a flurry of memes portraying him as an "alt-
knight." This led to the founding of a Proud Boys fight club, dubbed
the "Fraternal Order of Alt-Knights," and the addition of a final merit

badge or "degree." Thereafter, any Proud Boy who "kicked the crap out of an antifa" will have ascended to the order's highest ranks. A member of Anarchist People of Color sent out a Signal alert telling activists of color to stand down to deprive Kessler of his badge. Seth went around to give the businesses on the Downtown Mall a heads-up and to ask that they refuse to serve Kessler. Solidarity Cville asked that local media be present.

At 7:00 p.m. a dozen Proud Boys began strolling about, shadowed by a reporter from WINA newsradio and followed by the eyes of leery business owners, oblivious restaurant patrons, and activists who had stationed themselves in "plainclothes" to monitor their movements. The police were omnipresent. When Kessler paid his tab at Miller's, the one downtown establishment that continued to serve him, his departure was met with applause. He began livestreaming. If "Antifa" wouldn't take the bait, he'd troll the police.

"This police officer right here laid hands on me; I didn't touch him!" he shouted.

"You are dreaming, bud!" a local countered. "What are you trying to prove, dude?"

Denied service at business after business, the men found themselves surrounded by a growing group of citizens, approaching a hundred people. The crowd included waiters and business owners who publicly berated Kessler and eventually chased them off. A local man came upon them all regrouping in a stairwell of the Market Street parking garage, and they set upon him. The man escaped to the police headquarters next door to press charges. The Boys left without a badge; Jason Kessler had once more been disgraced.

This was the first indication that an unallied portion of the community was ready to come out and confront Kessler, either out of moral conviction or because he was just so obnoxious. At the city council meeting that Monday, Brandon Collins, speaking on behalf of the Public Housing Association of Residents, insisted that regular folks understood what was at stake better than the council did. "I think it would be wise if our elected leadership show some spine to stand up to these assholes, excuse my language."

"You are out of order," Mayor Signer interjected. "We cannot use profanity. *Seriously*, Mr. Collins."

"My bad," he replied.

Emily Gorcenski wasn't going to let herself get distracted by the Klan. Her focus was on getting Jason Kessler's rally canceled. She saw herself as a propagandist, running an operation with two audiences. The first was the city council. She was aggregating intelligence from her DMs and amassing a dossier to prove the rallygoers were planning acts of violence. She believed there was sufficient evidence for the city to deny Kessler a permit. Her second audience was Richard Spencer, and she knew exactly which button to push. "Hey Richie, what's it like when your boy Kessler and his compadres are team #punchthenazi?" she tweeted at him. She attached a chat log containing threats against Spencer from a Kessler associate. If she could get Spencer to think there was a snitch in Kessler's entourage, she could drive a wedge between them. Then he might reconsider his participation in Unite the Right. And if Richard Spencer pulled out, others would follow, with the added boon that Kessler would again be humiliated.

She threw all she had at the wall.

CHAPTER 9

Invisible Empires

On Christmas Eve 1865, six Confederate veterans swore oaths to one another, took on aliases, and spoke in code. They masqueraded as ghost soldiers on horseback pretending they were still at war. Was the loss of white rule over Black bodies more disabling than the wholesale butchery they'd survived? Would they rather have expired in a "perfect halo of glory" than admit their sacred cause was in truth a wicked one? They called themselves the Invisible Empire, a slogan derived from their secret alliance with the Confederacy's most revered general. Rumor had it that Robert E. Lee wanted his connection to the Klan kept "invisible." In brotherhood with a man of stainless honor, they imagined they could reclaim their own.

The post–Civil War period saw an explosion of membership in fraternal organizations. By 1900 one in five American men had joined one or more of them. Like the Klan, these societies—Shriners, Odd Fellows, Freemasons, and countless college fraternities—liked to dabble in mysticism and perform occult rituals under vows of secrecy. Where some societies built hospitals and raised funds for medical research and scholarships, the Klan distinguished itself with vigilante campaigns of racial terror and financial grift. Then something changed. In the 1920s the Klan became respectable, even more powerful in the North and Midwest than it was in the South. As a result, anti-Catholicism and anti-Semitism surged alongside anti-Black sentiment. Klan leaders began to boast of millions of members at every level of government. Its roster included sixteen US senators, more than twenty members of the US House of Representatives, eleven governors, and two Supreme Court justices. As a "secret" society the actual numbers were elusive, but in 1921 even the UVA yearbook featured an image of the ghostly riders as a frontispiece for the section on student clubs and organizations.

Though it seemed more like a publicity stunt than a cloak-and-dagger affair, that same year the *Daily Progress* reported on a secret Klan ceremony at Monticello. Like the speeches that accompanied the installation of the Lee statue, the reporter's overheated prose bordered on satire. "The fiery cross, symbol of the Invisible Empire, cast an eerie sheen upon a legion of white robed Virginians," the June 28, 1924, account began. Meeting at midnight at the tomb of Thomas Jefferson, "hundreds of Charlottesville's leading citizens and professional men . . . sealed the pledge of chivalry and patriotism with the deepest crimson."

The Klan's emergence as a respectable institution of civic life began after the turn of the century. With Reconstruction and a populist uprising of agrarian cooperatives and trade unions soundly defeated, in 1902 a new state constitution had given Virginia's landed and business elites a monopoly on political power. With the institution of a poll tax, most Black citizens and illiterate and impoverished whites were disenfranchised. The men at Jefferson's grave enacting a blood covenant were celebrating the triumph that had eluded their Confederate forefathers. For the next half century, vast disparities in wealth and social status prevailed throughout the Commonwealth, aided and abetted by Northern investors. Virginia's oligarchs were given a free hand to exploit and maintain social control over their fellow citizens, just as they once had the enslaved. This was the "New South."

The arrival of the roaring twenties, combined with talk of a "New Negro" and a "Harlem Renaissance," ushered in crackdowns on brothels, moonshine operations, dance halls, and gambling dens. Enforcing prohibition was key to the consolidation of the Klan's power. Since the true sin of the fathers could not be spoken of, a fanatical handwashing had commenced instead: political and economic domination masquerading as Christian moral panic. The state supreme court allowed the sterilization of "mental defectives," a term often applied to "loose" women, as "moral degeneracy" was thought to be a symptom of feeble-mindedness. Mandatory screenings for venereal disease began. Films that treated the relations between whites and Blacks were sanitized by a board of censors. "Every scene or subtitle calculated to produce friction between the races [will be] eliminated," its mandate read. Racial covenants began appearing in property deeds. Two years later the Virginia General Assembly passed the Public Assemblages Act, mandating racial segregation of all public events and spaces. All these practices and policies codified racial apartheid and strict social conformity. In this way the semi-feudal powers of "Ole Virginia," or at least a warped Hollywood version of it, were reconstituted.

The Klan also exerted its power in less subtle ways. Three weeks after the blood oaths exchanged over Jefferson's grave, ominous leaflets appeared around town. "Do you believe in the tenets of the Christian religion, Free Schools, Free Speech, Free Press, Law Enforcement, Liberty and White Supremacy? Can you take a MAN'S OATH?" All others, deemed "undesirables," were told to leave town. The leaflet ended on a note of menace. "The eye of the unknown is constantly observing."
"THIS IS YOUR LAST WARNING."

Housed in the Beaux Arts McIntire Building across the street from the former Lee Park, the Albemarle Charlottesville Historical Society had long been the fiefdom of local history buffs. Not long before the KKK was due to return to the city, Jalane Schmidt learned that the bowels of the society held twenty-six Klan robes. The robes were discovered in 1993 in a shed in Belmont, a once white working-class neighborhood Black residents knew to avoid after sundown. Though the gift came with no restrictions, after consulting with the Lee statue defender Lewis Martin III, the society's director refused to release the names of the Klan members identified with the donated robes. It was as if the blood oath of secrecy still clung to these costumes, indelible as mildew. Faced with their stonewalling, Jalane emailed the press.

"It's probably some old respectable family name which adorns a current

Charlottesville building, street or park," she wrote to a *Daily Progress* reporter, intimating that Paul Goodloe McIntire, Charlottesville's storied
benefactor, likely partook in the midnight festivities at Jefferson's tomb.
After the appearance of Spencer's torch mob, Jalane had been talked out
of making UVA's president, Teresa Sullivan, publicly acknowledge the
historic links between Richard Spencer, the university, and the Klan.
Never again, she said.

In advance of the Klan rally, Jalane, Lisa Woolfork, a colleague in
the UVA English department, and Laura Goldblatt, a UVA grad student, began putting together media messaging. Bringing the robes into
the light was part of Jalane's strategy to engage the media on her terms,
much as she had reframed the discussion surrounding the Lee statue.
She and her colleagues brainstormed over cans of LaCroix, scrawling
talking points and hashtags like #BlocKKKparty on whiteboards. They
highlighted the work of activists disrupting Kessler's networking on
the Downtown Mall. Working with the Carter Woodson Center for
African American Studies at UVA, they made visible the continuities
between the frat brothers of the Invisible Empire and their avatars in
the Proud Boys. They showed not just how acquiescent Charlottesville
had been in previous eras when the Klan made an appearance, but also
how it had abetted and empowered it. Finally, they fleshed out the ways
white supremacy had been part of the university and city landscape
since the days of Jefferson.

People needed to understand, Jalane said, that both these rallies were
"less an invasion and more of a homecoming" for white supremacy.
In providing white supremacists and the Klan a Charlottesville backstory, she and her colleagues hoped to give journalists something as
provocative as the spectacle they had come to cover. But could their
framing compete with visuals of grown men in Klan hoods? Young
men with torches shouting "Blood and soil" in Charlottesville's historic
downtown? Where Mike Signer wanted the *Washington Post* to hawk
his boosterism, Jalane Schmidt wanted the media to provide historical context.

Two days before the Klan arrived, the historical society's new director
finally agreed to a private viewing of the Klan robes for local reporters.

Two of the twenty-six robes were brought out. Jalane invited Vice-Mayor Wes Bellamy and several members of the Blue Ribbon Commission to see them. She tweeted a picture with the caption: "Stashed away in the KKKloset . . ." Jane Smith, "the Archivist" who had unearthed the story of the midnight exchange of blood oaths at Jefferson's grave, was there, as was Don Gathers. "The Professor," a historian named John Edwin Mason, told the director he was failing to do his job by not providing the robes' provenance.

For Wes Bellamy the discovery of the robes served as a rebuttal to all those who said the city had never had any problems with race before he came. "These robes were found in Charlottesville . . . How can you tell me that is not all connected in some shape, form, or fashion?"

Al Thomas, the city's first Black police chief, had been in office for just over a year. A short-statured, light-skinned man who spoke with the twang of rural Virginia, he'd arrived from an even smaller and more insular Virginia college town. Lexington was home to two historic bastions of white Southern manhood, Washington and Lee University and the Virginia Military Institute. Perhaps this explained his reserve. At press conferences he was guarded in the way of a man who doesn't know whom he can trust. His conversation tended to be cryptic or laden with police-speak. Despite his professed passion for community policing, he didn't move as easily in Charlottesville society, white or Black, as his backslapping predecessor, Timothy J. Longo, had. After the Ferguson uprising, Longo had initiated a program of police community dialogue, a project that grew out of President Obama's Task Force on 21st Century Policing. They'd been meeting on Saturdays at community rec centers and parks. Thomas had shown no interest in continuing with that. The Black community saw little of him.

Richard Spencer's May 13 tiki torch rally and the "Take Back the Park" candlelit vigil that followed caught the police department flat-footed, revealing what Chief Thomas determined was an "operational blind spot." He directed his staff to draw up intelligence dossiers on Unite the Right's featured speakers and on the klavern behind the upcoming July 8 rally. Neither the Southern Poverty Law Center nor the

Department of Justice was initially consulted. There were no efforts to
contact jurisdictions that had hosted the Klan chapter that had secured
the permit. One officer spoke of contacting some of the men on the
Unite the Right speaker list "to see what they were about." It wasn't
until the third iteration of their intelligence dossier that criminal histories were included.

Thomas also sent detectives to the homes and workplaces of local
activists to ask about their plans. Members of Cville Pride, BLM, the
Anarchist People of Color Collective, and Showing Up for Racial Justice
were among those who received house calls. Though Mayor Signer
framed these visits as "outreach," Thomas called them "a comprehen-
sive intelligence gathering operation," as if civic-minded locals posed a
threat equal to the one posed by armed Klan members. For those unused to having their activism treated as suspect, this was unsettling.
They had jobs, Jalane Schmidt pointed out; they held mortgages and
paid taxes. When an officer appeared at a Showing Up for Racial Justice
meeting to take notes, Pam Starsia called a press conference objecting
to the police department's "intimidation tactics."

Consequently, local detectives were left to draw from DHS intelligence reports and on open source material gathered by the Virginia
Fusion Center, the intelligence arm of the Virginia State Police. As
a result, Charlottesville's homegrown activists were treated not as
members of their various organizations but under the blanket rubric
of "Antifa." The resulting reports were badly sourced and riddled with
logical fallacies. "Antifa's labeling of Trump . . . or other right-wing figures as 'fascist' or 'racist,'" a local detective wrote, was politically mo-
tivated. "Using words to cloak reality makes it easier to dispose of that
reality," he stated, thereby enabling them to "feel they have the right
to commit violence." One report cited a Proud Boys spokesman as a
credible source for "Antifa" intel. Another cited Milo Yiannopoulos as
an "Antifa" authority.

While some city residents were becoming more and more terrified, others were exasperated at the hits Charlottesville's reputation as a
small, peaceful, and family-friendly city was taking. First the Flaggers,
then that man Spencer, now the Klan, and next whatever riffraff would

attend Jason Kessler's rally. The day before the Unite the Right rally, the *Daily Progress* would run an unsigned editorial under the headline "How Did We Get Here?" The editorial traced the history of Lee Park and its prized statue, beginning with its unveiling in a moment of civic pride followed by almost a century of peace. That peace held until one man, Wes Bellamy, decided to disturb it. The editorial spoke on behalf of those for whom Jim Crow, segregation, lynching, and cross burnings were at once "long ago" and "never happened." With no reason to feel personally threatened, blessed with an inborn trust in the judgment of local law enforcement, they were free to treat the upcoming rallies as a scourge brought about by their race-obsessed vice-mayor.

In downplaying the apprehensions of those who felt menaced, the city's messaging invited a complacent white community to see Bellamy and his fellow activists as the real disturbers of the peace. That a Black police chief and a Black city manager agreed with the mayor and the editorial board of the *Daily Progress* underscored the power of this consensus. Wes Bellamy, meanwhile, had largely checked out, deciding to focus on completing the dissertation he would have to defend on August 11 rather than addressing the growing alarm. On the day of the Klan rally he would be in New York City with his wife, celebrating their first wedding anniversary.

Unable to question its assumptions, focusing on the wrong target, the city's leadership was incapable of assessing the real threat. This would impact how law enforcement and city officials prepared for Unite the Right. This was the true "operational blind spot." A member of Black Lives Matter spelled out the expected consequence: "If you 'take the bait' . . . you are fair game."

Upon founding their North Carolina klavern in 2011, thirty-year-old Christopher Barker and his high school sweetheart, Amanda, crowned themselves Imperial Wizard and Imperial Kommander of the Loyal White Knights of the Ku Klux Klan. Vegas Tenold met them later that year when the first of what would become their annual rallies was invaded by a pickup full of skinheads and the future leader of the Traditionalist Worker Party, Matthew Heimbach. To Tenold the Loyal

White Knights amounted to no more than "a handful of guys drinking warm beer in a field." The only truly loyal members, he claimed, were Mr. and Mrs. Barker. Tenold underestimated the Barkers' resourcefulness.

Christopher Barker's first arrest was for breaking and entering a church charity shop, stealing electronics, and destroying food and clothing donations meant for the needy. Over the next decade, his rap sheet grew to include forty arrests for DUI, violent assault, weapons violations, domestic battery, and attempted murder. Barker once put a cocked shotgun in his wife's mouth and threatened to pull the trigger. His personal heroes included the man behind the 1964 murders of three civil rights workers in Mississippi, and the Klansman serving a life sentence for the 16th Street Baptist Church bombing that killed four young girls in 1963. In 2015 he added Dylann S. Roof to his pantheon.

Many LWK members, however, believed Amanda was the real power behind the operation. If so, the holiday-themed membership drives were her brainchild. Every MLK Day, Loyal White Knights across the country leafleted their neighbors' lawns with flyers calling Dr. King a Communist pervert. On Valentine's Day leaflets targeted queers and on Christmas, Jews. The idea wasn't to recruit homeowners but to ride the wave of media that followed, stories invariably accompanied by a photo of the offending flyer showing the LWK web address and 800 number. New members were thus self-selected. By 2017 there were enough LWK members for the Barkers to live off membership fees plus whatever they were making off Loyal White Knight merchandise.

At the time of their planned July rally in Charlottesville, Christopher Barker was on probation for aiding and abetting a stabbing that had left a former Klan brother in the hospital. According to the reporter Nate Thayer, the stabbing took place in the Barkers' dining room in front of their two young children. The terms of Barker's parole stipulated that he could not leave North Carolina or associate with known felons, so it was left to his wife to take charge of the Charlottesville convoy. Just over fifty Klansmen, including nine women, planned to be there. Amanda had wanted her rally to take place on the courthouse steps, but she was persuaded to move it to Justice Park, the new name for Jackson Park, where she could assemble her troops in Stonewall Jackson's shadow.

Barker told her contact at the Charlottesville Police Department the real threat would be coming from the "black church [*sic*] holding a black panther meeting," referring to the pre-rally Clergy Collective service at First United Methodist she saw posted on Facebook. If they weren't checked for weapons, she said, Chief Thomas would be responsible for the bloodbath. She of course would be armed to the teeth.

"I will not let my people die," she wrote.

As the date of the Klan rally approached, an uneasy truce settled on the Clergy Collective. Its energies were now neatly divided between Seth Wispelwey's plans for the day and those of Rev. Alvin Edwards. Seth and Smash had marshaled a legion of volunteers. A Signal thread, Faithful Action, was established so that clergy members could keep in touch with one another during the day. A three-member clergy group was appointed to de-escalate tensions and was prepped on what to do if they ran into trouble. Medics and legal observers would be on hand. Rev. Phil Woodson would be out of town, but First United Methodist would open at 1:00 p.m. and offer refreshments, prayer, and music, followed by a 2:00 p.m. multifaith service. For those who wanted to join in public witness in the park, there would be bystander training. "Care Bears" would be equipped with red wagons filled with bottled water and snacks. Their supplies would be replenished throughout the day by a runner who would fill her backpack to ferry stores to the park from First United Methodist.

On the day of the Klan rally Chief Thomas's Command Center opened just before noon in a law office with a conference room that overlooked the park. There he could watch events unfold on monitors trained on the four zones of his operational plan. A Virginia State Police helicopter hovering overhead would provide a live feed. City Manager Maurice Jones would send out periodic texts to keep city council members informed. A virtual emergency operations center interface allowed those with access to see maps, share files, assign tasks, and access breaking information. Both Charlottesville police officers and Virginia State troopers would be equipped with radios.

By 1:00 p.m., all officers were in their assigned zones. The only discordant note was a Mine Resistant Ambush Protected tank idling on East Jefferson. The funneling of military surplus designed for war zones to local police departments, like the establishment of Fusion Centers, was a gift of the War on Terror, but the military hardware pipeline was established under President Bill Clinton. On her first sight of the Virginia State Police's Tactical Field Force in riot gear, Emily Gorcenski observed, "The only ones who showed up looking for a fight were the police." At 2:15 p.m., just as the park was beginning to fill up, an officer reported sighting an "Antifa" group equipped with gas masks and body armor. This was the last mention of "Antifa" in police reports. In the hundreds of photographs and videos I viewed, I saw nothing matching this description.

Kessler's sometime associate, the tall and grumpy John Heyden, was the first to get into it with counterprotesters. Heyden was a familiar figure at city council meetings, speaking out on the plight of longtime city residents like himself who lived on fixed incomes in a city filled with "tax and spend carpetbaggers." His sign read: "The KKK. Brought to you courtesy of Mr. Wes Bellamy and Kristin Szakos." He was met with middle fingers and chanting, grist for his mill. Later he found a fellow contrarian, an armed man in an NRA hat whose sign read: "No KKK racism. No BLM racism."

A handful of Bible thumpers were soon surrounded by dancing young women twirling rainbow-colored boas, clapping tambourines, and blowing whistles to drown out threats of damnation. Mothers arrived with children bearing signs. There was a man in a wheelchair and a woman in a hijab. There were clean-shaven white men and bearded Black ones. Some had long hair, others shaved heads. Some were tattooed and some were pierced. Asian women carried signs saying, "Yellow Peril for Black Lives." There were International Workers of the World signs, a glittery "Queers for Black Lives" sign, and a piece of white cardboard with the scrawled inscription "Fuck Yo Statue." A student-led drum corps arrived just after 2:00 p.m., accompanied by a saxophonist. They marched a few times around the park and then settled in the grass to rest and hydrate, still drumming.

Rev. Bates spent the morning overseeing "Unity Day" activities at the Jefferson School African American Heritage Center with "the Art Historian" of the BRC, Dr. Andrea Douglas. There was one PowerPoint presentation on the history of white supremacy in Charlottesville, another on local Black history, and some breakout sessions for people to talk to one another. These events were attended by an older, largely white crowd. To pay for them, Rev. Bates had solicited funds from the city's church leaders. With one exception, only Black churches contributed. His own church, Ebenezer Baptist, ended up providing the food for the community picnic in the local art park. In a reprise of Holly Edwards's Dialogue on Race, "Unity Day" amounted to mostly white people talking to one another about Black history.

By 2:00 p.m. First United Methodist Church was full.

After a brief welcome, Seth announced that following the service, people could either walk to Justice Park and bear witness, or follow Rev. Alvin Edwards to the Pavilion on the Downtown Mall for a "Unity Day Concert" of live gospel and bluegrass. Only a handful of people chose the Pavilion. The rest, around four hundred, chose to accompany Seth and Smash to Justice Park. Rev. Brenda Brown-Grooms and Apostle Sarah Kelley would remain behind at First United Methodist. Both had health issues that prevented them from being out on the streets. Instead, they would hold a prayer vigil for the duration of the rally.

This vigil was also a prudent way of not being drawn into the rift between Rev. Edwards and the young white ministers. It enabled the two women to remain true to their faiths and maintain their autonomy. Where Rev. Edwards's and Rev. Bates's congregations were made up of middle- and working-class strivers, Apostle Sarah's Faith, Hope, and Love Church of Deliverance had grown out of her work as a nurse, a graduate of UVA's hospital chaplaincy program, and a volunteer chaplain in a women's prison. Like Pastor Brenda at New Beginnings Christian Community, she ministered to misfits, rejects, and outcasts.

Then in her late seventies, Apostle Sarah was a generation older than Pastor Brenda. First Baptist by Union Station, where she taught Sunday school and started a gospel choir, had once been her church. There, Rev. Dr. Benjamin Bunn and his wife, Imogen, had been her spiritual parents. It was Rev. Bunn who instilled in her a fierce dedication to justice.

But it was her great-grandmother who taught her to survive. Sarah Kelley's frank account of her life showed the indelible imprint of slavery and its long afterlife. Her great-grandmother's husband, she told me, had suffered from what she called the "slavery mentality." As the son of an enslaved woman, he never knew his father and so knew nothing of being a father himself. Her great-grandmother Susan, also born of an enslaved woman, was left to raise nine children alone. By the time young Sarah arrived, left behind by her teenaged mother, Susan was caring for a household of sixteen. Sometimes she did that by stealing food from the kitchen at the Dolley Madison Inn, where she cooked and served three meals a day. Every Sunday the entire household was marched to First Baptist. Even when she became too old to leave her house, her great-grandmother tithed.

A young Sarah once opened the door to a white woman who brandished her husband's shirt, red with rage at the ring around the collar. "You tell your husband to wash his dirty neck and then my grandma don't have to be working so hard on the washboard," Sarah shouted before closing the door. She'd never amount to anything, her great-grandmother fumed. But she read Sarah books, making her repeat the words above her finger. Sarah started school at three because her great-grandmother lied about her age.

It wasn't a straight line from Sarah's childhood home to a long and happy marriage, motherhood, and numerable professional achievements, including many firsts as a Black woman. There was sexual assault and homelessness in her last year of high school. There was mental illness and drug addiction. How many generations does it take to reclaim a life defined by all that was stolen while living among people who acted as if it had never happened? Now, seven generations removed from slavery, Apostle Sarah still prayed for justice.

To survive, she had her Bible, the example of Rev. Bunn, and the memory of her indestructible great-grandmother. "I believe she loved me," she said. Precarity comes in many forms, and the expression of love is an extravagance not everyone can afford. Apostle Sarah told me the love she dispenses so freely to her outcasts and misfits is accompanied by bitterness. I supposed this was a polite word for anger, though neither anger nor bitterness was evident in her bearing. But she had eyes, a heart. She'd come of age amid the remains of a crime. She'd watched a proud woman work herself to the bone. She'd borne petty indignities inflicted by white coworkers. She'd seen all that had been denied to her people. How could she not be angry or bitter?

This was the life experience and true faith Apostle Sarah Kelley drew on for her prayer vigil at First United Methodist on the afternoon the Klan returned to Charlottesville.

Seth, Smash, and Rev. Elaine Thomas led the way to Justice Park, each carrying South African vuvuzelas. Some clergy had fiercely objected to the vuvuzelas. Weren't they an incitement? Pastor Brenda deputized Seth to field their concerns; she had no patience for it. As the crowds of people following them came into view of those already in Justice Park, the mood lifted. Singing "We Shall Overcome," they filled the streets from sidewalk to sidewalk. Some carried large origami-shaped cranes, symbols of hope and healing, made by Charis residents. Others carried preprinted signs: "Our lives begin to end the day we become silent about the things that matter. Martin Luther King, Jr." Practically all wore Klanbuster stickers, a meme modeled on the Ghostbusters logo. Grace Aheron, in heart-shaped sunglasses and a leopard print bandanna, left the park to hug Smash and whisper updates in her ear. Grace carried a Showing Up for Racial Justice banner with three demands. "Cease targeting Black families by social services. Find Sage Smith. Revoke the permit for the August 12th rally."

When events at the Jefferson School African American Heritage Center concluded, Rev. Bates also headed to Justice Park. He didn't go to bear prophetic witness or as the minister of Ebenezer Baptist. He went to see for himself. He found the behavior of the counterprotesters unsettling. They were "drumming up all this noise," he said, "half-dressed, wild, and crazed." Veronica Fitzhugh, a leader of Anarchist People of Color who would later be arrested, may have caught his eye. She was wearing sparkly butterfly sunglasses, a gold headband, a black bra and a black lace tutu with fishnet tights. "FUCKKK" was written on her chest and "White Supremacy" on her midriff.

Though he had hosted Seth's planning meetings at Ebenezer Baptist, and thus knew what to expect, Rev. Bates still could not square a pastor's role with what he witnessed that afternoon: clergy leading people through the streets. "I have an accountability, a responsibility, and authority that comes with my position," he said, still rattled. Recalling the sight of Seth, dressed that day in black robes with a red stole adorned with a Clergy Collective button, he added, bitterly: "You don't have that, Mr. Activist."

Seth admitted they hadn't really planned on what they would do once they got to the park. While they waited for the Klan, they sang until they ran out of songs. It was hellishly hot. The energy that had buoyed them as they left the church ebbed in the heat and humidity of a July afternoon. Kay Slaughter, a former mayor who had walked with them from First United, felt they were inexperienced. Some retreated to find shade. Others lined up at the barricades. With people standing shoulder to shoulder at the still-empty enclosure surrounding the Jackson statue, it was hard to find a spot.

Just before 3:00 p.m. there was a skirmish. A heavily bearded man wearing a shirt with a picture of an AR-15 and the caption "Refugee Repellant" was confronted by counterprotesters. His buddy was wearing a Confederate flag as a cape. Cops formed a ring around the two, and a layer of TV media formed around the cops. The TV media, in turn, were encircled by legal observers in yellow vests and carrying note pads. Counterprotesters formed the outermost ring, forearms marked with emergency phone contacts as they held their phones aloft trying to film. Smash tried to calm things, but she was swallowed in the crush.

Elsewhere, another pastor witnessed a group of around a hundred protesters surround two men wearing Confederate hats, shouting "Death to the KKK" in their faces. He worked to keep the two men from retaliating. Even if he wanted to get out his phone to call for help, he said later, he couldn't reach it, and no one would have heard him shout. Apart from those in robes, it became difficult to distinguish clergy from laypeople. Seth became absorbed in filming the scene and wondering if he would be arrested. He hadn't prepared for that, he realized with dismay. As the afternoon wore on, the cacophony of noisemakers and drums was unremitting. The syncopated thump of the helicopter created an atmosphere of menace.

Three o'clock came and went with no sign of the Klan. The activists had seen the Virginia State Police's Tactical Field Force enter their staging area at the Juvenile and Domestic Relations District Courthouse and figured out where the Klan would enter the park. From the covered garage behind the courthouse the Klan would cross East High Street to enter a barricaded corridor that led to the enclosure where they would have their rally. The media was already in there. To sustain the energy of the activists who'd locked arms at the entrance, a woman with a megaphone led them in a call-and-response. "When Black lives are under attack, what do we do?" she asked. "Stand up, fight back," the crowd behind her answered. After ten minutes she switched it up. "When trans lives are under attack . . ."

A half hour after the rally was meant to start, the police issued a warning. Activists blocking the entrance to the park had to disperse or face arrest. Four submitted to being handcuffed and were taken off peaceably. Then troopers in riot gear began clearing the passage across East High Street. Once cleared, they formed a human barricade from the garage to the park entrance, while local officers lined the barricaded passageway inside the park. Standing eye to eye with the counterprotesters, their backs to the arriving Klan, they appeared more like private security guards than police officers. "Cops and Klan go hand in hand" became the new chant, interspersed with "No KKK, no fascist USA, no cops."

These chants struck Rev. Lehman Bates as especially shocking. "I can't afford to say that the police and the Klan go hand in hand," he said later. "I can't do that."

The historic continuities between slave patrols, night riders of the Invisible Empire, and law enforcement had been much discussed of late. I imagined Black families didn't need the history lesson. They only needed to know their children knew how to conduct themselves in the presence of law enforcement. That is how Philando Castile, a nutrition services supervisor at a school in St. Paul, survived fifty-two traffic stops before the one that killed him. In Charlottesville, Black men made up 8.5 percent of the population, but accounted for more than half the arrests. Though protesters have a right to chant whatever provocations they want, it's easier for white activists to ignore the consequences. They've rarely faced them. In Rev. Bates's experience, his people would bear the brunt. And for what?

Jack White and his wife, Gayle, had come from Richmond out of curiosity, arriving early enough to secure a good spot on the barricades. As a young Black reporter for *Time*, White had covered the latter years of the civil rights movement. His wife, who worked in community outreach at Monticello, was a direct descendant of Peter Hemings, Sally's brother. Her Monticello colleague, Niya Bates, the former tutor to the young Zyahna, had come with them. A man with a Confederate flag on his cap stood next to them. They disagreed about the statues, White said, but had an otherwise civil discussion.

When, fifty minutes late for their hour-long rally, the Klan finally barreled into the bricked-over enclosure, White said they looked like puffed up circus clowns. A few wore full Klan robes in the kind of wrinkled satin of cheap Halloween costumes. Most wore black shirts with an Invisible Empire patch on one side and a Roman cross with a drop of blood inside on the other. Many were armed. They carried a selection of Confederate flags and homemade signs marked by misspellings. "Jews are Satan's children," read one. "Wes Bellamy go be a nig somewhere else." For the first ten minutes they stood around awkwardly, smoking cigarettes and staring sullenly at the protesters gawking at and jeering them. Their speeches could not be heard over the clamor. A Klansman made monkey noises at Black protesters.

The men Jack White saw that day were a shadow of the Klan he'd once reported on. Slouchy, pot-bellied, with bad teeth and terrible haircuts, they were more comical than terrifying. "If these were the best KKK guys they could come up with to symbolize white supremacy," he said, "then we had nothing to worry about." Charlottesville's response— scorn, laughter, boos, accompanied by tomatoes and fruit lobbed over the heads of the police—was entirely fitting. The Klan lasted just over half an hour before they were hustled out of the park, back into their cars, and escorted out of the city. Then the trouble started.

Though many left when the Klan did, the hundreds who remained were left trying to absorb what had just happened. Why had the police let them stay twenty-five minutes after their permit expired? "Who do you protect? Who do you serve?" they chanted. Why had cops faced residents, rather than the armed Klan? Advancing on a retreating line of state troopers in riot gear, bearing assault rifles and grenade launchers, protesters chanted: "We don't see no riot here, why are you in riot gear?" Emily Gorcenski, wearing a Black Lives Matter T-shirt, was among them. She tweeted a photo of a second Mine Resistant Ambush Protected tank.

"The cops are bringing out their toys," she tweeted, "since our rally was peaceful." A letter signed by several local civil rights organizations would later ask: What was the point of high-capacity AR-15s? The helicopter overhead? Why all the military-grade equipment?

The first declaration of unlawful assembly by the police came at 4:40 p.m. At 4:59 p.m., an officer pepper sprayed a twenty-eight-year-old white woman who had kicked him in his testicles while resisting arrest. Batons came out. Troopers in riot gear lined up in a phalanx across East High Street. In the Command Center, Chief Thomas denied a request to deploy chemical agents. Two minutes later Maj. Gary Pleasants, on the scene and carrying a megaphone, pronounced the gathering an unlawful assembly, warning that those who failed to disperse would be subject to tear gas and arrest. Few heard the warning. Many people's backs were turned. Emily heard conflicting commands.

Pleasants didn't convey his warning over his radio. On his own authority and outside the chain of command, he gave permission for the Virginia State Police to use CS dispersal powder: tear gas. At 5:07, twenty-two minutes after the Klan's departure, the Tactical Field Force deployed three canisters, catching both the counterprotesters and unmasked local officers by surprise. A future city councillor heard a state trooper say, just before firing, "You better watch yourself, Charlottesville."

Tear gas clouds appeared on the Command Center monitors. "What the hell just happened?" Chief Thomas demanded. Two minutes later, City Manager Maurice Jones texted city council members that the police were working to de-escalate the situation. Decades of research have shown that the use of tear gas does not diffuse tensions, it raises them.

Outside the Command Center, calls for medics went up. "We've got

pepper grenades being thrown," Emily reported. "Shit!" Her livestream
went dark, but audio continued. Calls for water and the appalling sound
of a man bellowing in pain could be heard.

"I got you," a nearby medic said calmly, before the pop of another canister. "Do you need water? Do you need me to flush out your eyes?"

"Yeah, give me a flush, give me a flush," Emily said.

Between 5:00 p.m. and 5:30 p.m., eighteen people were arrested for
failure to disperse, interference with arrest, obstruction of justice, disorderly conduct, and assault of a police officer. A military vet saw a
sixty-year-old woman pushed to the ground by a police officer, her head
hitting the concrete. He saw a handcuffed man sitting on the ground
get kicked in the face by an Albemarle County Sheriff's officer. Women
were flung to the ground. People were arrested for wearing face cover-
ings to protect themselves from the tear gas. Both Katrina Turner and
Rosia Parker, who suffered from asthma, were hit. A canister whizzed by
Seth's ear as he was filming. He covered his face with his stole and continued. Emily ended her livestream with the words, "There was no need
for this."

Later it was reported that the first declaration of illegal assembly
had been precipitated when a group of activists had tried to prevent
the Klan from leaving by blocking their exit from the garage. This
prompted the question as to why the passage hadn't been secured. It
also gave the governor a handle to upend the sequence of events to claim
that tear gas was used to disperse the crowds "so that the KKK could
go home." He later went further, declaring the KKK had been chased
into the garage.

This is a signature move. The police initiate an aggressive action,
framing it as a response to aggression on the part of protesters. In 1999
the police had tear-gassed people during the WTO protests in Seattle,
claiming it was in reaction to acts of vandalism that actually occurred
hours later. Behind a line of tanks, the police in Ferguson tear-gassed
a crowd of protesters, including children, asserting that Molotov cocktails had been thrown at them. "Any violence that occurred," a minister
on the frontlines insisted, "occurred after police attacked peaceful protests." In Charlottesville, more people were arrested after the Klan de-

parted than during the rally. This left the enduring impression that the police had waited for the Klan to leave before turning on a peaceful and legal assembly. After July 8, it began to dawn on some that the police might not keep them safe. "That was an interesting realization," Rev. Elaine Thomas of St. Paul's said.

Mayor Mike Signer had spent most of the afternoon at the "Unity Day Concert." He tweeted out photographs of the crowd and of himself and praised everyone who refused to take the bait. Receiving word that the Klan had left the city and unaware of what was developing a few blocks away, he tweeted, "I'm proud of the police and our community for balancing the 1st Amendment and our values." Kristin Szakos was in closer contact with those on the ground. In response to City Manager Maurice Jones's 5:47 p.m. report on the number of arrests, she texted, "teargas?" Jones replied, "we are working to confirm that." The Command Center was steps away from where the canisters had been launched. He could have simply stepped outside. An hour later, he verified what everyone already knew.

The Virginia State Police spokeswoman compiled a list of talking points. True to form she wrote, "At one point, a protestor began spraying the troopers on the frontline with OC spray." She said she had video evidence. She didn't. She attached a photo of a pepper spray can on the ground. The empty canister was rumored to have come from a homeless man's belongings. Mayor Mike Signer, arriving at the Command Center, repeated her claim on Facebook. His post drew immediate fire. The Virginia State Police decided not to release their talking points. There was no need to; Signer had given them cover.

Chief Thomas confronted Maj. Pleasants when he returned to the Command Center. "You're damn right I gassed them, it needed to be done," Pleasants said. To the public Thomas would prevaricate. Perhaps he needed Pleasants's support. Perhaps he couldn't afford to hang the state police out to dry before August 12. So, he, too, gave cover. "I was pleased with the professionalism and commitment of our law enforcement partners as our safety plan was well executed," Thomas said at the press conference that followed. For those who witnessed the confrontation in the Command Center, it was evident that Chief Thomas was not in command. Not of his senior officers. Not of the Virginia State Police. Later it was discovered that state and local police radios had been operating on different frequencies. This was not remedied in advance of Unite the Right.

Smash had been in far more volatile situations. The canisters came out of the blue, she said. There wasn't even scuffling going on, or even much in the way of yelling. One minute people were standing around and the next they were blinded, gasping, screaming, and begging for medical assistance. It gave her an idea of what was needed to prepare for August 12. They would require even more discipline. "We knew we had to get serious with our training."

Based on what he had seen, Rev. Lehman Bates came to a different conclusion. After submitting a report accounting for money spent on "Unity Day" counterprogramming, he resigned his membership in the Clergy Collective.

Out of the profusion of eyewitness accounts, documents, and after-action reports, one document captured the ambiguity, if you can call it that, of the understandings between law enforcement and white supremacists on the day of the Klan rally. Beginning in 2012, Christopher Barker had been an informant for the FBI's Joint Terrorism Task Force. He worked with two officers out of Greensboro, a half hour south of where he lived. One of them, a police sergeant named Steven Kory Flowers, was well placed to know something of Barker's long arrest record and violent proclivities. In advance of July 8, he sent an email warning to Chief Thomas. Attached to his email was a crude flyer Flowers claimed to have found circulating on social media. He characterized it as an advert calling all "Antifa advocates" to go to Charlottesville. The upcoming July 8 KKK rally was described as "The Battle for Charlottesville." It called on them to "stand against the Klan," and "shut it down." The sergeant warned Chief Thomas of the dangers posed by "criminal minded anarchists."

The flyer had the rally taking place on the steps of the City Circuit Court. This was on Amanda Barker's original permit application, but who else would have known that? The flyer's Halloween-themed typeface recalled for me those holiday leaflets the Loyal White Knights were known for. Had Amanda sent Sgt. Flowers this attachment? Was this an attempt to set up the counterprotesters? It bears noting that in all of Christopher Barker's flamboyantly violent history, he had never spent a single night in jail.

If there were invisible ties binding the Barkers and the Greensboro Police Department, there was a similar spirit at work at the Office of Intelligence and Analysis at the Department of Homeland Security. On August 9, two days before neo-Nazis, white supremacists, white nationalists, and neo-Confederates were to show up for the Unite the Right rally, it released a report on recent events in Charlottesville. "Domestic Terrorist Violence at Lawfully Permitted White Supremacist Rallies Likely to Continue," its headline read. The report conflated Richard Spencer's May 13 torch rally in Lee Park with the candlelit vigil of the following evening. Citing the *Daily Progress*, the report stated that on May 13, "anarchist extremists attacked white supremacists and several fights broke out."

Nothing in that sentence was true. The *Daily Progress* had reported no such attacks. The DHS sourced its reports on "domestic terrorist violence" from the far-right website Occidental Dissent. Furthermore, on the night of the torch rally, the police made no arrests. The musician who had confronted the torchbearers was the one who left with a bloody nose. At the candlelight vigil it was Jason Kessler who assaulted a woman of color. Apart from the charges brought against Kessler for his assault on a man who refused to sign his petition to remove Wes Bellamy from city council, and the assault charges (later dismissed) against Veronica Fitzhugh and Jeff Fogel, encounters between activists and white supremacists in Charlottesville had yet to go beyond shouting matches, dueling smart phone recordings, one incident of spitting, and another of a phone being knocked to the ground. Despite counterprotesters outnumbering the Klan twenty to one on July 8, the Klan emerged unscathed.

Still, on the eve of the Unite the Right rally, an intelligence analyst from the Department of Homeland Security predicted anarchist extremists would be the primary drivers of violence on August 12. This analyst went on to characterize "lawfully permitted" white supremacists' "preparations to counterattack anarchist extremists" as justified self-defense. That same week, the FBI's Domestic Terrorism Analysis Unit released a report of a new danger, at once racist, violent, and growing.

Not white supremacists, not white nationalists, not the alt-right: Black identity extremists.

CHAPTER 10

Deep, Abiding Love

In the summer of 2017 Robert "Azzmador" Ray had taken command of the Stormer troll army. With a full gray beard and greasy rattail, Azzmador looked at least a decade older than his fifty-one years. Like Andrew Anglin, Azzmador wasn't one to pussyfoot around his hatred of Blacks and Jews by calling himself a white supremacist. "Apparently that's the term you have to use to be clear with these idiots," he said. Judging by a recent surge in donations, his Daily Stormer podcast, *The Krypto Report*, was filling an unmet need for a more unvarnished language. "Jews have spent two millenia [*sic*] trying to purge it, but hate may be the most important attribute we have ever had." What happened two thousand years ago? A Jew was born in Bethlehem.

In June Azzmador had traveled from his home in East Texas to rallies in Houston and Austin. Showing up at the Texas capital, he held, was a watershed moment, the beginning of a national project to convince legions of far-right sympathizers to follow them into the streets. "The important thing is to show that people aren't afraid to leave the house." The fear of leaving the house was a constant refrain. The language used to talk about this fear, drawn from gaming, provides a glimpse into the fear-filled imaginings of the Stormer life. Being "lured into the woods" was when "Antifa" separated you from your pack, much as an enemy might in the pixilated terrain of a video game. Once "Antifa" gets you, the "noob" or newbie, into the woods, they will "steal your tendies." *Tendies* was slang for chicken tenders, a good part of the gamer's diet. Stealing your tendies was a euphemism for undergoing sexual assault or humiliation, even rape.

Azzmador wasn't alone in seeing historic developments in every meetup, only to have personal feuds undo whatever comradery and visibility had been gained. The blogger behind Occidental Dissent and the unofficial spokesman for League of the South, Brad Griffin, had seen many hopeful moments come and go. A native of Eufaula, Alabama, Griffin had been tracing the trajectory of this new generation of white supremacists from Spencer's earliest days hosting National Policy Institute conferences. Under the leadership of Dr. Michael Hill, Griffin had watched the League of the South evolve from a supposedly race-blind brotherhood of Johnny Rebs into a militant, neo-Nazi organization. Griffin had cheered on Breitbart as it "disemboweled" the Republican Party, replacing punditry on policy with cage fights over shifting cultural flashpoints. Steve Bannon and Milo Yiannopoulos were the stars in this firmament; Yiannopoulos had covered Gamergate for Breitbart. When the mainstream media lost its ability to monopolize the discourse, Griffin's Twitter count shot up, and he joined the company of those livestreaming far-right events and talking points on Periscope, Facebook Live, and YouTube. With access to the leadership channel on the Charlottesville 2.0 server, Griffin had a front row seat watching the Unite the Right rally come together.

Churning out memes, and directing troll swarms at Charlottesville's activists was fun, he said, but by taking their movement to the streets, people would see how cool it was to break taboos in the real world alongside like-minded souls. For Griffin and the League of the South, Charlottesville would be a "coming-out." Leaving the "internet closet," they could broadcast the arrival of a brash new generation in a public raid on a social justice warrior stronghold. "We're going to whack a hornet's nest. Hopefully, we can trigger them into coming out in force. . . . They will reveal themselves to be violent, intolerant, opposed to free speech, the insane enforcers of political correctness, etc. . . . They are the crybabies, hall monitors and diversity commissars that millions of White people resent at their workplace." After Charlottesville, he foresaw white nationalist summer festivals for young people. This envisioned future—Woodstock, not Altamont—was based on the assumption that the violent proclivities of far-right factions could be curbed.

Meanwhile, Azzmador believed there was a conspiracy afoot to pretty them all up for the "normalfags" in advance of the rally. He wasn't having any part of Vanguard America and Identity Evropa's frat boy getup. Even Anglin was now calling for sexy fitted T-shirts and jeans to make them appear "hip" and "cool." Well-trimmed beards, short hair, and gym memberships were the new order of the day. No one knew who was orchestrating the makeover. They would have asked Matt "Heimbowl," but he had a new baby. (Azzmador's Discord channel was called Bowl Patrol, in homage to Dylann Roof's bowl haircut.) They settled on Jason Kessler as the culprit.

Bowl Patrol was already up in arms over the fact that "Azz" was left off the lineup of speakers. Supposedly, Kessler was going to offer Azzmador a slot at the after-party. If that was the best Kessler could do, Azzmador told his boys, he would tell him to go fuck himself. If Baked Alaska is on that stage, "the Daily Stormer goddamn well belongs there." Eli Mosley claimed he had bullied Kessler into giving him a slot, but Azzmador had yet to hear. Finally, on July 27 he had a long talk with them both. They managed to mollify him.

"The plan is the same," Azzmador reported back. "Gas the kikes."

The closer the city got to August 12, the faster events unfolded. At the first city council meeting since the July 8 Klan rally, Chief Al Thomas was conspicuously absent, leaving City Manager Maurice Jones to explain police department actions. Tear gas was deployed not because the police had been pepper sprayed, he clarified, but because protesters had locked arms in defiance of the dispersal order. Tear gas was the most "effective, nonphysical, nonviolent" way of preventing people from being manhandled and arrested. This was another way of saying they were tear-gassed for their own good. That didn't go down well. A dozen or so activists, furious over the mayor's having sided with the police, had appeared at the dais to voice their outrage. Once again, the mayor had to suspend proceedings and deliver stern, long-winded lectures.

After a brief statement, Emily Gorcenski distributed twenty-two pages of screenshots to city councillors and staff. Her dossier included chat logs of a Virginia militia member who had been harassed by activists while hanging out with Kessler. Chatting with a man he imagined was sympathetic but who was, in fact, forwarding screenshots to Emily, this militia member expressed his expectation that people would be "finished off." Wes Bellamy would be "gotten rid of." Emily highlighted quotes from his Facebook account: "We are luring in BLM, SURJ, and Antifa from Baltimore, Philly, and DC. We'll kill 5 birds with one stone." "We . . . are bussing in people by the hundreds." "Just say when go time is and we'll walk in there with a thousand men and crush those little cunt rags for good."

For Emily, this man was one of hundreds, many with arrest records or documented histories of instigating violence in rallies across the country, due to arrive in less than a month for a five-hour armed occupation of her city's tiniest park. She included links from the Daily Stormer, articles in the *New York Times*, and information from the Southern Poverty Law Center. She cited Part 3.4.5 (b) of the Special Event Regulations stating the city could deny a permit if "it reasonably appears that the proposed activity will present a danger to public safety or health." She asked that Jason Kessler's permit be revoked. A letter-writing campaign echoing her points began the next day. Was Mayor Mike Signer going to do anything?

The decision on Kessler's permit wasn't Signer's to make. City Manager Maurice Jones had operational authority over permit negotiations. Within a week of receiving Kessler's application, it was deemed incomplete. The terms remained to be negotiated. Jones conferred with legal counsel. He couldn't ban the open carrying of guns because Virginia was an open carry state, but could he at least prohibit weapons like shields, bats, knives, or brass knuckles in the park? The Commonwealth's attorney told him he couldn't. He was wrong.

Charlottesville was subject to the Dillon Rule. Another legacy of "the Virginia Way," under this rule the only powers municipalities had were those explicitly granted by the state. Virginia political elites had long distrusted civic engagement; the machinery of governance was engineered to withstand public interference. This left liberally inclined localities at the mercy of conservative state legislatures, discouraging public accountability. Where the law was opaque, as with the city's vote to remove the Lee statue, matters ended up in court.

After Richard Spencer's May torch rally, city councillor Bob Fenwick had argued that the law was clear: the purpose of lit torches was to intimidate. Section 18.2-423.01 of the Virginia Code states that "any person who, with the intent of intimidating any person or group of persons, burns an object on a highway or other public place in a manner having a direct tendency to place another person in reasonable fear or apprehension of death or bodily injury is guilty of a Class 6 felony." There was a reason this 2002 law was on the books. It was tied to Virginia's history with the Klan. Because an older state law explicitly outlawing cross burning was deemed unconstitutional by the U.S. Supreme Court, the statute was rewritten to be "content neutral."

Unfortunately, the city prosecutor didn't believe Spencer's torch rally rose to the level of a crime: presumably the torches didn't intimidate *him*. Nor could Richard Spencer be charged for staging a rally without a permit because Signer had muddied the waters with his unpermitted Capital of the Resistance "press conference." Finally, though the intel Emily Gorcenski had collected was unsettling, the city's legal counsel concluded there was nothing there that constituted a credible threat to the safety of Charlottesville's residents.

It is hard to escape the feeling that this idea of a credible threat, both as a legal concept within a body of law surrounding the First Amendment, and in the literal sense of the adjective *credible* and the noun *threat*, exists in a realm beyond the reach of common sense. In this realm the words used by Nazis to describe their intentions, and by belligerent white men more generally, are provided more protection, a more generous allowance for creative license and hyperbole, than everyone else's words.

The law also treats the speech of armed individuals as equal to the speech of the unarmed. One might think the presence of guns in a public place, like the presence of burning objects, would change the character of what is being said. If flames are understood to be intimidating in a content-neutral way, why wouldn't guns be? The legal scholar and historian Farah Peterson writes, "The Second Amendment affords a white person the ability to clothe himself with constitutional authority even as he poses a direct threat to those around him." A Black person would be a fool to try something like that.

Was the federal government taking the threat of armed right-wing militants more seriously than the city prosecutor and the Commonwealth's attorney? In advance of the January 6, 2021, insurrection, an analyst at the Department of Homeland Security's Office of Intelligence and Analysis would log over five hundred pages of online threats, including calls for violence against members of Congress, maps of access tunnels, testimony that people were prepared to die, and tactical advice about smuggling arms into the Capitol. The FBI saw a post that read, "Congress needs to hear glass breaking, doors being kicked in." The intelligence wing of the Capitol Police intercepted posts that said, "We will storm the government buildings, kill cops, kill security guards, kill federal employees and agents," "start marching into the chambers," and "show up with guns and threaten them with death." It was all there.

Yet this DHS analyst concluded that none of this met the threshold of a "true threat." Like Charlottesville's city prosecutor, he didn't feel threatened. For him "threat" was a pure abstraction, never a working verb directed at him. Another analyst questioned whether it was even possible to "storm" the Capitol. According to the January 6 report, the special agent in charge of the intelligence division at the DC FBI field office insisted there was "nothing illegal" about people on social media discussing tunnels under the Capitol. If the speech, and ultimately the violence, directed against the most powerful people in America can be left unchecked, where does that leave the rest of us?

The chief of the Capitol Police described this as "a colossal intelligence failure." Was it, though? Law enforcement officers often make no secret of their sympathies with far-right groups. They wear Blue Lives Matter patches. They pose for selfies with militias. They stand by as armed mobs attack protesters and journalists. DC police officer Michael Fanone realized that, out of 3,000 on-duty DC police officers, only 850 showed up to defend the Capitol. At least 31 police officers from twelve states were part of the Capitol mob, along with a "disturbing number" of veterans and active duty servicemen.

Perhaps the DHS's Office of Intelligence and Analysis was blind to the face of white terror because it looked like its own. "Homeland Security" produced no warnings, bulletins, reports, or operational plans that would have enabled the Capitol Police to better secure the Capitol and themselves. Contrast this with the tall metal fence that shot up around the White House during the DC George Floyd protests the summer previous, or the generous deployment of sting ball grenades, sponge bullets, and other large-bore projectiles against Black Lives Matter protesters in DC. Such weapons went largely unused at the Capitol. A white officer testified that a member of the J6 mob told him, "Do not attack us! We are not Black Lives Matter!" The commander of the DC Guard waited for hours for permission to mobilize. Had African Americans tried to breach the Capitol, he said, "it would have been a vastly different response." As Ta-Nehisi Coates might say, this was not our system malfunctioning; it was our system working as it was designed to. The organizers of Unite the Right understood this.

During the July 17 city council meeting Mayor Signer proposed moving the Unite the Right rally to McIntire Park, a far larger park, away from the downtown. Though he framed this as a fresh proposal, he'd been on the phone all week promoting it. Trying once again to outflank the bad odor another rally would bring, he put out feelers to Rev. Dr. William Barber and Michelle Obama, John Lewis, and Jesse Jackson. Signer didn't stop to think what their presence might entail for the city's stretched local police force. Or the possibility that they might make Charlottesville a fatter target. Councillor Bob Fenwick thought Signer was using the crisis to raise his national profile, as he had with his "Capital of the Resistance" business. At the same time, Fenwick said, no one in the city administration had ever faced anything like this before.

There were obvious advantages to McIntire Park. There was plenty of parking. There were no local businesses or residents to worry about. But it was late. The more pressure Signer applied, the more the city

manager and police chief seemed to tune him out, as if they understood
that when it came to protecting the well-being of the most vulnerable,
institutions were inflexible. They also knew Kessler would stage his rally
in Emancipation Park with or without a permit. He had told them so.

Long before the trouble started, Seth Wispelwey had been playing with
acronyms for a new social justice organization. It was Smash who hit
on the right name. Seth had in mind a tight-knit, rapid response team
made up of clergy primed to show up "when shit (needs to) go down."
Once it became clear that the city council was powerless to stop the
Unite the Right rally, the need for a new organization became palpable.
And judging by the response they had on July 8, the community was
ready for more than prayers and gospel music. Congregate Cville would
provide it.

Smash and Seth made an odd pair. Where Smash was round and
short with the implacable air of a person secure in her faith, Seth was
tall and skinny, with the piercing stare of a perennial seeker. While
Smash spoke slowly and simply, Seth's words came out in a hectic rush.
By virtue of being a cisgender white man, he seemed ever ready to atone
for real and imagined transgressions. In a supporting role, however, he
could amplify Smash's voice with those Christian clergy, white men
largely, who had trouble hearing women's voices. He also maintained
a Rolodex of contacts in the wider social justice world. Smash, meanwhile, mobilized the volunteers that Congregate would draw on, maintaining text threads with sympathetic clergy from the Clergy Collective.
When the Starsias moved away in midsummer, Grace Aheron stepped
up her engagement with Showing Up for Racial Justice.

Congregate's first meeting was occasioned by a visit from a Pentecostal
preacher from St. Louis. When Tracy Wispelwey crossed paths with
Rev. Osagyefo Uhuru Sekou at the United Church of Christ Summit
for Justice in June, she told him about Richard Spencer's recent torch
march and the upcoming rallies. Proud Boys were roaming her city's
downtown, she said, harassing locals and frightening people of color.
The clergy were divided on strategy, and activists were being targeted
by trolls. Could he help? Rev. Sekou had a flight to catch to London the

next day, but he agreed to come for a night. Seth summoned twenty-odd friends and activists to their home. Out of security concerns, he didn't tell them anything. Before he left the next morning Rev. Sekou agreed to return in mid-July to prepare people for encounters with the police so they might avoid a repeat of July 8. Between the evening of July 19 at Sojourners and the afternoon of August 11 at St. Paul's Memorial Church, he held six workshops on nonviolent direct action.

Rev. Sekou was raised by his grandparents in the Arkansas delta, a region marked by vigilante and state-sanctioned violence against union organizers and Black people. The son and grandson of ministers, he was an ordained elder in the Church of God in Christ with decades of experience working for "the Movement." If Rev. Sekou's theological outlook was bread, the revolutionary ethos of the Pan-African Black Power and liberation movement of Kwame Ture provided the flour, the philosophical cool of the French existentialists and James Baldwin the leavening, and the spiritual truths of Black liberation theology its salt and sweet butter. Wherever his travels took him, in post-Katrina New Orleans, in post-earthquake Port-au-Prince, in occupied Palestine, and most recently in Ferguson, Missouri, he invariably found Jesus.

When he was still a student at Knoxville College, Sekou had taken a workshop at the nearby Highlander Center. The Highlander Center had sponsored workshops and training sessions for volunteers with the Student Non-Violent Coordinating Committee. A generation later, it would spawn Showing Up for Racial Justice. Sekou's instructor was the Methodist minister Dr. James Lawson. In 1956 Lawson had traveled to India to study satyagraha, a form of nonviolent resistance pioneered by Mahatma Gandhi in his long struggle against the British Empire. The tactics of satyagraha had been much studied among Black seminarians and, like the young Martin Luther King, Lawson made them his own. Rev. Sekou's own take on nonviolent resistance was grounded in his reading of the Gospels.

"God chose to be born of an unwed mother from an unimportant people in an unimportant part of the world living under military occupation," he would repeat again and again. In first-century Palestine, Roman law dictated the treatment meted out to subject people. Jews could be forced to carry a soldier's kit for a mile, and to give up their coats on demand. When Jesus told his followers to carry a Roman centurion's kit for two miles rather than one, it was defiance in the guise of submission. When Jesus instructed them to give every stitch on their backs to the Roman who demanded their coat, it was to provoke shame at the sight of their nakedness. Finally, when Jesus told his followers to turn the other cheek after a backhand slap, it was to invite a forehand slap, reserved for an equal. Turning the tables forced the occupier to acknowledge the humanity of the occupied.

These were parables; encounters with state-sponsored violence unfold unpredictably. Rev. Sekou taught people how to lock arms to make a human barricade. They were shown how to move in unison, how to stand up and sit down without breaking the line. They learned how to guard their vital organs from police batons, and how to de-escalate tensions. When a vulnerable community member was targeted, they were shown how to form a protective bulwark. Actions were staged as a kind of wordless theater, vying for the sympathies of a public inclined to suspect them. Their aim was to sharpen perception of what state violence on unarmed people looks like. A livestream clip or photograph might define the conflict. The songs Sekou taught them provided moments of relief from a rising sense of dread.

For Sekou, the essence of nonviolence was not the absence of fear but the presence of love. Love was the bulwark that enabled people to challenge, not individual cops, but the criminal justice system. If, as King believed, love was a weapon, it is one that disarms. This was the "deep, abiding love" of liberation theology. How are we going to show up? Rev. Sekou asked at that first meeting and every workshop thereafter. With deep, abiding love. Neither sentimental nor palliative, deep, abiding love had the iron vein of justice running through it. It was theological, but also tactical. It forced participants to ask themselves: *How much am I prepared to sacrifice?*

Over the course of the six workshops, a plan arose. They would arrive early, surround Emancipation Park, and block the rallygoers from entering. They would sing through their fears and wait to be arrested. This would require at least 200–250 people. As the date of the rally approached, more people began to show up: Jews, Muslims, Buddhists, Quakers, Christians, and nonbelievers. Katrina Turner and Rosia Parker of BLM were at every workshop. They followed Sekou's instruction to put their phones in the microwave, and to make sure they weren't followed.

Not everyone was on board. Seth spent fruitless hours trying to jog the conscience of his fellow white male clergy. Members of Anarchist People of Color were more focused on how they would protect and defend themselves. Queer people were often wary of religious authority, Smash said, and often had no experience of communities built on mutual trust. When still a seminary student, Smash had opened a house church that provided a sacred safe space, both for those who were ill at ease in traditional church settings and for those who had troubled histories with them.

Pastor Brenda couldn't take part in any direct action on the streets. If people needed to run, she said, they would have to return for her and that would put them in danger. Apostle Sarah had bad knees. Still, out of solidarity, both attended Sekou's workshops. One elderly Black woman proudly informed him she would carry her own bail money, so that the funds Congregate raised "could go to the babies." Her daughter talked her out of it. Grace Aheron was at the first meeting and, though she believed in the training, felt Sekou talked too much and was too much the dude. "I'm not going to be told what to do by this guy, no matter what his experience is," she said, adding, "God bless his heart." Instead, Grace and the "Puppetistas" of Charis planned a street performance narrated by a giant Sally Hemings puppet. At their peak, Sekou's workshops reached around one hundred people; even those who fell out found other ways to contribute.

By the end of July Congregate was in high gear. There were sign-up sheets for legal observer training. A friend of Bekah Menning's oversaw the Care Bears. Showing Up for Racial Justice took over bail bond support. Others signed on to security. The anti-fascist militias, Redneck Revolt and John Brown Gun Club, offered backup. Emily was monitoring the chatter on 8chan. Though she wouldn't provide me any names, she had an open line of communication with anti-fascists who followed her Twitter feed. They, in turn, put out a call on their networks for medics.

After the Klan rally, Smash and Seth had sent an email to the
Charlottesville Clergy Collective mailing list announcing the formation of Congregate. They made it clear that they still considered themselves members of the collective and that Congregate was established
solely for the purpose of training volunteers in nonviolent direct action
in advance of August 12. On the morning of July 23, Rev. Sekou was a
guest at the monthly breakfast. His visit coincided with one from Chief
Thomas. The reality of the looming rally suddenly seemed to register on
everyone, as did the scale and seriousness of Congregate's preparations.

Rev. Alvin Edwards's anger at being sidelined was unmistakable.
Seth bore the brunt of it. For those like Rev. Elaine Thomas or Rev. Phil
Woodson, who remained loyal members of the collective but had also
chosen to attend Sekou's workshops, it was painful. After describing his
trainings to the assembled clergy, Rev. Sekou fell quiet. He was raised to
respect his elders. He nonetheless believed that Rev. Edwards, and the
white ministers hiding behind him, were wrong not to support them. A
Quaker who was new to the Clergy Collective joined a planning and logistics committee to work out what sort of action the collective might undertake, independently of Congregate, but it soon became clear Rev. Edwards
wasn't interested. Later, the collective released a carefully worded statement. Because of the possibility of violence, they would not sponsor any
events. "We do NOT recommend that you be in Emancipation Park on
August 12 unless you have received training in non-violent, direct action."

On August 1 Smash held a press conference on the front steps of St.
Paul's Memorial Church. Seth, Pastor Brenda, and Rev. Elaine Thomas
stood with her as fellow clergy. Don Gathers, Jalane Schmidt, and
Katrina Turner were present, representing the Charlottesville chapter
of Black Lives Matter. Before a bank of local news cameras Smash announced Congregate's call for a thousand clergy to come to Charlottesville
to stand with them in support of their message: "Hate has no home here."
August 12 would be a national moment with implications for the entire
country, she said. When Pastor Brenda spoke, she said she was prouder
of Charlottesville than she ever thought she would be. Dr. Cornel West,
Rev. Traci Blackmon, the celebrated faith writers Lisa Sharon Harper and
Brian McLaren had already answered Congregate's call. Smash hoped

outsiders would make up the deficit in numbers. Seth raised $30,000 in twelve days.

In early August, Rev. Sekou realized, belatedly, they also needed to prepare for the threat of "civilian on civilian engagement." Tracy Wispelwey suggested bringing in Sarah Nahar of Christian Peacemaker Teams. Christian Peacemaker believed it was easy to be a pacifist when you are protected by the world's largest military. What if Christians were willing to sacrifice their lives the way soldiers are? In two workshops over two days, Nahar trained people in live shooter drills and sniper fire. She demonstrated how to move someone who's been shot and how to communicate under gunfire. To help people manage their fears, she described what happens emotionally when you are targeted by violent people. Finally, she taught them that the greatest power comes from absolute vulnerability.

Bonnie Gordon, the UVA music professor who had attended Wes Bellamy's press conference, had three children. Hebrew school had prepared them for the racism of the July 8 Klan rally, but not the anti-Semitism. Now her teenage son wanted to attend Rev. Sekou's workshops. She thought Unite the Right was no place for a fourteen-year-old Jewish kid and his legally blind mother, but she supposed he needed to know what to expect. Subjected to racial epithets and recordings of gunshots, they lasted fifteen minutes.

After each workshop, a smaller group would return to Seth and Tracy's house, where Rev. Sekou was staying, for dinner. They discussed how to maintain discipline and how not to "lose the middle." The DC chapter of BLM was pushing for a more radical stance, but Sekou felt this would not go down well in Charlottesville. He was counting on white activists and anti-fascists to keep the rallygoers contained. To have Black men with guns in the middle of that was a bad idea. As for the growing feeling of dread, Seth's meals took the edge off, as did Rev. Sekou's teasing and gallows humor. Weed also helped.

They kept returning to the question of how much real danger the rally-goers posed. Emily Gorcenski was reporting chatter suggesting the far right planned to kill people; they were sharing memes showing cars and farm machinery mowing down protesters. Those who had experienced the brute violence of private security at Standing Rock or the militarized police in Ferguson were tempted to think this was mere shitposting by seventeen-year-olds living in their mothers' basements. Others imagined that the violence wouldn't rise above Trump rally–type dustups. Eric Martin, a Catholic Worker, thought Rev. Sekou was being alarmist. *No one was going to die*, he thought to himself. Someone finally asked Rev. Sekou directly: What were the chances there'd be fatalities? He was blunt about the stakes. "It's not a matter of whether they'll try to murder someone, but whether they'll succeed."

The official threat assessment was laid out in a July 27 briefing that took place just outside Richmond at the offices of Virginia Fusion Center, the intelligence arm of the Virginia State Police. The Charlottesville Police Department was not invited. Governor Terry McAuliffe would later give the impression that the briefing focused on armed neo-Nazis and white supremacists, but Mike Signer remembered his briefing was all about the threat posed by "Antifa" and "black bloc." Descriptions of anti-fascist tactics predominated, including reports of leftist subversives bringing fentanyl and cans filled with cement, and Antifa stashing caches of bricks in the area around Emancipation Park. No one recalled being briefed on the threat posed by armed militias or armed neo-Nazis.

It wasn't just Fusion Center analysts who tarred everyone planning to protest the rally with the "Antifa" brush. Signer made a habit of it, too, as if the Downtown Mall had been under siege by black bloc all summer. In his book about the events of that summer, Signer included a militaristic "far left" poster in his photo section, captioned: "'Antifa' members produced their own images designed to galvanize those seeking to confront the United [*sic*] the Right ralliers." But the photograph (credited to Signer's wife) wasn't an "Antifa" poster but a Vanguard America one, featuring their logo: an eagle carrying a fasces with an ax. Meanwhile, on Discord, those planning to attend Unite the Right were giddy at the prospect of cracking heads.

In advance of the rally, the Virginia State Police held field training exercises without the Charlottesville Police Department and never shared their operational plan with Chief Thomas. While City Manager Maurice Jones couldn't get anyone at the FBI to return his calls, the state government seemed intent on withholding its expertise and cooperation from those who most needed it. This was all in due deference to the Dillon Rule, which put Chief Thomas nominally in charge, though his 95 officers would be far outnumbered by 600 state troopers and 115 members of the National Guard.

Meanwhile, officers of the Charlottesville Police Deptartment had been meeting with Unite the Right advance men for weeks. Every phone call and face-to-face meeting gave Jason Kessler and Eli Mosley an opportunity to warn of the danger posed by "Antifa." After the Klan rally, Eli Mosley reassured everyone that the police would be "incredibly hands on with Antifa," so they should sit back and let the police do their job. "In our communications [law enforcement] know that the left are the ones looking to do violence."

On August 2 Maj. Gary Pleasants, the officer who had okayed the use of tear gas on July 8, was scheduled to meet with city residents worried about the lack of communication with law enforcement. Though activists sometimes relied on go-betweens, many of them made a point of never engaging with cops. The woman who requested the meeting shared their qualms, but she wanted to clear the air so that August 12 wouldn't be a repeat of July 8. The night before their meeting, Pleasants canceled.

After their own Fusion Center briefing, the city council held a closed session to hear what a white-shoe law firm had to say about the legal case for moving the rally in the face of an inevitable court challenge from Kessler. The law firm came to the same conclusion the city's lawyers had: it was a tough case. Nonetheless, under pressure from Mayor Signer the city council voted in closed session to recommend the permit be contingent on the rally being held at McIntire Park. By then Gov. McAuliffe had become sufficiently engaged to realize the upcoming rally had the makings of a black eye for him. To cover his derriere, he called Signer and read off a series of talking points. The rally was a week away.

The day after the Fusion Center briefing, the closed council session, and the call from the governor, City Manager Maurice Jones finally relented. He told Jason Kessler his permit was contingent on his moving the rally. He cited the estimated thousand rallygoers who planned to attend, which was far more than Kessler's application estimate of four hundred. When Kessler refused to consider it, Jones canceled his permit. This had an electrifying effect on Discord chatter.

Kessler wrote to Nathan Damigo and Brad Griffin of Occidental Dissent: "We aren't moving the rally under any circumstances." Damigo followed up on the Identity Evropa channel. "City can shove their permit up their ass." Richard Spencer put out a YouTube video mocking the city. It was an open-and-shut case, he said, chuckling in disbelief. After asking Jason Kessler to swear up and down that his rally would be peaceful, the ACLU filed a motion for a preliminary injunction on his behalf, arguing that the rationale behind the rally was bound up with the Lee statue. A hearing was scheduled for August 11. Chief Thomas would have to draw up an operational plan for two locations.

Thomas secretly hoped Kessler's motion for an injunction would be granted. He believed he could better control things at Emancipation Park. According to one of his captains, Thomas suppressed actionable intelligence to weaken the city's case. Even the August 9 memo of the Office of Intelligence and Analysis at Homeland Security, concluding that the Unite the Right rally "could be among the most violent to date," was not included. Moreover, the Daily Stormer appeared to have a CPD source confirming this: "We have it on good authority that the chief of police is going to ensure that the protest goes through as planned, regardless of what the ruling kike/Negroid powers are attempting."

Violence in America has created its own media ecosystem. Mass shootings, school shootings, and cop killings of Black people can put a town or a city on the map overnight. Journalists from major newspapers or networks fly in, burdened with the skepticism or despair that comes from carrying these stories with them from place to place. All hope for at least one soul-piercing sound bite or image to distill the madness with the point of a switchblade. Often, all they have time for are interviews with victims' families and footage of stage-managed press briefings. There may be a long read months later or, years later, trial coverage.

With Unite the Right, the media had advance notice that a controversial and possibly violent event was going to take place in a small and pretty Southern city more associated with Thomas Jefferson than civil unrest. Consequently, an unpredictable spectacle was on offer. Citizen journalists who specialized in covering the rise of the militant right would livestream the rally on YouTube or Periscope or Facebook. Many of them would try to interview the major alt-right personalities. To preempt the far right's messaging and to frame the approaching rally from a local, social justice perspective, Rev. Sekou first approached the Movement for Black Lives coalition for help. They told him they considered the controversies over Confederate statues "a white people's problem," not bearing on their mission. Sekou then turned to Andy Stepanian of Balestra Media. Stepanian showed up with his team in early August.

Stepanian had spent three years in prison for having violated the Animal Enterprise Protection Act, an Orwellian law aimed at anyone trying to curb industrial practices involving acts of animal cruelty. From this experience he learned that the right communication strategies can shift public opinion. In the long lead up to the verdict that left the officer who shot Michael Brown a free man, Stepanian had represented the youth of Ferguson, Missouri, connecting them to mainstream media outlets so their voices could be heard. Until he arrived, it was police department spokespersons who framed the narrative.

Laura Goldblatt, the grad student working with Jalane Schmidt and Lisa Woolfork on media outreach, was grateful to have the experience and added capacity Stepanian provided. The three women had worked together in advance of the Klan rally, but the frenzy surrounding the approach of Unite the Right was overwhelming. Stepanian was adept at gaining people's trust, telling a compelling narrative, refining talking points, and juggling calls from the press. He did line edits and churned out press releases. He tightened up messaging. He was, like Goldblatt herself, focused, methodical, and plainspoken.

One of their tasks was to coach the activists they had chosen for Katie

Couric to interview for a Nat Geo documentary she was producing on the rise of hate in America. Both Rosia Parker and Katrina Turner were on the list. Flamboyant and fearless, they planned on showing up to confront the racists so that their children and grandchildren wouldn't have to. Goldblatt hoped their voices would be heard over the Nazi noise. Laura and Andy prepped Rosia, Katrina, Seth, Don Gathers, Zyahna Bryant, and Pastor Brenda.

On the afternoon of August 9, around thirty activists had gathered at the UVA conference room where Katie Couric and her crew were setting up. While they waited to be interviewed, Stepanian reviewed with the activist leaders a series of hypotheticals to get a handle on what kind of response they wanted to go with. Midway through, a white activist asked a question: How would they respond if someone was killed? He volunteered to draft talking points and write a press release before quickly changing the subject.

"Don't downplay this!" the activist shouted at him, thinking he was dismissing her concerns. "Somebody is going to *fucking* die this weekend."

Stepanian's face turned red. Could she not see that Katie Couric was right there? To the press such a statement could be read as histrionic or even threatening. He was so spooked he never got around to writing the in-case-of-death press release. Goldblatt was also upset. This was off message. Experienced activists knew you should never ever give the press a story you didn't want them to tell. Soon there was another fire to put out. As white supremacists from across the country were boarding flights, renting vans, and taking selfies of themselves kitted out with shields, weapons, and body armor, the *Daily Progress* ran its editorial blaming Wes Bellamy for Unite the Right.

As the clock ticked down, tensions flared. The Charlottesville chapter of Black Lives Matter held a meeting at the Unitarian church to clear the air. Katrina Turner, a small, fierce woman with curly gray hair, had found her voice as a young mother raising a special needs child. She had to fight to get him the care he needed. She and her best friend, Rosia Parker, were unfaltering BLM partisans. At meetings, however, it seemed that whatever they had to say went in one ear and out the other of college-educated folks like Jalane Schmidt and Lisa Woolfork. She and Rosia got their education in the streets. They didn't need lectures on their oppressors from Black folks who married white people. And she didn't like it when they shut white people out. When Katrina's son was unjustly arrested and brutalized by the Charlottesville police, she took her complaint to city council. There it was Star Peterson, the white teacher with a special ed background and stalwart of the Fuck You Kessler crowd, who was the first to reach out in support. Katrina's kin included both white and Black folks. Some white people had been through hell, too, she said. They needed to listen to everybody. She made her feelings known.

Meanwhile, Congregate did a walk-through of the liturgy planned for St. Paul's the night before the rally. Hotels were being booked, trips to the airport to meet arriving clergy arranged, and safe houses secured.

On the eve of Unite the Right, Andrew Anglin told his Stormer troll army their time had come. Who are we? he asked them, like a coach preparing a team to hit the field. "We are a generation of throwaways." He itemized their humiliations. Student loans for worthless degrees. Meaningless wars fought in, suffered for, and lost. Struggles with drugs, women, and feelings of emasculation. To relieve them of their shame, he directed their attention to the root cause of their tribulations: Jews. He told them to wear their fury as a badge of honor and draw from it a source of brotherly solidarity. "There is an atavistic rage in us, deep in us, that is ready to boil over," he wrote. "There is a craving to return to an age of violence. We want a war." Under the handle AryanBlood1488, Dylann Roof had been a habitué of the Daily Stormer. Who was listening to Anglin now?

The closer Azzmador got to August 12, the more excited he became. "I always come bare-fisted and bare headed," he boasted, "but my guys will be ready with lots of nifty equipment." While his guys were off buying pepper spray at Walmart, he was ordering up shields and arranging transport. There was a brief hiccup when Airbnb canceled all their reservations, but Azzmador swept in with Krypto coins and booked them all in a Waynesboro Days Inn. The Stormer account had a rough balance of $300,000.

To forestall "Antifa" or BLM taking the space set aside for the rally,

Azzmador planned to arrive early. He'd take on BLM first because Black people were easier to trigger. He imagined himself leading the charge, he saw their shields crashing into Black bodies with such force that they would spend the rest of their lives trying to forget the moment. How awesome this would be, he said, and how proud he was of them all.

Signing off, he posted a meme of Hitler in his Daimler-Benz with the caption:

GET IN LOSER WE'RE INVADING CHARLOTTESVILLE!

The Stormers were ready to leave the house.

INTERLUDE

A School for Backward Southern Whites

Growing up in Ivy, eight miles west of Charlottesville, I preferred the mountains, woods, and streams of Albemarle County to the tony, pastel-clad country club and garden society of "town." We lived in a hollow without TV or radio reception. Meriwether Lewis, whose birthplace was down the road, figured a great deal in my imagination. Pocahontas too. Monticello's director, James Bear, was a neighbor; his tomboy daughter was my friend. Though I was only vaguely aware, Mr. Bear was changing our understanding of Thomas Jefferson through archaeology; in material artefacts like textiles and pottery shards, he unearthed the silenced lives of those who left no other records. In 1967 he published an annotated edition of the memoirs of a Monticello slave.

That year my third-grade classroom at Meriwether Lewis Elementary included one Black classmate. Leon always sat at the same desk, never missed a day of school, and never said a word. No one ever spoke to him, not even the teacher. My father had attended Meriwether Lewis back when it was a high school. What was it like to grow up in a segregated school, I once asked him. He said that the worst thing about it, in retrospect, was that he hadn't noticed. I felt certain then that I would have noticed. I'm no longer so sure of that. I left too many other questions unasked.

While delving into the era of Massive Resistance during my spring 2018 residency at UVA, I began coming across the names of people I

knew as a child. When the governor shut down Charlottesville's public schools rather than integrate them, Nancy Manson, a friend of my
grandmother's, organized ad hoc schoolrooms in romper rooms and
basements. Anyone who signed up their children for classes had to
pledge they'd return to the reopened public schools when they were
integrated. Another neighbor, the wife of the county sheriff George
Bailey, became the principal of Rockhill Academy, one of the taxpayer-
subsidized segregation academies founded during this period.

While at UVA that spring, I met a woman named Wendy Baucom.
She had been at the first meeting of Showing Up for Racial Justice in
Bekah Menning's living room. As wife of UVA's dean of the School of
Arts and Sciences, she and her family lived on the Lawn. The pavilions
that line the Lawn are home to emeritus professors and senior administration officials. She told me she'd been at home when Richard Spencer
returned to his alma mater with hundreds of torch-bearing men the
night before the rally. In 2018 I was still teasing out what had happened
in the summer of 1956. Another year would pass before I realized I
needed to write about Unite the Right. Wendy Baucom introduced me
to Bekah Menning.

And what of that Charlottesville housewife? The one who introduced
me to the saga of John Kasper and Ezra Pound? I asked my father if
he had known her. He had a vague recollection that General George S.
Patton had relations in town, but his memory wasn't as sharp as it once
had been.

When Sarah Patton Lindsay was a child, these were her fairy tales.
That the South stood for something fine and brave. That Virginia was
exceptional in the same way that America, above all other nations,
was. And, because the best people in Virginia tended to marry each
other, Virginians were a breed apart from the regular run of Americans.
Finally, to be a Virginian was to live in accordance with the most exact-
ing code of chivalry, "for here the ideals of the nation were born." Her
mother and grandmother would drop their voices when they told her
she was born into the very first of the First Families of Virginia. She
took that with a grain of salt. Still, she never doubted she was a direct

descendant of the English and Scottish nobility who had first settled the colony. That she was of the same blood as the presidents, generals, and governors who followed them. If Virginia was a microcosm of America; Albemarle County was a microcosm of Virginia.

Her friends called her Patty.

It would be left to Patty's father, a doctor of divinity and field secretary for the Episcopal Church, to calculate what the Civil War had cost his family. He had grown up on a plantation of four thousand acres tended by 163 slaves, not far from Shadwell, where Thomas Jefferson was born. On the modest salary of a clergyman, out of a quixotic sense of Southern honor, or an unconscious act of penance, he had chosen to discharge his own father's many debts. While Patty's maternal grandfather had been Robert E. Lee's personal scout, her father's father had been a colonel under General Stonewall Jackson's command. To settle the colonel's accounts, Rev. Lindsay borrowed on his life insurance and sold or mortgaged the family land. After the war, conspicuous displays of wealth were considered disreputable. If you hadn't lost everything to the Cause, you hadn't sacrificed everything. After Patty's father's death, the Lindsays lived in genteel poverty. Patty and her older sister Alice grew up in hand-me-downs, without a car twenty miles from town, and no prospect of education.

As a young woman, Patty was introduced to the writer Allen Tate. Tate was both the critic who would soon review Ezra Pound's first thirty cantos, and one of the twelve Southerners whose 1930 manifesto, *I'll Take My Stand*, had found a sympathetic reader in T. S. Eliot. Patty had likely met him in the summer of 1931 when the University of Virginia hosted the Southern Writers Conference featuring Tate and his fellow Agrarians from Vanderbilt University in Nashville.

The Agrarians aspired to relitigate the Civil War. Exhuming the agrarian philosophy of Thomas Jefferson, they reframed the war as a defense of rural values and Southern folkways in the face of the depredations of Northern materialism and industrialization. Their vision of the New South translated into a racially exclusive, quasi-spiritual nostalgia for the prelapsarian, antebellum one. Tate's biographies of Stonewall Jackson and Jefferson Davis portray the Unionists as the true traitors.

His poem "Ode to the Confederate Dead" was the South's answer to *The Waste Land*. The work of the Agrarians can be found on a syllabus for a course titled "The Southern Tradition and Modernity" offered by the League of the South's Institute for the Study of Southern Culture and History. As recently as 2021, William Wilson, a colleague of Jalane Schmidt's in UVA's religious studies department, was listed among the institute's faculty, alongside the founder of the League of the South, Dr. Michael Hill.

Allen Tate prized the Lindsay sisters not for their cleverness or literary culture, but for their Virginia pedigree. "Me and Brer Lytle is a-coming to old Virginny agin in about two weeks," Tate wrote a year after they first met, in the Uncle Remus dialect he, along with Pound and Eliot, found so amusing. While Tate fell for Alice, his younger protégé, Andrew Lytle, was smitten with Patty. After a yearlong courtship, she accepted his proposal of marriage only to renege. I imagine she was unable to leave her beloved Albemarle for another debt-plagued farm in Depression-era Tennessee. However ennobling in Jeffersonian principle, agrarianism without the free labor provided by the enslaved had proved difficult in practice for the Lytle family. Lytle's 1931 biography of Gen. Nathan Bedford Forrest, the first Grand Wizard of the Invisible Empire, portrayed him as a "quintessential Christian warrior" with a soft spot for his human property.

Twenty years after her abandoned nuptials, married to a University of Virginia assistant professor and the mother of two teenage boys, Mrs. Roger Boyle was a forty-two-year-old housewife and freelancer, writing articles on domestic science for national women's magazines. The imminent arrival of a Black law student at Mr. Jefferson's University marked the beginning of her undoing. In 1950, the NAACP had won Gregory Swanson's admission to UVA's Law School in a case heard at the courthouse that later became the library across the street from Lee Park. Thurgood Marshall, of the NAACP Legal Defense Fund, his Richmond associate Spottswood Robinson III, and Mr. Swanson celebrated their win by posing for a photograph in front of the Lee statue. Much as the *Nature* article on Jeffersonian DNA would fifty years later, the Swanson case had set the university and the city abuzz and on edge.

Patty decided this was the moment for the good people of Virginia, her people, to show the world who they really were. She appointed herself Gregory Swanson's one-woman welcoming committee. She was convinced no one understood "the Negro," indeed no one *loved* the Negro as much as she did. When she approached Charlottesville's "New Negroes" for advice on how best to settle the young Swanson in, she was in uncharted waters. Until that moment, she'd never addressed a Black man using an honorific, much less one who was far more educated than she was. She was a little giddy and rather surprised at herself.

It thus came as something of a shock when she was met not with gratitude but with scarcely disguised hostility. Even Gregory Swanson took offense at her cringe-inducing Lady Bountiful airs when she volunteered to coach him on how to avoid stepping over certain social lines. Only a Black newspaper editor was brave enough to laugh in her face.

T. J. Sellers did not agree with Patty Boyle's conviction that the best people of Virginia would do the right thing by "our Negroes." In the early years of their acquaintance his chilly asperity sometimes reduced her to tears. But she kept going back. She soon began referring to their conversations as "The T. J. Sellers School for Backward Southern Whites." Two years into her apprenticeship, Sellers gave her a column in his paper, the *Charlottesville-Albemarle Tribune*, inviting his readers to contribute to her schooling. "If there really is all this good will toward Negroes in the South," one reader inquired politely, "why are you the only person who has noticed it?" She remained undaunted.

Boyle began submitting and publishing letters to the editors of Virginia's major papers about desegregation. She used various arguments, signed with variations on her name: Patty Patton, Sarah P. Boyle, Mrs. Roger Boyle, S. L. Patton, Sarah Lindsay. It was a fifties' version of sock puppets. Times had changed, she pointed out in one letter. It made good economic sense to bestow education on a deserving few, she argued in another. This was the Christian thing to do, went a third. When the editors wouldn't let her use pseudonyms, she bullied friends and her sister Alice into letting her write letters on their behalf, often rising before dawn so her cause wouldn't interfere with her housework. She undertook amateur surveys of UVA students and faculty. Her intent was to summon a groundswell of support for "our dusky brothers," among prominent Virginians. Virginians such as herself.

It wasn't long before Mrs. Boyle became the talk of the editorial offices at the *Richmond Times-Dispatch*. She had offered to write a weekly column charting the progress of desegregation in the state. The paper's longtime editor, Virginius Dabney, later to write the takedown of Fawn Brodie's 1974 Jefferson biography, told her this would only stir up the Ku Kluxers. Boyle called this the "let's not make a fuss school of thought" and did not subscribe to it.

Not long before the 1954 *Brown v. Board of Education* decision, Sellers accepted a job as managing editor at the *Amsterdam News* in New York City, leaving Patty Boyle to see for herself just what the best people of Virginia were really made of. That summer she took a course at the university to help her overcome her fear of public speaking. During the single public hearing of Senator Byrd's Commission on Public Education, held in Richmond that November, Patty Boyle spoke publicly of her support for desegregation for the first time, weaponizing her mighty clubwoman's voice.

"There is nothing in our hearts to make this change difficult if only we get a little help from our leaders," she declared. A handful of whites spoke up in agreement. A few advocated keeping the schools open but with minimum compliance. But sixty-eight segregationists, including most of the state's political leadership, held the floor for eleven hours, promising all hell would break loose if public schools allowed Black children to sit alongside white ones.

The bitterest pill for Patty Boyle to swallow? Not one faculty member from the University of Virginia showed up.

Two years later, on Saturday, August 18, 1956, Patty Boyle attended John Kasper's rally in McIntire Park. She went out of curiosity, standing apart from the riffraff in the stands, while Kasper led the crowd in a chant: "Honor, pride, fight. Save the White."

The South was looking to Virginia for leadership, Kasper declared. The "red-controlled Supreme Court" had chosen Charlottesville to be the first Virginia city to integrate. If they didn't make a stand now, the NAACP would soon be arranging marriages "between Nigras and Whites." He called for a school strike. Posters carried the names and telephone numbers of the handful of local people working on desegregation efforts, including Patty's. City residents were urged to make their feelings known to them directly. A flyer in lofty Poundian rhetoric called out those "homos, perverts, freaks, poodle dogs, hot eyed Socialists, Fabians, scum, liars for hire" intent on destroying their Southern way of life. Of the two hundred and fifty who attended the rally, one hundred and fifty took applications to Kasper's Seaboard White Citizens Council. Charlottesville was only Kasper's first stop; he had plans to stage similar rallies across the South.

Patty Boyle encountered John Kasper in person five days later when he crashed a meeting of the Virginia Council on Human Relations at Westminster Presbyterian Church. He bounded up to the pulpit, called out their thirty-odd members as "flat-chested high brows," and threatened to run them all out of town. His verbal fusillade was met with titters and a polite request that he leave. Adjourning early, they found a cross burning on the church lawn. To a friend who asked about him, Boyle was thoughtful. Kasper was a hollow man, she said, with no real beliefs. He watched events unfold with the dispassion of a man who sets fires to determine what makes them burn brighter and faster. "He gets great satisfaction out of seeing things happen, knowing that he's responsible." She found him sinister. Kasper skipped town that night, heading for the Deep South, never to return.

A few days later, Patty Boyle noticed the light of a burning cross shining through her bedroom window from her front yard. The next cross burning, on the lawn of a white Sunday school teacher who had written a letter in favor of desegregation to the *Daily Progress*, never properly caught fire. By the close of the school year she had sold her house and moved north. The last of the four crosses was found on the front lawn of a Black doctor's house in December, but it had burned out by the time he returned from the interracial meeting he'd just attended.

Boyle chose to see her cross not as a threat but as a sacred symbol of eternal love. The *Daily Progress* ran a photograph of her posing with it. She kept the cross for many years, pinned with the mock Latin motto:

"Illegitimi non carborund um" (Don't let the bastards grind you down). It's now in the Special Collections Library at the University of Virginia.

Immersing myself in Sarah Patton Boyle's papers in the spring of 2018, I watched the fairy tales Miss Patty Lindsay was raised on die a slow death. Poisonous letters addressed her as a stinker, scalawag, carpet-bagger, dirty slut, white trash, Judas, and the inescapable nigger lover. Every time her name appeared in the *Daily Progress*, bomb threats woke her in the middle of the night. But it was the moral cowardice of the Virginia elite that burned the most. She took it as a personal betrayal.

By the time Massive Resistance closed Charlottesville's schools, Boyle had long been a social pariah. Her husband's university colleagues shunned her. Her marriage was over. Her sister Alice had stopped returning her calls. Though she tried to maintain her sense of humor, she couldn't avoid knowing she was hated, and not just by the men who called her in the middle of the night, but by her own people. She wrote T. J. Sellers that she felt like a man without a country. There were times when she wished she was dead. Eventually, she stopped telling herself, *Now they've gone too far, and the decent Southerners will rebel.* Because they never *ever* did. Her decade-long effort to prick the consciences of Virginians had failed. It was the NAACP's unflagging legal challenges that defeated segregation, not Patty Boyle and the First Families of Virginia.

In September 1959, nine months after the Massive Resistance loop-hole laws were declared unconstitutional, a handful of carefully chosen Black children walked through the doors of an all-white public school. Among those climbing the steps of Venable Elementary were Thelma Townsend's sons, William and Marvin, Zyahna Bryant's granduncles. Her grandmother Vizena would follow them. The streets did not run with blood. The world did not end.

Three weeks into the school year, Patty Boyle felt a dark cloud lift. The air freshened. Old friends resurfaced. Apparently, she was no lon-ger the kiss of death. She was now a hard-charging Southerner. A rebel even. A sweet-faced woman grabbed her arm at the grocery store. "You'll never know what you meant to me through all this," she said. "You saved my faith in the South."

Patty Boyle nearly slapped her.

She'd once considered the warmth and graciousness of Virginians, like the natural beauty of Albemarle County, an outward manifestation of an inner spiritual grace. No longer. The sight of her beloved Blue Ridge Mountains left her cold. "What a different picture Virginia would have presented had they stood up to be counted in 1954!" she wrote to Gregory Swanson, UVA's first Black law student. When St. Paul's Memorial Church failed to speak up in support of Dr. King's March on Selma, Patty Boyle left the church she'd attended for eighteen years for Trinity Episcopal, a Black church in the 10th and Page neighborhood. She tithed there for the rest of her life, even after she left Charlottesville. She put on a brave face in her letters to T. J. Sellers in New York, but in truth she never recovered her bearings.

It might be argued that Boyle's disillusionment and sense of bitter personal betrayal arose more from bruised vanity than a fierce sense of injustice. But perhaps it doesn't matter what led Patty Boyle to make a fuss over integration. She listened, she learned, and, whatever it cost her, she never backed down. There is a tiny plaque bearing her name, and another for T. J. Sellers, on the bridge that crosses over the north–south tracks on West Main Street above the Amtrak rail station. When I'm in town I pass by it nearly every day.

John Kasper found more fertile fields of conflict in Alabama and Tennessee. He joined forces with Asa Carter, a Klan firebrand out of Alabama, who had given a speech at his Charlottesville rally. Carter is credited with writing Governor George Wallace's inaugural address demanding "segregation now, segregation tomorrow, segregation forever," a speech that echoed Ezra Pound's "Segregation Forever" leaflets Kasper left around Charlottesville in 1956. Before that year was out, Kasper would gain national notoriety, alarming those Pound defenders advocating for his release from St. Elizabeth's. Of the eighty-eight bombing incidents in the Deep South between 1955 and 1960, sixteen or more of them directly involved John Kasper and his close confederates.

"We got it Gramp," he wrote in triumph to Pound. "I repeat, the people are alive and are ready. . . . This is the proving ground, and we feel the eyes of the Nashun are on Alabam."

Kasper signed off with a Chinese character, a swastika, and a Confederate flag.

Mirroring the spate of Confederate statue commissions of the post-Reconstruction era, in the years following *Brown v. Board of Education*, dozens of Virginia public schools were named after Confederate officers. Charlottesville's schools weren't fully integrated until 1962. The state wouldn't stop paying for private school vouchers until 1968. That year my father finished writing a thin volume titled *Strike the Tent: In the Steps of Robert E. Lee's Army of Northern Virginia*. Its publication was timed to coincide with the centenary of Lee's death. Its frontispiece was a photograph of the Lee statue in Lee Park.

In the spring of 2020, I was in Charlottesville for the last of my monthlong spring residencies at UVA. I arrived days before the Covid lockdown. My commitments were canceled and my access to archives suspended indefinitely. I found a copy of my father's book on the shelves of my childhood home in Ivy. A yellowing clip of the *Daily Progress* review fell out when I opened it. "A most fitting tribute to Lee's memory," it read. The book was illustrated with moody photographs of Virginia's Civil War battlefields.

Though my paternal ancestors, prominent New England abolitionists, had fought on the side of the Union, my father had moved to Albemarle County as a young boy. He prefaced his account of Lee's campaign by saying that if the book seemed "a bit sentimental and slanted in favor of the men in butternut and gray," that was because he had told their story as "they would have wanted it to be told." I put the book aside. I was mourning the death of my mother; my father was dying of heartbreak. It wasn't the time to talk to him about the Lost Cause.

After his death later that summer and before returning home to New York, I picked the book up again and looked at his preface more closely. "Those who read into this story an attempt to glorify further the Army of Northern Virginia or revive the antagonism that led to its formation have missed the point." This was his point: "What men may sincerely believe they are fighting for is often unrelated to the consequences of their doing so." The Confederate soldier was "fighting for the extension of an institution—slavery—which was the complete opposite of individual liberty and freedom," which they imagined their cause to be.

While my father was finishing *Strike the Tent*, America was tearing itself apart over Vietnam. Was he revisiting the battlegrounds of the Civil War to fathom the scale of the bloodletting then underway? To comprehend the national compulsion behind yet another suicidal war? Or was he trying to understand the persistence of the delusion that every American war is a war fought on behalf of freedom. The Jeffersonian language of individual liberty and natural rights has too often worked in the service of white supremacy and civil insurrection, just as it has in wars of conquest and land theft. As the Unite the Right rally would show, freedom's war cry still haunts us, while true liberation still eludes us.

"If destruction be our lot," Lincoln wrote, "we must ourselves be its author and finisher."

PART III

Unite the Right

August 11 & 12, 2017

CHAPTER 11

Nameless Field

The morning before the Unite the Right rally, Emily Gorcenski posted a link to an Al Jazeera story about the coming weekend to her ten thousand–plus followers. "What we do on Saturday has consequences for the rest of the country and maybe the rest of the world," she wrote. "It may be the catalyst." Richard Spencer was making similar claims. Emily asked her followers to spread the word before finishing her coffee.

Two days before, she had learned from her sources about a possible Friday night torch march. Her instinct told her it would take place at UVA, but as of that morning she was still awaiting confirmation. Then, just after 10:00 a.m., she suddenly swapped out her Black Lives Matter T-shirt for a Charlottesville Pride one. She also holstered a 9mm. Her followers were confused. She needed her SIG Sauer, she explained, and BLM didn't endorse guns. More questions. Yes, the rally was tomorrow, but she was worried about today. She didn't elaborate, but she'd received the confirmation she'd been waiting for: the torch march would take place that evening at UVA.

Emily's most powerful weapon was her phone. She took a selfie of her outfit, the cuffed jeans, her favorite shoes. A noteworthy mountain of clothes was piled on the dresser behind her. It had only been five months since her surgery. She was happier than she'd ever been. She loved her wife. She loved their home in Fifeville. And she adored her cat,

Toby. The best part was when she would catch sight of herself in a shop window. She hadn't forgotten what it was like to have more emotions than she knew how to handle. She knew the men trolling her couldn't bear the thought that a person like her existed. Part of their hatred was aimed at her transness, but they must have also resented how well she understood them.

Jason Kessler had recently unblocked her on Twitter so that he could keep tabs on her. With her selfie she was conveying to him that she was onto their evening plans and wasn't defenseless. Most of the outside activists traveling to Charlottesville would arrive that night. There wasn't time to organize a collective response. Assuming Kessler wouldn't be mobilizing more than the usual forty to fifty people, Emily quietly decided to livestream the torch march herself. Fielding compliments on her outfit and dispensing shoe advice one minute, describing what the weight of a 9mm in her hand felt like the next, Emily was twirling her cape at trolls watching her every move, taunting them while addressing her followers' questions. Her DMs filled with death threats.

The Charlottesville police chief, mayor, and city manager were still advising everyone not to "take the bait." This chorus had been joined by the president of the University of Virginia, Teresa Sullivan. In an August 4 email to the university community, Sullivan acknowledged that many of the participating groups "express beliefs that directly contradict our community's values." Yet the prospect of anyone defending those values alarmed her. Beyond her fear of physical confrontation, Sullivan believed that showing up in any fashion would simply "satisfy their craving for spectacle" and "help their cause." To act according to one's conscience, one religious studies professor noted, was thus made an act of complicity. A law professor pointed out that in failing to meet the moment, the university was betraying their most vulnerable students and treating those who wanted to defend them like children. Jalane Schmidt tried to penetrate the institutional blinkers. In a draft of an open letter, she wrote, "You are discouraging our public protest against the very white supremacy that UVA helped to construct."

Instead, Sullivan invited students to attend Saturday's soccer game for a meet-the-teams rally. There would also be a series of panel discussions on the Constitution and local history. Where the League of the South's spokesman saw a pivotal historical moment, one that would bring the underground culture war to the surface where it would explode "like a volcano," Teresa Sullivan pitched Movie Night at Scott Stadium.

But there was another troublesome aspect to the university's position. They assumed the students and faculty would have a choice in the matter. Despite several red flags alerting them to the fact that the white supremacists were doing them the favor of coming to UVA's Grounds, the university administration was glacially slow to register this simple fact.

Emily scoffed at Sullivan's idea that these men were making a bid for attention. "People who want attention don't use private, invite-only Facebook groups," she wrote. "They don't use codenames. They don't obscure their faces in photos." Ignoring Nazis had never been an option for her. Queer people, including the trans people who populated Berlin's demimonde, were among Hitler's first targets. Three months after Hitler was made chancellor, the library of the Institute of Sexology in Berlin was burned to the ground. The criminalization of homosexuality was followed by mass arrests. Homosexuals were subjected to castration and experimentation, and disappeared in the camps alongside Jews, the disabled, and Roma.

Despite her newfound community of activists, Emily still had the habits of a loner. The truly hard part of any task, she said, wasn't technical. Success or failure was dependent on how well you organized stakeholders as a team, much as she once did as a raid leader in *World of Warcraft*. Such "soft skills" were generally looked down upon by tech people, because tech people by and large don't have them. Even to call such skills soft is misleading, she said. They are hard.

To that end, she worked with online anti-fascists monitoring rally organizers and their plans so that everyone else could focus on that evening's service at St. Paul's Memorial Church or on preparations for Saturday. With her blue checkmark, which verified she was who she said she was, Emily provided them cover. While they organized behind the scenes, she made herself a target, just as she had as a Paladin in *World of Warcraft*.

Then Emily got an alert that Christopher Cantwell was already in town and had arranged a secret meetup with subscribers to his *Radical*

Agenda podcast. Cantwell had become a target of anti-fascists as soon as his name appeared as a speaker on Jason Kessler's Unite the Right poster. One of Emily's contacts had slipped onto his listserv. Cantwell's meetup was scheduled for noon at the Walmart parking lot on 29 North. Emily got in her truck and set off.

Tyler Magill was a fixture of the local music scene and worked part-time as a DJ at WTJU, the student-run radio station. He wasn't on anyone's Signal feed. Until he met his wife, he told me, he had lived like an idiot. He'd been sober for over a decade and though he struggled with depression, he had a good therapist. In the early summer of 2017, however, the death of his father in sordid circumstances had reawakened the trauma of an ugly family history, one he summarized as "bad Faulkner." That was when he began hanging out on Gab. Founded in 2016, Gab was the "free speech" alternative to Facebook and Twitter, providing a safe space for hatemongers of various stripes. Gab became a place for Magill to keep tabs on the jerks who kept showing up in his town. Sometimes he would get into it with them. He would be the first to admit this wasn't the most mature move.

On Friday morning Magill got a call from a friend on the West Coast who wanted to send him something. Did he have a secure email account? Magill opened a Proton Mail account and downloaded his friend's docs. Somebody had infiltrated the Discord planning channel for Unite the Right, and Magill now had the screenshots in which the torch march was being discussed. His first thought was: *Oh Christ.* His second thought was that if he had this, then everyone else must too. There was no way a forty-seven-year-old schmuck like him would know something the UVA brass didn't.

His wife and child were off visiting his Alabama in-laws. After work he had to run some errands, but then he would head back to his office at Alderman Library, just above Nameless Field, where the torch march would assemble. From there they would march to the Jefferson statue. It was here, at the foot of the steps of Jefferson's Rotunda, that Tyler Magill would first cross paths with Emily Gorcenski and a man named Kristopher Goad.

Kristopher Goad is a tall, lean brunet with lustrous and long wavy hair, a disco era mustache, heavy bangs, and Groucho eyebrows. Someone told me that if the fascists disappeared tomorrow, anti-fascists would return to drinking beer and playing *Pokémon Go*. Goad had an ongoing *Pokémon Go* practice, a pastime that eased the toll anti-fascist work took on him. A sous chef based in Richmond, he first came across the Virginia Flaggers in 2014, long before they made common cause with Jason Kessler. Back then they were demonstrating in front of the Confederate Memorial Chapel, not far from where he lived.

The chapel, a Carpenter Gothic structure, stands out like a sore thumb from the glassy facade of the neighboring Virginia Museum of Fine Arts, a central meeting spot for *Pokémon Go* raiders. VMFA and the Virginia History Museum, Goad told me, were built on what was once known as the "Old Soldier's Home," a twenty-four-acre site that had housed aging Confederate veterans until the last of them passed into the hereafter in 1941. This left the chapel, dedicated to the Confederate war dead, without a clear purpose. In 1993 the state government leased it to the Virginia division of the Sons of Confederate Veterans, but when the lease came up for renewal, the state made it a condition that the Confederate battle flag be removed from the chapel's interior. The Flaggers' sidewalk protests began after that.

Goad outfitted his bike with a boombox and for the next three years spent part of every weekend introducing the Flaggers to his favorite rap artists. During this time League of the South secessionist stickers began appearing on their cars. As time went on, he noticed that the Flaggers seemed to become increasingly chill with white nationalists. When he pointed out a KKK grand dragon in their midst, they shrugged it off. Any successful organization, they said, had a few bad apples. So, he would photograph and document who came and went for no other reason than a civic sense of duty. It wasn't until he met Laura Sennett, of Daryle Lamont Jenkins's One People's Project, that he realized he wasn't the only one paying attention. As Goad didn't drive, he limited his activities to the Richmond area unless he could cadge a ride. He and a group of five friends intended to be at the Friday night torch march.

Gorcenski, Magill, and Goad weren't the only ones with advance notice. Four days after Jason Kessler first proposed a torch march to Eli Mosley, a Virginia State Police intelligence analyst got wind of it. Her July 14 intelligence memo included the nature of the demonstration (a tiki torch march), the date (the night before the Unite the Right rally), and a location (the Jefferson statue on UVA Grounds). This intelligence was shared with the Charlottesville Police Department. They passed it on to the Albemarle County chief of police and, of course, the University Police Department.

This was UVA's first red flag. Unlike Kristopher Goad, they seemed to have filed it away and forgotten about it. Apparently, the Virginia State Police had too. Governor Terry McAuliffe would later accuse the Charlottesville Police Department, which he portrayed as utterly incompetent, of failing to share their intelligence about the torch march with the source of their intelligence about the torch march.

The only thing Goad didn't know was where it would take place. Like Emily Gorcenski and Tyler Magill, he heard from the person who had infiltrated the Discord planning channel on Friday morning. The torch march would begin at Nameless Field at 9:00 p.m. and go from there to the Jefferson statue in front of the Rotunda. Goad was told to keep this to himself. The funny thing about Nameless Field, Goad said, was that there were people on Discord thinking this was a code name. As the day wore on, they kept asking: When are they going to announce where we're meeting? He found that funny. As soon as he arrived in town, Goad and his friends bypassed Nameless Field and went directly to the Jefferson statue.

Work started early for Lt. Steve Knick of the Charlottesville Police Department. At 7:01 a.m. that Friday he confirmed that an officer recently returned from medical leave, Tammy Shiflett, would be stationed with her cruiser at the intersection of Fourth Street NE and Market Street on Saturday. This was one of two car crossings over the otherwise pedestrian-only Downtown Mall. If Kessler's rally ended up in Emancipation Park, the plan was to have both crossings closed to traffic on Saturday. At noon another CPD lieutenant had a final meeting with Richard Spencer's security chief, Jack Peirce, to go over the zone inside the park allotted to the rally's VIP speakers. When asked what he knew about an event that evening, Peirce confirmed they had something planned but refused to provide specifics.

Just after noon, Albemarle County Police received reports of someone brandishing a weapon and threatening customers in the Walmart parking lot. This turned out to be Christopher Cantwell, the podcast host and scheduled speaker. Cantwell was a bullet-headed, barrel-chested, short-fused, and pathologically garrulous man in his late thirties. He was also something of a nervous Nellie. He'd been trying to reach Richard Spencer all morning. He wanted reassurance that he wouldn't lose his right to carry if Jason Kessler failed to secure a permit for Emancipation Park, but Spencer wasn't picking up his calls or answering his texts. Having driven eight hours from Keene, New Hampshire, Cantwell was getting peeved.

"I'm willing to risk a lot, including violence and incarceration," he texted Spencer, "but I want to coordinate and make sure it's worth it to our cause." "It's worth it," Spencer finally replied. Mollified, Cantwell had invited him to his meetup, dangling the promise of media. A journalist from Vice News was following him around. Spencer declined. "Way too dangerous this weekend. I must focus." Spencer was spied lunching with David Duke in the plush safety of Boar's Head Inn, a country club. Coming directly from his meeting with the Charlottesville Police Department, Jack Peirce joined them.

A few cars away from Cantwell's Ford Taurus, Emily sat in her truck, watching a county police officer question him. Despite misdemeanor convictions for criminal trespass, criminal possession of stolen property, criminal possession of a firearm, public intoxication, drunk driving, and speeding, Christopher Cantwell was at his happiest chatting to law enforcement. He believed, not unreasonably, they were on his side, serving as a kind of superego to curb his worst impulses. Indeed, after checking his gun permit, they let him go. Emily tweeted a photo of Cantwell being questioned at Richard Spencer and Brad Griffin. "Tsk tsk, so many leaks," she wrote, trying to sow suspicion that she was everywhere and knew everything. Spooked, Spencer sent a go-between to the 7:00 p.m. Unite the Right leadership meeting at McIntire Park.

The Fusion Center intel about the torch march on UVA Grounds never made it to the desk of UVA president Teresa Sullivan. As far as she knew, the Nazis would confine themselves to Saturday's rally at Lee's graven image downtown, a distant one and a half miles from UVA's white colonnades. She had reassured the Board of Visitors that the university was fully prepared for the arrival of several hundred white nationalists in the city. "Of course, we anticipate that some of them will be interested merely in seeing Mr. Jefferson's architecture and Lawn," she wrote. Seth Wispelwey believed that everyone knew the march would take place at the university by Friday morning.

After a meeting with the Charlottesville Police Department in which the torch rally was discussed, a UVA police captain named Donald H. McGee elevated his concerns to the higher-ups. He outlined the dangers of a "tiki torch march" on UVA Grounds. "There is concern," he wrote to Chief Mike Gibson and others, "that the location could be the Rotunda or Lawn area since Mr. Spencer, an alum, will likely be at the Friday event." This was the second red flag. McGee touched briefly on the fire hazard posed by torches. Citing the Hibachi grills provided to the fifty-three distinguished fourth-year Lawn residents, he assumed the university had no regulations against open flames. No one disabused him.

Jefferson's "Academical Village" is a UNESCO World Heritage Site, so one might imagine there would be a regulation somewhere regarding open flames. Failing that, there was always Section 18.2-423.01 of the Virginia Code. This was the code about "burning objects" the city prosecutor failed to enforce after Spencer's May 13 torch rally because he didn't feel torches rose to the level of a crime. This alone would have provided a legal means for the university to stop the torch march before it began. By the time the university came around to drawing up its August 11 report, everyone knew there was, in fact, a 2013 UVA policy explicitly forbidding open flames on Grounds. This was why Eli Mosley and Jason Kessler were being so furtive.

Supposing the university administration might discount anything a "brown-skinned, outspoken professor" had to say, Jalane Schmidt used an intermediary to share what she knew. That person contacted Emily L. Blout, an assistant professor in media studies and, as wife of Mayor Signer, the self-described "First Lady of Charlottesville." Blout alerted the provost at 3:00 p.m. about the possibility of an alt-right march on Grounds. Jalane's info had it beginning at the Jefferson statue and ending at St. Paul's, where Congregate was holding its 7:00 p.m. service. Word was passed to Chief Gibson, the Department of Emergency Services, and the university spokesperson. This was the university's third red flag. Blout also left word with Chief Al Thomas's assistant. The starting time wasn't given, and there was no mention of torches.

For the next five hours officers from the University Police Deptartment would try to track down the source of the rumor. Ostensibly, they were in search of further details. More likely, they wanted to judge the source's credibility and find a reason to disregard it. Another "confidential source" had the march taking place at a public park outside city limits. This was likely planted by the torch march organizers, but was seized upon as another reason to do nothing.

James Baldwin's essay "The White Problem" was written amid the assassinations, church bombings, and civil uprisings of 1963. "In order to avoid believing [what he had to say], white men have set up in themselves a fantastic system of evasions, denials, and justifications, [and this system] is about to destroy their grasp of reality, which is another way of saying their moral sense." Pastor Brenda would have said that white people cannot see the truth, even when it is unfolding in front of them. They prefer the lie.

At a 4:30 press conference, Chief Thomas fielded a reporter's question about the rumors of a torch march at UVA. Thomas was so cagey that Mayor Signer was left with the impression that the message his wife left with his assistant never reached him. Maybe Chief Thomas was pretending he knew more than he did. Or maybe he didn't want word to get out and bring in more protesters. Who could say?

As Thomas's press conference ended, Christopher Cantwell was arguing with Jason Kessler in McIntire Park. Cantwell wanted him to tell the police about the march. "We need cops involved because if [Antifa] attacks us, we're going to fucking hurt them." Cantwell wanted law enforcement there to stop him from getting into a fight. "Especially with torches," someone said. Kessler eventually gave Cantwell the name of his police contact. Cantwell told Sgt. Wendy Lewis about the march but refused to provide her specifics. She conveyed the info Cantwell gave

her to Capt. Angela Tabler at the University Police, who was still trying to get more information on the provost's source. Lewis told Tabler
that Cantwell didn't appear to realize that "Nameless Field" was an actual location.

At 7:41 p.m., the University Police Department shared an It's Going
Down post about the torch march with the Albemarle County Police
Department, nearly an hour after Emily Gorcenski had retweeted it. By
then the pews of St. Paul's were filled for the Congregate service that
evening, and those in charge of security were turning people away. Still
reluctant to acknowledge what was bearing down on them, the UPD
email said the post "appear[ed] to confirm" an event involving torches
on UVA Grounds. At 7:47 p.m., a fourth-year student pulled President
Sullivan aside as she was greeting students moving into their Lawn
rooms for the fall term. He showed her the It's Going Down post. The
post included where and when the torch march would take place.

"Have you seen this?" he asked her.

"Well, this is news to me," she replied.

After getting off the phone with Sgt. Wendy Lewis, Capt. Tabler
tried to reach Kessler, but he was still in the 7:00 p.m. leadership meeting at McIntire Park. Finally, Eli Mosley answered Kessler's phone.
In their five-minute conversation Mosley told her their march would go
up University Avenue to the Jefferson statue, assemble there for fifteen
minutes, and then leave. He said their numbers weren't as large as he had
hoped. He promised they would leave the area spotless. He also swore
they would not march through the heart of the university. He said nothing about torches.

How might the University of Virginia have used its institutional resources to prepare itself and its students, faculty, and staff for the weekend of Unite the Right? Its law school might have offered crash courses
in civil disobedience and opened a bail fund. Its hospital might have donated medical supplies. Its medical school might have offered courses
in emergency first aid. Executive VP and COO Pat Hogan or Chief
Mike Gibson might have sent out a community alert on the Emergency
Notification System that would have appeared on everyone's phones.
They might have at least supplied Lawn residents with Super Soakers.

Instead, the entire administration was sleepwalking, bewitched by a dream of their own making.

A later investigation reached the conclusion that the university "over relied" on the information the organizers had provided. This information "turned out to be deliberately misleading." President Sullivan had assumed Kessler and Spencer would abide by the Honor Code they had signed as UVA students. It was left to music professor Bonnie Gordon's ten-year-old son to point out the obvious. Hitler swore up and down he wouldn't invade Poland up until the day he invaded Poland. Nazis lied. It was in their nature to lie.

At 8:00 p.m., Richard Spencer sent out a blast to his listserv. "As I write, the stage is being set for a historic moment for our movement and our people in Charlottesville."

"I think we are good for right now," University Police Chief Mike Gibson wrote eleven minutes later. "My folks are watching this closely," he told his fellow police chiefs. As for himself, he'd gone home. Meanwhile, City Manager Jones wrote to Pat Hogan, the university's chief operating officer. "Pat, I just heard about Kessler March tonight. Do you need assistance?" Hogan was said to be at the beach. "I think Mike Gibson has ample coverage," Hogan replied. At 8:30 p.m. Chief Gibson learned that the torch march was all over social media. There were repeated offers of help from other jurisdictions, but the chief was sitting tight. "We'll see how this plays out." Fielding a 9:00 p.m. request for safety instructions from the vice-president of the student council, he had little to offer. At 9:10 p.m. his officers reported that tiki torches were being delivered to Nameless Field.

St. Paul's Memorial Church was consecrated at around the same time as the Lee statue was unveiled. Built in Greek Revival style, its stepped portico is framed by four Doric pillars. A slated gable roof is topped by a spire. Inside, the nave and transept are unadorned; the six bay casement windows are clear glass. Standing on the portico, turned slightly to your right, you will have a view of the Rotunda and the North Plaza across University Avenue. There the statue of Thomas Jefferson stands on a rust-colored marble plinth.

Will Peyton, the new rector at St. Paul's, had returned to the church at 4:00 p.m. that afternoon to discover Rev. Sekou and around one hundred people undergoing training in nonviolent resistance in the sanctuary. Rev. Elaine Thomas, his associate pastor, had asked his permission, and he had given it. But when he overheard Rev. Sekou talking about a torch march and instructing people on what to include in a letter to their loved ones in case they should be killed, he was alarmed. The meeting afterward was tense.

What did they know? Was the church in danger? Did they need to post police officers in and around the church? No one would give him a straight answer. Everyone kept looking at Andy Stepanian, Congregate's press liaison, but he kept quiet. He knew Rev. Sekou wouldn't work with the police. He also knew Rev. Sekou wouldn't object if the rector arranged to have officers present. But he would neither suggest it nor agree to it. The rector went ahead and requested officers, but at the last minute they reneged. Congregate had to scramble to find their own security. This was how Willis Jenkins, Bekah Menning's husband and a professor of religious studies, came to be on the front portico when the church doors opened at 6:00, an hour before the service was to begin.

Student volunteers helped him search people's bags for weapons. The John Brown Gun Club had seven men stationed around the perimeter. One had stashed a gun under a car close by. Otherwise, everyone doing security was unarmed. Jenkins thought some of the men were being overzealous. They wanted certain doors locked. They spoke of snipers and lines of sight. But then a few young men refused to have their bags searched. During the service, activists would monitor the social media threads of Kessler, Spencer, and Brad Griffin. That information was fed back to Jenkins and his security team.

Jalane Schmidt, Rev. Phil Woodson, and Rev. Elaine Thomas sat in the chancel with Dr. Cornel West and Rev. Traci Blackmon, who was to give the sermon. In the Congregate livestream, Seth loomed head and shoulders over everyone. Smash wore her usual backward baseball cap with her white robes. Around a piano to the right of the pulpit stood Pastor Brenda in a purple clerical stole and a tall striking woman with a gorgeous voice named Yolonda Jones. As residents filled the pews, they sang "Wade in the Water," "Oh Freedom!" and songs written specifically for the occasion by Rev. Tracy Howe Wispelwey. Yolonda's husband, Will Jones III, was again shadowing Wes Bellamy as his unofficial security. The vice-mayor had successfully defended his dissertation that morning and was now Dr. Wes Bellamy.

The service began with a brief welcome from the new rector. Dr. Cornel West followed with thanks to his hosts and gave a shout-out to his former students, Jalane Schmidt and "your beloved mayor," Mike Signer. Another shout-out went to the organizing work of Sister Smash, Brother Seth, and his fellow freedom fighter, Brother Sekou. "Anytime he calls, I come running." Then he introduced fifty-four-year-old Rev. Traci Blackmon, the first woman minister of Christ the King United Church of Christ in Florissant, Missouri, and a galvanizing force behind the Ferguson protests.

Rev. Traci Blackmon had a headache and a low fever when she stepped up to the pulpit. Seth was worried about how well she'd manage. She began her sermon with a story about her native Alabama. In March 1965, Rev. Martin Luther King Jr. put out a clergy call that brought a forty-year-old nun and a number of her fellow sisters to Selma. Sister Mary Antona Ebo, from a semi-cloistered order based in St. Louis, hadn't seen the newsreel footage of "Bloody Sunday" that had interrupted the Houston–Notre Dame football game the previous Sunday. She'd had no training in nonviolence. She was there on the orders of the St. Louis cardinal. A front page photograph of this serene and smiling Black woman in a full habit put Sister Mary Antona in the history books. One of the last acts of her life was to lead a prayer vigil for Michael Brown.

Selma was in the air. Even the Wispelweys' seven-year-old felt it. Here was another church, as filled with apprehension as Brown Chapel AME Church had been on the night before Sister Mary Antona and her sisters marched on the Edmund Pettus Bridge. And just as Selma had Rev. Ralph Abernathy and Dr. King there to "rile up the crowd," Charlottesville had the feverish Rev. Traci Blackmon.

Mayor Mike Signer sat with his wife near the front. He had spent the morning doing media. Katie Couric had interviewed him for her documentary at the Daughters of Zion cemetery. Fulfilling one of the recommendations of the Blue Ribbon Commission, the city council had earmarked money for the restoration of this neglected resting place. "The African Americans buried here," Signer told Couric, "were just as much founding fathers and mothers of Charlottesville as Thomas Jefferson, James Madison, and James Monroe." Couric was sitting behind him at St. Paul's.

An hour or so into the service, Signer got word that the federal judge had ruled for Jason Kessler and the ACLU. The Unite the Right rally would take place in Emancipation Park after all. The decision gave the rally a legitimacy and visibility that money couldn't buy. The Virginia chapter of the ACLU would later acknowledge that "history can be an unforgiving tutor." The national office decided it would no longer represent white supremacist groups who demonstrate with guns. Chief Thomas's officers would spend the evening breaking down barricades set up in McIntire Park, and reassigning officers to zones downtown. Signer was too dismayed and restless to sit still. He and his wife got up and left.

Elsewhere in the city, Joe Heim of the *Washington Post* had heard the rumors. He texted Richard Spencer just after 8:00 p.m. "Is there [a] happening tonight that you know of?"

"Yeah, I'll keep you up to date. I'd be near campus tonight, if I were you."

"Good to know. Thanks. Time frame?"

"After 9 pm"

"The Lawn?"

"Nameless Field," he explained. "We are starting there and marching to the statues at UVA. Hundreds and torches."

When Signer reached home, he saw Spencer had tweeted at him and Wes Bellamy, trumpeting their court victory. "I told you we'd defeat you days ago. Why didn't you just give in?"

At 8:43 p.m., the Charlottesville police received an anonymous call from a man saying he had an AR-15 and in five minutes would begin opening fire inside St. Paul's. Officers were dispatched. In the sanctuary a Signal thread was lighting up phones. A man identified as a white nationalist had tweeted a photograph from inside the church. Seth thought he was trying to livestream the service. No one knew what he looked like, so he and Smash tried to figure out where he was sitting from the angle of the photograph. Everyone in the church had been searched. They didn't want to panic people unnecessarily. At 8:56 p.m., another threat to the church was called in. Willis Jenkins, Bekah Menning's husband, recalled two cruisers with flashing lights passing by, but he received no word of either threat.

Rev. Blackmon's sermon was about prophets and dreamers. Where were the prophets and dreamers now? she asked. "Prophetic resistance like that of Sister Ebo," she said, "isn't possible without those who can dream of peace amid war, those who have the presence of mind to speak of love in the face of hate."

"When dreamers rise up," she said, "giants fall."

It was dark outside when Rev. Blackmon began telling the story of David and Goliath. Across the street only the tennis courts by Nameless Field were brightly lit. A few dark figures stood along University Avenue, as men in white shirts passed them to descend a grassy slope into the darkened field. The night was sultry. Tyler Magill, the part-time DJ, sat on a bench on Newcomb Road just below the university library and above Nameless Field. The tiny rectangles of phone lights below him began to proliferate, like stars coming out in a night sky. About thirty members of the media carrying cameras headed toward the parking garage where a truck was unloading tiki torches. A man was filling them with fuel at a nearby table.

Rev. Blackmon described the weapons Goliath brought to the field where the fight with David was to take place. They were the same weapons they have always brought, she said. David came armed only with his faith. "You are coming to me with a sword, a sphere, and a javelin," David said to Goliath, "but I am coming to you in the name of the Lord Almighty God."

"We don't come to this weekend simply as individuals," Rev. Blackmon told the assembled. "We come as the army of God, equipped with the spiritual weapons of our faiths." What were these weapons? In place of hatred, they brought love. Faced with violence, they asked for peace.

"Can you see beyond the giants," Rev. Blackmon asked, "to see the hand of the Lord?"

Andy Stepanian was in the room off the transept with Chris, a member of the John Brown Gun Club. Chris was a polite young man with long blond hair, armed with a baton and pepper spray. "It's just such an honor to be here to be able to support the good work that you're doing," he said shyly. But Stepanian was restless. When he first heard about the torch march, he had written a threat assessment. He figured, as Emily Gorcenski and Kristopher Goad had, that they would see around fifty to seventy-five people on Friday night, with about five hundred showing up on Saturday.

He knew Seth wouldn't be thrilled, but the pull of needing to know what was happening across the street was overwhelming. Stepanian left the church by a side door to make his way to Nameless Field. In the dark it was hard to tell who was on which side. He was wearing a white Oxford shirt and had grown out his beard to easily comingle. When he crossed the path of two armed men it took him a while to realize they were with the John Brown Gun Club. He came across another group of people near some bushes. They looked at him warily until he said, inanely, "How's it going?" Bizarrely, he saw two activists he knew from growing up in Long Island. After a brief exchange, he made his way down to where the torch march was staging. Men were arriving in small groups from every direction.

When Stepanian tried to describe what he saw and felt during the twenty minutes he spent in Nameless Field, he prefaced it by saying he didn't believe in the devil. When they were handing out the torches, he said, every so often one of the men would let out a howl. This would set off another howl, as if they were feeding off one another. He compared it to the hot summer nights of his childhood, when he and his friends would sneak out of their houses to meet up on their bikes and set off for the beach, each of them brimming with anticipation of unspoken possibilities. That was an innocent version. In Nameless Field, the current of energy that surged from one man to the next felt deeply malevolent. Among those leaving the garage to pick up torches, Stepanian was shocked to recognize prominent YouTubers, influencers, and provocateurs like Baked Alaska. He saw the Proud Boy Enrique Tarrio. He estimated the Nameless Field numbers to be around 750. He approached the media present to ask them to check out the church service and pleaded with them not to platform Nazis.

"This is what drives them. Don't give them that shot," he said.

Jason Kessler, walking up, overheard him.

"Did you hear that, people? He wants me to get shot." Kessler accused him of being a spy sent by George Soros to kill him.

"Jason, you don't even know my name," Stepanian said. A man in a polo shirt approached. He was wearing a headset and an earpiece and leaned in to speak to Kessler while pointing a can of bear spray at Stepanian.

"Permission to engage, sir," he said.

Goliath didn't just come out of nowhere, Rev. Blackmon said. He came from the camp of the Philistines. He was their mouthpiece. "Sometimes we give all our attention to the mouthpiece. But until we close the camp, there will always be another Goliath." There was another, often overlooked, detail of the story of David and Goliath, she said. The slinging of the small stone that knocked the giant down and killed him was not the end of the story. The real end was when David knelt and cut off Goliath's head.

Every so often Seth would check his phone under his robes, texting with Smash and Sekou in response to bits of intel. For a service that was meant to bring everyone together on the eve of a great threat to their community, some were waiting for an attack on the church, and others were wondering where Rev. Blackmon was going with Goliath's head.

Rev. Blackmon acknowledged that the vision of a severed head might make some people uncomfortable. She was, as Dr. West had said, a peacemaker. But there was a time for peace. Now was the time to fight. When she spoke about the arrival of these men, she didn't mean to imply that they hadn't always been here. The vote on the Confederate statues, the Trump administration, all of this was simply bringing to light what had been there all along.

She told the congregation they had celebrated too soon. They celebrated when the schools were integrated, when Jim Crow was defeated, and the vote was won, she said. Watching Congregate's shaky video recording of Rev. Blackmon's sermon at my desk in Brooklyn, I thought of the explosion of joy on the streets the night Obama was elected. I had been intoxicated by the idea that America had achieved some measure of absolution for its crimes. Instead, here we were, and are still, riding a shock wave of backlash that threatens to overturn, once and for all, the idea that all men were created equal.

The reason David needed to cut off Goliath's head and raise it above his own, Rev. Blackmon said, was to send a message to the camp of the Philistines, whose campfires were flickering not far away. What Goliath had brought into the city would not be tolerated.

Her voice now slowed and softened.

"I can remember as a little girl. A little girl in Birmingham, Alabama. I can still remember standing on the street, on the sidewalk, and watching the Klan rally go by. Flags, hoods, passing me by. I can still see it in my mind's eye."

Students in a green Toyota SUV pulled up at the parking garage where Andy Stepanian was just about to be bear-sprayed and told him to get in. He asked to be dropped off at the Thomas Jefferson statue, a quick right turn up University Avenue. There he discovered a group of around twenty students. They weren't the activists he had gotten to know at Rev. Sekou's trainings and his media work, but an entirely different group. He told them there were more people coming than they imagined, and he didn't think it was a good idea for them to be there when they showed up. He suggested they accompany him back to the church.

The reception he got was like, "Who the fuck are you?" and "Where did you come from?" One person told him, "This is our ground." Another pointed toward the Lawn and said, "I live right there." Another said, "We aren't leaving, forget that." There was no way to convey, in what little time he had, what it meant to be completely outgunned. Stepanian knew that if he was nineteen and some random forty-year-old showed up to tell him what to do, he'd ignore him too.

"And so, I said that we would keep the front doors of the church open, and that if they needed to come in, to please come in."

Born in 1963, Blackmon was too young to recall the three Klan bombings of Bethel Baptist Church in Birmingham but, growing up in a Baptist family, she would have heard of them. She would have heard, too, about the 1962 fire bombings of New Bethel Baptist, St. Luke's AME Zion, St. James United Methodist, and Triumph the Church and Kingdom of God in Christ. Finally, there was the 1963 bomb placed by the KKK under the Sixteenth Street Baptist Church steps that killed those four young girls. And these were just the Birmingham churches.

"They are coming back," she said. The Klan was rising.

And why was the Klan still rising? Rev. Blackmon lifted her head to look out over the congregation as if she expected an answer.

"The Klan is still rising BECAUSE *WE*"—and here Rev. Blackmon brought her fist down so hard on the pulpit the microphone crashed—

"HAVEN'T. [*Bang!*]

CUT. [*Bang!*]

THE DAMN HEAD OFF!"

An altar call hadn't been part of the planned liturgy. Arising out of Pentecostal and evangelical traditions, altar calls are often highly emotional. Typically, a pastor will invite people up to the altar rail to accept Jesus as their savior. A blessing is said over their heads, and they will have been saved for all time. In progressive churches, including Episcopalian ones, there are no altar calls. Still, when Sekou told Smash to call one after Blackmon concluded her sermon, she went with it. She began with questions. Who are we? Who will we be tomorrow? Who will we be after tomorrow? She invited people to join them on the streets the next day, so their bodies could absorb the violence and spare those for whom the violence was intended. As Jesus had done. When the clergy in the chancel stepped forward on either side of her, she invited the congregation to come up and receive their blessings. She was elated when dozens of people began forming lines.

"I think people were feeling the weight of the moment," she recalled.

"The Spirit of God was moving." The Spirit of God allowed her to forget earlier concerns over the threat to the sanctuary. After the altar call was over, various local and visiting clergy offered prayers.

Smash can't remember when the church was put on lockdown. She remembered that when anyone approached the door wanting to leave, they were dissuaded. She remembered trying to keep the singing going. Many were so far up the mountaintop they had no idea that there was any kind of danger.

Kay Slaughter, a former mayor and a long-standing member of St. Paul's, was sitting next to Katie Couric. Couric showed her what she was seeing on her phone, a feed of hundreds of torches lined up in Nameless Field. "Oh my god," Slaughter said. "You've got to tell them," meaning the people leading the service. When Couric got up, Slaughter assumed that was what she was going to do. Instead, she went out the church doors and stood on the front portico to see if the marchers were going to cross the street and attack the church. Slaughter saw Rabbi Tom Gutherz at the end of her pew. She told him there were men with torches outside. Could he get word to the rector? "Why don't you tell him?" he said. Though St. Paul's was her church, she didn't think she had the standing. She thought a rabbi had more standing.

For a long time, Rabbi Tom Gutherz had difficulty grasping how a controversy over Confederate statues had led to Nazis in Charlottesville. He couldn't see how the Jews fit in. In the aftermath of August 12, a local journalist made a documentary on the events of that weekend and failed to interview a single person in the Jewish community. Like the rabbi, he could not see how the Jews fit in. The great replacement theory underlying the chant "Jews will not replace us" is the same fascist talking point dressed, not in white supremacy, but in white nationalism. Only now Jews were conspiring to flood the country with migrants, refugees, and Muslims. "It wasn't all about us," Rabbi Gutherz insisted. "It *definitely* wasn't all about us." But people had to understand that Jews were the glue that held the ideology of white supremacy and white nationalism together.

Like Rabbi Gutherz, Bonnie Gordon and her ten-year-old son had come directly from the early Shabbat service at Congregation Beth Israel. At 9:52 p.m., she got a text from a friend.

"Holy shit!! Are you on the lawn?"

"We are in the church what is happening on lawn?"

"Huge march . . . Torches as far as you can see. Chanting Jews cannot replace us." "Fuck off commies this is our town now" "Blood and soil." Attached to the text was a link to a Facebook livestream. Her friend told her she should leave. But it was too late. The church was on lockdown. Gordon's ten-year-old was quietly taking it all in.

"I knew we shouldn't have come to a church on Shabbat," he finally blurted.

Soon people's cell phones were exploding. The rector got up. "We're going to need y'all to sit and prepare to duck and take cover," he said.

Willis Jenkins had been getting Signal reports showing the progress of the torch march. The speculation on the thread all night had been that the torch march was conceived of as a counter to the service at St. Paul's and timed to intimidate it. Everyone assumed the church was the march's destination and target. Some heard that the church was already surrounded. Rev. Sekou, Rev. Elaine Thomas, and Smash joined Willis Jenkins and Katie Couric on the portico to see what was happening. Thomas recalled the surreal feeling of seeing the torches yet at the same time hearing the singing coming from inside the church. It was as if there was a storm outside, she said, and the church was providing safety and shelter.

While they were on the portico, an agitated woman came up and told them there were students at the Jefferson statue and they needed help. This was how they learned about the students. Smash told her to wait; they would figure out who to send over. She, Sekou, and Seth retired to a room to talk. "I really thought we were gonna figure it out," Smash said later. "I honestly don't remember that conversation at all. I don't know who decided what. Instead, we started to fill up water jugs."

It was Rev. Sekou who had made the call. They had people in wheelchairs. They had children. The safety of those in the church was their priority. He couldn't send anyone over because he didn't know for certain what they would be walking into. Furthermore, the students had not told them of their plans. He went back out and told Katie Couric that the situation was going to get bad. She should go back inside.

Guilt is a wayward and inexplicable emotion. We call it guilt whether or not we are entirely culpable. We can't always find the logic behind the need to accept blame. Is there a better word than *guilt*? Willis Jenkins called it *moral trauma*. Moral trauma appears to open a wound that can be more troubling than the presumed offense warrants. As a teacher, Willis believed he should have gone over to help the students. White supremacy had shaped his perception that the police would protect them. *You naive white moderate*, he later castigated himself. *Haven't you been listening?*

Smash would deeply regret the decision to lock the church doors and not send anyone over. She had been leaning too much on Sekou to make decisions about what she and her community were going to do. After it was all over, she decided she wouldn't do that anymore. Later, she wrote a letter of apology to one of the students. She didn't say the decision Rev. Sekou made was the wrong one. It might even have been the one she would have made. Believing that her profound and lingering sense of guilt, her moral trauma, derived from her feeling of helplessness, she imagined that if the decision had been hers, she would have been more at peace with it.

Inside the church, people were getting worried. Public transport shut down at 10:00 p.m. How would they get home? Seth's daughter had a panic attack and wouldn't let him go. Bonnie Gordon's ten-year-old was terrified. Rev. Sekou returned to the chancel and took the microphone. He said they had company, but they were going to sing loud enough to be heard. Then he launched into a round of "Over My Head, I Hear Freedom in the Air" which segued into "Oh Freedom!" followed by "Woke Up This Morning with My Mind Stayed on Freedom." His robes swept the floor as he paced back and forth, his locs flapped as he jumped. Spared the details of what was happening, the historian John Mason of the Blue Ribbon Commission, the man I nicknamed "the Professor," thought all was well. The windows rattled, and the floors shook with the stomping. The church was transformed into lungs of life and joy, trepidation and terror.

Rev. Traci Blackmon tweeted:

"They are coming for the church!"

"They won't let us go outside."

"Y'all these KKK are marching with torches!"

CHAPTER 12

The Torch March

Jon Ziegler of Rebelutionary Z.tv was broadcasting simultaneously on Facebook, YouTube, Periscope, and YouStream. Independent video journalism had taken off in 2015 when cheap tech enabled anyone with a phone to become a videographer. Sometimes the livestream business was about getting footage and licensing the spicy bits to mainstream media, and sometimes it was about finding a niche and building up followers and paying subscribers. As a citizen journalist Ziegler had amassed sixty thousand followers while livestreaming the Ferguson uprising, where he was twice arrested. Again and again, he'd witnessed how peaceful protesters, if they made any move to defend themselves against a heavily militarized police force, were framed by mainstream media as violent.

On the evening of the torch march, Ziegler would cross paths with Chris Schiano, of the nonprofit left-wing media collective Unicorn Riot, and the independent journalist Jake Westly Anderson, whom he knew from Ferguson. Ford Fischer of News2Share was also milling about. The *Washington Post* had two journalists in Charlottesville, one in the church and another in Nameless Field. Though some journalists came from as far away as South America and Europe, the *New York Times* sent no one. Mainstream television news outlets were nowhere in sight.

Ziegler's first interview was with a red-bearded, red-shirted marcher with an unlit torch and a GoPro camera on his chest. A neo-Nazi from northern Virginia, Red Shirt liked to pass himself off as a MAGA normie. He had been at Richard Spencer's May 13 torch rally in Lee Park and had also hung out in town with Jason Kessler and his Proud Boys crew. He told Ziegler the May 13 torch rally was no different from the candlelight vigil that followed it. A torch was simply a bigger candle. Ziegler disagreed. "There is clearly a difference between a torch and a candle." He tried to get him to admit that a mob with lit torches was threatening. Overhearing, a man next to Red Shirt said, "The thing is, we don't care what you are going to call us." Red Shirt also thought Ziegler should just come out and say what he was thinking. Ziegler said he didn't know what he was talking about.

"People around here are saying it resembles the KKK or something," Red Shirt said.

"I wasn't even thinking of that," Ziegler countered. He was thinking of peasants storming castles. "Give me an example of a time in history when marches with torches meant peace."

"A vigil," Red Shirt replied, "a funeral."

"They don't march with torches, they carry *candles*," Ziegler said, fully exasperated and bringing the debate full circle. "Give me an example in the United States." But Red Shirt wasn't interested in the United States. He was interested in Viking funeral rites. Their movement, he said, was all about channeling their European heritage.

"I think you are kind of making stuff up as you go here," Ziegler said gently. "I appreciate the dialogue, but you aren't giving me facts of any kind. You are just saying you are connecting to history, but I don't know what history you are talking about."

"Okay," Red Shirt said before melting into the dark as the final call for security went out.

On the surface, this entire exchange seems pointless. Yet Red Shirt got right to the question of intent to intimidate, almost as if he'd been coached on how not to be charged under Section 18.2-423.01 of the Virginia Code. He was also echoing Jason Kessler. A French journalist told Kessler that torches were provocative. "That's why we use it," Kessler replied, saying what generally went unsaid before quickly changing the subject to Viking funeral rites.

The obvious problem here was that Kessler wasn't staging a funeral; he was staging a demonstration. Would the founding fathers be marching with them? Ford Fischer of News2Share asked him. "Of course, they would. They were revolutionaries, just like we are." Whether demonstrating for white civil rights, "heritage not hate," or fomenting a fascist revolution against the tyranny of the royally woke, all such rationales for carrying torches might have provided a get-out-of-jail-free card. Or would have, had anyone seen fit to arrest them on the charge of violating Virginia's law against burning objects, a Class 6 felony.

Emily Gorcenski had finally got her livestream up on Twitter and Periscope. "They are going to march up this hill where they are gonna slip and fall on their ass and we are going to have Nazi bowling and it's going to be fucking hilarious," she said. For those just tuning in, she provided some background about Thomas Jefferson and his relationship to the University of Virginia and slavery. A stream of hearts ran alongside her screen, some accompanied by snide comments, others with simple questions. She wandered over to where Eli Mosley was barking orders.

Mosley, the jaded Iraq War vet, the exterminator, the *Judenjäger*, had waited his whole life for this moment. The torch march and rally heralded the start of a juggernaut, the Racial Holy War he had long dreamed of. Though Samantha Froelich helped with the planning of the VIP after-party, she hadn't come to Charlottesville. She was afraid there would be violence and hoped the city would shut it down. This left Mosley better able to focus on the task at hand. He'd worked hard to put the pieces in place without arousing suspicion. His team of men with headsets and handheld radios fanned out in the darkness following his commands. "I run this as a military operation," he told a *Cavalier Daily* reporter that night. "I was in the army." Their numbers were now well into the hundreds.

"Listen up, everyone, crowd around, crowd around. You in security, listen up, this is the deal." A cacophony of hoots and yips coming from the torchbearer lines interrupted him. Security, Mosley announced, wouldn't be carrying torches. Security needed their hands free. "You are going to line up on either side of the torches, okay? We are going to have two separate columns on either side of the two [torch-bearing] columns in the middle. One on the right and one on the left."

"If I yell left side, left side," Mosley continued, "then that means Antifa is coming from the left so everyone doing security makes a wall on the left side to protect the torchbearers, and men on the right side go through the formation and join those on the left side." If anyone was too frightened to confront Antifa they should pick up a torch; if they hadn't yet got a torch they should get to the front of the line and "*fucking, get one.*" Mosley wasn't fooling around.

"You guys waging a war?" Emily asked in a slightly sarcastic tone.

"Standing up for our civil rights," Mosley replied, before he looked at her. "Get the fuck out of my way, you fag."

"This whole security theater is because they are afraid of Antifa," Emily said, back to addressing her livestream. She began trolling the marchers, pointing out that she was striding through their lines without any of them registering the presence of their biggest nightmare. She promised to record every glorious moment of their humiliation. In the background, Mosley could be heard calling for Sacco Vandal on his megaphone. Vandal, the ex-marine calling for white sharia law who'd been at Pikeville, was one of his lieutenants.

While Emily was down in Nameless Field, Jason Kessler, fresh off his ACLU-engineered court victory, was on Newcomb Road carrying a lit torch. This drew the media to him like moths to a streetlight. "As of today, the Constitution was upheld, and the people who founded this country have a chance to take it back," he announced to the assembled cameras. Kessler conflated the removal of monuments not with "cultural genocide" that Amanda Barker of the Loyal White Knights had spoken of, but actual genocide. Chris Schiano of Unicorn Riot asked him what evidence he had such a genocide was underway. Kessler deflected. "Read my *V-Dare* article," he said, referring to a right-wing newsletter named after Virginia Dare. When Schiano persisted, a member of Kessler's security detail knocked the phone from his hand.

Minutes later the call to light the torches went out. A river of fire emerged from the darkness and Nameless Field erupted in a chorus of piercing screeches, yips, and low-timbre howls. President Sullivan, standing outside her Carr's Hill residence on the other side of University Avenue, texted the dean of students at 9:45 p.m., saying she could hear them. Dean Allen Groves had heard them too.

"All right, we have got the flame going," Emily noted. The firelight gave those following her livestream a better look at their glistening faces. Some were in helmets. Emily took a close-up of a gaunt-faced, weak-chinned man who had been vigorously nodding his head while Eli Mosley was giving out security instructions. Emily called him Swastika Pin because his white polo shirt had a swastika pin where Ralph Lauren, né Ralph Lifshitz, usually placed his polo player. The polo shirt and khaki pants combo mandated by Vanguard America and Identity Evropa was just the sort of preppy-with-trust-fund LARPing that Lauren made a fortune from.

Swastika Pin was accompanied by a goofy-looking man with a cowlick, a foul-mouthed man in a distinctive, large-checked, black-and-white shirt, and a short goateed man wearing a necklace and brawling gloves. Cowlick was later identified by Miami anti-fascists as a Tampa Realtor. Emily subsequently identified Checked Shirt as an Identity Evropa member from St. Charles, Missouri. In 2018 he would be convicted on domestic terrorism charges for attempting to hijack an Amtrak train. Brawling Gloves has yet to be identified.

"Oh my god, that's fucking disgusting," someone was overheard saying on Emily's feed. Swastika Pin pointed at her. "I can see his dick, eww, gross." Anti-fascists would later connect Swastika Pin with the Kessler livestream follower who threatened to "smash that tranny faggot's face" and boasted that his face would be the last thing Emily Gorcenski would ever see. Swastika Pin was a Milwaukee DJ.

Emily ignored him. Two brunettes in sunglasses carrying torches caught her attention. Both women turned away from her phone. "When you have to wear sunglasses at night, it's a pretty good sign you are embarrassed by what you are standing for," Emily said, loud enough for them to hear.

"I like your shoes, though, they're pretty cute."

And then Emily heard Christopher Cantwell. He was, as usual, talking.

"Chris, how was the Walmart meet-up," she asked cheerfully.

"I'm sorry?" Cantwell replied. "How's the Walmart meet-up? Who are you? Are you the fucking asshole who made a false report? Is that who you are?"

When the line of torches began to snake across Nameless Field, Emily moved up to Newcomb Road to get a shot of them ascending the grassy slope. A security man slipped and grabbed at the wet grass— "Nazis slipping down the hill!" she exclaimed gaily—but most took the stairs. Standing next to her, a gray-haired man with a neatly trimmed beard turned to her and said, "My father would spin in his grave like a dreidel if he saw this." Emily nodded but remained determined to be snarky and unimpressed.

A young Black man shouted, "All y'all suck, bitch ass motherfuckers. I'll fight all y'all motherfuckers. Y'all on the wrong side." To someone's reply, "We're on your side," he said, "Aw hell no. I'm heaven sent. Y'all some bitches, though." In Jon Ziegler's livestream, an American Vanguard banner floated by.

Tyler Magill thought they would turn left when they got up to Newcomb Road, walk a hundred or so feet north to University Avenue, then turn east for the short walk to the Rotunda and the Jefferson statue. Instead, the march turned right, accompanied by scurrying videographers with selfie sticks, crouching photographers with heavy backpacks, and a few students with phones. "Sacco, you got any other guys?" Someone called out, "I got a gap." Magill decided to run ahead and warn people. To students sitting on the Lawn, he shouted, "Don't be here, this is a bad place." He worked his way up and down the quadrangle. Soon the Lawn was empty as students retreated to their Lawn rooms.

The fifty-three student rooms on the Lawn date to 1817. Each has a window at the back, a fireplace, and a front door that opens directly onto a covered brick passageway. To use the bathroom, Lawn residents must leave their rooms, walk outside, and down some steps to a back alleyway where the bathhouses are located. With the door closed, a peephole and a mail slot provide students shut inside their only view of the Lawn.

Emily noted that the man who shouted, "Leftist piece of shit" and lunged at her was wearing an 88 on his shirt. Security pushed him back in line. "What's this I've been hearing all week that it is the left that starts violence?" she asked. Emily assumed everyone following her knew that the number 8 referred to the eighth letter in the alphabet; and that 88 is HH, short for Heil Hitler.

The torches passed the University Bookstore, the back exit of the parking garage and Newcomb Hall, the student center. Mosley's lieutenants worked to consolidate the line with shouts of "Hasten the pace," "Keep it tight," and "Close the gap." The marchers were jittery. They had declared their manhood. They had mocked leftists, LGBTQ people, and Jews. But they had yet to fully cohere. A shout of "Jews did 9/11" was followed by nervous laughter. When a French journalist asked them if they longed for the old days of the Klan, one said yes, another said no.

A string of comments ran alongside Emily's livestream. "This is terrifying," one said. "This is what happens when PC culture gets pushed on folks too hard for too long," another wrote. Unshackled from tiresome and dreary PC culture, the torch marchers were now free to give gleeful public expression of their private animuses. They jockeyed like schoolboys with fart jokes to see who could be the nastiest. Only they weren't schoolboys.

The last exchange between Capt. Angela Tabler and Eli Mosley was at 9:52 p.m. By then she knew the torch march was not following the promised route. When she called Mosley to ask him about this, he said they had rerouted to avoid "Antifa." Tabler passed along Mosley's reassurances to her fellow officers that all was going well. Mosley was being modest. Everything was going swimmingly. There was no evident police presence in either Jon Ziegler's or Emily Gorcenski's livestream.

Then a single voice shouted, "You . . . will not . . . replace *us*."

"You are eminently replaceable," Emily shouted back. But the rest of the line soon joined the chant, alternating with "Jews . . . will not . . . replace *us*," with someone adding a little tag, "Into the ovens!" Something about the rhythm of this chant finally united them. After that, it became harder for livestreamers to engage them individually. When they switched to "Blood and soil," Emily paused to comment. "Blood and soil is a Nazi chant from the 1920s. Originally coined in the nineteenth century, this was used to rally people to the Nazi cause." By then the torch columns had reached the end of Newcomb Road and had turned left onto McCormick Road, the central artery through Grounds used by the UVA bus service. The march was doubling back north, heading up a slight incline. Here Emily finally saw a single police officer. At 9:56 p.m. President Sullivan received word they were heading to the South Lawn; she relayed this to Dean Grove.

Nineteen minutes into her livestream, Emily wanted to give those watching a sense of how many marchers there were. Rather than running alongside to keep up with the front, she decided to stop and wait for the end of the march to get to her. I had the sense she was trying to absorb the scale of the spectacle and what it meant, for those following her on Periscope and for herself. The snark was gone.

"I want you to watch this. I want you to remember this. This is hundreds of people carrying torches, chanting Nazi chants." The double line of torches streamed by her, bracketed by security. "This is America in 2017. This is Charlottesville, America." The torches kept coming. "I'm on the Grounds of UVA's campus directly in front of the Clark engineering library where I have spent quite a bit of time in my life studying and researching in peace. And in front of it are hundreds of white supremacists marching with torches." After a minute of quiet streaming, she announced, "Folks, this is the end."

But it wasn't the end. The torches were still coming.

President Sullivan updated Dean Groves at 10:01. "They are at the amphitheater." The chant became "Whose streets? Our streets," before returning to "You will not replace us." Tyler Magill saw the first of them appear at the end of the South Lawn, two hundred and forty yards away, backlit by the lights of Cabell Hall. The yips started as the columns turned up the Lawn. "Whose town? Our town," they chanted. Christopher Cantwell got in the face of a man who got too close. Though Emily tried to convince me the marchers had gotten lost, that they had no idea where they were going, I believe the Lawn had always been Richard Spencer's destination. He had once staged Shakespeare productions on the Lawn. As an undergraduate witnessing the controversy over Sally Hemings, he absorbed this cardinal fact: Thomas Jefferson was central to his vision of returning America to a time when superior white men ruled it.

On Ziegler's livestream a Black man said, "Fuck *all y'all.*"

A fearful white woman in a black tank top grabbed his arm: "Just leave them alone."

"No! I'm not gonna stop. I'm not gonna stop. 'Cause this shit ain't gonna stop."

Deciding to get out in front again, Emily headed to the East Pavilions. The columns were snaking their way to the center of the Lawn, where they would turn toward the steps of the Rotunda. She stopped briefly to pan the line of torches. "This is the scale," she said. "They're worried about Antifa. As if we can pull these numbers." An FBI agent had called her that week; he'd received a tip she was planning to attack the rallygoers. "Agent Wolf, if you are watching this livestream, I've found your domestic terrorists."

Wendy Baucom, the wife of the dean of Arts and Sciences, heard the chanting from her kitchen. She had been at the service at St. Paul's but had left after Rev. Blackmon's sermon. Her husband was in South Africa, and she wanted to be home to make dinner. She opened the front door of Pavilion X, the southernmost of the East Pavilions facing the South Lawn, and saw the torches. Two doors down was a biracial Jewish student. Baucom had met her earlier that day as she was moving in. They had spoken of the looming rally. Baucom now imagined her alone in her room watching what was happening through her mail slot and hearing the chant "Jews will not replace us." Given that Baucom was alone with her five children, it would have been nice had someone thought to check on her. But she didn't expect that. She was more concerned for the students. So, she went out, banged on the student's door, and brought her back to Pavilion X. They went up on the balcony to watch.

Wendy Baucom had always been ambivalent about living on the Lawn. The truth of it was that neither she nor her husband were UVA alums, so she wasn't as passionate about the university as nearly everyone around her was. Yet that night she felt extremely protective of all of it. She was thankful she'd left St. Paul's to be with her children, but what of everyone else still there? She assumed the torches were headed to the church.

"Even Leftists have to admit this is amazing," @ts819216 commented on the spectacle Emily was capturing with her phone. It was. Emily over-heard a cop ordering the marchers to ground the drone flying overhead. The grounded drone was a small victory. With the right soundtrack, with the domed Rotunda as backdrop, framed by Jefferson's Pavilions, this might have been Richard Spencer's greatest production.

When the march stopped so that everyone could catch up, Emily began running. The sound of chants, the slap of her feet on the brick walk-way, echoed off the East Pavilions. The stream of comments rising on the right side of her livestream quickened. They were mocking her.

"Is somebody chasing you?" "Runnnn, girl!"

She dashed around the east side of the Rotunda and took the steps down to the North Plaza where the Jefferson statue stood. At around the same moment, Kristopher Goad, the sous chef from Richmond, ran up the steps on the west side to look down on the Lawn. It was hard to take in. Columns of torches stretched into the distance. He ran back to the students he and his Richmond friends had found milling about on North Plaza when they first arrived. "God, there's hundreds of them, what are we gonna do?" Everyone looked at one another. "We're gonna stand by the statue. Where else are we gonna go? Are we gonna run away from everywhere all over Charlottesville? Or just hold our ground right here?" Everyone agreed. *Cool*, Goad thought. He and his friends made an outer protective ring around the students who had now moved to encircle the statue. He was vibrating with adrenaline but had never felt so sure of himself. And so angry.

When Emily arrived, people were conferring over where the torches would first appear. "Yeah, they are coming up the Lawn," one said. "They are coming through the gardens," another said. The gardens behind the Pavilions once housed slave quarters. Jefferson cleverly hid them from view with eight-foot-high serpentine walls.

"This is important to all of us," a man began, as if to remind them why they were there. Before he could continue, the first cameras arrived with their klieg lights, and a woman's voice shouted, "Heads down, y'all. Heads down." They began their chant. "No Nazis, no KKK, no fascist USA." Emily blocked her phone camera while she spoke to a man on the outer circle.

"There are a fucking lot of them."

"Yeah, I know," he said.

"We have a handful of activists who have linked hands around the statue," Emily narrated as she circled the statue and filmed the students' feet. There were five to a side. Above their heads, four angels representing Liberty, Justice, Equality, and Freedom of Religion encircled the liberty bell on which Jefferson stood with a copy of the Declaration of Independence. One angel carried a scroll on which Moses Ezekiel, a Jewish sculptor, had inscribed the names of God: Jehovah, Brahma, Atma, Allah, Zeus, and Ra. The surrounding plaza appeared nearly empty.

"This is what we have to stand against them," Emily said, arriving at the back of the statue. There, facing the Rotunda steps, five students held aloft a banner reading "VA Students Act Against White Supremacy." This banner would be the first thing the torch marchers saw.

Emily turned the phone around. Her face radiated distress. Fifty thousand people were watching her livestream. "Where *the fuck* are the rest of you?" she asked. "This is twenty people, standing against what is coming."

Tyler Magill sat down on the Rotunda's steps, facing the Lawn, and lit a cigarette. It was just after 10:00 p.m. The torches were coming toward him. He saw Jason Kessler in the lead, his face slick with sweat and rapturous in the torchlight. "I was fairly sure I was gonna die," he said. Instead, they marched around him, arriving at the top of the Rotunda's steps to fan out on the south portico, pausing to admire the view down the Lawn. The columns of torches stopped. Someone blew a ram's horn. Those in the lead walked out over the west terrace of the Rotunda and turned to the steps leading down to the North Plaza. Word went down the line of torchbearers still on the Lawn: "All right, we're moving, we're moving." A few of them broke ranks and raced forward. Men began grunting and whooping. Tyler Magill stood up and threw away his cigarette to sprint around the east side of the Rotunda and down the steps.

"The situation is very tense," Jon Ziegler reported from the top of the steps as two cops raced around the east side of the Rotunda. He was still talking about his interview with Red Shirt and hadn't registered the presence of the students at the statue, but a nearby marcher had. "Yeah! Let's replace *them*," he shouted. If the plan had ever been to march to the church with their torches, the presence of the students may have distracted and waylaid them.

Emily's phone captured the first of them descending the steps. Behind her, the students' chanting quickened. Tyler Magill arrived at North Plaza just as the torches began to encircle them. As he approached the statue a student with a blond ponytail pointed at him in alarm. Magill lifted both his hands and shouted, "I'm cool, I'm cool," before stationing himself in front of a student in a wheelchair. He joined Kristopher Goad, Goad's Richmond friends, Emily Gorcenski, and Dean Groves in a loose outer circle of men and women standing between the oncoming marchers and the students. BLM activists from a DC chapter had also shown up.

Filming at the top of the Rotunda's steps, Jon Ziegler caught the moment when the line began snaking around the statue of Thomas Jefferson. Richard Spencer, who had been leading the march with Jason Kessler, held back, letting the torches pass by him, transfixed by the view. Jake Westly Anderson had registered the presence of the students at the statue and the oncoming marchers. "The situation is something I've never seen before in all my years of reporting," he later related. That the police, standing off to one side, made no effort to insert themselves between the oncoming torchbearers and the students he found shocking and suspect. The circle of flames closed.

"And then, you know, that was all she wrote," Tyler Magill said. "We were surrounded."

Natalie Romero, in sandals and a tank top, had her back to the west side of the Jefferson statue. Her friend Devin Willis, a member of the Black Student Union, was to her right in a white button-down shirt and jeans. Natalie was less than five feet tall, with black and wavy hair. They were both rising second-year students and both on scholarship. They were part of a group of twenty students from across the Commonwealth who had gathered that night at a professor's house for a spaghetti dinner to work on their protest signs. Devin had prepared a daylong program at McGuffey Park, to keep everyone occupied during the rally. The students were also organizing a counterprotest for Saturday.

They had hoped to finish their posters in time to attend the service at St. Paul's, but when they got word of a pre-rally to take place that evening, either on the Lawn or at the Jefferson statue on the North Plaza, their plans changed. They decided to stage a counterprotest at the statue and to bring along the banner they had just finished. Assuming that the pre-rally was public knowledge, they imagined they would be joined by others. Devin anticipated it would be something like the July 8 Klan rally. Kessler's people would say their piece, and they would say theirs. As a diverse group of students, they had more standing to assert what the Jefferson statue meant than Jason Kessler and Richard Spencer. They didn't know about the torches.

It was just beginning to get dark when they arrived at North Plaza. A member of their group, a queer, nonbinary, and multiply disabled student, was in a wheelchair. They didn't see any Nazis. Their plan was to hold hands and form a human chain around the statue, but since nothing was happening, they stood around talking, looking for updates on their phones, and waiting for more people to show up. Natalie wished she had a hat. They'd all been warned about the threat of doxing. Some had UVA hats and could hide their faces under the bills. She felt exposed.

At first the roar came from a distance. Devin realized he'd been wrong about how many there would be. Based on the sound, there were clearly hundreds of them. As the roar got closer, they could make out the chants. "Blood and soil!" "White power!" "You. Will. Not. Replace. Us!" Devin described their arrival as an "ocean of light and flames" tumbling down the steps, moving toward them like a lynch mob. They were making monkey noises, but whatever else they said he drove from his head as soon as he heard it.

Natalie looked up at the Rotunda in time to see them descending the steps in a swarm. The night sky, lit up with torches, seemed to radiate their rage. Someone filming shone a blinding klieg light in her eyes.

She realized she and Devin, the only people of color on the statue, were dangerously exposed. A group of grown men soon loomed above her. They looked enormous. She felt like a trapped mouse. One would call her a stupid bitch and the others would echo it. Then they began chanting, "Go back to wherever you came from." The heat of their torches was dense, suffocating.

"If you want to know what it looked like," Emily said, "this is what it fucking looked like," turning her phone around. As the plaza filled up, the marchers moved in closer. "It's our town now," they shouted in students' faces. The circle of fire surrounding the students was ten deep, then twenty.

Emily now appeared visibly frightened, but she kept livestreaming. "When fascism came back forty people stood against hundreds." Filming from inside the circle of massing torches, she captured Swastika Pin getting in the faces of the men standing between the oncoming marchers and the students. The cowlicked Tampa Realtor and the goateed man with combat gloves stood by him. Swastika Pin had a crazed look. He soon shifted his focus to Emily. While she filmed Swastika Pin's sweaty face, a short, bearded man shoved a phone on a selfie stick in hers.

"You are not even a woman," the future Amtrak terrorist said to her while her phone focused on Swastika Pin, next to him. "What kind of mental illness do you have that you want to cut off your parts? That's fucked up." She turned her phone to him.

"Do you have a big open wound between your legs?" Amtrak Terrorist asked. "Are you XX or XY?"

"Where are all your friends at, *bitch*?" said Swastika Pin.

"We outnumber you," said Amtrak Terrorist. "We run this shit. Not you."

Behind her, the students chanted, "Black lives matter!"

Swastika Pin turned his attention to the man standing next to Emily and threatened to fuck his wife. Men with blank faces looked on over his shoulder. Tampa Realtor wore a goofy smile.

"Black lives matter! Black lives matter!" the students chanted, their voices pitched with fear.

Briefly turning her phone away from Swastika Pin and toward the students, Emily's feed picked up Prof. Walt Heinecke walking by. Heinecke had hosted the spaghetti dinner. He had been on his way to Rev. Sekou's post-service workshop at St. Paul's when he heard the students had gone to the statue. He ran over and offered to help them escape. Some chose to hold on. Others he pulled away. Dean Groves also intervened; his hand was burned in a torch strike; Devin noticed his natty suit was sliced open. Swastika Pin opened his mouth as if to swallow Emily's phone. Then he turned away to throw a punch at someone. Emily's phone was knocked from her hand, ending the feed. Ford Fischer of News2Share captured Swastika Pin and Amtrak Terrorist whaling away on the students and their protectors.

Azzmador had caught Tyler Magill's attention. Seeing that the Albemarle police and UVA police were forty feet away, standing and staring, Magill had an idea. He knew he wouldn't win a fight, so he tried goading Azzmador into throwing a punch so that the police would come and arrest him.

"Come on and kill me, you fuckin' pussy," he shouted, hands on his hips, looking annoyed. Someone shoved him hard to one side. Or perhaps he was hit in the neck with a torch. He remembers seeing a flash of light. The injury to his carotid artery wasn't discovered for several days, when he was moments away from dying in the emergency room of the university hospital. By then, parts of his brain had died.

"Of course, if Azzmador *had* punched me, nothing would have happened," Magill said, still suffering partial blindness.

While fists flew around him, Kristopher Goad's face maintained a focused look, arms at his side as he chanted, "No Nazis, no KKK, no fascist USA," bobbing up and down. He saw a bald man in a Radical Agenda T-shirt raise his arm and point a can at one of his Richmond friends. Goad managed to shout, "That man has mace!" before the spray came, directly in everyone's eyes. Unicorn Riot captured the moment. Goad had never been maced before. Once it was in the air, he said, it seemed to stay there, affecting everyone in the vicinity, including Emily Gorcenski. The bald man who had maced them may not have known this, because he was soon pulled out of the melee pouring out obscenities and screaming in pain. Goad believed he had maced himself.

When a torch landed at Natalie's feet, she thought they were going to set her on fire, like a witch. Then there was silence, as if someone had pushed a mute button. She watched men attacking people around her, swinging their torches, pepper spraying everyone. She tried to climb up the statue, but she kept slipping. The bodies of people being beaten kept hitting her. To her left, a fourth-year student named Caroline Bray ducked her head behind the banner as she chanted. When Caroline could no longer hear her own voice over the roar of the torchbearers, her heart dropped. "That's how loud they were," she said later.

Devin kept his head down out of fear of being doxed, to avoid flying objects, and to keep himself from freaking out. At some point some kind of liquid splashed on his shoes and on the pedestal. It smelled like lighter fluid. Now they were going to burn them alive, he thought. It was a mistake to have come. He had so much to live for. He, too, tried to climb up the statue to get away from the path he imagined the fire would take. He managed to get up on the cement lip. A fight broke out in front of him. "White lives matter" rang in his ears. He saw the student in the wheelchair grabbed and pepper sprayed.

A law student named Elizabeth Sines had been filming from the upper portico of the Rotunda, posting her footage on Facebook Live. The UVA police stood by as the torch marchers plucked one student after another off the statue, punched them, kicked them, and used lit torches to beat them before casting them aside. Her roommate, standing next to her, said it looked like what happens when a cancer attacks a healthy cell, destroying it and then moving on to the next one.

Conferring with the others surrounding the statue, Devin said he was ready to try to break free. The remaining students surrounded him and Natalie protectively, but as soon as they moved away from the statue, they were all set upon, pummeled, and pepper sprayed. They made it to some wooden benches not far away. Watching the marchers celebrate—grown men in overwhelming numbers who had just beaten up a handful of students—infuriated Devin. Despite the pain he was in, he joined the others when they stood up with the banner, which they had managed to save, to start up another chant. When Dean Groves approached him about leaving the area, Devin said no. One livestream showed a student, holding the edge of the banner. She was unable to join the chant of "Black lives *matter*! Black lives *matter*!" because she was hyperventilating. Natalie couldn't recall exactly how she got out, but she too joined the students holding up the banner, her face hidden under a hat provided by an anti-fascist.

Richard Spencer stood on the north portico of the Rotunda, ten feet from the law student Elizabeth Sines. A tight circle of security surrounded him like the spokes of a wheel as he waited for the statue to be captured and the torches to be put out. At 10:15, Kessler, amid cheers and chanting, sent a text to Spencer directing him to "come out front." Someone gave Spencer a megaphone, but its batteries were dead, so he made his way down to North Plaza, where he was hailed like a returning conqueror.

"We own these streets," he bellowed repeatedly, shaking his fist as he stood where the banner had been. He applauded them for having risked their lives on behalf of their ancestors. "Antifa was no match for your brawn," he told them. *Brawn?* I thought. *Seriously?*

Lisa Draine, the arts administrator who had attended the Mother's Day candlelight vigil with her daughter Sophie back in May, sat in a pew at St. Paul's waiting out the lockdown. Lisa tended to dress more conservatively than her peers, fashioning a coordinated look often accented with scarves in autumn colors. She generally wore her honey-blond hair stylishly pinned up. Both her college-aged daughters had spent the summer elsewhere. The eldest, twenty-three-year-old Rebecca, was sitting next to her. She and Rebecca had attended Rev. Sekou's workshop on nonviolent direct action at the church that afternoon. Sophie had only returned home two days before. Now a rising fourth-year student, she was elsewhere preparing for the next day's rally with her friends.

When the church leaders finally let them go, everyone was made to exit through a side door into a back alley. More curious than afraid, Lisa ventured out onto University Avenue and saw a jittery line of fire. She and Rebecca crossed the street and stumbled through some bushes. By the time they reached North Plaza, around 10:10 p.m., most of the torches had been extinguished and were lying on the ground or stuffed in trash cans. People were running around, some fighting, some sitting on the ground getting their eyes washed out. There was a strong smell of chemicals.

When Lisa heard people chanting "Black lives matter," she turned to Rebecca and said matter-of-factly, "I bet you Sophie's here." They found her in a huddle of friends looking dazed. Sophie had been one of the students holding the banner. Caroline Bray had been standing next to her during the siege at the statue. Neither believed they would make it out alive. Sophie and Caroline had gone to Charlottesville High School together.

City police officers had been waiting across the street all this time. They had twice offered their assistance to the University Police, the second time after they saw the torches appear at the top of the Rotunda's steps. The Virginia State Police also had officers stationed nearby, but they weren't granted permission to enter UVA Grounds until 10:16 p.m. By the time they crossed the street, it was too late. Not finding any commanding officer present, the CPD took charge, declared an illegal assembly, and gave the order for everyone to disperse. Once that was done, they formed a line to sweep those who remained off North Plaza. Emily Gorcenski went down the line in a fury, berating them all. By the time the police line began to move, the only people left were the press. Katie Couric, in a dazzling white dress and carrying an oversize pocketbook, tried to talk to them. She was taken by her elbow and escorted off.

When Seth Wispelwey pulled out of the alley behind the church to drive the theologian Brian McLaren to his parked rental, men in polo shirts were swarming all over University Avenue. Some were carrying baseball bats; others held extinguished torches. Jason Kessler suddenly appeared in the windshield like an apparition. Inevitably, McLaren had parked in the same garage as the fascists. From there, Seth ferried Rev. Traci Blackmon and Lisa Sharon Harper, the Black theologian and writer, to their hotel on West Main. There they began a conversation that would continue the next morning. Did they need to change their plans? Did they need to show up earlier? If so, how would that impact the timing of the sunrise service? Seth scoured his phone to find out what exactly had happened at the statue. Everyone understood that these men were now convinced law enforcement had granted them permission to do whatever they pleased the following day.

As if to prove as much, Augustus Sol Invictus, one of the rally's speakers and coauthor of Richard Spencer's "Charlottesville Statement," pulled up in front of their hotel. Andy Stepanian went out to photograph his license plate. Seth impulsively followed only to get trapped with Invictus between two sets of glass doors where he was caught between the desire to stand his ground and not wanting to fight a leader of the Proud Boys militia. Invictus left, but the women were furious that Seth had allowed Invictus to follow him into the hotel. Not for the last time, he was left to consider how much he had to learn.

Nearly everyone was trying to absorb how a group of Nazis could parade down the Lawn bearing torches and attack undefended students while University Police officers stood by and watched. President Sullivan later affirmed the marchers' right to access the University Grounds as well as their "First Amendment rights to freedom of speech and assembly." The failure to send out an alert was laid at the students' feet. "Don't expect us to be reading the alt-right websites. We don't do that," Sullivan snapped at Caroline Bray. "Now you guys have a responsibility here, too." UPD chief Mike Gibson downplayed the threat that 500–750 armed fascists posed. More officers on the scene wouldn't have helped, and besides, he told Caroline, no one was seriously hurt. Plus, the violence didn't last long. When Caroline persisted, he said, "I think the question that you're asking is, should we have [acted] sooner? I wasn't there so I can't answer that. Does that help?" The vice-rector of the Board of Visitors clarified. "Sometimes the very best response is to simply ignore them because they are ignorant fools and do not deserve our attention."

While some needed time to process the realization that these men had come to hurt people, Pastor Brenda needed no time at all. Waiting for a car to come collect her after the service, she was overcome by a sense of grief so overwhelming she couldn't even cry.

All bets are off, she said to herself. *All bets are off.*

CHAPTER 13

Emancipation Park

When Brian Moran, Virginia's public safety commissioner, visited Emancipation Park the day before the Unite the Right rally, he was shocked at just how tiny it was. A neat square of green, slightly elevated from the street, the park is contained on three sides by low stone walls. Bushes mark each of its four corners, framing stepped entrances that lead to walkways that once ended at the pedestal on which sat the Robert E. Lee statue. Today the square is known by the more humdrum name of Market Street Park, and the paths end at an empty rectangle of grass.

The Unite the Right rally that took place in Charlottesville on August 12, 2017, was not a saga of clashing armies, directed by uniformed men on horseback, sending runners down the lines with orders to advance or retreat. It was a riot. It was a demonstration and a counterprotest. It was a media spectacle and a crime scene and a prayer vigil.

To portray the multiple, nearly simultaneous, explosions of violence that took place in and around the park is a near impossibility. Some were orchestrated, but many were spontaneous. Because pivotal moments sometimes unfolded at the same time in different places, a linear chronicle is impractical.

But first, the lay of the land.

Imagine a map. At its center is the statue of Lee and Traveller. Lee faces the Albemarle Charlottesville Historical Society on Second Street NE. On the day of the rally the Virginia State Police posted a sniper on its roof. To the west, behind Lee, is First Street N, on which sits Hill and Wood Funeral Home. A sniper was posted on its roof too. Along the park's northern edge is East Jefferson Street. Here Rev. Phil Woodson's First United Methodist Church faces the park. Except for a mansion behind a high privet hedge, the church and its parking lot take up the entire block between East Jefferson and East High.

On the day of the rally, three of the four streets surrounding the park were barred to both car and pedestrian traffic, leaving Market the only street abutting the park open to pedestrians. These three blocks— First Street N, East Jefferson, Second Street NE—were each block- aded with bike rack barriers threaded with police tape and stocked with thirty-two Charlottesville police officers apiece. One unit of VSP Rapid Response officers was posted at the funeral home on First Street N. Otherwise, state troopers were not assigned to zones in the park's im- mediate vicinity.

There were two entrances to the park on Market Street. One was at the park's southwest corner, across from the funeral home, tightly framed by high bushes. Chief Thomas's operational plan had originally desig- nated this entrance for the public. But when Jack Peirce told them the shuttle vans would drop off rallygoers at the foot of Market Street, about a quarter mile west of the park, they switched the side of the park reserved for rallygoers from east to west. Now the public would use the grander southeast entrance, across from the Jefferson Madison Regional Library on Market between Second Street NE and Third Street NE.

Between the rallygoers' side of the park and the side designated for the public was a fourth staging area for the police. Two rows of bike rack barriers made an eight-foot-wide, T-shaped channel inside the southern half of the park. The northern half, which included the Lee statue, was cordoned off to everyone but police and the VIP speakers, so a tiny park was made even tinier. The T-shaped channel took up even more space, forming a corridor between the east and west side of the park, and between the park and pedestrians on Market Street. Suggestions that officers be posted on Market Street itself were ignored by CPD brass.

Directly across Market Street was the surface lot at the back of a Wells Fargo Bank. This lot was the fifth and final staging area and included some state troopers. Because of its proximity to the Command Center, located on the bank's sixth floor, the Virginia State Police insisted this zone also be barricaded. Here, too, officers would be stationed behind racks, like onlookers. In the Command Center, Chief Al Thomas's attention would be fixed on monitors fed by surveillance cameras installed in and around the park, and a livestream from a helicopter manned by two state troopers.

One block east of the Lee statue, down East Jefferson, sat the historic Congregation Beth Israel. As a member of the Clergy Collective, Rabbi Tom Gutherz had been focused on issues pertaining to racial justice. At the Klan rally he had seen posters referencing Jews as baby killers, yet, like most people, he associated the Klan more with racial terror than attacks on Jews. Then came Kessler's Unite the Right poster, with its Nazi-era typeface and its storm troopers. Security briefings from the ADL featured screen grabs from the Daily Stormer. After that there was no escaping the threat these men posed to the Jewish community. For the first time ever, they hired a private security guard. They also moved the temple's Torah scrolls elsewhere. One of them, taken from a Czech synagogue during the Nazi occupation, was to have become part of Hitler's planned Museum to an Extinct Race but was repossessed by the Allied Forces. After the war, the temple acquired it and honored it in memory of those killed during the Holocaust.

Emily Gorcenski tweeted out the map showing Saturday's road closures. She was concerned that rallygoers would be funneled downhill, to the south, crossing Market Street and the Downtown Mall to Water Street. A conversation picked up by a police body camera confirmed this was the plan. "If this turns south, they'll just rush across the Mall," one officer said to another. "That's the plan, just get everyone out of here and vent them to Water Street." Away, that is, from the historic district, its businesses, and wealthy white neighborhoods. Just beyond the surface parking lots on Water Street was Friendship Court, one of two low-income housing estates built to accommodate those left homeless by the razing of Vinegar Hill. The white nationalists had identified it as a "niggerhood." Emily was merciless. "Fucking amateur hour at CPD."

August 12 dawned in fog. By 7:00 a.m., there was 100 percent humidity. Working with Congregate, Deacon Don Gathers of Charlottesville's chapter of Black Lives Matter had organized a "Love over Fear" sunrise service at First Baptist. Dr. Cornel West gave the sermon and Rev. Sekou brought everyone to their feet with a galvanizing reprise of "Woke Up This Morning with My Mind Stayed on Freedom." A drum set and pounding piano woke up everybody else. The service closed with another altar call. Rev. Sekou invited those who had participated in the trainings and planned to bear witness to receive a blessing. A smaller group than that of the previous evening came forward.

Don Gathers left the church at 7:30 a.m., brandishing a mop handle to lead about 150 singing, faith-infused members of the public down West Main Street to the Jefferson School African American Heritage Center a few blocks east. The inseparable Katrina Turner and Rosia Parker, Gathers's fellow BLM members, were just behind him. The service had emboldened them. With Katrina's son Timmy acting as their security, they were ready to face the devil himself.

Vice-Mayor Wes Bellamy, in a white Menace II Supremacy T-shirt, was still smarting from criticism of his absence on the day of the Klan rally. He told Will Jones III from the barbershop that he couldn't hide; he needed to attend the sunrise service and join the BLM–led community march to McGuffey Park. He promised to leave after that. Katie Couric left the church with half her camera crew, leaving the other half to follow the clergy. Rev. Elaine Thomas provided the benediction as they set off, her hair especially curly in the humidity. Andy Stepanian had gotten very little sleep. Dressed in a black tie and white dress shirt, he accompanied the community march.

The procession swelled when they picked up the hundred or so people waiting for them in the Jefferson School parking lot. "God bless you, Charlottesville," Don Gathers greeted them. "We will reclaim our city!" Bellamy announced that there would be no police escort, just legal observers, so they had to look out for one another. Joining the march were city councillor Kristin Szakos, Dr. Andrea Douglas, the "Art Historian," and "the Professor" John Edwin Mason, the angsty conscience of the Blue Ribbon Commission. His sign read: "Prejudice, an Emotional Commitment to Ignorance." Kay Slaughter, the former mayor, was also there. Lisa Draine showed up alone in a BLM T-shirt and jeans, her honey-colored hair pulled back under a blue baseball hat. She hadn't attended the sunrise service. She wasn't a morning person. She was looking for her friend Ann Marie Smith, someone she knew from Congregate, but couldn't find her. She wasn't answering her texts.

The procession set off, passing through what had once been Vinegar Hill. As they approached North Downtown, the route forked. The rally-goers would go right for the steep climb up Market, which was closed to traffic. The community procession went left for a similar hike up High Street, which was open. Just before 8:30 a.m. Prof. Walt Heinecke welcomed them all to McGuffey Park. Wes Bellamy followed his remarks with the declaration "This is *our* town." The mood was buoyant. Members of the Clergy Collective got ready to speak.

Heinecke, the host of the Friday night spaghetti dinner, had secured permits for both McGuffey and Justice Parks. McGuffey was two blocks west of Emancipation; Justice two blocks east. Between these two parks students, legal observers, visiting clergy, and counterprotesters would have a safe space to gather or retreat to. McGuffey would have snack and first aid tents. Bonnie Gordon, the UVA music professor, would play the viola as part of the daylong program Devin Willis had arranged. Her music department colleague, a hip-hop artist named A. D. Carson, would recite a poem titled "Mourning in America." Devin would talk a little about what had transpired at the statue the night before.

Grace Aheron had spent the previous day picking people up from the airport and bringing them back to Charis. She'd arrived at McGuffey Park early, with a dozen friends piled in Rowan's van, and was amazed to have found a parking space. The large Sally Hemings puppet with a papier-mâché head came with her, along with black paper birds on sticks marked with the hashtag #defendcville.

Grace had thought a lot about crafting an alternate narrative for the media to cover. She'd probably spoken to Jalane's partner a hundred times a day that summer. Her Puppetistas planned to hit the streets to retell the story of the statues, the Klan rally, the tear-gassing, the fight over the permit. She would then pivot to tell what they wanted to see happen that day, and what they wanted the world to look like in the future. Jalane, Lisa Woolfork, and Laura Goldblatt would be doing media liaison work in a safe house nearby, keeping an eye on Congregate's livestream, Emily's Periscope, and various Signal threads. Presumably, they would alert the media when the puppet performance began. Andy Stepanian would be out on the streets with the media, reporting back to them on what was happening.

"As I write this people are getting in cars and getting to Charlottesville after what they saw last night," Richard Spencer wrote in an email to the National Policy Institute listserv that morning. Megan Squire, the computer scientist who had monitored Unite the Right on Facebook, and her husband, Tony Crider, were among those getting in their cars. They had both watched Emily's livestream the night before. The students at the statue were the same age as her college students, Megan said, the same age as her children.

A local photographer named Ézé Amos had been at the sunrise service and had photographed the community procession to McGuffey Park. At 8:30 a.m., he was taking pictures of two dozen state troopers carrying riot gear up Second Street NW, when a lone man in a fashy white polo shirt following behind them caught his eye. After watching the torch march footage, twenty-year-old James Alex Fields Jr. had left Maumee, Ohio, and driven all night to reach Charlottesville. Before he left, his mother texted him: "Be careful." He texted back: "We're not the ones who have to be careful." Fields was the driver of the car that would later kill Heather Heyer. When he stopped to look at his phone, Ézé took his picture. The sound of the shutter made Fields look up. Ézé snapped again. It's an unsettling photograph.

After the doors of First Baptist shut behind Don Gathers, Seth and Smash realized they had a problem. To avoid putting people of color, Jews, or Muslims in harm's way, they had intended to have only white people participate in direct action. But the white people they had counted on had largely left with Don Gathers. This included those clergy who had come to town in response to the clergy call, as well as the laypeople who had lined up to receive blessings at the altar calls. They'd hoped for 250 people. Among the fifty or so who remained behind, many from vulnerable communities, some were having second thoughts.

Rev. Sekou had never denied the danger; left unsaid was that there was safety in numbers. Their original plan was to surround the park, prevent the rallygoers from entering, and be arrested. While two of the four entrances of the park were now behind barricades, they still had only enough people to line up on the Market Street side of the park. What would that accomplish? Some felt it was too dangerous to proceed. They would be as outmatched as the students had been. Others were not on board with being arrested. One minister, unaware of what the commitment to participate in nonviolent direct action entailed, said his congregation wouldn't see his arrest as a Christian act.

Everyone was given a chance to speak. Everyone was free to bow out. A queer minister who was something of a leftist celebrity suggested that their talk of holding space reflected a territorial theology that reeked of settler colonialism. The Christian thing would be to let the rally happen unopposed. No one reacted kindly to that. Smash realized that some of those who had come from out of town arrived with different expectations of what they were there to do. Those who'd been training for weeks were on the same page. The disconnect between the locals and the out-of-towners would be felt in various ways as the day wore on, both among the clergy, and among factions of the counterprotest. Yet, whether they joined them on the streets or not, the clergy and lay activists Congregate had mobilized for August 12 outnumbered every other group—anti-racist, BLM, anti-fascist, DSA, anarchist, or black bloc—that showed up.

To lay the matter to rest, Rev. Sekou said, "We have a plan. We have local leadership in Smash and Seth. I'm going to go with what they say." Rev. Traci Blackmon, who'd already been targeted by trolls, chose to live to fight another day. She would show her support by doing a Facebook livestream. Lisa Sharon Harper, the Black theologian, was torn. Cornel West kept quiet. He was there to go to jail, he said, not to run his mouth.

Among those who accompanied Seth and Smash to Emancipation Park that morning was Dr. Jeffrey Pugh. A white ordained minister, a colleague and friend of Megan Squire and Tony Crider at Elon University, he was on the cusp of retiring to Charlottesville. As a professor of religious studies, Pugh gave lectures on the relationship between anti-Semitism, white supremacy, and the church. He believed the failure of German church leaders to confront Hitler's Brown Shirts in the streets doomed them. Beth Foster, a redhead in glasses, didn't know anyone there. She had driven up with a group of anti-racists from Chattanooga. A longtime ally of Daryle Lamont Jenkins, she donned a stole and joined the clergy ranks. Bekah Menning, the reluctant rabble-rouser, cofounder of Showing Up for Racial Justice, and dedicated member of Congregate, was terrified. The question "Would she have braved the walk over the Edmund Pettus Bridge?" was her touchstone. She placed her trust in Smash and Seth's vision of faithful nonviolence.

Standing alongside Bekah was Lisa Draine's friend and Bekah's buddy for the day, Ann Marie Smith. Smith was the mother of three who'd been awakened by Zyahna Bryant's remarks at Wes Bellamy's press conference. A meditation practice she had begun during a brutal struggle with cancer had steered her to Buddhism; her close-cropped head reminded her both of her vows and the illness that led her to them. A year earlier she'd begun the chaplaincy program at UVA hospital. Absent a local Buddhist sangha to complete her internship, she ended up with the young people at Charis. Ann Marie had resisted the pull of Rev. Sekou's charismatic gospel. People coming from Abrahamic traditions, she told me, tend toward a binary way of thinking about good and evil. Still, over the objections of her husband, she committed herself to civil disobedience. Her stole featured a lotus, a prayer wheel, a Star of David, and a cross.

Brandy Daniels was a tall, striking-looking woman with long chestnut hair and a sly sense of humor. Raised as a Christian evangelical, she'd been kicked out of Wheaton College for dating women. After that, she joined an organization that traveled around the country trying to engage students at Bible colleges and conservative seminaries. Like Rev. Sekou, she'd been trained by Jim Lawson in nonviolent direct action and had been arrested many times. She had just arrived in town to do a postdoc in theology at UVA. Her multicolored stole was draped over black robes.

Eric Martin, the Catholic Worker, was also no stranger to jail cells. Smash was one of his dearest friends. He was always going to be there. Bee Lambert was a local atheist in her seventies with long gray hair. At the Klan rally she had carried the sign that read "We are your white enemies." Back in the sixties, she'd been a member of the Student Nonviolent Coordinating Committee and, with her husband, spent years on the lam from the FBI. She too donned a stole and prepared to be arrested. In the end, Lisa Sharon Harper bravely threw in her hat. As they left First Baptist, Jeffrey Pugh tweeted, "Charlottesville under Code Red. Violence and injury likely."

Walking two by two, they headed east down West Main Street in solemn silence, passing the Lewis and Clark statue to enter the westernmost end of the Downtown Mall. Wes Bellamy, escorted from McGuffey Park by two state troopers, crossed paths with them there. He was en route to Rev. Alvin Edwards's Back to School Bash in Fifeville's Tonsler Park. Nazis or no Nazis, for the minister of Mount Zion First African Baptist and leader of the Clergy Collective, backpacks and school supplies were still needed. For many in the Black community, carrying on with their day-to-day commitments to one another was not, or not simply, an act of resistance. It was who they were.

Turning up First Street N, the clergy walked ten abreast. Bee Lambert smiled serenely in the center, her arms linked with Smash on one side and Cornel West on the other. Eric Martin was on one end in cargo shorts next to a New York woman in a hijab. They exchanged jokes to leaven the mood, but Seth shushed them. Rev. Sekou was on the other end next to Lisa Sharon Harper. Behind them was a rabbinical student wearing a kippah and prayer shawl, along with activists and out-of-town clergy of many denominations. Legal observers in lime green caps took up the rear. Police cruisers sat crosswise on Market at First Street N in front of the funeral home and at Second Street NE. Two satellite trucks sat in front of the library. The clergy arrived just after 9:00 a.m. The street was eerily quiet.

Holy shit, Jeff Pugh thought when he saw the militias. They had been forewarned that the rallygoers would have guns. But no one was prepared for the militias. Beth Foster from Chattanooga had been in protests all over the South and had never seen them before. "It was like arriving in an occupied American city," she said. Even the Virginia State Police were disconcerted. "What are they, like, military?" one trooper asked another. "They're more armed than we are."

Thirty-two members of the Pennsylvania Lightfoot Division had shown up, falsely claiming they were there with the blessing of the Charlottesville Police Department. Some militias sported Punisher patches on their helmets and wore bulletproof vests and gloves with built-in brass knuckles. They bristled with pistols and AR-15s. They wore knives strapped to their legs and chests and were equipped with earpieces and radios. A cohort of Three Percenters from New York wore bandoliers. When questioned, they said they were there to keep the peace. As the clergy spread out along the Market Street curb facing the park, nearly filling the gap between the southwest and southeast entrances, militia members posted themselves on the sidewalk in front of them.

Rev. Sekou cut the tension by starting a round of "This Little Light of Mine." Photographers stood on the knee-high stone wall that marked the edge of the park taking pictures over the shoulders of militia members. Then each person in the clergy line offered a brief, spoken prayer. Rev. Sekou went first: "We come in the name of love." Lisa Sharon Harper prayed for the protection of the city. Cornel West spoke in the name of John Coltrane and his *Love Supreme*: "Let us never be afraid of facing hatred. And let us bear witness to love, knowing that justice is what love looks like in public." Smash asked forgiveness for the sin of white supremacy. "Help us realize the white supremacy in ourselves."

"Is this every lesbian clergy member in America in one place?" The photographers swiveled to see a smirking rallygoer leaning against a tree outside the barricades, one of the early arrivals. He demanded they recite a Bible verse to prove they were legitimate. Brandy Daniels was used to being jeered and spat at and knew better than to respond to provocation. She heard "nigger lover" a few times and, because she was standing near two rabbis, anti-Semitic slurs. It was the militias she found confusing. Some were friendly. One Three Percenter thanked her for being there. Later, he joined them in song.

"God, thank you for making me a straight white man," Seth said, interrupting the insults, "so that I can stand with those who are so de-humanized and made to feel that they don't belong."

As the prayers progressed down the line, people carrying cups of coffee strolled behind them. Some clergy turned their back to the park and faced the street as it was not clear from which direction the rally-goers would arrive. Rev. Sekou would periodically check in on people, while Smash remained rooted in place, her heart pounding. The prayers were still moving down the line when they heard the first chants of "Blood and soil." Everyone turned to see where they were coming from. Twelve minutes after the clergy reached Market Street, the photographers sprinted off to meet the new arrivals.

The Fusion Center briefing had emphasized the importance of keeping counterprotesters apart from the rallygoers, the need for separate entrances and exits, and supervised transport to and from the venue. Sgt. Tony Newberry of the CPD, and Jack Peirce, Spencer's security man, had worked out a plan for the VIPs, but there was no plan to keep the rest of the rallygoers separate from the counterprotesters or to supervise their transport. Only the two white vans of the seventeen scheduled speakers would be escorted by unmarked police cars down McIntire Road to East High Street to disembark at First Street N. There they would be waved through the barricades to enter the rear of Emancipation Park from East Jefferson Street, at the foot of the steps of First United Methodist. That, at least, had been the plan. All that remained to be settled that morning was what time the vans would depart McIntire Park where Unite the Right was staging. Sgt. Newberry was eager to get them settled in the park before the streets filled with counterprotesters. He'd been trying to get a firm answer from Peirce since 7:00 a.m., but Peirce wasn't answering his calls.

At 8:45 a.m. the CPD reported that rally attendees had begun to gather in McIntire Park. They relayed sightings of David Duke, Mike "Enoch" Peinovich, Richard Spencer, and Jason Kessler. The first vans were being loaded for the relays to Emancipation Park. The Virginia Department of Emergency Management estimated that over one thousand of them were in the downtown area, with buses still arriving. Finally, at 9:00 a.m., Jack Peirce broke the news to Sgt. Newberry that the Unite the Right speakers would make their own way to the park.

A Portland detective had warned the CPD. This was their MO: Convey their respect for the work of policing the violent Antifa, sign off on their plan, go rogue. Every shuttle van had its own armed security; there was never any need for a police escort. Like other warnings from outside the department or from lower down in the chain of command, the detective's warning never penetrated what one officer described as the "brick wall" of upper management. Sgt. Newberry refused to believe Peirce had purposefully misled him.

In the end, both rallygoers and VIPs arrived at the park from every direction. They parked in and around Court Square, at the Jefferson School, or in surface lots and garages on both sides of the Downtown Mall. Many parked in residential neighborhoods adjacent to downtown. Shuttle vans dropped off rallygoers at the foot of Market Street, from which they made their way to the park on foot, passing by scores of counterprotesters. Other vans arrived in relays running on a loop from McIntire Park to Second Street NE, where a lone CPD forensic technician armed only with pepper spray was posted on East High. After disembarking, they would get into formation, circle the long way around to Emancipation Park so that they might stage a dramatic entrance, flaunting their various uniforms, flying their flags, brandishing their shields. As with the torch march, speeches couldn't compete with a choreographed spectacle of menace.

This, of course, was Eli Mosley's plan. He arrived in the first shuttle, dropped off on East High Street near the forensic technician and her cruiser. Accompanying him was a pint-sized Texan in mirrored aviators named Thomas Rousseau. Rousseau was the eighteen-year-old upstart commander of Vanguard America. Dillon Hopper had been locked out of Vanguard America's servers in a Rousseau-engineered coup. As a result,

Hopper had not come to Charlottesville. With Mosley and Rousseau were forty Vanguard America men, all in shiny black helmets equipped with face shields and blindingly white shirts embossed with an eagle and fasces. Technically, Vanguard America was part of the Nationalist Front, so one would have thought they'd be marching alongside Matthew Heimbach et al., but Rousseau, unlike Hopper, disdained to be seen with the grubbier neo-Nazis and Trad Workers.

With Second Street NE closed to foot traffic, the group walked two blocks east, in the opposite direction from Emancipation Park, turning right at Fourth Street NE, to arrive, in all their finery, at Justice Park. Mosley wasn't lost; he was on parade. Among the events planned for Justice Park that day was a speech on racial justice delivered by Jeff Fogel, the civil rights attorney arrested the night Jason Kessler was banned from Miller's. There would be a Quaker worship service and a teach-in on systemic racism. Tyler Magill provided live WTJU programming. Legal observers staged at the Jackson statue.

Kristopher Goad saw a member of the John Brown Gun Club intercept Eli Mosley to tell him he had the wrong park. The Vanguard America lines continued down Fourth Street NE before turning right on Market. As they closed on the library, they started chanting. Emerging from the shadow of the satellite trucks, Mosley threw his shoulders back and began to strut, his eyes trained on the distance. Cameras clicked like a field of locusts. Lined up at the top of the steps on the public side of the park were James Alex Fields Jr. and five stray Vanguard America men. Richard Preston, a ponytailed and goateed Imperial Wizard of the Confederate White Knights, a klavern out of Maryland, skulked behind them. Seeing the white polos, Mosley made a beeline for them. No one stopped him. Daryle Lamont Jenkins, who had driven down from Philadelphia the night before with a carful of allies, talked with Andy Stepanian at the bottom of the steps as the last of the Vanguard America men filed by.

Told by a police officer he was on the wrong side of the park, Mosley turned on his heel, skirted the steps, and hopped off the low wall onto the sidewalk. The Vanguard America men followed him, chanting, "You will not replace us." James Alex Fields fell in behind them. The men passed the suddenly silent clergy line. The police looked on dully from their pens. The first formation of rallygoers had encountered little resistance beyond Star Peterson, the special ed teacher, shouting, "Black lives matter!" Peterson had been at the statue the night before, working as a medic and washing pepper spray out of people's eyes. Everyone else seemed mesmerized. Even the militias stepped aside to let them pass.

Reaching the southwest side of the park, the Vanguard America men took up positions inside the park behind the row of barricades facing the clergy line. Fields would soon be photographed there with a VA shield, provided to him by a member of Rousseau's Texas entourage. Mosley stationed himself at the top of the steps at the park's southwest corner and began checking his phone. Behind him stood a Proud Boy in dark glasses, holding a coffee and wearing a lumberjack shirt under a bulletproof vest.

This was Enrique Tarrio, a man who would soon take over leadership of the Proud Boys from Gavin McInnes. Tarrio had first strolled up and down Market with a group of unaffiliated rallygoers and militias, as if testing the waters. Accompanying him was a rabid anti-communist in a red tricorne MAGA hat wearing a white linen suit with Pepe the Frog embroidered on a lapel. Another blasted an air horn.

In the clergy line, Brandy Daniels noted the rallygoers weren't staying in the park. They would come out to stir things up and then retreat. One bumped into her, trying to knock her over. As more rallygoers showed up they would hang around outside the park before going in.

Just before 10:00 a.m., Tanesha Hudson, a thirty-five-year-old activist who briefly joined the clergy line, asked one of the officers in the enclosure in front of her why none of them was on the streets. It was the right question.

"When things happen," he assured her, "we'll respond."

Hudson had seen these same police officers chase young Black men on very little pretext. She'd never seen them stand and watch. She shot back.

"*When* they happen? You're supposed to *prevent* them from happening."

During this exchange Eli Mosley left Emancipation Park with twenty-five men, including helmeted militias, two men in Radical Agenda T-shirts, the anti-communist in the red tricorne MAGA hat, and an older man in a Hitler T-shirt. Mosley wore the sort of earpiece seen on body-guards, with a mike clipped to his button-down shirt and a radio on his belt. Presumably this is how he had arranged to meet up with nine members of the Rise Above Movement, the ultranationalist and racist neo-Nazi fight club out of Southern California that Nathan Damigo had trained with in advance of Berkeley. They were led by a willowy man in dark glasses and peroxide hair topped by a Tintin-style flourish. Both Tintin and an aerospace engineer from Northrop Grumman had just re-turned from a trip to Italy and Germany, where they met with far-right leaders. Among the men accompanying them to Unite the Right was one who can be seen pounding a man in the background of Damigo's viral Berkeley video.

The Rise Above Movement men arrived with taped-up hands and brawling gloves. Northrop Grumman wore a mouthguard. While Mosley conferred with them on East High, his flag-bearing troops started down Second Street NE, passing the parking lot of First Methodist United Church. The RAM men took up the rear, only to be stopped by the bar-ricades on East Jefferson, where they were forced to turn around. Near the First United Methodist parking lot, they ran into a line of follow-ers of the communist leader Bob Avakian blocking their way. A curly-haired woman in a Revolution Now T-shirt taunted them, as Mosley paced back and forth in front of his lines. "We have a plan to defeat not just these fools in front of us," she shouted through a megaphone, "but the whole system that generated them." There were other such groups in town like this one, piggybacking on the counterprotest, but with their own agendas and leaflets.

A bearded white man from Chattanooga in a black cap had been filming Mosley's people with his phone. Tintin grabbed him by his neck and sleeves while someone else punched him. A man with earlobe gauges wearing a Radical Agenda T-shirt joined in. The Chattanooga man fell on the sidewalk and was set upon by Vanguard America mem-bers. The Revolution Now woman who had been goading them tried to intercede but retreated with a bloodied head. The man's girlfriend ran in only to have her forehead sliced open with a head butt. Both had accompanied Beth Foster to Charlottesville and were committed to nonviolence. Volunteers in the church parking lot looked on in disbelief. The attack seemed to come out of nowhere. Another Revolution Now woman tried to pull the girlfriend out of the melee, but she too was set upon.

A man in a mustard-colored shirt finally pulled her to safety, her face a sheet of blood. Flecks of blood now dotted Eli Mosley's white button-down shirt. The fight spilled into the church parking lot. The unarmed forensic technician, ordered to stay at her post, watched and waited for the state troopers standing nearby to act. After five minutes, they ambled over. This was sufficient to put a stop to the attack. Mosley retreated the way he had come, snapping at everyone to keep moving. He had been looking for a fight, and the Rise Above Movement men helped him find one.

"The Nazis just continued to march on," the Chattanooga woman recalled in disbelief. Her forehead required twelve stitches. When a fifty-eight-year-old pilot asked a state trooper why they had not intervened, he was told that they were under orders not to get involved in every little skirmish. When he pointed out the fight amounted to more than that, the trooper conveyed to him, with an aggressively expressionless face, that he couldn't have cared less. Behind this blank stare, the pilot imagined him thinking: *What the hell's up with this guy? Why is he even here?* As if he wasn't certain he liked people like him, with his Obama T-shirt, any more than he liked the rallygoers.

Five minutes after the attack near the church parking lot, when a counterprotester tried to steal a green Kekistan flag from a rallygoer on Market, two officers in the Wells Fargo Bank parking lot jumped over the barricade to intercede. Watching from across the street, a local officer posted at the zone closest to where the attack had taken place asked his zone commander: "What happened to not going outside the gate if they are beating the crap out of each other?"

"Yeah, well, that was somebody else's zone," was the reply. This was the first and last instance of a police officer leaving the barricades to de-escalate a potentially violent encounter. Subsequently, that officer and every other officer in the bank parking lot zone were ordered to "save their energy."

Grace and the Puppetistas arrived on East High within minutes of the fracas. It took her no time at all to realize a puppet performance couldn't compete with street warfare. They had all girded themselves for a police crackdown. They hadn't expected no police response whatsoever. She couldn't overstate people's shock over this. "They were, like, 'wait . . . *what*?'"

By 10:20 a.m., Eli Mosley was back at his perch at the southwest entrance, welcoming the arrival of Sacco Vandal. The Virginia Department of Emergency Management estimated the crowd inside the park had reached fifteen hundred.

The clergy line was wilting in the midmorning heat and humidity. Standing and kneeling became sitting on the curb. It was still overcast; the sun wouldn't fully emerge until close to noon. Then, at 10:21 a.m., the energy on the street shifted. A phalanx of anti-fascists, chanting "*Antifascista*" and "*No pasaran*," arrived on Market, marching behind a black Fascist Scum banner. Behind them were an array of Democratic Socialists of America flags, Anti-Fascist Action black flags, and a banner carried by the Carolina Anti-Racists. The anti-fascists included equal numbers of women and men and a smattering of people of color. Nearly all sported sunglasses, hats, and kerchiefs. Megan Squire marched in with the Raleigh-Durham branch of the Industrial Workers of the World General Defense Committee. Among them, too, was Lacy MacAuley, a flame-haired anarchist from DC, equipped with a megaphone. She parked herself at the southwest entrance, directing her chants at Mosley and arriving rallygoers.

"We don't want a fascist state! We say no to racist hate!"

A multiracial troupe of eight women from Richmond who called themselves the Seven Hill Autonomous Queers also arrived with the anti-fascists. They had helmets painted pink and carried pink-and-black shields. In all the videos I watched, I counted only three men and one woman who might reasonably be identified as "black bloc." They were equipped with gas masks, black body armor, black helmets, scarfs, and sunglasses and weren't at all shy about directly engaging with rallygoers. Enrique Tarrio, standing on the edge of the park, pointed them

out. In response, the black bloc woman yelled, "Fuck you, Nazi trash."
After blowing her a kiss, Tarrio mouthed, "You don't know what I am."
Tarrio was an Afro-Cuban Proud Boy allied with white supremacists
and white nationalists. He was also a federal informant. Did *he* know?

When the anti-fascists tried to enter the side of the park set aside for
the public, the militias stopped them, thinking the entire park was reserved for the rallygoers. Apart from a group of singing Quakers and a
man with a sign offering hugs to anyone who wanted one, few members
of the public had ventured into the side of the park allotted for them.
When Rev. Sekou decided to make his move, he, too, was unaware that
the entrance he chose to block was the public entrance.

Word came down the clergy line, telephone style. If people felt comfortable, they would now move to the southeast steps so that arriving
rallygoers would be unable to enter the park. Such an action would
also draw attention away from Eli Mosley and the anti-fascists at the
southwest entrance. Sekou gave the clergy a minute to think about it
before he gave the order to move.

Of those fifty who had marched from First Baptist, half decided to
mount the southeast steps. The New York woman in the headscarf and
the seventy-something atheist Bee Lambert were among them. After
confirming with her "buddy," Bekah Menning, that they would both be
joining the action, Ann Marie Smith asked a friend to text her husband
and let him know that she was about to get arrested and that he should
meet her at the jail. But when the zone commander on Second Street
NE saw the clergy mount the steps he assumed their intention was to
prevent the counterprotesters from engaging with rallygoers. He wasn't
about to arrest them. The entire state and city police force appeared content to let others do their work for them while they watched from the
safety of their pens. The clergy lined up in rows, with half facing the park
and half facing Market.

While they waited with linked arms, vans carrying Azzmador and his
crew of around fifty Stormers pulled up two blocks north on East High.
Ten Stormers in helmets emerged first, carrying square black shields with
a ghostly spray-painted Punisher skull at the center; Azzmador's three
bearded lieutenants, two beefy and one skinny, carried round shields

with sonnenrads (an occult symbol aligned with neo-Nazi ideologies) inside red circles. Another carried the tube with Azzmador's prize banner calling for the end of Jewish control of America. Seeing another fifty Identity Evropa men marching toward them, having been turned back by the barricades on East Jefferson, Azzmador's column headed east on High Street with the Identity Evropa men falling in behind them.

Azzmador's livestreamer peeled off to film Don Gathers, Rev. Phil Woodson, and others lining up to guard the periphery of First United Methodist's parking lot. In the aftermath of Eli Mosley's incursion, they weren't taking any chances. After some confusion about which way to go, Azzmador turned right on Third Street NE, which took them by Congregation Beth Israel. "Yeah, I'm the Jew Hunter General," he crowed to a woman on the sidewalk. Azzmador had, in fact, mistaken First United Methodist Church for the "synagogue of Satan." Reaching Market, his men began grunting like football players.

By then, preprinted signs saying "Smash White Supremacy," "Make Racists Afraid Again," "Black Lives Matter," and "KKKessler Is Nazi Trash" filled the stretch of Market in front of the park, alongside black Anti-Fascist Action flags, red, black, and green Pan-African flags, and red Industrial Workers of the World flags. The IWW was founded in Chicago in the early twentieth century; its presence in American labor history had ebbed and flowed ever since. IWW members, who call themselves Wobblies, now joined everyone heading toward the intersection of Market and Second Street NE. Reaching Rev. Sekou on the southeast steps, they asked, "What do you need us to do?" Sekou told them to leave the intersection and the area in front of the steps open.

"Shields to the front" Azzmador called out, bringing those with Punisher shields scurrying to form a phalanx alongside the three sonnenrad shields. Once in place, they restarted their grunting, advancing down the sidewalk. After the line of shields passed the satellite trucks in front of the library, the chant became "Get the reds out." They stopped at the corner of Second Street NE.

Azzmador's livestreamer panned the vista in front of them, capturing a street packed with counterprotesters, blocking their way west down

Market. Daryle Lamont Jenkins was filming them at the foot of the southeast entrance, the clergy lining the steps behind him. A Hispanic man in a MAGA cap holding an American flag stood in the empty intersection taunting the anti-fascists. A woman with a megaphone chanted "Black lives they matter here!" next to Azzmador's lines.

Azzmador weighed which way to go. Proceed through the massed ranks of anti-fascists and counterprotesters on Market? Or take the easy route through the clergy? Because the police were inconsistent in ejecting rallygoers from the public side of the park, a Confederate flag beckoned from behind the clergy.

"You dress like a whore, Black lives do *not* matter, and Hitler did nothing wrong," Azzmador said to the woman shouting at them. He was biding his time.

"Nazi scum off our streets," the crowds across the intersection chanted.

"Walk through them fucks!" a Stormer shouted from the back of the line.

At this moment, Bekah Menning was arm in arm with Ann Marie Smith on the left side of the steps facing forward. Cornel West stood behind them, his arm linked with the redheaded Beth Foster from Chattanooga, also facing forward. On the right side of the handrail that ran down the middle of the steps was the chestnut-haired Brandy Daniels and the black-robed Rev. Sekou facing the street. Eric Martin, the Catholic Worker, stood on the right, at the top of the steps with a clear view of the streets. Behind them all, on each side of the steps, Smash and Seth stood sentry facing the park. They believed it was important to face the park, because that was where the rallygoers were. As a result, both were unaware of Azzmador's arrival, trailed by one hundred men.

Eric Martin's father had been a cop. Consequently, he had a habit of looking at things the way a cop would. When he arrived on Market and saw the way the barriers were arranged, his first thought was that this was bad police work. His second thought was that things were going to go south quickly. He was right.

Azzmador finally decided: he would take the easy route through the clergy. "Forward march!" he shouted. Ten men in green helmets carrying Punisher shields stepped off the curb with Azzmador behind them. Andy

Stepanian, at the foot of the steps, tried to engage one of the green helmets, but the man just moved around him, heading up the left side of the steps. Someone shouted, "Kill the faggot priest!" Brandy Daniels stared grimly ahead as the shields plowed through Bekah Menning, Ann Marie Smith, Cornel West, and Beth Foster. Seth, facing the park, was caught by surprise and got pushed into the bushes. One of Azzmador's red-bearded lieutenants spat "Fuck you, faggot" in his face as he struggled to his feet.

The clergy "opened up like a crack whore's legs," Azzmador later boasted, adding that he had looked Cornel West in the face and told him he was "for the rope." Beth Foster found the venom directed at West, bone-chilling. When a Stormer raised a club above his head, she feared for his life. West, however, appeared unfazed, she said, and even addressed one of the men as "brother." While they were still filing by, Rev. Sekou started singing.

Smash wasn't in the least interested in a new round of "This Little Light of Mine." She was furious. "What the FUCK just happened?" she burst out. How many hours had they practiced holding the line? "If we're going to be up here, we need to hold the line. If you can't hold the line, then get off the line," she said crossly. Bekah and Ann Marie were gutted and poured out apologies. Sekou reassured them. "No, it's okay. It's okay. But like, hold, hold it next time, right?" Smash wasn't so understanding. The failure to hold the line compounded the mistake they had made the night before, of not sending anybody over to help the students at the Jefferson statue. Smash believed she had again failed the community. Later, she and Seth learned it was Cornel West who had told those on the left side of the steps to let the marchers through.

After the last of the Stormers and Identity Evropa members filed into the park, Seth followed Smash's tongue-lashing with a pep talk. By then both he and Smash had moved to the front, where they had a view of the street. But now the Wobblies and members of Redneck Rebellion wanted to know what the hell was going on. The black bloc woman who'd clashed with Enrique Tarrio changed her chant from "Kill. All. Nazis." to "Stop. Protecting. Nazis," followed by "Protect. Us. Instead." There was a hasty conference with Rev. Sekou behind an array of IWW flags.

"What are you doing?" they asked. "It looked like you all were letting them in."

Sekou told them they were caught by surprise. A long-haired Wobbly piped up. "Reverend Sekou, I know who you are, I respect your work, but they will not touch you on our watch." Sekou reminded him that they were there in the spirit of nonviolence.

"Sir, they will not touch you on our watch."

Sekou accepted their protection. Anti-fascists and anti-racists moved their phalanx east of the Second Street NE intersection, blocking Market from sidewalk to sidewalk, with another line of anti-fascists arrayed in front of the southeast entrance.

Daryle Lamont Jenkins greeted Azzmador at the top of the steps. "Show us your collection of porn, you fat bastard," was Azzmador's reply. The man with the hugs sign offered Azzmador a bottle of water. He ignored him. It didn't take long before Azzmador realized he was on the wrong side of the park. After conferring with his shield wall, it was back out into the street, avoiding the clergy by clambering down the low stone wall to the left of the steps. They ran a gauntlet of curses from the anti-fascists during their quick trot to the southwest entrance but arrived unharmed. The Vanguard America shield wall behind Mosley opened to admit them. On his arrival, Azzmador was given a rowdy welcome, showered with backslaps and name-checks, hoots, and hollers.

Not three minutes later, at 10:46 a.m., a line of men looking extremely sharp in dark glasses and navy suit jackets heralded the arrival of Richard Spencer at the southwest entrance. "Let him in!" The crowd erupted in cheers; phones came out. Spencer's security pushed back overly eager fans vying for selfies, widening a corridor that enabled him to pass unmolested by the masses. Eli Mosley evicted a blond photographer who snuck in after him. Azzmador was quickly forgotten.

"I love the smell of mace in the morning," Spencer shouted.

"Hail Spencer!"

"Spencer, great to meet you." A foppish-looking livestreamer in a black suit approached him, hand extended. Spencer's security stepped between them. "No handshakes right now, guys."

"Loved your AMA," a woman said.

"Oh good, glad you watched."

"Yeah, made us up our game," she replied.

"Hey Richard," another fan piped up holding a phone. "Can you say hi to someone for me?"

"All right, from afar."

"Say Hi, Stacy."

"Hey, Stacy." Spencer gave a thumbs-up and smirked.

Jason Kessler was next to arrive, forcing Azzmador to step aside to make way for his security detail. The smell of some chemical wafted in from Market.

"Do you feel that," the foppish livestreamer asked a faintly mustachioed man in a suit and MAGA hat, "when you breathe it in?"

"Yeah, I felt it." The man looked as if he hadn't seen the sun in a while.

"It's tear gas," the fop said. "Antifa was talking about burning poison ivy."

Four Wobblies now posted themselves at the foot of the southeast steps, offering the clergy a thin layer of defense. Sandwiched between them was Megan Squire in a gray head wrap. Within minutes, everyone on the street was again looking east. A new wave was coming—not down the sidewalk, as Eli Mosley and Azzmador had. The next wave was streaming out of the multilevel Market Street parking garage and filling the street.

Matthew Heimbach of the Traditionalist Worker Party told Vegas Tenold that he had tried to reach law enforcement to find out how he should access the rally site, but they never got back to him. Tenold took him at his word. But Heimbach knew there would be shuttles from McIntire Park; it was on the Discord planning channel. His Nationalist Front cadres had always planned on going rogue. They all assembled on the garage roof where the chief of operations for the League of the South gave a speech reminding them why they were there. "This is the greatest assemblage of white identity Aryans that I, personally, have ever seen. None of us here are alt-right or alt-lite. We're here because we are the *hard* right." It was up to them, he said, to take the park.

The first to emerge from the garage was League of the South founder,

Dr. Michael Hill. He was wearing brawling gloves and carrying a stick. Next to him was his national chairman, the bare-fisted Michael Tubbs, and Matthew Heimbach. Both Tubbs and Hill were well over six feet tall with matching white goatees. Compared to Heimbach's happy warrior grin, they were grim-faced. Both wore dark glasses and vests adorned with Southern Cross patches. There the similarities ended.

In 1994, while still a professor of British history at Stillman College, an HBCU in Tuscaloosa, Alabama, Michael Hill had founded the League of the South. In the years since, he'd become the driving intellect behind the movement for Southern secession. He was now the director of the Institute for the Study of Southern Culture and History, the educational arm of the League. Tubbs, on the other hand, was a former US Special Forces soldier. He had spent four years in prison, convicted of domestic terrorism after having stolen military equipment with a plan to bomb Black- and Jewish-owned businesses in Jacksonville, Florida. A giant of a man with long, graying hair, he rallied his men like a symphony conductor, a can of bear mace in his pocket. Immediately behind Hill and Tubbs were the ranks of the Southern Defense Force, the militant wing of the League of the South. Equipped with a dozen heavy white plastic shields emblazoned with the black Southern Cross, they made up the League of the South shield wall.

Charlottesville is a city of rolling hills. From the Market Street garage to Emancipation Park, Market Street first dips then, approaching the library, flattens out as it passes the park. The League leadership appeared at the crest of Fifth Street NE near the garage before descending. A contingent of Southern Cross and Confederate flag bearers rose in their wake. Then came the neo-Nazi Jeff Schoep and his National Socialist Movement banner, held aloft by two black-booted women. The NSM cadres included the Blood and Honour Social Clubs of New York and Pennsylvania. These were bulked-up men in biker gear with tattooed heads and faces who appeared fresh from the prison yard. A neo-Nazi who hadn't got the memo barring swastikas carried a Nazi flag. They, too, crested the hill. They were followed by sixty black-shirted Trad Worker Party cadres who were equipped with twelve clear surplus police riot shields and construction helmets painted black with the TWP logo in white. I counted over 225 men and women in the Nationalist Front lines.

David Duke was in the middle. Brad Griffin of Occidental Dissent marched with his wife and livestreamed on Periscope. No one noticed Emily Gorcenski, doing her own Periscope from the sidewalk as they passed by. Emily had spent the night in an Airbnb with a bunch of Southern anarchists. After filing assault charges against Christopher Cantwell that morning in a practically empty police station, she'd been hanging out on the periphery of Justice Park with a crew of armed women. "I think I did everything I needed to do last night with my video showing what was going on," she told those following her on Periscope. Having promised her wife she wouldn't go near the rally, this was the closest she'd get to Emancipation Park. She knew they were looking for her.

At 10:50 a.m. Rev. Traci Blackmon began a live on-camera interview with Joy Reid on *AM Joy*, a weekend morning show on MSNBC. Rev. Blackmon faced the barricaded Wells Fargo parking lot. Behind her a river of counterprotesters was flowing steadily down Market toward the Second Street NE intersection. Over her shoulder the clergy could be seen on the steps. Out of sight were thirty or so anti-fascists who had formed a line to prevent the Nationalist Front cadres from progressing farther down Market and from entering the park where the clergy stood. Tony Crider, Megan Squire's husband, narrated the scene on Facebook Live. "All right. Here comes the big wave. This should be interesting." He panned to the clergy at the top of the steps, with his wife and the four Wobblies standing guard below.

"On this corner we have the entrance, with the clergy and IWW." Crider then walked around the empty cruiser parked in the middle of the intersection. "And here we've got . . ." The full view of the brigades bearing down on the anti-fascist lines blocking Market stunned him into silence. A woman's voice from the anti-fascist lines could be heard screaming, "We need more people!" The Seven Hill Autonomous Queers and BLM crews raced across the intersection to support the line. Cameras followed. Chants of "Nazi scum, off our streets" filled the air.

Two and a half minutes into the *AM Joy* broadcast, at 10:52 a.m., Rev. Blackmon was in the middle of describing the previous night's service at St. Paul's when she was suddenly swept away by her security. She had only enough time to shout "Gotta go gotta go."

Bekah Menning would never forget the spectacle of downtown Charlottesville descending into utter lawlessness. From her place at the top of the steps, she was reminded of that scene in *Lord of the Rings*, when the Elves confront the hordes of Orcs. Only here the Elves were the anti-fascists. The clergy, she supposed, were the earnest and peaceable Hobbits, protecting all that was sacred from all that was evil. Ann Marie Smith, meanwhile, was having an out-of-body experience. She realized later that whatever pact she imagined existed between them and the police had been a delusion. Brandy Daniels's first thought was, "Oh my God, we're gonna die and the police won't do anything." Her second was, "Okay, here goes." Rev. Sekou turned around and told them all to stay locked. The theologian Jeff Pugh turned to Cornel West and said, "We can't get the guys with the khakis and the white shirts, you know, we have to get these guys."

Tubbs hadn't hesitated upon reaching the intersection. He and the first wave of his shield wall crashed through the middle of the anti-fascist lines. He went directly after a tall white man with dreads who had placed himself front and center and sent him sprawling. At the moment the two groups clashed, the clergy could be seen on *AM Joy*'s live feed abandoning the steps. Jeff Pugh heard Rev. Sekou say, "Okay, our day here is done." Brandy Daniels heard, "Nope, this isn't worth it. Everyone disperse." The four Wobblies, plus Megan Squire, stepped up to take their place. Some of the anti-fascists fell back and lined up in front of them.

A second wave of shields barreled through in Tubbs's wake. The sticks, the collapsible batons, the pepper spray all came out and the two sides began whaling on each other. Counterprotesters launched balloons filled with blue paint. Tony Crider, still streaming, tried to describe the scene. "The cops," he began. "Well, the cops have left."

After a brief cutaway to a confused and concerned Joy Reid, the feed returned to the scene. On live morning television, a man was lying on the street next to the empty police cruiser being hammered and kicked by men holding white shields adorned with black Southern Crosses. When

AM Joy's producer couldn't reach Rev. Blackmon, Andy Stepanian got on the phone to describe the assault underway, unaware he was standing in front of the live feed. "They're using clubs, bats, and fortified brass knuckles," he narrated.

Stepanian had lost the clergy. The anti-fascists had created a corridor so they could make their escape, but no one knew where they had gone. Cornel West later credited the anarchists and anti-fascists with having saved the clergy from being crushed "like cockroaches."

During the first two minutes of the day's second full-scale riot, one white woman stood out. Though people later spoke of her with awe, no one knew who she was or where she came from. Tall, strapping, with long black hair sectioned off in braids and bare arms and legs etched with delicate plant tattoos, she stood at the far end of the anti-fascist frontlines. She escaped the direct hit of the shield wall but had caught the attention of a Trad Worker man in search of his viral moment. She leaned away from his blow to her head and then launched herself at him with such speed and force that he stumbled backward in surprise. She fell, grabbing his shirt as he kicked and punched her wildly, trying to get out of her grip. She pursued him into a crowd of older men holding Southern Cross and Confederate flags and heavyset Trad Worker men in black helmets, until she was surrounded. More men set upon her, kicking and beating her with sticks and fists. One grabbed her hair and pulled her to the ground. Others shouted, "Stop! Get out of here. Get the fuck out of here!" "Leave. Leave. Leave," they grunted.

"This is public property, you idiots," she yelled back as she rose, struggling to her feet, flailing, stone-faced, and fearless. "You better watch your back."

Only after a point-blank blast of mace to her eyes from a League of the South member in a batter's helmet did she retreat. Tony Crider later captured her sitting alone, leaning against the Jefferson Madison Regional Library sign on Second Street NE, calmly scrolling. The disruption she caused obliged Michael Tubbs to turn around, retrace his steps, and restore his lines. The anti-fascists had time to rally, but their line was now depleted by injuries, so the cadres of the Nationalist Front simply walked around them. Unable to proceed down Market—blocked

by the Seven Hill Autonomous Queers, anti-fascists, and Wobblies—
Tubbs also headed for the southeast steps.

Four Wobblies, two men, two women, had furled their flags, and
locked arms with Megan Squire, forcing the Nationalist Front to enter
the park on the left side of the steps, single file. The Wobblies were
pushed and shoved. They were called faggots. Fat and ugly. One Wobbly
suffered a cut above the eyes and bled tears. They were locked together
so tightly, Squire said, that the next day her arms had sleeves of bruises.
Squire ripped into Matthew Heimbach as he passed. She unleashed a
verbal tirade on the neo-Nazi Jeff Schoep, "so intense that he blew me
a kiss." One of the last flags to pass by, she noted sadly, was a Virginia
state flag. She thought, *Okay. They're in their park, they asked for that park,
I think that's the last one. They're done.*

They weren't. No sooner had they arrived than the Southern Defense
Force and Trad Worker Party cadres turned around and pushed their
League of the South and police surplus shields into the backs of the
Wobblies until they were forced off the steps. By 11:03 a.m., the Tubbs-
led lines had taken over the public side of the park and the full sweep
of the southeast steps. Reinforcements came from the other side of the
park by pushing their way through the crowds, streaming east down
the sidewalk where the clergy line had first stood. Members of Rise
Above Movement were the first to arrive.

A shield wall was put in place at the foot of the steps. Here fights between counterprotesters and rallygoers would break out intermittently,
until pepper spray sent them back to their places. The street was soon
covered in vomit and blood. IWW members retreated to the sidelines.
For eleven minutes, five unarmed people dressed in street clothes had
held half the steps without fighting back. In a day of few victories, this
was one. Later, they would pay the price.

A woman standing near the barricades on Second Street NE was
caught on a police camera looking back and forth at the fights over the
steps to the police in front of her, waiting and watching for a reaction.
With the cries for medics sounding in the background, she couldn't
bear it any longer. "This is shameful! I am a teacher; I am a community

member. Take care of your people! What the fuck are you doing?" The police stood silently, empty-eyed stares fixed on their faces.

Joy Reid's producer was still trying to locate Rev. Blackmon. An MSNBC reporter was found to give another live report. Describing where she was standing and what she was seeing, she noted, "I can hear drums going off in the distance."

The students had arrived.

CHAPTER 14

A State of Emergency

Lisa Draine, who had once worked on a photography exhibition at the newly opened Jefferson School African American Heritage Center, sometimes found its founding director, Dr. Andrea Douglas, hard to figure. While listening to various speakers hold forth at McGuffey Park that morning, Douglas had turned to her and remarked, "Just another day in the hood." Douglas, "the Art Historian" of the Blue Ribbon Commission was a stylish New Yorker, the daughter of Jamaican immigrants. Her air of reserve was matched by an all-consuming dedication to the center and the local Black community. Yet her subtle and sardonic sense of humor was often lost on people.

Lisa's daughters, Sophie and Rebecca, had left home early that morning. In response to her texts asking where they were and if they were coming to McGuffey, both eventually dropped by, but it wasn't their scene. They left with Devin Willis to rendezvous with the students who had been at the statue the night before. They were preparing a counter-protest at the nearby Bridge Arts Initiative. Despite the beating he received, Willis had risen at 5:30 a.m. so that he could be at McGuffey to put up tables and decide where to park the porta potties.

After her daughters left, Lisa got restless. She decided to venture out. The Downtown Mall was a ghost town. She bought a coffee at the only place open and headed east to the Bridge. A group of around twenty young people were preparing to disrupt the rally's speakers with drums, whistles, megaphones, and noisemakers. Some had been at the statue the night before and were sharing their experiences. Others were choosing what instruments to carry. Then her daughters saw her.

"What are *you* doing here, *Mom*?"

She told them she didn't want to be alone. They rolled their eyes.

"Look, you guys just got back to town. I've been here doing the work all summer long. I kind of need to be here and want to be here." After that they just ignored her.

"Okay, we're going to walk over to Market Street now," a student organizer announced. "Everyone, make sure you have a buddy."

Lisa turned to her daughters, but they had buddied up with each other. When the organizer asked who was unhitched, Devin Willis piped up: "I don't have a buddy." Lisa went over and introduced herself as Sophie's mom. The group arrived at the intersection of Market and Second Street NE shortly after the anti-fascist lines had been breached by Tubbs's shield wall. Forced to enter the park single file, there was now a Nationalist Front logjam at the southeast steps. The spectacle of the students' arrival, drumming and chanting "Black lives matter," was diminished by the thumping helicopter overhead and the atmosphere of chaos the Nationalist Front lines left in their wake.

When the students formed a line across Market, those with free hands locked arms and faced east in anticipation of the arrival of more far-right brigades. Others, wary of being doxed, covered their faces with cymbals, baseball hat rims, bandannas, and posters. Natalie Romero had come prepared with a pink UVA hat, a long-sleeved shirt, a black bandanna, and an anorak in case she got maced again. She had made the mistake of taking a shower to get last night's pepper spray off. That had set her whole body aflame and she ended up weeping in her bath-tub. Still, she found the nerve to come. She took a spot near a group of white students next to the empty police cruiser on Second Street NE. She was light-skinned enough to hope she wouldn't be noticed, but the Nationalist Front cadres waiting to enter the park diverted just to spit at her and tell her to go back to where she came from.

Just as the students were settling in, Chief Thomas in the Command

Center ordered all his officers to get in their riot gear and gather on East Jefferson. He was willing to let the crowds on Market fight it out so that by the time everyone was suited up in riot gear and gas masks, he could declare an unlawful assembly. Unfortunately for those on the streets, the riot gear wasn't in easy reach. The officers in the bank parking lot vanished, leaving only a few state troopers behind the barricades surrounding the park and no officers inside it.

The sudden disappearance of the police occasioned another level of shock. There was now no one to tell Michael Tubbs or Matthew Heimbach they were on the wrong side of the park. It hardly mattered; they hadn't come for a selfie with Richard Spencer. They weren't there to give media interviews as David Duke immediately did. Nor had they come for the speeches. They'd come for Black Lives Matter and "Antifa." With the police gone, someone took the initiative and pushed over the barricades dividing the park. As soon as they began walking over the downed bike racks to join their comrades, the anti-fascists started up the southeast steps to retake the public side of the park.

Then it was "Pull back! Pull back! Hold the line!"

Lisa Draine wanted to protect Devin Willis from the fascists, but where would they come from? Devin was facing east toward the Market Street garage; she was behind him. Should she be in front of him? Or should she turn around to face the shield wall that was slowly migrating into the intersection to provoke the Black counterprotesters waving tricolor Pan-African flags? In the bushes at either side of the steps, in the streets, at the police barricades, were livestreamers, photographers, legal observers, and curiosity seekers with phones aloft. Everyone was jockeying for position to get a shot of the fight about to take place between those on the street and those in the park. At 11:06 a.m. the first water bottles were launched. Tony Crider announced: "The fight begins." The black bloc woman seemed to be everywhere: "Kill. All. Nazis!" she shouted.

At 11:07 a.m. Rev. Blackmon was back on the phone with Joy Reid. "It is getting more volatile out here," she said. Projectiles were reaching the police tent where she was taking shelter in the bank parking lot, behind the MSNBC camera. "They are beginning to throw things, and

we have lost contact with three of our ministers who had to run." Rev.
Sekou, Cornel West, and Seth were missing. Rev. Blackmon saw nothing like the mobilization and militarization she had faced in Ferguson.
The few remaining state troopers just stood there. "Nothing is sacred
here, Joy. This is a sad day in America, and I'm afraid that there will
be many more like it." While Rev. Blackmon was on air, City Manager
Maurice Jones declared a local and regional State of Emergency.

At 11:25 a.m., holding a white rag over his face while trying to look at
something on his phone, Devin picked up his water bottle and dropped
out of the student line. Lisa followed him. Five minutes later, one last
group of men came down Market from the east, chanting "USA,
USA," through a bullhorn and then, Braveheart style, "FreeeeeeeDOM,
FreeeeeeeDOM, FreeeeeeeDOM." The Hiwaymen were a band of violent, racist, homophobic neo-Confederates. They wore bulletproof vests,
helmets, and brawling gloves and carried furled American flags. Ahead
of them was pure bedlam. "Do you smell it?" their leader said through
his bullhorn. "The smell of gas around you?" The drums of the student
line continued even as the air thickened with chemical irritants.

Just as the Hiwaymen arrived, a smoke bomb was sent flying from
the southeast corner of the park into the street. Retrieved by a counterprotester, it sailed back. As smoke clouds billowed above the quickly
emptied intersection, a single officer appeared in the police enclosure on
Second Street NE with a small bullhorn. Thirty minutes remained before the rally officially began.

"This event has been declared an unlawful assembly," the officer announced. "You are to leave the area now or you will be arrested." No one
heard a word. Jon Ziegler of Rebelutionary Live TV went up to him and
told him to get his big megaphone out. He suggested an LRAD, a high-
decibel sound cannon, "like the ones you used on Black Lives Matter,"
he added. Ziegler's sarcasm was likely lost on the officer. The instruction
to leave the area, the threat of arrest, wasn't even directed at the rallygoers in the park, but at the counterprotesters in the streets.

Lisa Draine didn't hear the declaration of illegal assembly. There was
fighting everywhere, she recalled. In the crush to escape the poisonous
air, she lost Devin. She was filmed walking by the Hiwaymen lined up

on Market with her blue hat pulled down and her nose under the collar of her BLM T-shirt. Sophie and Rebecca were among those scattering, holding bandannas over their mouths. Once the pepper spray dispersed, Lisa went back to look for Devin. The Hiwaymen had launched themselves into the melee, shouting slurs and knocking him to the ground. Lisa eventually found him on the library steps. In the meantime, she had lost her daughters. Before too long she got a call from Rebecca.

"Where are you?" Rebecca asked.

"I'm here, where are you?" Lisa said. Rebecca was with Sophie at Justice Park.

"You have to get out of there," Rebecca said. "They've declared an illegal assembly. If you don't leave, you'll be arrested."

"I can't leave without Devin," Lisa replied.

When Devin's girlfriend arrived with protest signs, Lisa took a picture of them. She suggested they go to Justice Park, but Devin wanted to hang out on the library steps for a while longer. She was reluctant to leave him, but he said he would be fine.

Once more she was on her own.

Not long before the declaration of an unlawful assembly, while the Nationalist Front was still filing up the southeast steps, a group of bored rallygoers on the southwest side of the park began debating the risks of venturing out. Now that they owned the park, they wanted the streets. "We are taking the fucking field," one man exulted.

Eli Mosley and Thomas Rousseau were still stationed at the southwest entrance, keeping media out but giving interviews. Behind them was the Vanguard America shield wall, which included James Alex Fields Jr. and the Amtrak Terrorist. An especially obnoxious rallygoer, clutching the flag of the Texas chapter of Vanguard America, was standing at the top of the southwest entrance and getting into it with the "Kill. All. Nazis." black bloc woman on the street. This was thirty-year-old William Henry Fears IV. At twenty-three, Fears had been convicted of having kidnapped a woman at knifepoint.

"Got a boyfriend?" Fears asked her, leering crazily. "You look like you love to fuck."

The black bloc man behind her waved his hand. "You say that like it's a bad thing," he shouted.

Ignoring him, Fears kept at her. "Gonna fuck him?"

The "Kill. All. Nazis." woman turned around and gave her black bloc boyfriend a smooch.

"Honey, you look like you like getting choked," Fears said. In a 2019 plea deal, Fears would agree to a five-year prison term for choking his girlfriend. Stepping back to let late arrivals into the park, he waved goodbye. "I'll see you tonight, honey. I'll hit you so hard you'll fall in love with me."

A group of men began assembling at the top of the southwest steps. "Who's going to start the battle? Who's with us?" one said.

Fourteen men in helmets, armed with guns and heavy broom handles, lined up to go out. Fears was in the lead. Tampa Realtor from the torch march joined, carrying a flag. A few minutes after they headed into the streets, another contingent lined up, including Nationalist Front men who'd walked over the downed barricades from the east side of the park and wanted to hit the streets again. The students were still drumming. The Hiwaymen were just arriving. The announcement of an illegal assembly was about to be called. The smoke bomb left the park. A fight broke out at the foot of the southeast steps. A woman holding an anti-fascist sign was overcome with pepper spray. More smoke bombs followed.

"Careful, careful, back up!" a far-right livestreamer shouted to the helmeted man in front of him whose shoulder he gripped as he advanced east on Market. "Higher ground, higher ground!" Upon reaching the southeast steps, which were now enveloped in smoke, pepper spray, and fighting, they jumped up the hill. "Shields up! Shields up! Projectiles, projectiles!" Water bottles landed around them. The livestreamer moved his camera down to film the street from between the legs of the shield wall.

Pepper spray cleared half the intersection, causing both sides to retreat while water bottles flew back and forth. William Fears IV stood at the top of the steps waving his flag. "Load up," he yelled at those behind him. "They are fucking charging us."

"Go ahead, motherfuckers," Imperial Wizard Richard Preston said to the anti-fascists who'd returned to the foot of the southeast steps, brandishing his 9mm. "I'll shoot you." A man with a Pan-African flag replied, "Fuck you." Preston had occupied the public side of the park all morning, lobbing water bottles and caressing the gun in his holster. A counterprotester lifted the *C-ville Weekly* dispenser and tried to throw it at him. It fell short.

"We are getting ready to charge them," a man in the park was overheard saying, as William Fears waved his Vanguard America flag, feet from advancing counterprotesters with BLM flags and a white "Fuck Fascism" banner. "Get out of our city!" the Pan-African flag man shouted. "You don't live here." Fears tried to stab him with his flagpole. In Jon Ziegler's livestream I was shocked to see that Bee Lambert, the seventy-something atheist, former member of SNCC, was among those moving up the southeast steps. She still looked serene and happy.

Behind Fears, Michael Tubbs raised his arms facing the park and men raced to line up before him. Suddenly, Baked Alaska, a scheduled speaker, was being hauled up the southeast steps, a victim of pepper spray. Taking advantage of the hubbub, Tubbs wheeled around, shouted "Follow me!," and launched himself down the steps, trailed by Fears and a stampede of League of the South and Trad Worker Party men wielding shields and billy clubs, body-slamming anyone in their way. The first man Tubbs hit was dragged off the street by counterprotesters. The *C-ville Weekly* dispenser flew into the street with a bang. Daryle Lamont Jenkins tried to retrieve a large plywood "Alt Right Scum, Your Time Has Come" sign, featuring a beheaded Pepe the Frog, but it was snatched away by Tubbs and hauled up the steps as a prize. Imperial Wizard Richard Preston railed from the safety of the park: "I want to shoot one of these motherfuckers. Let me fucking at 'em. Fuck. I've fucking had it with these fucking faggots."

Bee Lambert retreated to the street, unfazed, a pink kerchief perched delicately over her nose. "Some kind of spray in the air," Jon Ziegler commented. "That's powerful shit." Daryle Lamont Jenkins was in the thick of it, diligently documenting, until a Proud Boy militia type hit him with pepper spray, and he had to be pulled out. The Seven Hill Autonomous Queers took his place at the foot of the steps. Jenkins later identified Trad Worker Party men as the instigators of a lot of the violence. The militias had mysteriously vanished. Bloodied counterprotesters were dragged off the streets to safety; bloodied rallygoers were hauled up the southeast steps. Tubbs and his men returned to the park to regroup.

Apart from the four-member black bloc crew, the counterprotesters were not as well prepared for street fighting as their adversaries were. They had a few signs that could be repurposed as shields, but the citizen journalists had more helmets than they did. I presume many carried pepper spray. Mostly, they used what they could find or snatch to protect themselves and fight back. This amounted to flagpoles and the sticks to which their printed signs had been stapled, garbage can lids, and water bottles. They were met with heavy shields, stun guns, ax handles, smoke grenades, clubs, hammers, copper pipes, collapsible batons, and copious supplies of chemical irritants in various forms.

One side or the other also sent eggs, plums, and tomatoes flying, along with water bottles filled with urine. The anti-fascists claimed the pee bottles came from the fascists. The fascists claimed they came from "Antifa." A bag of someone's excrement hit an older live streamer from New York named Sandi Bachom. A heavily armored man with a GoPro on his helmet dared the anti-fascists chanting "From the Midwest to the South, punch a Nazi in the mouth" to take their best shot. He came away with a bloody goose egg on his cheek and was later doxed by Texas anti-fascists. Christopher Cantwell, another headliner who was late to arrive, was pepper sprayed. As he lay sprawled on the ground at the top of the southeast entrance, carrying on like a big baby, Swastika Pin reassured him: "We're going to fucking kill them. I promise you that." The Hiwaymen walked around him.

Three minutes after the announcement of an unlawful assembly, Richard Spencer tweeted his response. After showing a clip of the VSP Tactical Field Force and local officers in riot gear on Second Street NE preparing to enter the park, he turned the camera on himself. "This is an absolute outrage. We had a permit. As you can see, there are militarized police who are moving in. This is a peaceful assembly!" He had to shout to be heard above the pandemonium. "We will see them in court!"

The turmoil on Market had arrived in Emancipation Park.

A Charlottesville officer came up to Spencer while he was filming:

"In the name of the Commonwealth, this has been declared an unlawful assembly—"

Spencer didn't let him finish.

"*HOW!?*" he shrieked. "You are going to have to drag me out of here,"
he said, wagging his finger. He turned the camera back on himself and
said petulantly, "I'm not going anywhere." Spencer's manner was that of
a man who knew he had nothing to fear from the police; it was the anti-
fascists waiting on Market who terrified him.

Eli Mosley was darting from one side of the park to the other to give
Matthew Heimbach, Sacco Vandal, and anyone else who would listen
the option of being arrested with Spencer and other VIPs, now waiting in the northwest corner of the park. Otherwise, they should head
to McIntire Park. Around a dozen chose Spencer's corner. Even before
the Tactical Field Force filed in from East Jefferson at 11:44 a.m., many
had already left.

Thomas Rousseau and Vanguard America were among the first to
leave. Both Rousseau and Dillon Hopper would be defendants in the
Sines v. Kessler trial. Hopper, the founder of Vanguard America, insisted
that James Alex Fields had never been a member; he'd been given a
shield without ever having been vetted. After Unite the Right, Rousseau
would relaunch Vanguard America as Patriot Front to escape the association with Fields.

Close behind Rousseau was a red-faced Brad Griffin, followed by
Azzmador, and his Daily Stormer crew. Eluding a felony warrant for
his malicious release of gas on the night of August 11, Azzmador would
eventually join Andrew Anglin on the lam. The Daily Stormer would be
forced to relocate to the Dark Web. Both would be named defendants in
Sines v. Kessler. Kessler, the lead defendant, marched out behind them,
surrounded by his Identity Dixie security detail.

Trailing behind Kessler, taking a selfie, was Augustus Invictus, another defendant. A minute behind him, was James Alex Fields Jr., still
carrying his Vanguard America shield. Jeff Schoep's neo-Nazi foot soldiers, an assortment of League of the South, and Trad Workers followed
Fields. David Duke was on their heels. A van picked up Azzmador on
McIntire Road, a shirtless and teary-eyed Cantwell jumped in after

him. Both Richard Spencer and Christopher Cantwell would represent themselves at the *Sines v. Kessler* trial, cross-examining the students they'd laid siege to at the Jefferson statue. Cantwell would look
for Antifa under every red bandanna and ask every plaintiff if they knew
Emily Gorcenski.

Seven minutes after the arrival of the Tactical Field Force, Michael
Tubbs and his minions finally abandoned the southeast steps to retreat
to the rallygoers' side of the park. Counterprotesters, anti-fascists, the
black bloc crew, and livestreamers swarmed up the southeast steps in
hot pursuit. Eli Mosley was now racing around the park trying to stave
off their advance. Members of a hastily summoned shield wall managed
to pull the bike rack barricades back up and arrange themselves and
their shields behind them only to have the counterprotesters push them
back down, forcing them to retreat. During the standoff, the DC anti-
fascist Lacy MacAuley took a break from the barricades to give an interview to Ford Fischer of News2Share.

"I believe this is their last desperate grab to cling to their remaining
white cis male privilege. The world is not going in their direction," she
said with unflappable self-assurance.

Twenty feet in front of her, a bearded man in a trucker hat stood behind the purloined "Alt-Right Scum Your Time Has Come" plywood
sign, next to a line of shields. PVC pipes and sticks flew overhead like
javelins. "This is where we make our stand," said a happy teenager in
a white construction helmet with "Commie Killer" written on it. One
megaphone bleated: "Charge!" and "Shields to the front!" Another:
"Retreat!" William Fears darted hither and thither in front of the shield
wall, waving his Vanguard America flag at the advancing anti-fascists,
thumping his chest, and inviting them to fire the first shot of the race war.

The Tactical Field Force lined up on both sides of the Lee statue before hesitantly advancing. The lines of riot police acted as a kind of pin-
cer movement with the lines of the anti-fascists, together funneling the
rallygoers toward the crowded southwest exit. There was now a logjam
and people were panicking. "Keep moving," a man in line shouted, his
voice edged with desperation. Imperial Wizard Preston was once again

working himself up into an obscenity-laced lather. A man who'd been pepper sprayed squawked, "I can't see shit!" A woman shrieked, "Noah, I'm scared!" "You are pushing us right into our enemies," the rallygoers whined to the police.

This was true. As they emerged from the park, some were met by pepper spray from the anti-fascists awaiting them on Market. The vast majority, however, made their way to McIntire Road none the worse for wear. Still, the fear of venturing out contributed to the gridlock. At 11:52 a.m., a shirtless twenty-three-year-old Black man named Corey Long was standing at the bottom of the southwest steps when he picked up a can of spray paint someone had thrown at him. After spraying a few rallygoers with paint as they emerged, among them Imperial Wizard Preston, Long decided to light the spray up. Taking shelter next to him was a stooped and fragile white man. He looked lost.

As a Virginia Klansman in camo shorts reached out from the top of the entrance, trying to hit Long and the old man with a flagpole, an impressive plume of flame shot out of the paint can. Preston, who had circled back, pointed his 9mm at Long's head before bringing it down to get off a shot into the ground. A former Charlottesville mayor witnessed it. On the street nearby, Rosia Parker, of BLM, heard it. A reporter from Buzzfeed News filming inside the park thought it was a firecracker. So doubtless the officers standing in front of the funeral home not twenty feet away heard it too. The former mayor approached them to point out the man who had just fired a gun. They made no move to arrest him. In a criminal complaint he filed later that day, the former mayor wrote that before the gun went off, someone, most likely Preston, shouted, "Kill that nigger."

People had lined up along the outer ring of the park barricades lining Market Street, spellbound by the sight of fascists running around like headless chickens trying to hold their ground against the steadily advancing anti-fascists. Jon Ziegler of Rebelutionary Live TV had been so glued to this drama that he failed at first to notice that the line of riot police was being resisted by a gaggle of smartly coiffed men in navy suits, their shoulders pressed into riot shields. An Identity Evropa flag flew overhead. In his five years covering protests as a citizen journalist,

Ziegler had never seen anything like this. The BuzzFeed News reporter had covered Berkeley. He, too, thought this development "highly unusual."

"You wanna know what white privilege is?" Ziegler asked those following his livestream. "*This* is white privilege. *Right here!*" He addressed his trolls: "You can do this. Black people cannot." Still haunted by his experience covering Ferguson, Ziegler tried to talk to a local officer in riot gear near the end of the line. "You know if these were Black people you would be arresting them. Go home and think about this, please. The reality is everyone would be tear-gassed, beaten, and arrested."

Ziegler returned to narrating the scene. "The cops are just pushing with shields. No batons out. No pepper spray. . . . [Spencer] now gets to attack cops, apparently," he noted dryly. Actively resisting their advance, Richard Spencer screamed at the cops that he was on their side. But the usual magic wasn't working. The cops weren't following his script. Was he going to have to face down the anti-fascists?

Sacco Vandal stood to one side, looking vexed. Nathan Damigo was somewhere in the crush. A photograph of a white man in a fashy haircut, face down in the grass with a cop cuffing him, would soon go viral. The arrestee was identified as Richard Spencer, but it was likely Damigo or one of three Spencer associates arrested for failing to disperse. Named in the *Sines v. Kessler* suit, Damigo declared bankruptcy to forestall any claims on his military pension.

As the line of riot cops got closer to the clashes taking place between anti-fascists and Mosley's shield wall, the OC spray came out. "Finally!" Ziegler exclaimed, then paused. "I'm tasting it. This is the weakest pepper spray I've ever felt on my face." Spencer's men kept pushing back. Ziegler was now utterly disgusted. Recounting the scene to Katie Couric and her film crew a short while later, he said Charlottesville had put America's hypocrisy on full display. He was met by the expected deflection, the *whatabout* two-step.

"There was also some violence by counterprotesters, right?" Couric asked.

The compulsion of the mainstream media to equate two things that are not the same, the writer Rebecca Solnit has written, upholds their fiction of fairness, their "aesthetic of objectivity." This is delusional. It reflects a willed obliviousness to the fact that journalists will be the first to be targeted by a fascist regime. In the meantime, the result is a systematic warping of reality that effectively neutralizes the work of dissenting voices. Even before the president weighed in with his "both sides" comment, I saw this time and time again in the coverage of Charlottesville. The level of violence instigated by the heavily armed and armored far-right forces was far and away more intense and premeditated. There was simply no comparison.

Meanwhile, the men in Mosley's shield wall were still banging sticks on their shields. The foppish-looking livestreamer who had tried to shake Richard Spencer's hand that morning was accompanied by a sidekick with a set of speakers in his backpack. "Victory," the soaring film score of *Lord of the Rings: The Return of the King*, now added to the air of unreality at the southwest entrance.

"Eli! You going back?" The foppish livestreamer shouted.

"Yes," Mosley answered distractedly, before darting off, still intent on keeping his shield wall from giving way.

The black bloc quartet was now in the park. The "Kill. All. Nazis." woman was arguing with the rabid anti-communist in the red tricorne MAGA hat. While one comrade pulled her away, another in a gas mask pepper sprayed Tricorne, putting an end to the argument. Tricorne immediately started howling. "He got me right in the eye! Oh *fuck*!" A distracted Sacco Vandal arrived with a water bottle, but the riot line was closing in. Richard Spencer was maced just as "Victory" reached its soaring climax.

Forty-two minutes after the 11:31 a.m. declaration of unlawful assembly, the last of the rallygoers were pushed out of the park, some choking on pepper spray, others resisting to the end, shouting, "Don't erase us. We support you!" to the riot police. Northrop Grumman of the Rise Above Movement escorted a blinded comrade down the steps. Jon Ziegler got pepper sprayed as he left and was temporarily out of action.

The departing fascists walked down Market to McIntire Road, passing sidewalks filled with jeering locals and cries of "Shame!" DSA and IWW flags filled Second Street NW. People from McGuffey Park gathered on the hill below McGuffey Art Center to see them off. Some held up middle fingers. A Black man who had shackled his wrists to an iron ring around his neck rattled his chains. Rosia Parker and Katrina Turner watched their departure with raised fists. A Black man in a BLM T-shirt pointed and laughed. Another Black man held aloft a large framed photo of Barack and Michelle Obama. An older white woman made a shame-on-you gesture intended for children. The Black man with the "Fuck Yo Statue" sign from the Klan rally was there with the same sign. "We're Charlottesville," the BLM man said. "Get the fuck out of our town."

Clare Ruday, in a purple tie-dyed shirt, worked in the public health department. Her husband was away, and she'd left her children at home. That morning, she had parked in a garage south of the Downtown Mall while her friend and colleague Casey, along with thirty members of BLM Richmond, awaited her at McGuffey. She'd crossed Market Street at a particularly wild moment and was glad Casey had told her not to bring a sign because they were being snatched away and used as weapons. While she and Casey stood watching the departing rallygoers, Clare kept fielding calls from a colleague manning the triage tent at the Rescue Squad base on McIntire Road. Even there, fights were breaking out. Her boss, the health director, was insisting Clare leave, her colleague told her. It was too dangerous. But Clare was intent on protecting her BLM friends from the Nazis. Clare was from an old Virginia family. The Nazis, she noted, wore the same clothes she and her prep school peers used to wear. A Nazi threw a smoke bomb at them. Casey ran and kicked it back.

Grace Aheron and her partner, Rowan Hollins, sat nearby. Grace had been texting her mother every ten minutes to tell her she was fine. When she heard the governor had declared a state of emergency, she thought surely now there would be mass arrests. The procession down Market was a parade of horrors, but it was a big moment. The Nazis were leaving! Rowan agreed. A *huge* moment. But then, she said, they turned around and came back.

After leaving the park, Michael Tubbs had reassembled around sixty-odd League of the South men at the bottom of Market. Perhaps he wanted another go at the anti-fascists, or perhaps he just wanted to return to their cars in the Market Street garage. Either way, by the time he and his men got to the top of the hill below McGuffey Art Center, eight members of Black Lives Matter stood in front of them. "If I catch your ass in the street, you'll be unconscious, you little bitch," a Black man said to the hastily assembled League of the South shield wall. "Back the fuck up," he warned. A Black woman gestured frantically for reinforcements. As people raced to join those blocking Market, the man with the photograph of the Obamas held it up above his head in the middle of the street. Tubbs's shield wall now faced off against around twenty-five people, of all ages and hues.

Sidling up to Michael Tubbs, the foppish livestreamer asked, "What's your play?"

Tubbs gave him an absolutely withering look.

Anticipating a new offensive, the livestreamer told his sidekick to fire up a selection from his Two Steps from Hell playlist. Two Steps from Hell was a music production company that specializes in music for movie trailers and movie ads. Orchestral sound is combined with ancient-sounding chants to evoke "huge emotion, tense anticipation, and breathtaking intensity." The music swelled.

Suddenly, there was a disturbance ahead. Someone shouted, "Spencer!"

Richard Spencer, overcome with pepper spray, was being half carried down the street. His security detail, along with around thirty rally-goers, broke through the back of the BLM line and Tubbs's surprised shield wall. Tubbs didn't even look at Spencer as he was rushed past. Instead, he used the confusion to charge the hill. "The Strength of a Thousand Men" emanated at high volume from the sidekick's backpack. Clare Ruday and her friends from BLM Richmond locked arms at the bottom of Second Street NW, but Tubbs and his men marched straight past them up Market.

Eli Mosley had emerged from Emancipation Park much as Spencer had, incapacitated. Sacco Vandal guided a blinded Mosley to an alley behind Hill and Wood Funeral Home. Mosley had taken this alley to meet up with the Rise Above Movement men that morning, enabling him to evade the counterprotesters on Market. Under the watchful guard of Three Percenter militias, he and Tricorne were treated by street medics.

The "Kill. All. Nazis." black bloc woman tried to get at Mosley but was pulled back by her partner so they could focus on the Michael Tubbs procession moving east up Market. The man with the Obama photograph fell in behind them, as did the man in chains. The sight of the rallygoers returning infuriated those who'd just watched them leave. The black bloc woman joined in flag-snatching attempts on Tubbs's lines. Emancipation Park was now teeming with men in blue. As Tubbs passed the intersection at Second Street NE, riot cops raced to line up at the edge of the park, as if their duty to protect and serve began and ended there. At the top of the southeast steps, watching Tubbs walk by, stood Bee Lambert, backed by a line of riot cops. She never did manage to get arrested. The police would make fewer arrests that weekend than on the day of the Klan rally.

Lining the sidewalk in front of the library, anti-racists shouted, "Nazis Go Home!" IWW flags were amassed on Third Street NE, but by the time Tubbs reached the top of the hill at Fourth Street NE, the streets were largely emptied of counterprotesters. Here, Officer Tammy Shiflett stood by herself next to her cruiser. Tubbs's men were being trailed by photographers and livestreamers. They were harassed by the black bloc crew and shadowed by a half dozen clearly agitated young Black men. Among them was Corey Long, who had fashioned the makeshift flamethrower. A heavyset man waved a purloined baseball bat with a Confederate flag on it, taunting those returning to the garage. Someone's voice was caught on a livestream trying to incite them.

"Do something, do something, do something, my nigga, do something."

After leaving the steps, the clergy had hung around Market for a while. They soon realized that it wouldn't have been clear to anyone what they were trying to achieve by being there, aside from putting themselves in harm's way. "I don't remember how long we were there," Eric Martin recalled. "But eventually we just said, we can't do anything in this moment. We fucked up." They went to a café on Water Street, just south of the Downtown Mall, to regroup. Though Rev. Sekou believed he had made the right call to leave the steps, he still regretted it. In the heat of the moment he, like Cornel West before him, had overstepped local leadership. It was Smash's call to make. After venting her feelings about everything that had happened, Smash stood up and invited people to join her back on the streets. They had trained to protect their community, so that was what they were going to do. From that moment, no one doubted Smash was in charge.

They left the café just before noon, leaving some behind. Arm in arm, they walked up Second Street NW. The closer they got to Market Street, the stronger the smell of chemicals. As small groups of white nationalists and militias percolated throughout the downtown area, emotions were high, and slugfests broke out like small fires. Seth saw Tom Perriello, a local resident and former US congressman who'd lost the recent Democratic primary for governor, break up one fight.

The hill below McGuffey Art Center and the street adjoining it were filled with those who had just watched the return of Michael Tubbs. As soon as the clergy appeared, a resounding cheer went up. To those, like Eric Martin, who believed they had failed, it was salt in their wounds. But Seth was moved. Law enforcement hadn't stopped the white supremacists from hurting people. And other city officials were nowhere to be seen. Only community members, activists, and medics had stayed on the streets and looked out for one another. Smash had made the right call.

"I think people were cheering because at least someone was coming to just be with them," Smash said simply. The clergy lined up with linked arms across Market, where Black Lives Matter had just faced down Tubbs. A rump brigade of League of the South flagbearers was forced to turn around and double back to McIntire Road. Then, when a line of riot police began advancing down Market, the clergy moved to where Clare Ruday, Katrina Turner, and cadres of Richmond BLM had prevented white nationalists from proceeding up Second Street NW to McGuffey Park.

On Fourth Street NE, Officer Tammy Shiflett had no gas mask or protective gear. As Michael Tubbs's column passed her en route to the garage, she called for backup. Instead of sending reinforcements, her supervisor told her to stand down. Passing her, the foppish livestreamer's sidekick took out his phone to select a new number from his playlist.

"Heart of Courage" starts with a melancholy string section, something to score an after-action scene of a vast battlefield strewn with dead soldiers. As Tubbs approached Fifth Street NE, the music suddenly turned percussive, a preamble to a rising dramatic action.

It wouldn't be long.

DeAndre Harris, a twenty-year-old special education teacher's aide and hip-hop artist, had accompanied his friend Corey Long as they trailed the Tubbs procession up Market. Upon reaching the garage, Long attempted to grab the Confederate flag belonging to the state chairman of the North Carolina chapter of League of the South, a family lawyer named Harold Ray Crews. Harris went to Long's aid, and a tug of war over the flag ensued. Someone had given Harris a Maglite flashlight, and he lashed out at Crews's shaved head. At the exact same moment, a League shield man pepper sprayed both Harris and Long. Long took off; Harris turned away to run and fell. He got up to follow Long into the garage only to fall again, breaking the wooden arm at the ticket punch. Then he was set upon. The Market Street garage is literally next door to the Charlottesville Police Department.

The attack on DeAndre Harris began fifteen minutes after Corey Long lit up his spray can. It lasted ten seconds and was livestreamed by at least eight people, including the foppish livestreamer, who laughed and described it as "glorious." The New York Daily News journalist who shot the video that went viral, Chuck Modiano, was the only one who tried to stop it. All in all, seven men chased Harris, surrounded him, and took turns beating and kicking him. They attacked him while he was on the ground, while he was trying to run away, and after he fell a second and a third time. One hit him on the head with a wooden tire thumper. An eighth man pulled a gun on him. At least two members of League of the South participated in his beating, as did a member of the Trad Worker Party's shield wall. The Proud Boys were represented by a MAGA hat–wearing member of the Fraternal Order of Alt-Knights. A man carrying a Vanguard America flag was among the attackers. Harris weighed about 135 pounds.

Five of the seven attackers were eventually identified. They were a self-selected group. Unlike those who left Emancipation Park soon after the declaration of an unlawful assembly, some of Harris's attackers had followed Tubbs's orders to hold the steps. At least two of them participated in Eli Mosley's shield wall inside the park. The teenager in the white Commie Killer construction helmet was identified by his high school classmates. Another, yet to be identified, was the bearded man who used the purloined Nazi scum sign as a barricade in the standoff. Yet another was outed after he crowed about his part in the attack on Facebook. The seventh man was identified from documents that came to light during the *Sines v. Kessler* trial that took place four years later.

A city sheriff witnessed the beating and followed Harris to the stairwell where he had taken shelter. Harris's friends joined him before moving him across the street to wait for an ambulance. After moving her cruiser, Officer Tammy Shiflett joined them. Harris's injuries included a concussion, a head laceration that required eight staples, a fractured wrist, knee and spinal injuries, and a chipped tooth, as well as countless abrasions and bruises.

While the Harris attack unfolded in the garage, the Confederate flag–bearing Harold Ray Crews and a lanky, elderly League of the South man were set upon by the black bloc crew. Crews was bludgeoned in the back of the head with what looked like a truncheon, while the "Kill. All. Nazis." woman grabbed the older man, pulling him down in the middle of Market to beat him about the head with her fists until she was pulled off him by her fellow black bloc members. In all the videos I watched of that day, this was the only instance in which leftists initiated a violent attack. Officers tried to break it up, including two with Tasers, but no one was arrested, even though the attack took place directly in front of the police station.

Crews would try to pass off his head injury as one inflicted by DeAndre Harris. Without the footage from Buzzfeed News, a Black man would have paid the price for the actions of zealous white leftists. While Tubbs and his men disappeared into the garage, about thirty other rallygoers, including Commie Killer, still carrying his plank, the Vanguard America man, the Proud Boys fight club man, the foppish livestreamer and his sidekick, left the scene. There were many such rump brigades now, roaming the city on foot, in cars, and in pickup trucks, looking for trouble.

"Whoever knows where we are going," someone shouted, "get to the front!"

After ceding control of Market Street to riot cops, Smash and the clergy headed to McGuffey Park. They crossed paths en route with Rev. Elaine Thomas and Rabbi Tom Gutherz, who were coming from First United Methodist. The two had been keeping an eye on the rally from its front portico while Pastor Brenda and Apostle Sarah maintained their vigil in the sanctuary. Even here, pepper spray had wafted in.

Blake Montgomery, a reporter with BuzzFeed News, saw the robed gathering as he was walking west down East High. Montgomery had begun his live feed inside Emancipation Park a few minutes after the announcement of an illegal assembly. Rather than accompany the exodus to McIntire Park, he had joined those following Tubbs and so captured the assault on DeAndre Harris and the attack on the League of the South family lawyer. From there he went to Justice Park. When Lacy MacAuley left to march down East High leading over a hundred counterprotesters with her bullhorn, Montgomery fell in with her until the clergy caught his eye. In his experience covering counterprotests to the far-right, clergy were a novelty. Smash explained they represented different faiths, but they shared a commitment to not letting the sin of white supremacy go unchallenged.

Smash and her clerical retinue, Emily and her crew of armed women, Lisa Draine and her daughters, Blake Montgomery of Buzzfeed, and the flame-haired Lacy MacAuley with her megaphone reached McGuffey not long before the happy but faulty news of Richard Spencer's arrest. At 1:08 p.m. WTJU reported that a photograph of Spencer face down on the grass was being shared at McGuffey. The day, like Buzzfeed's live feed, seemed to be coming to an end. It was miserably hot and humid, and Montgomery was still suffering the effects of the pepper spray he'd inhaled at the garage. After a final interview with Lacey MacAulay, he would log off. There was a sense, Lisa Draine recalled, that it was over, and the activists had won. No one was keen on following the fascists to McIntire Park.

So, they lounged under the trees or sat on the swings of the playground and chatted. Seth Wispelwey ate half a peanut butter sandwich. Smash had a burrito. The DJ was playing reggae, and the vibe of a street party was coming on. Elizabeth Sines, the law student who had filmed the attack on the students from the Rotunda's portico, described the scene as "the resistance camp at the end of the world." Emily introduced herself to Kristopher Goad by telling him the bald man who'd maced them the night before was Christopher Cantwell. "No shit," Goad said. He had filed a police report, but because he didn't have a name, he couldn't press charges. He would later press charges. Clare Ruday and Casey, like many others, were waiting for a signal that it was safe to head to their cars. The governor's declaration of a state of emergency had led to flurries of calls from all over the country. Clare's mother was texting her saying, "You're not out there, are you?"

Lisa Draine thought she might head home. Sophie and Rebecca were with Sophie's UVA friends. Natalie Romero, eating an orange, had joined them on the swings. Except for Sophie's high school friend Caroline Bray, Lisa didn't know any of them. Caroline's mom, Daryl, offered to give her a ride so she wouldn't have to walk alone to the Jefferson School where she'd parked that morning. When Lisa went to tell her girls she was leaving, they told her that a group of white supremacists was menacing residents at Friendship Court, so they were heading there. Lisa didn't feel like she had to go to that. She was tired. The family had a week at the beach coming up.

Unbeknownst to any of them, Eli Mosley had left McGuffey just as the Justice Park crowd arrived. While the streets were in an uproar over Tubbs's return, Sacco Vandal, carrying a guitar, had snuck him out of the alley behind the funeral home to get further treatment at McGuffey. Led to a cot, Mosley lay down like a lamb, wailing about his eyes but still intent on radioing commands to his lieutenants.

"Where am I?" he finally asked.

"The Black Lives Matter tent," a medic told him. He stiffened.

"This is Switzerland," a nurse said. "We'll treat you, but you have to put that radio down."

When Mosley reached McIntire Park, he changed into army fatigues. He'd recovered sufficiently to think of returning to the park to collect the sound equipment abandoned in the scramble. Before the VIP after-party, Richard Spencer would tweet another video responding to the rally's cancellation. He had some choice words for Wes Bellamy and Michael Signer. Though he tried to sustain a waggish tone of contempt for them and their little provincial town, his temper kept flaring.

"You think we are going to back down? No. We are going to make Charlottesville the center of the universe. We are going to come back here so often your heads are going to spin."

CHAPTER 15

The Dodge Challenger

For a long time, I wondered how Heather Heyer's phone had ended up at First United Methodist. Her brother was the first to call it. He'd seen footage of a car driving into a crowd of protesters and wanted to make sure she was okay. Whoever answered couldn't tell him where she was, but promised to hold on to the phone until she could come get it. Heather's mother was also trying to find her. She had called the University of Virginia and Martha Jefferson hospitals. Both told her they didn't have a patient with that name. Twenty minutes after his first call, Heather's brother called again. He told the person who answered his sister's phone that she had been killed in the car attack.

Though Rev. Phil Woodson didn't know Heather personally, he was certain she had been at his church, though anyone could have found her phone on the street and turned it in. Those not taken to the hospital from the scene of the car attack had been brought to First United Methodist. Of course it doesn't really matter how her phone got there. Knowing the answer will not alter the trajectory of the afternoon or distract from the horror of how she was killed. The blast radius of James Alex Fields Jr. and his Dodge Challenger will remain incalculable, multiplied hundreds of times by his victims, their families, those on Fourth Street, in the churches, parks, safe houses, ambulances, fire trucks, and those in area hospitals who had dutifully prepared for a mass-casualty event.

Anyone who has been through a traumatic experience knows how certain sensory cues lodge like tiny land mines in the brain. Unable to take in the enormity of all that is happening, a phantom joins them, forcing the traumatized into an exhausting state of vigilance, alert for the omens that herald the threat's return. Witnesses to the car attack described the percussive sound the car made when its metal met the flesh of its victims. Like a metal baseball bat being drawn across a wooden fence, the law student Elizabeth Sines said. It wasn't a crash sound, Emily said. It was *thug, thug, thug,* then *pop,* when the Dodge Challenger hit the car in front of it. Because so many rallygoers traveled in white vans, the sight of white vans can summon the phantom. Proximity to crowds. The sound of a helicopter. The smell of citronella or burnt rubber. The incantatory rhythm of "You. Will not. Replace *us!*"

It isn't just trauma. There's loss. A witness to the car attack said afterward she was unable to do her job. First demoted, she was eventually let go. Marriages and friendships foundered. Parents watched their children dissolve into anxiety and panic. There's grief. An entire life is forced into a plot of before and after; the years preceding August 12 flattened into preamble. There are the outbursts of rage that come out of nowhere, again and again. And chronic pain. Thoughts of suicide. Nights spent staring into the dark. The incandescent fury that turns accusations of indifference—where were you?—into accusations of complicity. And that final bequest: the hideous urge for vengeance.

Other details labor under the weight they are asked to carry in the name of healing. Placing Heather at First United Methodist Church falls here. For church members volunteering that day, having had Heather's phone established a connection between their beloved church and the thirty-two-year-old woman who became a symbol and a martyr for many out on the streets. "If you're not enraged," Heather's last Facebook post read, "you're not paying attention." Imagining Heather in a sanctuary filled with the prayers of Apostle Sarah and Pastor Brenda, imagining her anywhere other than the street where she was killed, is a consoling thought. But as I got closer to the car attack, the logic of that consolation eluded me.

So, I looked for her elsewhere. Heather had never taken part in a street protest. She had to ask what this *Antifa* she kept hearing about was. The torch march changed her mind about staying away. With her on Saturday afternoon were two close friends, Marissa Blair and Courtney Commander, from the family law practice where they all worked.

I first encountered Courtney and Marissa at the First Baptist service that took place on the second anniversary of August 12. Marissa had been slotted to speak that evening, but as she struggled offstage to compose herself, other speakers, like Pastor Brenda, stepped up to take her place. In time, Marissa found the strength she needed. Courtney stood next to her, in a half embrace. Marissa spoke with painful eloquence about Heather and what she had endured since her murder. She ended with a fierce injunction, as if it were torn from her heart. "We must *love* the *hate* out of them." I thought of her often after that. I still do.

Later, I caught a glimpse of Courtney in the Showing Up for Racial Justice livestream of the Klan rally. By then I had gotten to know both her and Marissa slightly. By then I knew it was Courtney's torch march footage that had changed Heather's mind about joining them on the streets. The possibility that Heather was only there out of friendship must have weighed on them. And then there is this painful thought. Both Marissa and Courteney were women of color: if either of them had been killed, would they have served so well as martyrs?

Heather explained her decision to join them not as an act of friendship but solidarity.

"When people are wailing in the streets," Smash had said, "God is there."

An hour before the car attack, a group of anti-government paramilitary men and women marched back up Market Street, where they were met by chants of "Go home, Nazis." Unlike Michael Tubbs's procession, a line of riot police forced them to turn down Second Street NW, toward their cars. Though a one-legged Hiwayman with a red, white, and blue beard marched with them, many of them were wearing Three Percenter patches.

"Threepers" take their name from the disputed claim that only three percent of colonists fought against the British during the American

Revolution. They see themselves as liberty-loving revolutionaries, intent on challenging anyone, above all the federal government, when rights are being trespassed. In their words, they came to Charlottesville to "maintain order" and "to locate individuals being infringed upon." Like Alexander Stephens's postwar claim that the "great principle of Independence and Sovereignty" was the true cause of secession, Threepers are the latest iteration of Americans who co-opt patriotism in service of an obsession with personal liberty, whether it is the liberty to own people, to flaunt their weaponry, to tout their racist views, or to overturn the results of an election. Several Threepers would face conspiracy charges for their role in the January 6 insurrection.

After crossing over the Downtown Mall, the militia came to the two surface lots on Water Street. Instead of getting in their cars and leaving, they continued east on Water and turned up Second Street SE. Both the locals and the activists shadowing them told them repeatedly that they were headed toward the "hood." They didn't stop. In other words, they weren't lost. They were looking for trouble in the name of keeping the peace, parading as patriots while baiting the residents of a Black neighborhood. When an older Threeper was hit in the head with a rock, they began to reconsider the wisdom of this. By then they were across the street from Friendship Court.

Back at McGuffey Park, Emily received a Signal text requesting she bring her crew to Friendship Court. After sharing it with twenty close allies, wary of aggravating tensions, she asked for more details. There was talk of sending out scouts. Star Peterson wanted to head out right away. Kristopher Goad felt they shouldn't go alone. They needed numbers. While Emily hesitated, a standoff ensued between the Threepers and a small group of agitated residents standing in front of Friendship Court.

"You are invading these people's homes," the Threepers were told.

"You came to where we live at," a Friendship Court resident said.

When the Threepers finally, grudgingly, began to leave, they were seen to their cars by watchful residents and activists. Then someone threw another rock. A man wheeled around.

"Don't fucking do that. They leaving. Let them get the fuck out of here. If they cross the street, then you can fuck them up, but they ain't crossed the street."

With a neat auburn braid swinging from the crown of her head, Heather Heyer passed in front of a livestreamer's phone as she walked alongside those accompanying the militia back to their cars. She had to leave for her second job as a waitress soon. Reaching the parking lot, she tried to talk to a militia woman who looked about her own age. Heather was in a black T-shirt and jeans. This woman was also dressed in black. Returning to Courtney, Heather said the woman told her, "I can't engage with you. Because you don't have a good argument."

An older woman, helping the Threeper hit by the rock return to his car, railed against the coward who had thrown it and the ingratitude of those whose rights they had come to protect. She was interrupted mid-rant by a commotion behind her. Sandi Bachom, the livestreamer from New York, had tripped and cracked her head on the curb on South First Street. Two militia members jumped to administer first aid. One barked, "Watch my back!" A crowd collected. The thudding of a helicopter above them was joined by a whining drone. The asphalt radiated heat. The sun bore down, and tensions rose.

In the drone footage, I saw Courtney first, with her red backpack and topknot. Then Marcus Martin, Marissa's fiancé, in a white singlet, red baseball cap, and red Jordans. Marissa, with a tiny backpack and pale blue cap, kept close to him. When the black-clad mobile field force arrived, looking like a line of toy soldiers, Marcus moved to the surface parking lot between South First and Second Street SW. Marcus was on parole and wanted to keep clear of any possibility of trouble. Marissa followed him. This lot was three feet higher, with a better vantage point from which to record what was happening on the street below.

And then I saw Heather. She stood behind Marcus and Marissa as they perched near the lip of the lot that overlooked the knot of militia surrounding Sandi Bachom. Unable to see over the heads of those in front of her, Heather stepped away to stand in the shade of a small tree at the edge of the lot. After a minute or so she returned to standing behind Marcus and Marissa. Suddenly she was clapping. I looked away to see Smash in her white robes followed by a caterpillar of clergy walking across the mostly empty lower lot. Word of rocks thrown, and an in-jured militiaman, had made its way to McGuffey. Seth assumed it was the militia member being treated. It was very hot, he said. Heather re-turned to the shade. When Marcus and Marissa left, she followed them out from under the tree and disappeared.

Nikuyah Walker, the late Holly Edwards's protégée, looked on as a sweaty Ford Fischer of News2Share interviewed a scrawny militia mem-ber with a nasal Southern accent. Walker was running as an Independent for a seat on the city council. To Mayor Signer's utter consternation, she would win her seat and go on to unseat him as mayor. The campaign slogan on her T-shirt read "Unmasking the Illusion." Walker overheard the militiaman telling Fischer that, unlike the people following them and calling them Nazis, everyone else understood that "we, as a group, are not here for one side or the other." She interrupted.

"So why *are* you here?"

"To help maintain order between the two groups."

"But your group is the only group that's left. What are you maintain-ing order of?" Her voice was pointed and casual.

"We were trying to, but we have been encircled by protesters." They were now encircled by riot cops and clergy.

"But that's over now. Why don't you go home?"

"We stopped here once that lady fell off the curb and hit her head," he stammered. "They kept pushing us forward."

"Where's your cars at?" She wasn't quitting.

"Right up there," another man said, pointing to the upper lot. "That's where we was trying to get to. But as you see, there's a wall of people there."

"So, if this area is clear, y'all will leave? Go home?"

"Yes, if you can clear this area. We will leave."

Even after Walker had cleared the wall, a man who'd been arguing with the crowd got into his car only to get out again. Another sped up and nearly ran someone over as he left.

To Emily Gorcenski's chagrin, the Friendship Court alert she'd re-ceived was widely shared. Even after Threepers departed, the streets south of the Downtown Mall continued to swell with counterprotesters.

This was just one of the ways in which the militias took a volatile situation and made it infinitely worse.

Continuing his livestream, interrupted when his phone overheated, Ford Fischer walked east on Water, commenting on Jeff Schoep's parade of neo-Nazis across the street. Unremarked upon was a gray Dodge Challenger with tinted windows that passed by him before coming to a stop at the Second Street SE traffic light. Three blocks away, Jon Ziegler of Rebelutionary Live TV squatted on Fifth Street SE trying to launch a drone. Schoep soon passed by him, with the black-booted women still flying the NSM banner, followed by a dozen or so Vanguard America polos and khakis, Trad Workers, and a lone Confederate flag bearer. They were all en route to the Market Street garage. In the aftermath of Charlottesville, Schoep and Heimbach, both named in the *Sines v. Kessler* lawsuit, would step down from the organizations they'd founded and disavow their Nazi beliefs. Nobody believed them.

"So, this is the scene in Charlottesville right now," Ziegler narrated to his followers on News2Share. "There are many groups of Nazis making their way back to their cars, followed and tailed by small groups of counterprotesters and media."

Like the woman with an English accent who approached Ziegler to ask where Friendship Court was, many of those who received the alert were not locals. At 1:20 p.m., one hundred people from Justice Park walked down Fourth Street NE, crossed the Downtown Mall, and headed for Friendship Court. Around the same time, several hundred left McGuffey Park with the same intention. The Justice Park folks got there first and were told that the militia had left, so they turned around and headed back toward Water.

Walking down Second Street NW and crossing the Downtown Mall, the McGuffey Park crowd turned left on Water Street. Lisa Draine's daughters were among them, accompanied by Sophie's UVA friends. They chanted "Black Lives Matter" as they marched. Clare Ruday from the health department and her Richmond friend Casey had left the park with them. Seeing the McGuffey Park crowd coming down Water, some dressed as clowns, Heather decided to stay a bit longer before leaving for her waitress job. Reaching Fourth Street SE, they met up with the Justice Park folks, including Megan Squire and her IWW comrades. Squire was just following the crowds wherever they took her.

For Emily, watching all her friends and allies come together provided a moment of the purest joy. They had worked so hard. Her heart was full.

"We were divided the entire day and that moment we were all in one place. We saw that we were okay. The mood was jubilant. We were singing. People were chanting. Everyone was celebrating. We beat the Nazis. Everything was fine."

Jon Ziegler, walking west from Fifth Street SE, heard the roar before he saw them. "Looks like a large group of counterprotesters up here," he narrated. "Appears to be counterprotesters, anti-racist protesters, a large gathering marching through the streets." IWW flags floated toward him. The marchers slowed, pooling at the intersection of Fourth Street SE and Water, their happy faces turned toward the tail end of the Justice Park people walking toward them from Friendship Court. The chant "Whose streets? Our streets!" went up. Some pointed east and started walking toward Ziegler. Others pointed north, up Fourth Street SE. Ziegler's livestream captured a man saying he didn't care which way they went. He wanted a beer. A woman happily took this up. "Man wants to drink a beer! Man wants to drink a beer!" It was decided. They would go up Fourth Street to the Downtown Mall and find a beer.

Katrina Turner, her son Timmy, and Rosia Parker had been told by a police officer to avoid the Downtown Mall, where the riot police were apt to arrest them. But people were saying, go left, go left. Katrina tried to speak up, but their security detail wanted to follow the crowds. They had the walkie-talkie, so she relented. Memories of what happened next, for her, were scrambled. For some, time slowed down and details stood out. For Katrina everything happened in a blurry rush.

Niya Bates had been slated to give a talk at UVA that day on the work she was doing at Monticello to "correct the narrative." When the governor declared a state of emergency, the day's programming was canceled, and the university went on lockdown. Her thesis supervisor told her she wasn't safe on Grounds. She took a roundabout route home only to discover six Jeeps of armed rallygoers parked at the end of her street. One pulled out to follow her. She kept driving around until he got bored and left. Reaching home, she put her gun next to the door and turned on CNN. Charlottesville looked like Ferguson, she said. Looking at her phone, she saw that her Delta sorority sister Marissa Blair was livestreaming on Facebook. She clicked on that and watched as Marissa turned left off Water Street, onto Fourth Street SE. Then the livestream went crazy.

James Alex Fields Jr. had driven his 2010 Dodge Challenger all the way to Tenth Street SE before circling back to Market. He passed the police station and the parking garage before turning left on Fourth Street NE. This was where officer Tammy Shiflett and her cruiser had been posted until the attack on DeAndre Harris. A street that was meant to be closed to traffic was now open. A plastic sawhorse had been moved aside. Fourth was a narrow one-way street, made narrower by a black Toyota truck that had pulled over to the curb on the right. A maroon Honda Odyssey, followed by a silver Toyota Camry with a black top had pulled up beyond the truck, and stopped at the intersection of Water, unable to proceed because of the crowds. Fields drove down Fourth Street SE and stopped briefly behind the Camry before backing up. He paused in the middle of the Downtown Mall and idled there for over a minute while the counterprotesters debated which way to go.

When the crowds began to funnel up Fourth, they flowed around the stopped cars to fill the street and the sidewalks. Megan Squire and her Wobblies were on the east side of Fourth Street SE. Marcus Martin, whose red hat floated above those in front of him, saw Fields's stopped car ahead of them. Marissa was to his right, switching back and forth from selfie mode to filming Heather and Courtney in front of her. Just as Courtney passed the bed of the Toyota truck, she turned around to smile at Heather, slightly behind her in the middle of the street, her thick braid still swinging. Natalie Romero could be seen over Heather's shoulder. Lisa's daughter Sophie, in a purple-and-maroon-striped jersey, was walking beside her sister, Rebecca, a few feet in front of Courtney.

At 1:41 p.m. Fields started backing up once again, but then he shifted into drive and hit the gas. Those in front saw him barreling toward them and were able to leap out of the way. The views of those behind them, unless they were tall enough to see over the heads of those in front, were obscured. Tiny Natalie Romero saw nothing. She was passing the Toyota truck when she was hit. Marcus caught a glimpse of the oncoming car in time to push Marissa out of its path, to the east side of the street, where Megan Squire was standing. Then he was hit, thrown into the air, his left leg and ankle shattered.

A frame in the series of photographs taken by Ryan Kelly, a *Daily Progress* reporter, showed the position of people beyond the Dodge Challenger just before the impact sent a hectic flock of shoes, hats, sunglasses, water bottles, and bodies into the air. Marissa, identified by her light blue cap, stood between Timmy, Katrina Turner's son, and Heather. Sophie was directly behind Heather and slightly in front of Marcus. Rebecca saw the car coming because she was tall and looking ahead, but Sophie had run into a friend and her head was turned toward her. The last thing Sophie remembered was hugging her and saying, "Wow, you're back!" Sophie went over the Challenger's roof, rolled off the back, and fell on the street behind the Toyota truck.

In Kelly's disquieting Pulitzer Prize–winning photograph, IWW flags and protest signs proclaiming Love, Solidarity, and Black Lives Matter line up alongside a stop sign to form the backdrop. Water bottles burst in the air alongside six pairs of airborne legs. The figure of a hatless Marcus Martin dominates its center. He is hovering above the street behind the Dodge Challenger. His left leg is painfully twisted. Above him, a pair of glasses that look like Heather's are suspended over the roof of the car. Next to his left foot a phone is floating in the air. Between the Dodge and the cab of the truck is an upside-down man whose falling shirt reveals a beautiful tattoo on his lower back. Heather is just beyond him. Her eyes are closed, as if she is lost in thought. Shoes litter the street. People are running toward the Challenger, toward the injured.

Natalie fell on the street next to the bed of the Toyota truck. Someone pulled her to the sidewalk. The activist and medic Star Peterson had both legs and her back broken. As several men beat on the back window of the Dodge Challenger with sticks, breaking the glass, Fields reversed at full speed. That was the moment that the law student Elizabeth Sines realized this wasn't an accident. That whoever was driving was trying to kill as many people as possible.

Had Natalie not been moved, Fields would have run over her legs.

Sophie narrowly escaped that fate. A Richmond activist had her pelvis crushed in six places when she got caught between Fields's reversing car and the Toyota truck. Her face slammed his back window, breaking her orbital socket and briefly knocking her unconscious. When Fields's reversing car reached the Downtown Mall, one of Marcus's red Jordans bounced off his dragging front bumper. Then he was gone.

Marissa's hands were trembling so violently she couldn't turn her phone off, so it recorded her cries for Marcus. Courtney was next to her, slightly hurt, but they had seen the car reverse and, afraid it would return, briefly ducked into an alley. Marissa then retraced her steps and found Marcus's red hat. It was covered in blood; the street was covered in blood. Then she heard her name being called. Someone took her hand and brought her to Marcus. He had managed to move off the street in time to avoid being hit a second time. Medics swarmed around him. She didn't know where Heather was.

Natalie Romero was immediately surrounded by medics asking her what she needed. Her phone. She wanted to call her mother. No one could find it. She felt something dripping down her face. To keep herself from lying down, she gripped a parking sign. If she fell asleep, she worried she might not wake up. Natalie had a skull fracture and, in an iron act of will, didn't pass out until she was in the ambulance.

Someone pushed Katrina Turner to the ground. She thought it was a gunshot. She saw people in black clothes flying in the air and people running toward her. Her son Timmy and her friend Rosia had disappeared. She wondered what was going on and began calling for them. "Where y'all at? Where y'all at?" she shouted. Security arrived at her side. "They picked me up and they took me around the corner and kept on telling me, you gotta leave, you gotta leave." She phoned her other son. He told her to leave. But she couldn't. She had to find Rosia and Timmy. That was clear. Everything else was jumbled.

Clare Ruday was around the corner when the car hit. She heard an explosion and saw things flying. She thought a bomb had gone off, so she ducked down next to the maroon van that had been pushed into the middle of the intersection by the force of the impact of Fields's car on the silver Camry behind it. Clare heard people screaming for medics. She was a nurse. A medic's mindset is to assess, do what's possible to stabilize a patient, and wait for transport. A medic carries gloves, wound ointment, gauze bandage rolls and squares, medical tape, liquid soap, antiseptics, and trauma shears to cut off clothing. Used to having all the resources of a hospital at hand, all Clare had in her bag was a bottle of sunscreen, water, and some painkillers.

Emily had been in the Water Street–Fourth Street crosswalk, preoccupied by the fear of a police kettling orchestrated by the helicopter thudding above. She had just told her crew they had to get people off the street and back to Justice Park when the car hit. Enveloped in silence and sharply focused, she pulled out her gun and asked herself, *Where is my target and what is my range?* She registered a man hitting the back of the Dodge with a flagpole. With him in range, unable to see through the car's tinted windows, and the sun's glare, she didn't have the shot.

"If he had come down for a second pass," she said, "I would have stood in his path and put every bullet that I had into that windshield." Only after reholstering and running partway up the street did she hear the screams. When she breeched the line of advancing cops, one drew a gun on her. "I stood in front of his gun, and I said, 'Officer, this is a rescue situation, not a combat situation. We need medical assistance.'" His face was as white as a ghost. "He had no idea what to do."

When Rebecca found Sophie, she and a medic made a seat with their arms to move her into the alley Marissa had first retreated to. She told the first cop who showed up they needed an ambulance. He told her that the ambulances couldn't get through because of "you people." She was confused: "What are you saying?" The next thing she saw was a BearCat rolling down Fourth Street with a man standing in the turret pointing a gun at them.

Clare saw a Black teenager with a cut on her forehead sitting on the ground. Still thinking a bomb had gone off, she was worried about a second bomb, but the girl had gotten separated from her mother and was beginning to panic, so Clare tried to keep her calm. She wanted to move her off the street, but when a medic showed up, he told her she might have a neck or spinal injury. After he took over, she saw Casey helping a woman lying on her back in the street. The woman had deep cuts and her pants were torn. Casey was trying to hold pressure on her femoral arteries to keep her from bleeding out. Clare took one leg while Casey kept pressure on the other. Above them another woman was doing chest compressions, but Clare just focused on maintaining pressure. She did think to ask Casey, who had been a few steps ahead of her, if she was okay. She had seen it all, but she was okay. The woman under them was Heather.

I imagine everyone impacted by the car attack has studied the Ryan Kelly photograph to calculate how much distance stood between them and Heather Heyer. In its tight frame, I counted the faces of at least eighteen onlookers, some startled, some still unseeing. The early toll of those injured was nineteen, though UVA treated twenty. Martha Jefferson received another ten. Later this was revised to thirty-six confirmed victims, but even this might be an undercount because some were unwilling to come forward. The friend Sophie had been greeting ended up under the Toyota truck. She was so terrified she left the scene before the ambulances arrived and drove home to northern Virginia. She didn't even tell her parents.

Rosia Parker was filmed walking the street in a daze, looking for Katrina. She began helping the two women in the Camry that Fields's car had hit, both of whom were injured, one seriously. They turned out to be friends of her daughter's. Katrina's son Timmy had seen the car coming in time to get out of its way. He had taken off after it shouting, only to give up and circle back. A reporter asked him what happened.

"They just literally came down the street, at eighty miles per hour to fucking hit us, just now," he said blinking through his glasses and gesturing at the bloody chaos behind him. "We told city council we did not want them here. *They let them come.* We told the police we did not want them here. *They let them come.* . . . This is my town. We did not want them *motherfuckers* here. And now we got bodies on the ground and they're trying to revive somebody."

When the clergy got back to the café from the parking lot, Katie Couric was interviewing Cornel West in one corner. Andy Stepanian was reworking Congregate's victory press release on his laptop in another. Smash was also being interviewed. Seth had been on his feet all day and his phone was blowing up. He had just sat down for a smoke on the outdoor patio when a woman ran up hyperventilating and crying, saying something about a blue Jeep hitting a bunch of people. That they had to come; it was bad. Seth stuck his head inside and shouted, "Clergy, we got to go."

Andy Stepanian yelled, "Nobody tweet," because he knew that everybody gets information wrong in the early moments of a crisis. He told everyone to stay calm, even as the café emptied. Seth asked Smash if he could run and she nodded, buttoning up her robes. She'd be right behind him. Grace Aheron and Rowan looked up at Seth as he left, mouthing thank you, thank you. Eric Martin, Rev. Sekou, and Don Gathers left with him. Bekah Menning and Beth Foster from Chattanooga followed. Stepanian worried that if he started running, he might incite panic, so he started off in a brisk walk to set an example. Two blocks ahead of him, Seth heard screaming. A fire truck came up behind him, siren going.

The first thing Andy Stepanian saw was Chris, the polite young man from the John Brown Gun Club he'd met at St. Paul's. He was wearing a Dakota Access Pipeline T-shirt and lying half in the street and half on the sidewalk. "Did a car hit you?" Andy asked. "Was it a Jeep?" Medics were putting Chris in a neck brace and splinting his leg, which had a compound fracture. "Is it okay if I take your picture?" Chris gave him a thumbs-up.

Stepanian was confused. How had Chris gotten so far? A little farther on, he saw people scattered everywhere. It was as if a bomb had gone off and they had all got up in shock and run before collapsing. Some were leaning against buildings. When he got to the intersection, he saw a gurney and someone performing chest compressions. And then his brain crashed. He said that it was as if the operating system he had created for himself while incarcerated short-circuited. From that moment he lost the ability to live in the here and now. It has never returned.

Just as Seth reached the corner of Fourth Street the BearCat rolled down. Kneeling by the medic giving Heather CPR, Seth asked her how they could help. Get everyone out of here, she said. Sekou and Seth turned around and moved people to the sidewalks. They separated the injured from those in shock. They used anti-fascist banners to make privacy barriers around the wounded so they couldn't be photographed. Seeing Seth, a man yelled out, "Father! This woman needs help." Seth recognized him as the black bloc man who'd chanted "Don't Protect Nazis" at them after the Azzmador assault. He thrust the woman, who was heaving in sobs, into Seth's chest. After holding her a few minutes, Seth asked if it would be all right if his colleague stayed with her so he could mobilize the clergy. Smash took her in her arms. A few feet away, the black bloc woman was photographed holding the bandaged head of another victim.

Clare hadn't been with Heather long when the ambulance arrived. Firefighters and Rescue Squad people all converged on them. A cop in full riot gear began screaming at them, telling them to leave. Clare began screaming back. If he wanted them to leave, she shouted, he had to take their place. He refused. A firefighter medic stepped in. He saw that Heather was gone. He asked Clare, Casey, and the woman doing CPR to help turn the patient on her side so they could slip a gurney under her.

It was then that Clare realized the true extent of Heather's injuries. Still, tourniquets were tied, and CPR continued. Casey doubled over in sobs as the gurney was lifted. Clare's arm had been slashed when Heather's pants were cut off. Still, she helped carry the gurney to the ambulance. Clare suffered from a disease that would put her in a wheelchair within a year. Just before her legs gave way, a medic caught her. After the ambulance left, she was treated for shock. The cut on her arm was dressed. She showed me the scar. She never saw Heather's face.

Beth Foster from Chattanooga recalled seeing a militia member arguing with people in shock while surrounded by bodies in pain. "I remember him saying something about how it's their fault. They shouldn't have been in the street. That this is what you get when you get in the street." She paused, as if struggling to remember more, and then gave up. "Stuff like that. Yeah."

I've heard this time and time again. Sometimes from people I love. How do you explain that those protesting the arrival of Nazis on their doorsteps shouldn't be blamed for the death and destruction Nazis always bring? When did the act of protest become more troubling than the presence of Nazis?

James Alex Fields Jr., who kept a framed photograph of Hitler and a copy of *Mein Kampf* by his bedside, was convicted in both state and federal court of Heather Heyer's murder and sentenced to life plus 419 years.

Lisa Draine hadn't been home thirty minutes when Caroline Bray's mother called. "Lisa, you need to get to the Downtown Mall," Daryl said. "Sophie has been hit by a car." While her husband drove, Lisa tried to get Rebecca on the phone. As they walked down the Mall, they saw Daryl coming toward them. At Fifth Street Daryl gave them Sophie's string bag, which Caroline had given her, and a bloody towel. Daryl thought Sophie had been put in an ambulance. So, they raced off to UVA hospital because that was the closest. In the parking garage, Lisa finally reached Rebecca. "What's happening?" she asked. "We're waiting for an ambulance," Rebecca replied. They were still on Fourth Street, a block from where Daryl gave her Sophie's things. Rebecca said an ambulance was coming and she would call back. When she did, it was to tell her mother that Sophie was being taken to Martha Jefferson.

When Lisa and her husband arrived, they found Rebecca at the emergency room entrance. When they asked where her sister was, she broke down in tears. She told them how she had to beg to be allowed to accompany Sophie in the ambulance. But they wouldn't let her into the hospital. She said something about Sophie having a gash on her head and maybe a concussion.

So, Lisa and her husband had a bloody towel and a weeping daughter, but they didn't know what had happened and the guard wouldn't let them in. They were told there was a mass casualty situation. Ambulances were arriving, patients were admitted, and more people were not being let in. Similar scenes were taking place at UVA hospital. Lisa's husband told the guard he was a doctor. Now they learned that people weren't being let in because the hospital was on lockdown.

First the guard let her husband in. A while later, he let Lisa and Rebecca sit in the waiting room. Lisa didn't want to press Rebecca, so they just sat there in silence with around twenty others in shock. Periodically, Lisa would get text updates from her husband. Sophie is getting a CAT scan. Sophie doesn't have brain damage. Now they are stitching up her head. Her leg is badly injured, but it is too swollen for them to assess, so they are just going to splint her for now. In between these updates, which came every hour or so, Lisa tried to imagine what had happened. She was relieved her daughters had been together and thankful that the ambulance crew let Rebecca accompany Sophie to the hospital. At some point she looked up and saw that the CNN newscaster on the waiting room TV was talking about Charlottesville. Before she realized it, she was watching footage of a car ramming into a group of protesters.

And that was how she learned what had happened to her daughters.

Pastor Brenda and Apostle Sarah had been kept posted throughout the day by those who stopped by the sanctuary. In the Sunday school room, a member of the Clergy Collective monitored online threats. In Fellowship Hall Care Bears dispensed snacks and water while Bekah Menning's friend texted her runners to make sure they were safe. Those stationed in the parking lot continued to check IDs and collect phones, keeping their eye on the metal detector. White men were not allowed entrance unless someone vouched for them. Some of the street medics posted there were doctors and nurses. They didn't need to be told what to do when people began arriving with injuries from the car attack.

Apostle Sarah was glad she was too old to be out on the streets; she wouldn't have wanted to witness something like that. Certified trauma specialists took over the chapel and moved the benches around to create little sections, so people could have privacy while they struggled to emerge from the dissociative state that accompanies shock. At one point a woman came in and sat down. She said she had given a woman

CPR and needed to know how she was. When she was told that her patient had died, she began howling. To this day Apostle Sarah remains haunted by the sound of this woman's grief. She and Pastor Brenda now lead the Charlottesville Clergy Collective.

Pickup trucks filled with rallygoers were rampaging all over the city. One barreled over the curb into the church parking lot to harass those manning the outside tables. A man pulled out a gun, watching as they ran for the doors, yelling, "Lockdown! Lockdown!"

Kristopher Goad remembers two men in the back of one truck shouting slurs. He and a friend started running after them, but then he got worried. "Don't run, don't run too fast," he called out. "If we run too fast, it will just be two of us." His friend turned and pointed, saying, "Look behind you." About twenty-five people were sprinting with them.

Rabbi Tom Gutherz had been at First United Methodist since Shabbat services finished at 10:45 that morning. Though the streets had already descended into mayhem, he still walked the two blocks from the synagogue wearing his prayer shawl and kippah. From the portico he could see the rooftop snipers and the hundreds of state troopers and city police dedicated to the park and its statue. Yet not one officer could be spared to protect his synagogue. An hour after the car attack, at 2:45 p.m., a tweet targeting it arrived: "Let's meet at three o'clock, torch those Jewish bastards."

In early evening, a bomb threat was called in to Boar's Head Inn, the country club where Richard Spencer and David Duke had lunched the day before. Responding, the helicopter that had been monitoring the streets all day crashed, killing both troopers aboard. Two months after 9/11, a plane went down just after takeoff from JFK. Everyone on board and five people on the ground were killed, including a woman who had escaped from the North Tower of the World Trade Center. In those days, it felt like everything was connected. There were no accidents, only the unfolding of conspiracies.

The downing of the helicopter on August 12 reminded me of that.

For those watching from around the world, Charlottesville's fate as the global synonym for "white supremacy" and "white nationalism" was sealed when the president of the United States declared there were "very fine people on both sides." He doubled down several days later to describe the violence of an imaginary "alt-left." "Nobody wants to say that, but I'll say it right now. You had a group . . . that came charging in without a permit, and they were very, very violent." Trump's remarks seemed to open the gates of hell. The next eighteen months saw a surge in white supremacist violence across the country. For some city residents, the shield of complacency they had worn all their lives was gone for good. Few Black residents ever had one.

Charlottesville was given little time to mourn. The next day Jason Kessler called a press conference in front of city hall. He was mobbed by enraged citizens. Tyler Magill stalked him as he escaped through the bushes. That night a vigil for Heather Heyer at the Jefferson School was canceled due to a "credible threat." The Seven Hill Autonomous Queers returned from Richmond to guard the entrance to the rescheduled memorial service later that week. When the city council voted to cover the Lee statue in a black plastic tarp as a gesture of mourning, men with guns showed up to rip it off. They would haunt the parks for years.

Far-right stickers appeared on lampposts and street signs. Cars were spray-painted. Someone called in a bomb threat to the school that Wes Bellamy's daughters attended. Lit tiki torches appeared on activists' lawns. On September 30, 2017, "Jack Corbin" posted eighty-six names on Stormfront.org under the headline "Antifa in Charlottesville Revealed." Don Gathers, running for city council, was specifically targeted. The list would reach over eight hundred names, until a Philadelphia anti-fascist group identified Corbin as Daniel McMahon of Brandon, Florida.

The phone at First United Methodist Church rang off the hook as men with basement radio shows called to ask why they only cared about Black people and weren't letting white people in. Someone on a far-right podcast mentioned having seen a group of preschoolers walking to the McGuffey Park playground. "What do you call a group of Jewish kids," he asked. "Is it a gaggle or is it a boxcar?" Henceforth, the children played in the backyard of the music professor and mother, Bonnie Gordon. All this made it harder to sustain the idea that all these men had come to Charlottesville from elsewhere. They didn't all check in to the Motel 8, Rev. Phil Woodson said. They didn't all fly in and book an Uber to drive them around. They had always been here.

Eight weeks later, Richard Spencer made good on his promise to return with a fifteen-minute torch march to the shrouded Lee statue. Like Wile E. Coyote's full-on pursuit of his nemesis, he had yet to register he was no longer on solid ground. Eli Mosley, who had finally ousted Nathan Damigo and taken over leadership of Identity Evropa, was also on borrowed time. "Is this what war felt like, Eli?" Spencer asked sarcastically as they prepared to disembark from their vans, as if he already knew Mosley's jig was up. His make-believe would be laid bare by the same *New York Times* Op-Doc crew that accompanied them to Charlottesville that evening. Mosley had never been to Iraq. He wasn't a vet. He'd joined the National Guard and never left Pennsylvania. Samantha Froelich would testify against all of them in the *Sines v. Kessler* trial. Mosley, a defendant, would serve time in prison for withholding documents during discovery.

The two white vans pulled up on High Street and Second Street NE. Spencer led the way with a torch through dark and empty streets. A lone police car followed, radioing in their progress. Arriving at Emancipation Park, they trumpeted their return and promised to keep coming back. Spencer's speech was rote. The chants were the same. A group of residents stood silently in the dark. Some went over to the synagogue, just then celebrating Sukkot, to let them know they weren't alone.

"We came, we triggered, we left," Spencer told the *Times* crew. At 8:11 p.m., he posted a video boasting of the success of "Charlottesville 3.0" on Twitter.

I watched the Op-Doc not long after an audio appeared online of Richard Spencer venting over the phone to Milo Yiannopoulos the night of August 12. Spencer's voice cracked with the rage of a man whose power play had gone south. "They don't do this to fucking me! We're going to ritualistically humiliate them. Little fucking kikes, they get ruled by people like me. Little fucking octoroons! My ancestors fucking enslaved those pieces of fucking shit!" Nervous laughter could be heard in the background. Perhaps the VIP after-party was underway. Still, someone had the presence of mind to record Spencer's rant. Treachery was a feature, not a bug, with these folks.

Before the end of the year, Richard Spencer left the public stage, blaming Antifa for making his life on the college circuit impossible. In 2022 he described himself as "politically moderate," with a simple desire to "live his life" as a private citizen. He dismissed the events of August 11 and 12 as "yesteryear." Then, toward the end of 2023, he was back, this time to kiss the ring of a man he'd once dismissed as a child. Nick Fuentes had been an undergraduate when he attended Unite the Right. Since then, he'd amassed a "Groyper" troll army with its own froggy mascot and had dined with Trump and Ye at Mar-a-Lago. In a podcast video uploaded on Twitter, Spencer fawned on him like a fond uncle.

What accounted for Spencer's comeback? Worldwide protests had erupted over Israel's genocidal siege of Gaza. Just as he had exploited the controversy over the Lee statue, he now seized on the Zionist stranglehold on American politics to gin up anti-Jewish sentiment. Jason Kessler, Nathan Damigo, and Mike Peinovich were all-in. The "rules-based international order" that grew out of one genocide was upended by another, conducted by the descendants of the first and abetted by the Western democracies that had liberated many of the death camps. This was now our legacy.

But all that was years away. On August 12, 2017, Richard Spencer's rage was focussed on Charlottesville, a city he now vowed to destroy, a city whose residents would one day look up from its smoking ruins to see him looking down at them.

"That is how the fucking world works."

After numerous delays, the *Sines v. Kessler* suit against the fourteen organizers and promoters of the Unite the Right rally and the organizations and platforms they helmed arrived in court on October 28, 2021. Marissa Blair's marriage to Marcus Martin had ended in the aftershocks of the car attack. The expectation that their wedding would provide the happy ending that had eluded everyone else doubtless contributed. Yet both testified as plaintiffs, as did Devin Willis, Natalie Romero, Rev. Seth Wispelwey, and the student Wendy Baucom rescued from her Lawn room. The law student Elizabeth Sines was the lead plaintiff.

Members of the Charlottesville Clergy Collective took turns showing up in support. The jury awarded the plaintiffs $24 million in damages, only to have a federal judge reduce it to Virginia's statutory cap of $350,000, plus $2 million set aside for compensatory awards. It is uncertain how much the victims will end up seeing. Though some of the men behind the Unite the Right rally have paid a price, this was hardly justice. As Rev. Traci Blackmon might say, until we close the camp of the Philistines, "there will always be another Goliath."

On the fifth anniversary of the attack, Heather's mother, Susan Bro, visited Fourth Street SE, now Heather Heyer Way. She sat on a chair next to the place on the pavement where her daughter was killed. Someone held an umbrella above her head to shade her from the sun. Tyler Magill arrived with his wife and daughter to pay their respects. Jalane Schmidt, Lisa Draine, and Bonnie Gordon all came. Star Peterson sat on the curb with a friend, her surgery scars inscribed on her legs. Dozens left messages drawn on hearts for Heather.

Marissa Blair arrived much later in the day. I caught sight of her standing alone at the edge of the crowd that had gathered to hear Wes Bellamy speak. She smiled warmly when she saw me and said she had spent the day by herself. She appeared to have made her peace with all that had happened, but I didn't inquire too closely because I wanted to believe she had.

EPILOGUE

Charlottesville hired Tim Heaphy, a former U.S. attorney and city resident, to undertake an independent review of the city's and state's handling of the summer's events. His conclusions were unsparing. On August 12 Chief Al Thomas had established no unified command structure; coordination between local and state law enforcement was nonexistent. Mike Signer's interference in city operations forced the police to prepare for two locations. The Commonwealth's attorney misadvised the police department about their power to restrict weapons other than firearms. And, though Heaphy found a lawyerly way of saying so, Chief Mike Gibson of the University Police Department had been out to lunch. Fatefully, too, the CPD commander who relieved Officer Tammy Shiflett of her post on Fourth Street NE failed to replace her. This left a street meant to be closed to traffic wide open. Those were the highlights. Heaphy would later be appointed chief investigative counsel to the January 6 Commission.

Heaphy's FOIA requests to Virginia state agencies, including the Virginia State Police, the Department of Emergency Management, the National Guard, and the Office of the Attorney General, were rebuffed. The VSP's refusal to cooperate with his investigation, Heaphy said, was consistent with their aloofness before, during, and after the rally. In Governor Terry McAuliffe's published account of that weekend, the Heaphy report went entirely unmentioned. Instead, McAuliffe blanketed state law enforcement with high praise. He described the drumbeat of

warnings the hapless city of Charlottesville ignored, as if he hadn't ignored them as well. He got the date of the Klan rally wrong. City Manager
Maurice Jones and Chief Al Thomas, both Black men, took the fall.

For those activists who worked to prepare the city's defenses, Heaphy's
postmortem confirmed their bleakest views. They had always been on
their own. Both state and local law enforcement admitted they had dis-
counted the "noise" about the rallygoers' potential for violence because
it had come from the activists. During the trial of James Alex Fields Jr.,
prosecutors played a recording of the banter of the state troopers manning the helicopter above Water Street just before Fields's car tore into
the crowd below them. Lisa Draine was sitting with the victims of the
car attack when she heard a state trooper refer to the counterprotesters
below them as "motherfuckers."

"That's what they thought of my children," she recalls thinking. "That's
what they thought of all those who were on the street, you know, standing up for what is right. *Motherfuckers*."

To eclipse the footage of Spencer's fiery pageant, the university organized a candlelight vigil retracing the steps of the torch march from
Nameless Field. Bonnie Gordon asked her ten-year-old if he wanted to
go. Was Brother Cornel going to be there? She didn't think so. Antifa?
She wasn't sure. That decided it. He wasn't going. A photograph of thousands of candles with the Rotunda as backdrop stirred many hearts. But
for those who had been there, the sight of flames on the Lawn brought
back the nightmare and sharpened their sense of having been thrown
to the wolves. When Wendy Baucom passed by armed guards posted
on the Lawn she wanted to know where they had been on August 11.
No one in UVA's administration reached out to Lisa Draine's daughter,
who underwent two surgeries on her shattered leg and months of rehab,
to ask how she was.

Bekah Menning remembers not talking with people for a while. It
was too hard to go over the details with those who hadn't been there. The
fact that she had failed to hold the line was a lingering source of shame.
For a period, Emily Gorcenski worked with deskbound anti-fascists to
identify rallygoers. With the help of a reporter from ProPublica, she
outed a lance corporal in the U.S. Marine Corps as a member of the

violent, neo-Nazi Atomwaffen Division. He had boasted on Discord of having drop-kicked her. After a Twitter account associated with Jason Kessler posted her home address, she was swatted. She eventually left the country. In November 2018, German law enforcement contacted her in Berlin with a message from the FBI. A militia member of the Atomwaffen Division had traveled to Germany with her in his sights. Smash and the Wispelweys left town after the first anniversary, which was like August 12 all over again, only with a heavy-handed police presence. Rev. Elaine Thomas and Rev. Phil Woodson also left.

Local activists and clergy raised funds to cover medical bills for car attack victims and lawyers' fees for Corey Long and DeAndre Harris. They attended every day of Fields's trial. "We keep us safe" was their rallying cry. By then anti-fascists had gone to work to identify DeAndre Harris's attackers in the Market Street garage. Among these internet sleuths was an elfin city resident named Molly Conger with the nom de guerre @socialistdogmom. After Unite the Right she quit her job and on October 31 described her reincarnation in a tweet. "To my teenage self: one day you will be a gay, socialist nazi hunter. Hang in there, the future is wild." She had her first death threats before the year was out.

Conger sat through the hearings on the Klansman who fired the gun at Corey Long, and those of DeAndre Harris's attackers, scribbling furiously in appalling handwriting. No one was even looking for a seventh DeAndre Harris attacker when Conger found him. She worked up her notes into much discussed Twitter threads, supplemented with photos of her two dachshunds and screenshots of FOIA'ed documents from the Charlottesville Police Department. Though targeted by Proud Boys, she reported on the January 6 insurgency in a wig and outed two Virginia police department employees, one in Charlottesville, who participated. As a side hustle she began paying compulsively close attention to municipal governance. If you aren't following Molly Conger's mordant coverage of city council meetings, you don't live in Charlottesville.

In December 2023 Conger reported, "I've been stalled out on a couple things lately that I wouldn't have imagined were connected until they all came together." Working with the Unicorn Riot data dump, she found a veteran of Unite the Right carrying the flag of Thomas Rousseau's

new outfit, Patriot Front, in a recruitment video for a group of Polish fascists. A former U.S. marine, he'd been an earpiece-wearing Mosley lieutenant the night of the torch march. This is the legacy of Unite the Right:
when not running for political office, alums were networking with fascist groups in Europe. Self-taught in the arts of open-source intelligence gathering, Conger tells people, "If you've ever stayed up all night
scouring Instagram for pictures of your ex's wedding, you can do this."

Life is trying to gut it out, the computer scientist Megan Squire told
me, in a voice of infinite weariness, as she tried to summon her thoughts
on August 12 years later. Everyone who stood with her on the steps was
targeted by Daniel McMahon aka "Jack Corbin." He was finally arrested and sentenced to prison for a host of cybercrimes. Not everyone was able to withstand the attacks, she said. "It is really hard. They
threaten us in the street. Harass us through the mail." If she didn't live
where she lives, she wouldn't be as committed to the work. "They created me," she said. "Otherwise, it is all just theoretical, writing papers,
living in an ivory tower." Squire is now a Senior Fellow at the Southern
Poverty Law Center. Her most recent article reviewed annual reports
from six donor-advised funds to determine which hate groups received
funding and how much. In 2021, Project Veritas and Turning Point USA
received more than half of the $22 million distributed.

"I keep hoping for the best and seeing the worst," Jeff Pugh, a member of the clergy line, said to me in the fall of 2020, soon after the
plot to kidnap the governor of Michigan was reported. Trump's campaign rallies had reached a fever pitch of incoherence. Trucks bedecked
with Trump flags blocked highways; boat flotillas took over marinas.
Hospitals were filled with people dying of a disease that the president
insisted the press was exaggerating. "I don't know another way of saying it," Pugh said. "We're in the shit. America is Charlottesville now.
Everywhere is Charlottesville."

Even so, the May 25, 2020, footage of a white police officer's slow
suffocation of George Floyd on a busy street in broad daylight set off
waves of protests across the country, most of them in predominantly
white counties. In the middle of a pandemic, an estimated 15–26 million people thronged America's streets, blocking highways and bridges

in the largest civil rights demonstration in US history. If ordinary white people are risking arrest, beatings, teargas, or being shot by a teen-aged vigilante, perhaps it isn't too late. A Black photographer out of Charlotte said that what he witnessed on August 12 was "more fucked up" than anything he'd seen in Ferguson or Standing Rock. He'd never been more frightened for his life. But he'd also never seen white people, counterprotesters, "so in it" as they were that day.

During the summer of the George Floyd protests, Confederate statues all over the South were taken down from their plinths. In Charlottesville, an anonymous cabal of older white people conspired in meetings held under the subterfuge of "Bible study" to topple the life-size Johnny Reb statue in Court Square in the dead of night (the Lee statue was beyond their powers). In Richmond, the plinth of the co-lossal Lee was tagged with graffiti, and every night images of Floyd, Harriet Tubman, or Frederick Douglass were projected on it. For weeks the grassy circle where Lee stood was filled with music, dance perfor-mances, pickup games, and food trucks. Covering the protests, Molly Conger was arrested and spent the night in a Richmond jail. Kristopher Goad was arrested several times. In Charlottesville, Zyahna Bryant led marches and hosted block parties while her grandmother Vizena danced in the street. Jalane Schmidt and Andrea Douglas gave walk-ing tours of both parks under the eyes of self-appointed, armed guard-ians of Lee and Jackson.

On July 10, 2021, a month after the Virginia Supreme Court held that the monument protection law did not apply to city monuments erected before 1997, Zyahna Bryant gave a short speech in Emancipation Park. Mayor Nikuyah Walker followed her. Behind them a crane sat waiting. Seth and Tracy Wispelwey returned to town for the occasion. Kristopher Goad stood in front of the Albemarle Charlottesville Historical Society as the twenty-six-foot-tall statue of Lee and Traveller was trussed and roped, lifted and mounted on a flatbed truck, and carted away. Stonewall Jackson was next, joining a cavalry charge of Confederate statues heading west for a 2024 exhibition at an LA art museum. Niya Bates and Don Gathers witnessed his departure from under a tree. Tweeting a photo-graph of the empty Jackson plinth, Conger recalled the sacrifices made by those who worked to open the view. The removal of the Lewis and Clark and Sacajawea statue, at the top of East Main, was followed by the departure of *Conqueror of the Northwest* and his armed crew. Two months later, Richmond's Lee was ignominiously sliced off at the midriff before being transported off to the oblivion of a city storage facility. His new owner, the Black History Museum and Cultural Center, has yet to figure out what to do with him.

That fall, under the aegis of the Jefferson School African American Heritage Center, Dr. Andrea Douglas submitted her plan to take possession of the Lee statue, melt it down, and recycle the bronze for a new work of public art that would be presented as a gift to the city. An essential element of what she later came to call the "Swords into Plowshares" project, was community outreach and engagement, thereby continuing the conversation Dr. Holly Edwards began with her Dialogue on Race. Trained facilitators in beauty salons, barbershops, libraries, assisted living facilities, and the Jefferson School are soliciting feedback from city residents on what kind of artwork they want to see. Like the 2016 vote to move the Lee statue, the 2021 Swords into Plowshares project weathered legal challenges from good ole boy diehards. The website of the Jefferson School African American Heritage Center was hacked. When Jalane Schmidt pointed out that a descendant of one of the largest slaveholding dynasties in Virginia was among the men suing the city, she was herself sued for defamation. Both she and Andrea Douglas were cyberstalked.

Yet they prevailed.

On October 21, 2023, the Lee statue was consigned to the cauldrons of a small Southern foundry, melted in a crucible, and turned into six thousand pounds of bronze bricks. It was the first Confederate statue not to end up in the purgatory of a city storage facility or donated to a Civil War battlefield. Douglas and Schmidt were present, as was their spokeswoman, Lisa Draine. Whoever undertakes the Swords into Plowshares commission, whatever final form the artwork takes, the dedication and vision of these women have anchored the community in ways that will be fully appreciated only in retrospect.

Can the story of America be melted down and retold?

Who will tell it?

When I first began thinking about this book, I'd hoped I'd find an ending, or a vision of a future, cordoned off from the ongoing peril. Throughout my research, I tried to sustain the illusion that I knew where I was heading, as if I were not treading water in Charlottesville and in Brooklyn, piecing together what happened that weekend and trying to figure out what it foretold. I had just begun to write when the insurrection of January 6, 2021, took place. I had dreaded such an eventuality; I did not foresee it. Is it national vanity to believe fascism won't eventually arrive at our door in the middle of the night? The world is always ending somewhere, often at our hands, or with our bombs. Perhaps is it now our turn to plunge over the world's roaring rim.

So, I didn't find the ending I hoped for, and I don't think I'd trust myself if I had. Perhaps I'm more at home in the present looking back. Perhaps this is no longer my world to make sense of.

On the third anniversary, Lisa Draine curated a series of 120 black-and-white poster-sized portraits. Staring out from a brick wall on Second Street SW off the Downtown Mall were the faces of those whose stories I have tried to weave together here, but there was also a silhouette representing those who didn't want public recognition, had security concerns, or preferred others be raised in their place. One such person wrote to me that she didn't want to revisit the past; she wanted to "read about how to dismantle shit."

Such dismantling, Emily Gorcenski, Andy Stepanian, and Megan Squire will agree, must begin with content moderation on social media platforms and the disruption of AI algorithms. I don't see any of this happening when one of our political parties is controlled by extremists for whom content moderation is censorship and disinformation a vital tool of partisanship. Yet, as became clear when Israel's siege of Gaza was met by massive protests in major US cities and on college campuses, when powerful interests are threatened, both Democrats and Republicans are amenable to suppressing dissent. Both are eager to expand and militarize the police and invest in ever more sophisticated surveillance technology. A tiny pro-Palestine encampment on UVA Grounds didn't last five days before it was set upon by armed state troopers in riot gear, spewing mace in students' faces while fraternity brothers chanted "Arrest them! Arrest them! Arrest them!" For those who had heard President Sullivan defend the August 11 marchers' right to free speech and assembly, this was a bitter moment.

The mainstream media has trimmed its sails to accommodate prevailing winds. Kristopher Goad says they take up the talking points the far-right hands them because they are ideologically closer to them than they are to anarchists or socialists or anti-fascists. They would rather write think pieces about woke censorship and cancel culture on college campuses, he said, than report on actual students violently attacked by Nazis. Until they sit down with avowed communists, Goad says, that won't change. He has no expectation this will ever happen. Still, @GoadGatsby is out there every day, on TikTok and X, haunting the halls of Virginia's capital. Citizen journalists like Jon Ziegler and Ford Fischer, anti-fascists like Daryle Lamont Jenkins, and the anonymous infiltrators and anarchist contributors to Unicorn Riot and It's Going Down, are clear-eyed on how the media exerts its power to maintain the status quo.

Joe Biden used the events of August 11 and 12 in the ads that launched his 2020 and 2024 campaigns for president. Over footage of the August 11 torch march, he described "Charlottesville" as representing a defining moment for America. And it did. But his promise to restore the soul of the nation was premised on the wishful assumption that we are not the men and women marching with torches but the students at the Jefferson statue and the counterprotesters in the streets. Biden won't be the last to impose a consensus where there is none, nor the last to commandeer the valor of Charlottesville's activists. To know who they are and what they stand for, we have to listen to them. We must regard them not as radicals, Black identity extremists, or Antifa, but as ordinary Americans standing up and fighting in a myriad of ways for what is right.

"We never know who we are," Zyahna once wrote, "until we have to."

Deborah Baker
Charlottesville, August 12, 2024

ACKNOWLEDGMENTS

Will Jones III, the sage of the barbershop and Wes Bellamy's sometime security guard, is a running evangelist. When he first arrived in Charlottesville, he didn't see many runners like himself in his neighborhood. To maintain a connection with the Black community, he mapped out a running route that took him from the parking lot of the Jefferson School African American Heritage Center, through the city's Black neighborhoods and housing estates, past the Daughters of Zion cemetery and Mount Zion Baptist, before circling back under the railway tracks to end up where he began. Eventually he cajoled a few friends, including Bellamy, out of the gym and into the streets. Running together, he said, was "a way to get through something hard together."

In the early months of the lockdown, I was in Charlottesville and my family was in New York. The world seemed to be holding its breath. No one was answering my emails. I had yet to convince anyone, including myself, that I was the right person to write this book. Then Wes Bellamy announced he was organizing a run to raise money for the family of Ahmaud Arbery. Arbery had been running when he was chased, cornered, shot, and killed by white men in a pickup truck. For months no one was charged in his murder. In the small crowd of people who showed up for Ahmaud Arbery that Saturday in May 2020, I found the company I needed to keep.

Will Jones III had named his nascent run crew Prolyfyck after the opening lines of rap artist and entrepreneur activist Nipsey Hussle's

"Victory Lap." Prolyfyck's motto was "We here," and its philosophy was to leave no one behind. During lockdown, more and more people showed up before dawn to run or cruise with Will and his friends three times a week. In the heavy heat of a Southern summer, through the icy dark of winter, "Littlez," "Ballhawk," Juanika, Zeneida, NeNe, Erica, Greg, Caroline, Kat, Derrick, the Sues, Mike, Shelomith, Ben, Delphine, Holly, Kristen, Paul, Rachel, Kendrick, Cheryl, Lisa, Jessica, Barbara, Jude, Tina, Jenny, Lena, Tobiah, Wes, Marissa, Courtney, and countless others found community on the streets and outside the lines of Charlottesville's once indelible social arrangements.

I humbly acknowledge the many local reporters, citizen journalists, and online sleuths whose work I have drawn on here. I hope Molly Conger will forgive me for any errors of fact. And I'm deeply grateful to all those who answered my questions, who made introductions, provided documents, tech help, and encouragement in those early days: Rev. Brenda Brown-Grooms, Garnette Cadogan, Bekah Menning, Emily Gorcenski, Shawn "Spelunker" Breen, and Bonnie Gordon foremost among them. I'm thankful to the Silvers Foundation for the seed money and to Ethan and Fiona of Graywolf Press for keeping the faith. But it was those daybreak Prolyfyck walks with Vizena Howard and Lisa Draine that carried me through my long season of doubt.

Thank you.

SOURCES

Archives

Sarah Patton Boyle Papers. Albert and Shirley Small Special Collections Library, University of Virginia.

Ezra Pound Papers. Yale Collection of American Literature, Beinecke Rare Book and Manuscript Library.

Gregory Swanson Papers. Moorland-Spingarn Research Center, Howard University.

Books and Reports

Bellamy, Wes. *Monumental: It Was Never about a Statue.* Newport News, VA: Black Gold Publishing, 2019.

Berry, Damon T. *Blood and Faith: Christianity in American White Nationalism.* Syracuse, NY: Syracuse University Press, 2017.

Boyle, Sarah Patton. *The Desegregated Heart: A Virginian's Stand in Time of Transition.* New York: William Morrow, 1962.

Bryant, Zyahna. *Reclaim: A Collection of Poetry and Essays.* Self-published, Charlottesville, 2019.

Cabell, James Branch. *Let Me Lie: Being in the Main an Ethnological Account of the Remarkable Commonwealth of Virginia and the Making of Its History.* New York: Farrar, Straus, 1947.

Carpenter, Humphrey. *A Serious Character: The Life of Ezra Pound.* Boston: Houghton Mifflin, 1988.

Cheuk, Michael, ed. *Standing Up to Hate: The Charlottesville Clergy Collective and the Lessons from August 12, 2017.* Norman, OK: Good Faith Media, 2023.

City of Charlottesville. Blue Ribbon Commission on Race, Memorials, and Public Spaces: Report to City Council. December 19, 2016.

Cone, James H. *Black Theology and Black Power.* Maryknoll, NY: Orbis Books, 1997.

de Rachewiltz, Mary, David A. Moody, and Joanna Moody, eds. *Ezra Pound to His Parents: Letters 1895–1929.* Oxford: Oxford University Press, 2011.

Eliot, T. S. *After Strange Gods: A Primer of Modern Heresy.* The Page-Barbour Lectures at the University of Virginia, 1933. London: Faber and Faber, 1934.

Ellis, Joseph. *American Sphinx.* New York: Random House, 1996.

Freeman, Douglas Southall. *R. E. Lee: A Biography.* New York: Charles Scribner's Sons, 1934.

Genovese, Michael A., and Alyssa Landry. *US Presidents and the Destruction of the Native American Nations.* New York: Palgrave Macmillan, 2021.

Glaude, Eddie S., Jr. *Begin Again: James Baldwin's America and Its Urgent Lessons for Our Own.* New York: Crown, 2020.

Gordon-Reed, Annette. *Thomas Jefferson and Sally Hemings: An American Controversy.* Charlottesville: University of Virginia Press, 1997.

Hahn, Steven. *Illiberal America: A History.* New York: W. W. Norton, 2024.

Hawley, George. *The Alt-Right: What Everyone Needs to Know.* Oxford: Oxford University Press, 2018.

Heaphy, Timothy J. *Independent Review of the 2017 Protest Events in Charlottesville, Virginia.* Richmond, VA: Hunton & Williams, 2017.

Holloway, Pippa. *Sexuality, Politics, and Social Control in Virginia, 1920–1945.* Chapel Hill: University of North Carolina Press, 2006.

Jordan, Winthrop D. *White Over Black: American Attitudes toward the Negro, 1550–1812.* Chapel Hill: University of North Carolina, 2012.

Kenner, Hugh. *The Pound Era.* Berkeley: University of California Press, 1973.

Kincaid, Jamaica, and Robert Atwan, eds. *Best American Essays.* New York: Houghton Mifflin, 1995.

Lytle, Andrew Nelson. *Bedford Forrest and His Critter Company.* Nashville: J. S. Sanders, 1931.

MacLean, Nancy. *Democracy in Chains: The Deep History of the Radical Right's Stealth Plan for America.* New York: Penguin, 2018.

Martin, Eric. *The Writing on the Wall.* Eugene, OR: Cascade Books, 2023.

McAuliffe, Terry. *Beyond Charlottesville: Taking a Stand Against White Nationalism.* New York: Thomas Dunne Books, 2019.

Mogelson, Luke. *The Storm Is Here: An American Crucible.* New York: Penguin Press, 2022.

Moore, John Hammond. *Albemarle: Jefferson's County, 1727–1976.* Charlottesville: University Press of Virginia, 1976.

Nelson, Louis P., and Claudrena N. Harold, eds. *Charlottesville 2017: The Legacy of Race and Inequity.* Charlottesville: University of Virginia Press, 2018.

Neus, Nora. *24 Hours in Charlottesville: An Oral History of the Stand against White Supremacy.* Boston: Beacon Press, 2023.

Pound, Ezra. *Guide to Kulchur.* New York: New Directions, 1970.

——. *Jefferson and/or Mussolini.* London, Stanley Nott, Ltd, 1935.

——. "The Jefferson-Adams Letters as a Shrine and Monument" (1937). In *Selected Prose, 1909–1965.* New York: New Directions, 1973.

Reeve, Elle. *Black Pill: How I Witnessed the Darkest Corners of the Internet Come to Life, Poison Society, and Capture American Politics*. New York: Atria Books, 2024.

Rockwell, George Lincoln. *This Time the World*. New York: Parliament House, 1963.

Saunders, James Robert, and Renae Nadine Shackelford. *Urban Renewal and the End of Black Culture in Charlottesville, Virginia: An Oral History of Vinegar Hill*. Jefferson, NC: McFarland, 1998.

Sekou, Osagyefo Uhuru. *Urbansouls: Reflections on Youth, Religion, and Hip-Hop Culture*. St. Louis: Chalice Press, 2017.

Signer, Michael. *Cry Havoc: Charlottesville and Democracy under Siege*. New York: PublicAffairs, 2020.

Smith, J. Douglas. *Managing White Supremacy: Race, Politics, and Citizenship in Jim Crow Virginia*. Chapel Hill: University of North Carolina Press, 2002.

Spencer, Hawes. *Summer of Hate: Charlottesville USA*. Charlottesville: University of Virginia Press, 2018.

Tenold, Vegas. *Everything You Love Will Burn: Inside the Rebirth of White Nationalism in Americca*. New York: Nation Books, 2018.

Thomas, Jeff. *The Virginia Way: Democracy and Power after 2016*. Charleston, SC: History Press, 2019.

Von Daacke, Kirt, and Andrea Douglas. *After Emancipation: Racism & Resistance at the University of Virginia*. Charlottesville: University of Virginia Press, 2024.

Webb, Clive. *Rabble Rousers: The American Far Right in the Civil Rights Period*. Athens: University of Georgia Press, 2010.

Whitman, James Q. *Hitler's American Model*. Princeton, NJ: Princeton University Press, 2016.

Wiencek, Henry. *Master of the Mountain: Thomas Jefferson and His Slaves*. New York: Farrar, Straus and Giroux, 2011.

Important Internet Links

Integrity First for America Sines v. Kessler Trial Transcripts
https://www.integrityfirstforamerica.org/sines-v-kessler-trial-transcripts
Integrity First for America Sines v. Kessler Searchable Database for Trial Exhibits
https://www.integrityfirstforamerica.org/exhibits
Southern Poverty Law Center, Hatewatch
https://www.splcenter.org/hatewatch
Unicorn Riot Discord Leaks
https://discordleaks.unicornriot.ninja/discord/
Ignite the Right: Identifying organizers and attendees of Unite the Right
https://ignitetheright.net/
The Devil's Advocates: When hate goes on trial, the devil gets a lawyer.
https://the-devils-advocates.ghost.io/
Anonymous Comrades Collective
https://accollective.noblogs.org/

Periodicals

Aheron, Grace. "Listening to the Land: Eco-rooted Activism at the Charis Community in Charlottesville, Virginia." *Anglican Theological Review* 103, no. 2 (May 7, 2021), 186–95.

Barnhisel, Greg. "Hitch Your Wagon to a Star: The Square Dollar Series and Ezra Pound." *The Papers of the Bibliographical Society of America* 92, no. 3 (Sept. 1998), 273–95.

Cohen, William. "Jefferson and the Problem of Slavery." *Journal of American History* 56, no. 3 (Dec. 1969), 503, 526.

Dorr, Gregory Michael. "Assuring America's Place in the Sun: Ivey Foreman Lewis and the Teaching of Eugenics at the University of Virginia, 1915–1953." *Journal of Southern History* 56, no. 3 (2000), 257–96.

Endo, Miko. " 'The Word "Mixed" without the "Indian" Would Be Better': Virginia's Racial Integrity Act and the Destruction of the Indian Race in the Early Twentieth Century," *Native South* 7 (2014), 92–107.

Gordon, Bonnie. "In the Aftermath of Charlottesville." *Musicology Now*, Sept. 8, 2017.

Herman, Sarita M. "A Pedestrian Mall Born out of Urban Renewal," *Magazine of Albemarle County History* 68 (2010), 79–110.

Leffler, Phillis K. "Insiders or Outsiders: Charlottesville's Jews, White Supremacy and Anti-Semitism." *Southern Jewish History* 21 (2018), 61–210.

Leidholdt, Alexander S. "Showdown on Mr. Jefferson's Lawn: Contesting Jim Crow during the University of Virginia's Protodesegregation." *Virginia Magazine of History and Biography* 122, no. 3 (2014), 230–71.

McCutcheon, Priscilla. "The 'Radical' Welcome Table: Faith, Social Justice, and the Spiritual Geography of Mother Emanuel in Charleston, South Carolina." *Southeastern Geographer* 56, no. 1 (Spring 2014), 16–21.

Pound, Ezra, "Obituary of Ford Madox (Hueffer) Ford," *The Nineteenth Century and After* 127 (August 1939), 178–81.

Rorty, James. "Hate-Monger with Literary Trimmings: From Avant-Garde Poetry to Rear-Guard Politics." *Commentary*, Dec. 1, 1956.

Sexauer, Cornelia F. "A Well-Behaved Woman Who Made History: Sister Mary Antona's Journey to Selma." *American Catholic Studies* 115, no. 4 (Winter 2004), 37–57.

Urofsky, Melvin I. "The Levy Family and Monticello." *Virginia Quarterly Review* 78, no. 3 (Summer 2002), 395–412.

NOTES

Introduction

3   **Spencer had just . . . candidates' debate.** Hawes Spencer, *Summer of Hate: Charlottesville USA*. Charlottesville: University of Virginia Press, 2018, 108.

3   **"This is the beginning . . . around the entire world."** Based on a YouTube video that has since been removed.

4   **After a recent . . . for six months.** "Judge Halts Removal of Lee Statue for 6 Months," *US News and World Report*, May 4, 2017.

4   **Regnery had poured . . . Koch or Soros, Inc."** Aram Roston and Joel Anderson, "The Moneyman Behind the Alt-Right," BuzzFeed News, July 23, 2017.

4   **White nationalists . . . the Republican Party.** George Hawley, *The Alt-Right: What Everyone Needs to Know*. Oxford: Oxford University Press, 2018, 7.

4   **In an article . . . going to be president.** Evan Osnos, "The Fearful and the Frustrated," *New Yorker*, August 24, 2015.

5   **The remixes . . . also went viral.** Valerie Tevere and Angel Nevarez, "A Punch in 4-4 Time," *BOMB*, March 15, 2017.

5   **To the men . . . "time has come."** Based on a YouTube video that has since been removed.

5   **"They are trying to take away . . . is *your* future!"** Eyes on the Right, "White Nationalists and Neo-Confederates Agree: Removing Confederate Statues Is a Form of 'Ethnic Cleansing,'" *AngryWhiteMen*, blog, May 27, 2017.

6   **"They want to put . . . not replace us!"** Based on a YouTube video that has since been removed.

6   **A man in a kippah . . . on the ground.** Timothy J. Heaphy, *Independent Review of the 2017 Protest Events in Charlottesville, Virginia*. Richmond, VA: Hunton & Williams, 2017, 26–27. Hereafter, Heaphy report.

6   **Activists trailed . . . Black friends were.** UVA Students United, "Richard Spencer Rally at Jackson Park," Facebook, May 13, 2017.

6   **The route took . . . they were gone.** Heaphy report, Timeline, 178.

6   **Chants of "Blood and soil" . . . lit up the dark.** @craftypanda, May 13, 2017.

7   **Then the men . . . *Cabaret*.** IFA Trial Transcript. Samantha Froelich Deposition, 26.

7   **Wes Bellamy, Charlottesville's . . . started going off.** Wes Bellamy, *Monumental: It Was Never about a Statue*. Newport News, VA: Black Gold Publishing, 2019, 95. Statement at Prolyfyck after statues came down, July 12, 2021.

8   **"giant sleeping dragon of American history."** David Blight, "The Civil War Lies on Us Like a Sleeping Dragon," *Guardian*, August 20, 2017.

9   **White people knew . . . "Why the lying?"** Michael Cheuk, ed., *Standing Up to Hate: The Charlottesville Clergy Collective and the Lessons from August 12, 2017*. Norman, OK: Good Faith Media, 2023, 48.

9   **When they dragged . . . the lies inescapable.** Interview with Rev. Brenda Brown-Grooms, November 12, 2019.

12   **This holy land . . . "belonged in white hands."** Michael A. Genovese and Alyssa Landry, *US Presidents and the Destruction of the Native American Nations*. New York: Palgrave Macmillan, 2021, 45. Joseph Ellis, *American Sphinx*. New York: Random House, 1996, 248–50.

13   **By the early twentieth . . . "Anglo-American" power.** Andrew Lawlor, "How a Child Born More Than 400 Years Ago Became a Symbol of White Nationalism," *Washington Post*, May 24, 2018.

13   **Dr. John Woodson . . . English privateers.** "Ancestor Spotlight," *Roots and All: A Genealogy*, blog, July 18, 2014.

13   **As scholars have since . . . enslaved Africans.** James Oakes, "How the 1619 Project Distorted History," *Jacobin*, December 27, 2023.

13   **In 1625 . . . census of residents.** Beth Austin, *1619: Virginia's First Africans*, Hampton History Museum, December 2019.

14   **Of the twenty-three Africans . . . in colonial Virginia.** "Heritage," sermon by Rev. Phil Woodson, First United Methodist Church, August 11, 2019. Woodson's count of Africans, thirty-two, differs from historical consensus. See Claudrena A. Harold's "Chronology," in Louis P. Nelson and Claudrena N. Harold, eds., *Charlottesville 2017: The Legacy of Race and Inequity*. Charlottesville: University of Virginia Press, 2018, ix, which says there were twenty-three. The Spanish were also known to keep slaves, but their storyline rarely dominated accounts of early America.

14   **A Woodson ancestor . . . problems with race.** Interview with Rev. Phil Woodson, May 10, 2021. Michael Bragg, "Politicians Decry White Nationalist Torch Rally in Lee Park," *Daily Progress*, May 15, 2017.

14   **Not long before . . . *Between the World and Me*.** Clergy Collective minutes, February 15, 2017.

14   **The book's 2015 release . . . when she did.** Benjamin Wallace Wells, "The Hard Truths of Ta-Nehisi Coates," *New York Magazine*, July 12, 2015.

14   **As part of his personal . . . race-conscious man.** Interview with Rev. Phil Woodson, May 10, 2021.

15   **"Silence and inaction" . . . hear Christ's call.** Rev. Phil Woodson sermon, May 14, 2017.

Prologue: The Unveiling

18 **Virginia once boasted . . . was no exception.** Interview with Rev. Lehman Bates, July 23, 2020.

19 **"great and heroic sons . . . wisdom of Thomas Jefferson."** Albert LeFevre, "Presentation Address," in Robert Aitken, *The George Rogers Clark Statue: The Unveiling of the Monument to George Rogers Clark.* Charlottesville, November 3, 1921. Special Collections, Alderman Library, University of Virginia.

19 **In the mid-1970s . . . antique stores.** Sarita M. Herman, "A Pedestrian Mall Born out of Urban Renewal," *Magazine of Albemarle County History* 68 (2010), 80.

19 **In 1918 . . . gifted to the city.** Correcting the Narrative: A Timeline of Events Related to Racism and White Supremacy in Charlottesville Virginia, October 13, 2020, http://correctingthenarrative.org/posts/timeline-white-supremacy-cville/.

20 **In anticipation of . . . lined the streets.** "Klan Parade Drew Big Crowd," *Daily Progress*, May 19, 1924, 1. As quoted in *The Illusion of Progress: Charlottesville's Roots in White Supremacy*, Carter G. Woodson Center. See also Kirt von Daacke and Ashley Schmidt, "UVA and the History of Race: When the KKK Flourished in Charlottesville," https://search.lib.virginia.edu/sources/uva_library/items/uva -lib:2590120;https://news.virginia.edu/content/uva-and-history-race-when-kkk -flourished-charlottesville.

20 **A Black barber . . . by their shoes.** African American Genealogy Group of Charlottesville and Albemarle County, Virginia, *Tenth Anniversary Cookbook*, June 2005, 70. As quoted in *Blue Ribbon Commission on Race, Memorials, and Public Spaces: Report to City Council*, December 19, 2016. Appendix, 51.

20 **On the much-awaited day . . . an honorable verdict.** *Proceedings of the Thirty- Seventh Annual Reunion of the Virginia Grand Camp Confederate Veterans, and of the 29th Reunion of the Sons of Confederate Veterans*, https://archive.org/details /ProceedingsOfTheThirtyseventhAnnualReunionOfTheVirginiaGrand Camp/.

21 **The Master of Ceremonies . . . statue *at all.*** *Blue Ribbon Commission Report*, 99. Quoting from Judge R. T. Duke's diary, May 4, 1924.

21 **Two weeks after . . . in its ruins.** *Blue Ribbon Commission Report*, 52–54. *Daily Progress*, June 2, 1924, 1. June 4, 1924, 1. June 23, 1924, 1.

21 **According to the *Daily* . . . considerable excitement.** *Blue Ribbon Commission Report*, 55. "Burning Klan Cross Draws Large Crowd," *Daily Progress*, June 16, 1926, 1, https://search.lib.virginia.edu/sources/uva_library/items/uva-lib:2598916.

Part I: A Beautiful Ugly City

Chapter 1: Lee Park

25 **The Black community was skeptical.** Interview with Vizena Howard, February 8, 2022.

25 **Some called him "Fresh Prince."** Wes Bellamy and Will Jones III in conversation.

25 **Some saw him . . . bigger things.** Charlottesville City Council meeting, December 5, 2016. Public comment by Will Jones, https://www.youtube.com /watch?v=cmM2Nb4-Bwc.

26   **The week before . . . figured it out.** Bellamy, *Monumental*, 10–11.

26   **Then, in October 2015 . . . only to *localities*.** Interview with Kristin Szakos, August 30, 2022.

26   **The most iconic . . . of the Confederacy.** Fourteen feet high, Lee and Traveller stood on a wide sixty-foot marble pedestal, completely dwarfing the eight-foot statue of Jefferson Davis which stood atop a spindly sixty-five-foot Doric column farther down Monument Avenue.

27   **Almost as soon as he put . . . vibrating with death threats.** Interview with Garnette Cadogan, August 11, 2022.

27   **She was often . . . like a spectacle.** Zyahna Bryant, *Reclaim: A Collection of Poetry and Essays.* Self-published, Charlottesville, 2019, 14.

27   **Standing on the corner . . . George Zimmerman.** Interview with Vizena Howard, February 8, 2022.

27   **Fifty people showed up in support.** Amdie Mengistu, "This Teenager Made History and Pissed Off Racists Everywhere," *Vice*, February 28, 2018.

27   **She remembers a . . . constantly of organizing.** Interview with Niya Bates, July 15, 2020.

27   **But Zimmerman's acquittal . . . another protest regardless.** Bryant, *Reclaim*, 21, 26.

27   **"I am reminded" . . . she wrote.** Benjamin Wallace-Wells, "The Fight over Virginia's Confederate Monuments," *New Yorker*, November 27, 2017.

28   **They were accompanied . . . I-95 outside Richmond.** Associated Press, "Confederate Flag to Fly over I-95 Near Richmond," August 7, 2013.

28   **"I went to support" . . . were capable of.** Interview with Bonnie Gordon, October 3, 2020.

29   **Zyahna had been . . . "Charlottesville I was."** Interview with Ann Marie Smith, September 17, 2020.

29   **For Zyahna it began . . . included her surname.** Rob Shimshock, "Virginia Social Justice Warriors Want to Tear Down Robert E. Lee Statue," Breitbart News, March 31, 2016.

29   **Threatening letters . . . went to school.** Theresa Vargas, "The Girl Who Brought Down a Statue," *Washington Post*, July 17, 2021.

29   **The heckling became . . . "I never thought about."** Interview with Jane Smith, October 20, 2021.

30   **Since Zyahna's call . . . screw being safe.** Bellamy, *Monumental*, 30–31.

30   **"Sometimes it takes someone . . . 'good trouble.'"** Interview with Vizena Howard, February 8, 2022.

30   **Phil Woodson, then an . . . First United Methodist.** Interview with Rev. Phil Woodson, May 10, 2021.

31   **"The more you stir . . . lot of people upset."** Chris Suarez, "Tensions Rise as Push to Pull Statues Makes Its Case," *Daily Progress*, March 22, 2016.

31   **The ladies arrived . . . Robert E. Lee look-alike.** Spencer, *Summer of Hate*, 59–60.

31   **In victory, Grant . . . "might over right."** Elizabeth Varon, "The Original False Equivalency," in Nelson and Harold, *Charlottesville 2017*, 40, 45.

32   **"to prevent [his] celebrity ... a source of income."** James Branch Cabell, *Let Me Lie: Being in the Main an Ethnological Account of the Remarkable Commonwealth of Virginia and the Making of Its History.* New York: Farrar, Straus, 1947, 171.

32   **One Scottsville woman . . . "above the law."** Scottsville Ladies of the Confederacy Facebook page.

33   **"You Black nigger . . . break you down."** Wes Bellamy, statement after statues came down, July 12, 2021.

33   **Through his spokesman . . . "to our community."** Moriah Balingit, "Virginia Board of Education Member Resigns after Vulgar Tweets Surface," *Washington Post*, December 1, 2016.

33   **UVA's student newspaper . . . black women succeed.** Anna Higgins and Tim Dodson, "Homophobic, Sexist, Anti-white Language Abundant in Charlottesville Vice Mayor's Tweets," *Cavalier Daily*, November 28, 2019.

34   **In his early years . . . a young Black man.** Bellamy, *Monumental*, 9.

34   **He'd outrun a childhood . . . was in college.** Wes Bellamy and Will Jones III in conversation.

34   **Councillor Kristin Szakos . . . bluff his way out of it.** Interview with Kristin Szakos, August 30, 2022.

35   **"When you're talking about . . . should be ashamed."** Charlottesville City Council meeting, December 5, 2016, Wes Bellamy, Bob Fenwick, public comment by Nikuyah Walker.

36   **"My name is Jason Kessler" . . . days were numbered.** Charlottesville City Council meeting, December 5, 2016, public comment by Jason Kessler.

Chapter 2: The Blue Ribbon Commission

37   **Three months after . . . and Public Spaces.** Charlottesville City Council meeting, May 28, 2016.

37   **The commission's charge . . . Black Charlottesville.** *Blue Ribbon Commission Report*, 4.

37   **From the middle . . . "reflect current values."** Chris Suarez, "Tensions Rise as Push to Pull Statues Makes Its Case," *Daily Progress*, March 22, 2016.

39   **Garnett Mellen traced . . . at its center.** Blue Ribbon Commission, July 27, 2016, Jefferson School Community Forum, Garnett Mellen.

39   **Her mother had warned . . . in the park.** Blue Ribbon Commission, July 27, 2016, Jefferson School Community Forum, Mary Carey.

39   **She was simply . . . "expunging of another."** Jane Williamson letter to Blue Ribbon Commission, June 23, 2016.

40   **One man likened . . . would it end?** Blue Ribbon Commission, July 27, 2016. Jefferson School Community Forum, Scott Warner.

40   **Did people sincerely . . . "honor that history."** Blue Ribbon Commission, July 27, 2016, Jefferson School Community Forum, Zyahna Bryant.

41   **"The forte of the Old . . . *belles lettres*."** Cabell, *Let Me Lie*, 123. Willa Cather left for Nebraska at a tender age; Tom Wolfe and William Styron jumped ship for New York.

42   **In 1916 Russians . . . an armored car.** Joseph Brodsky, "Homage to Marcus Aurelius," in Kincaid and Atwan, eds., *Best American Essays*. New York: Houghton Mifflin, 1995, 2.

43   **They called themselves . . . on his bookshelf.** Interview with Lewis Martin III, October 30, 2019.

43   **Freeman protrayed Lee . . . "enigma to be solved."** Douglas Southall Freeman, *R. E. Lee: A Biography*. New York: Charles Scribner's Sons, 1934, 494.

43   **Martin held forth . . . end of the deal."** Blue Ribbon Commission, July 27, 2016, Jefferson School Community Forum, Lewis Martin III.

44   **Ten minutes after . . . toward the Lee statue.** Blue Ribbon Commission hearing, September 22, 2016, Buford School Community Forum, Jalane Schmidt.

45   **At the time . . . was another resource.** Interview with Jalane Schmidt, September 25, 2019.

45   **At the time of the Civil War . . . "being accounted for."** Blue Ribbon Commission July 27, 2016, Jefferson School Community Forum, Jalane Schmidt. In 1860 the total population of Albemarle County and Charlottesville was 26,625. Of that number, 13,916 were enslaved Blacks, 606 were freemen, and 12,103 were white. Schmidt first used 54 percent, which included 606 free Blacks. She later corrected her figures to 52 percent, which accounted only for those enslaved. John Hammond Moore, *Albemarle: Jefferson's County, 1727–1976*. Charlottesville: University Press of Virginia, 1976, 115.

45   **After that the Deacon . . . The Professor did too.** Interview with Jalane Schmidt, September 25, 2019. Interview with John Edwin Mason, August 29, 2021.

46   **He called these four distinct narratives . . . "*were not soldiers*."** Blue Ribbon Commission, September 1, 2016. Prof. Gary Gallagher presentation.

47   **David W. Blight . . . "process of national reconciliation."** David Blight, "Europe in 1989, America in 2020, Death of the Lost Cause," *New Yorker*, July 1, 2020.

49   **"to understand our past to benefit our present and our future."** Blue Ribbon Commission, September 22, 2016, Buford School Community Forum, Stephanie Marshall.

49   **"Everything that is Black" . . . in the sidewalk.** Blue Ribbon Commission, September 22, 2016, Buford Community Forum, Mary Carey.

50   **Porter's great-great-grandfather . . . "different standpoint."** Blue Ribbon Commission, September 22, 2016, Buford School Community Forum, Lee Porter.

50   **While they often disdained . . . "presentism."** Interview with Lewis Martin, October 30, 2021.

51   **I learned later . . . tone deafness.** Interview with Rachel Lloyd, September 15, 2021; interview with John Edwin Mason, August 29, 2021; interview with Jane Smith, October 20, 2021.

51   **"Typically, I'll say . . . at West Point."** Blue Ribbon Commission, September 22, 2016, Buford School Community Forum, Lewis Martin III.

52   **Only a commissioner . . . to put them.** Interview with Rachel Lloyd, September 15, 2021, Blue Ribbon Commission, November 1, 2016.

53 **Then one commissioner . . . was watered down.** Blue Ribbon Commission, November 1, 2016, Sue Lewis, Margaret O'Bryant.

53 **The Deacon said . . . results of the vote.** Blue Ribbon Commission, November 1, 2016, Don Gathers.

54 **Jalane Schmidt called on . . . with white supremacists.** Blue Ribbon Commission, November 10, 2016, Walker Upper Elementary Community Forum, Jalane Schmidt, Pam Starsia, Lindsay Beutin, Zyahna Bryant.

55 **In an email . . . playing with fire.** Jalane Schmidt to Blue Ribbon Commission, November 12, 2016, re: "Liberation Day": Slave holiday from the Status Quo.

55 **They voted unanimously . . . vote for Relocate.** Blue Ribbon Commission, November 28, 2016, City Space. *Blue Ribbon Commission Report*, 10.

55 **The Professor asked him . . . "hatchet in his hand."** Interview with Don Gathers, March 11, 2020.

Chapter 3: The Art of Trolling

57 **In the weeks after . . . in the works.** Jaweed Kaleem, "There's Nothing Wrong with Being White: Donald Trump's Election Brings 'White Pride' out of the Shadows," *Los Angeles Times*, November 17, 2016; Serge F. Kovaleski, Julie Turkewitz, Joseph Goldstein, and Dan Barry, "An Alt-Right Makeover Shrouds the Swastikas," *New York Times*, December 10, 2016; John Woodrow Cox, "Let's Party Like It's 1933: Inside the Alt-Right World of Richard Spencer," *Washington Post*, November 22, 2016.

57 **Showtime was putting . . . for a documentary.** IFA Exhibit #2850, Video of Nathan Damigo on Periscope.

57 **"America was . . . belongs to us."** Daniel Lombroso and Yoni Appelbaum, "Hail Trump! White Nationalists Salute the President Elect," *Atlantic*, November 21, 2016.

58 **This was a term . . . of the US economy.** Unless in direct quotations, I haven't used the brands or terms white supremacists use to define themselves—"alt-right," "alt-lite," "Identitarian," and so on—since the old words work just as well.

58 **With a knowing . . . of Trump's brain.** John Herrman, "Why the Far Right Wants to Be the New 'Alternative' Culture," *New York Times*, June 27, 2017.

59 **The Jewish financier . . . provided it.** Andrew Marantz, "Does Hungary Offer a Glimpse of Our Authoritarian Future?" *New Yorker*, June 27, 2022.

59 **Some foresaw . . . idea of an ethnostate.** Allison Kaplan Sommer, "White Nationalist Richard Spencer Gives Israel as Example of Ethno-state He Wants in U.S.," *Haaretz*, October 19, 2017.

59 **Spencer even called . . . other plans.** Suzanne Schneider, "The Disturbing Alliance Between Zionists and Anti-Semites," *Forward*, February 19, 2017.

59 **And when, in a debate . . . answer to that.** Josh Nathan-Kazis, "'Alt-Right' Leader Ties White Supremacy to Zionism—Leaves Rabbi Speechless," *Forward*, December 7, 2016.

59 **In 2012 Spencer . . . "dispose of them?"** Ramon Lopez, "Answering the Alt-Right," *National Affairs*, no. 57 (Fall 2017).

60   **One journalist . . . "his own amusement."** Vegas Tenold, *Everything You Love Will Burn: Inside the Rebirth of White Nationalism in America*. New York: Nation Books, 2018, 224.

60   **Rand and Sherry Spencer . . . another letter.** Rand and Sherry Spencer, "An Appeal to Whitefish: Live and Let Live," *Daily Inter Lake*, December 18, 2016.

60   **A downtown commercial . . . targeted by protesters.** Christine Hauser, "After Neo-Nazi Posting, Police in Whitefish, Mont., Step Up Patrols," *New York Times*, December 20, 2016.

60   **When Sherry Spencer's . . . Auschwitz gate.** Lois Beckett, "I Was the Target of a Neo-Nazi Troll Storm," *Guardian*, April 20, 2017.

61   **The campaign spread . . . anyone could do.** Luke O'Brien, "The Making of an American Nazi," *Atlantic*, December 2016.

61   **Two people involved . . . on his podcast.** Interview with Andy Stepanian, March 26, 2021.

61   **Some gamers . . . something arty.** Simon Parker, "Zoe Quinn's Depression Quest," *New Yorker*, September 9, 2014.

61   **A writer named . . . primary demographic.** Leigh Alexander, "'Gamers' Don't Have to Be Your Audience. 'Gamers' Are Over." *GamaSutra*, August 28, 2014.

61   **The threats multiplied . . . review coverage.** Kyle Wagner, "The Future of the Culture Wars Is Here, and It's Gamergate," *Deadspin*, October 14, 2014.

62   **While couch surfing . . . online sources.** Parkin, "Zoe Quinn's Depression Quest."

62   **Quinn discovered . . . of young men.** Casey Johnston, "Chat Logs Show How 4chan Users Created #GamerGate Controversy," *Ars Technica*, September 9, 2014.

62   **"come for the misogyny and stay for the fascism."** Interview with Andy Stepanian, March 26, 2021.

62   **To push back . . . in their game.** Emily Gorcenski, "Making God," November 25, 2023, https://emilygorcenski.com/post/making-god/.

62   **In 2017 Steve . . . Breitbart reporter.** Elle Reeve, *Black Pill: How I Witnessed the Darkest Corners of the Internet Come to Life, Poison Society, and Capture American Politics*. New York: Atria Books, 2024, 111.

63   **Coordinated online gender . . . on the Capitol.** David Gilbert, "Gamergate's Legacy Lives on in Attacks Against Kamala Harris," *Wired*, August 12, 2024.

63   **his troll army . . . of social media.** "Daily Stormer Book Clubs (SBC)," https://www.adl.org/resources/backgrounders/daily-stormer-book-clubs-sbc.

63   **A reporter for . . . create new realities.** Jacob Siegel, "Is America Prepared for Meme Warfare?" *Vice*, January 31, 2017.

63   **Responding to . . . trigger people.** Heidi Desch, "Spencer Says Threats of Armed March Just a 'Joke,'" *Daily Inter Lake*, December 28, 2016.

63   **"Everyone is blowing . . . Trolling even."** Tenold, *Everything You Love*, 228.

63   **Six days after . . . high-power rifles.** Luke O'Brien, "The Making of an American Nazi," *Atlantic*, December 2017.

63   **Whitefish went on . . . never showed.** Lois Beckett, "How Richard Spencer's Hometown Weathered a neo-Nazi 'Troll Storm,'" *Guardian*, February 5, 2017.

63   **Anglin's loyalties . . . whoever they might be.** In 2016 Andrew Anglin voted for
      Trump by absentee ballot from the Russian town of Krasnodar. Hatewatch, "Neo-
      Nazi's Bitcoin History Suggests Russian Darknet Link," SPLC, July 15, 2021.

64   **Queers weren't white . . . he equivocated.** Anon., "Queer Fascism: Why White
      Nationalists Are Trying to Drop Homophobia," *Antifascist News*, November 6,
      2015.

65   **"I think of myself . . . of culture.** IFA Trial Transcript. Richard Spencer Cross,
      November 5, 2021, 23.

65   **Spencer believed . . . trade school.** Richard Spencer, "What It Means to Be
      Alt-Right," August 11, 2017.

65   **"It was as if" . . . became white.** Rebecca Futo Kennedy, "On the History of
      'Western Civilization,'" Part I, https://rfkclassics.blogspot.com/2019/04/on
      -history-of-western-civilization-part.html.

66   **The phrase *Judeo-* . . . and Europeans.** Spencer, "What It Means to be
      Alt-Right."

66   **In an essay . . . in its glare.** Joseph Brodsky, "Homage to Marcus Aurelius," in
      Kincaid and Atwan, *Best American Essays*, 4.

67   **Damon T. Berry . . . "biological extinction."** Damon T. Berry, *Blood and Faith:
      Christianity in American White Nationalism.* Syracuse, NY: Syracuse University
      Press, 2017, 3.

67   **Spencer's Big Idea . . . "goofballs in Dockers."** *Alt-Right: Age of Rage*, documen-
      tary, directed by Adam Ghala Lough, interview with Richard Spencer [38:55].

67   **He titled it "The Charlottesville . . . race discrimination.** Richard Spencer,
      "Why and How I Wrote the Alt-Right Manifesto," Altright.com, 2017, https://
      altright.com/2017/08/11/a-note-on-the-charlottesville-statement/.

67   **"Race is real . . . often called Aryan."** Spencer, "What It Means to Be
      Alt-Right."

69   **He subscribed to . . . creates its own reality.** IFA Trial Transcript. Cross of
      Richard Spencer, November 4, 2021, 30.

69   **Samantha Froelich also . . . Identity Evropa.** IFA Trial Transcript. Samantha
      Froelich Deposition, November 1, 2021.

70   **The posters were . . . "Protect Your Heritage."** Megan Squire, "A Spotter's
      Guide," https://docs.google.com/presentation/d/1OpwJwIWHKdD6sJ4derXf
      w7EfIJGprfS0wXCb-YsOdnQ/edit?pli=1#slide=id.g266929b63a_1_0.

70   **In an interview . . . all the time.** "White Nationalist Opens Up to the Young
      Turks," https://www.youtube.com/watch?v=muf3XYTXfHk.

71   **Damigo had dropped . . . "pieces missing."** Gabriel Thompson, "My Brother
      the White Nationalist," *Pacific Standard*, November 26, 2018.

72   **His father . . . War on Terror.** *Alt-Right: Age of Rage*, October 30, 2018, Daryle
      Lamont Jenkins, Mark Potok, Richard Spencer.

72   **Met by a chorus . . . marveled at that.** Richard Spencer, "The Trump Betrayal,"
      Alt.Right.com.

73   **New members . . . first one "against the wall."** IFA Trial Transcript. Samantha
      Froelich Deposition, 12, 15, 19.

75 **This led to his . . . to Identity Evropa.** IFA Trial Transcript. Nathan Damigo Direct, 184.

75 **Mosley met Richard . . . not have happened.** Emma Cott and Andrew Michael Ellis, "How an Alt-Right Leader Lied to Climb the Ranks," Op-Doc, *New York Times*, February 5, 2018.

75 **In the last week . . . and Eli Mosley.** IFA Trial Transcript. Samantha Froelich Deposition, 15, 19–20, 22, 24.

Chapter 4: Holy Works

78 **One of its founders . . . outside the church.** Priscilla McCutcheon, "The 'Radical' Welcome Table: Faith, Social Justice, and the Spiritual Geography of Mother Emanuel in Charleston, South Carolina," *Southeastern Geographer* 56 (Spring 2016), 1.

78 **Dylann S. Roof . . . Burger King.** The nine congregants were Rev. Clementa C. Pinckney, Cynthia Graham Hurd, Susie Jackson, Ethel Lee Lance, Rev. DePayne Middleton-Doctor, Tywanza Sanders, Rev. Daniel L. Simmons, Rev. Sharonda Coleman-Singleton, and Myra Thompson. Frances Robles, "Dylann Roof Photos and a Manifesto Are Posted on Website," *New York Times*, June 20, 2015.

79 **Rev. Edwards was not alone . . . where to turn.** Interview with Rev. Alvin Edwards, May 5, 2021.

80 **Out of Rev. Edwards's . . . Collective was born.** Charlottesville Clergy Collective, "Statement on the Anniversary of the Mother Emanuel Shootings," June 16, 2016, 6–7.

80 **During a sermon . . . evangelical temperaments.** Interview with Rev. Elaine Ellis Thomas, April 15, 2021.

80 **Rev. Edwards . . . "Little Miss."** Interview with Rev. Brittany Caine-Conley, May 6, 2022.

80 **Some of the Black . . . only white person.** Interview with Rev. Elaine Ellis Thomas, April 15, 2021.

81 **"a land of dreams and opportunity."** Liam Stack, "Ben Carson Refers to Slaves as 'Immigrants' in First Remarks to HUD Staff," *New York Times*, March 6, 2017.

82 **"Being black in America . . . dispossessed are."** James H. Cone, *Black Theology and Black Power*. Maryknoll: Orbis Books, 1997, 151.

82 **While she pastored . . . the dark side.** Interview with Rev. Brenda Brown-Grooms, November 12, 2019.

83 **Over a hundred . . . chosen to attend.** Clergy Collective minutes, January 17, 2017.

83 **Pastor Brenda remembered . . . Just like that.** Interview with Rev. Brenda Brown-Grooms, November 12, 2019.

83 **"drag queen, the young Syrian . . . of the Christian Empire."** Brittany Caine-Conley, "God's Insistence," as quoted in Eric Martin, *The Writing on the Wall*. Eugene, OR: Cascade Books, 2023, 8.

83 **They understood racism . . . bear witness.** Interview with Rev. Brittany Caine-Conley, May 6, 2021.

84 **Moved by the spirit . . . existential commitment.** Interview with Rev. Tracy Howe, August 16, 2021.

85 **Growing up in . . . for Episcopal youth.** Interview with Rev. Brittany Caine-Conley, May 6, 2021.

86 **As a UVA student . . . young children.** Interview with Laura and Steve Brown, September 13, 2020.

86 **While her partner . . . by the Wispelweys.** Interview with Grace Aheron and Rowan Hollins, September 2, 2020.

86 **People of all ages . . . with Jesus's teachings.** Amy Sowder, "Episcopal-Supported Intentional Community in Charlottesville Embodies Radical Discipleship—and Permaculture," Episcopal News Service, August 18, 2017; interview with Grace Aheron and Rowan Hollins, September 2, 2020.

86 **The Charis mission . . . environmental destruction.** Grace Aheron, "Listening to the Land: Eco-rooted Activism at the Charis Community in Charlottesville, Virginia," *Anglican Theological Review*, May 7, 2021.

86 **Inspired by the writings . . . heard at Charis.** Interview with Jordan Lahey, September 24, 2020.

87 **If Grace had . . . began to attend.** Interview with Grace Aheron and Rowan Hollins, September 2, 2020.

88 **The first challenge . . . to her hesitancy.** Interview with Bekah Menning, September 28, 2019.

88 **Grace kept people . . . showed up later.** Interview with Ann Marie Smith, September 17, 2020.

88 **Bekah Menning . . . more radical place.** Interview with Bekah Menning, September 28, 2019.

Chapter 5: A Beautiful Ugly City

89 **A sizable contingent . . . their presence felt.** Bellamy, *Monumental*, 90.

89 **First, however . . . affordable housing.** Charlottesville City Council meeting, January 17, 2016, Mayor's State of the City Address.

90 **At her funeral . . . of her silent presence.** Interview with Rev. Brenda Brown-Grooms, April 14, 2021; comments on Holly Edwards by Joy Johnson and Nikuyah Walker, Charlottesville City Council meeting, August 6, 2018.

90 **Knowing she was dying . . . "ugly city."** Interview with Kendrick Edwards, August 3, 2020; phone conversation with Rev. Brenda Brown-Grooms, August 13, 2020, and her sermon, June 16, 2020.

91 **Gordon-Reed's . . . simple common sense.** Annette Gordon-Reed, *Thomas Jefferson and Sally Hemings: An American Controversy*. Charlottesville: University of Virginia Press, 1997, 107–9.

91 **"It's all about . . . writing history."** As quoted in Eddie S. Glaude Jr., *Begin Again: James Baldwin's America and Its Urgent Lessons for Our Own*. New York: Crown, 2020, 77.

92 **Yet even science . . . stance of skepticism.** Henry Wiencek, *Master of the Mountain: Thomas Jefferson and His Slaves*. New York: Farrar, Straus and Giroux, 2011, 203–4.

92 **"Jefferson was a man . . . dogs and horses."** William Cohen, "Jefferson and the Problem of Slavery," *Journal of American History* 56, no. 3 (Dec. 1969), 503–6.

93 **She remembered it . . . choices they faced.** Interview with Niya Bates, July 15, 2020.

93 **"You can't stand . . . knows how long."** Elle Reeve, "Vice News, Charlottesville: Race and Terror." *Vice News*, August 14, 2017 [17:03].

94 **What kind of man . . . "her life better."** Interview with Tanesha Hudson, November 9, 2020.

94 **My ancestors . . . implicated them regardless.** Steven Hahn, *Illiberal America: A History.* New York: W. W. Norton, 2024, 160.

94 **"We figured out . . . the bottom line."** Documentary, *That World Is Gone: Race and Displacement in a Southern Town*, 2010. https://www.fieldstudiofilms.com /that-world-is-gone/.

94 **Prevented from . . . Black intellectuals.** T. J. Sellers, "Mr. Jefferson's Mulatto Mistress," *Amsterdam News*, March 8, 1980.

95 **White speculators . . . which it stood.** Sophie Abramovitz, Eva Latterner, and Gillet Rosenblith, "Tools of Displacement: How Charlottesville, Virginia's Confederate Statues Helped Decimate the City's Historically Successful Black Communities," *Slate*, June 23, 2017; Jordy Yager, "A New Page: Longtime 10th and Page Residents Are Seeing a Shift in the Neighborhood," *C-ville Weekly*, December 1, 2017.

95 **Eugene Williams . . . forced to leave.** Interview with Eugene Williams, April 15, 2019; Boyd Zenner, "Who's That Knocking at My Door? Uncertain Times for Charlottesville's Fifeville Community," *Albemarle Magazine*, June–July 1989, 52.

95 **Brenda Brown-Grooms . . . remains standing.** Interview with Rev. Brenda Brown-Grooms, November 12, 2019.

96 **Black neighborhoods . . . to remedy it.** Interview with Eugene Williams, April 15, 2019.

96 **In the years . . . Tonsler Park.** Zenner, "Who's That Knocking?" 27, 42.

96 **His tires were slashed . . . phone was tapped.** Interview with Rev. Alvin Edwards, May 5, 2021.

96 **The university turned . . . on Fifeville.** Zenner, "Who's That Knocking?" 52.

96 **The idea wasn't . . . history of friendship?** Interview with Frank Dukes, August 2, 2022.

97 **Yet his efforts . . . "my elders had."** Interview with Rev. Lehman Bates, July 23, 2020.

97 **It was Councillor . . . "me the money," he said.** Charlottesville City Council meeting, January 17, 2016.

98 **Holly had been . . . as his issue.** Interview with Kendrick Edwards, August 3, 2020.

98 **When Mary Carey . . . hadn't really understood.** Bellamy, *Monumental*, 90.

98 **"You will die" . . . found loosened.** Wes Bellamy speech to Prolyfyck run crew after statues came down, July 12, 2021.

98 **Just that day . . . promptly seconded.** Charlottesville City Council meeting, January 17, 2016.

98 **During the Q&A . . . the night before.** Interview with Kristin Szakos, August 30, 2022.

99 **She made a motion . . . No one seconded.** Charlottesville City Council meeting, January 17, 2016.

99 **Until Bellamy . . . powers of persuasion.** Michael Signer, *Cry Havoc: Charlottesville and American Democracy under Siege.* New York: PublicAffairs, 2020, 95–96.

100 **After a few rounds . . . to throw up.** Signer, *Cry Havoc,* 97.

100 **More time was . . . for the Black community.** Charlottesville City Council meeting, January 17, 2016.

100 **Black residents who'd . . . one man fumed.** Bellamy, *Monumental,* 90.

101 **Kristin Szakos . . . "absolutely nothing."** Chris Suarez, "Council's Statues Vote Ends in Deadlocked Frustration," *Daily Progress,* January 18, 2017.

Interlude: Heart of Whiteness

105 **By 1955 . . . for the 1955–56 school year.** Dallas Randall Crowe, "Desegregation of Charlottesville, Virginia Public Schools, 1954–1969." PhD diss., University of Virginia, 1971, 35.

105 **Another outlet noted his smoldering charisma.** James Rorty, "Hate-Monger with Literary Trimmings: From Avant-Garde Poetry to Rear-Guard Politics," *Commentary,* December 1, 1956, 534.

105 **On July 12 . . . Lane High School.** "Judge Paul Denies Three Motions to Dismiss Desegregation Suit: Hints Decree Favoring NAACP," *Daily Progress,* July 12, 1956.

105 **Over twelve hundred people . . . orders to desegregate.** Moore, *Albemarle,* 449; "Mass Meeting Backs Proposal to Ignore Integration Orders," *Daily Progress,* July 24, 1956, 1, 3, 11.

107 **Like his father . . . communists and Jews.** Dan Wakefield, "Charlottesville Battle: Symbol of the Divided South," *Nation,* September 15, 1956, 210–13.

107 **"That Jew has been . . . in its schools."** Kasper, "Open Letter to the White Citizens of Charlottesville," August 7, 1956, Ezra Pound Papers, Yale Collection of American Literature, Beinecke Rare Book and Manuscript Library, Yale University (hereafter Ezra Pound Papers).

107 **The city's silent . . . "they'll explode."** Wakefield, "Charlottesville Battle," 213.

107 **"Another politician . . . a Citizens Council."** Kasper, "Open Letter," Ezra Pound Papers.

107 **In 1924 Charlottesville's . . . the local chapter.** "Mass Meeting Backs Proposal to Ignore Integration Orders," *Daily Progress,* July 24, 1956, 1, 3, 8, 11.

107 **After paying a . . . membership applications.** John Kasper, "Virginians Awake," Ezra Pound Papers.

108 **Dr. Henry Garrett . . . the *Brown* case.** Nancy MacLean: *Democracy in Chains: The Deep History of the Radical Right's Stealth Plan for America.* New York: Penguin, 2018, 49.

108 **UVA's Board of Visitors . . . integration efforts.** James J. Kilpatrick, "Anti-Semitism in the South," *Richmond News Leader,* July 7, 1958.

108   **He lamented the . . . profoundly radical mission.** MacLean, *Democracy in Chains*, 50, 66.

109   **At the outbreak . . . read and write.** W. H. Page, "The Rebuilding of Old Commonwealths," *Atlantic Monthly*, May 1962, 654.

109   **Like Senator Byrd . . . were his constituents.** Jeff Thomas, *The Virginia Way: Democracy and Power after 2016*. Charleston, SC: History Press, 2019, 19.

109   **Why should the . . . Jeffersonian language.** MacLean, *Democracy in Chains*, xv–xvi, 50, 66.

109   **"What had the world . . . from mongrelization."** Kasper, "Open Letter," Ezra Pound Papers.

109   **Virginia's defiance . . . aggravate the crisis.** Clive Webb, *Rabble Rousers: The American Far Right in the Civil Rights Period*. Athens: University of Georgia Press, 2010, 6.

110   **Key to John Kasper's . . . left-wing sympathies.** Rorty, "Hate-Monger," 534.

110   **At Columbia . . . Machiavelli and Stalin.** Humphrey Carpenter, *A Serious Character: The Life of Ezra Pound*. Boston: Houghton Mifflin, 1988, 800.

111   **"Nothing highbrow . . . in the mass mind."** John Kasper to Ezra Pound, April 10, 1956, Ezra Pound Papers.

111   **Pound's culture war . . . aged twenty-two.** Ezra Pound, "Obituary of Ford Madox (Hueffer) Ford," *The Nineteenth Century and After* 127 (August 1939), 178–81.

111   **By the mid-1930s . . . the *Chicago Tribune*.** Greg Barnhisel, "Hitch Your Wagon to a Star." *Papers of the Bibliographical Society of America* 92, no. 3 (September 1998), 273–95.

113   **At times . . . incomprehensible.** Mary de Rachewiltz, David A. Moody, and Joanna Moody, eds., *Ezra Pound to His Parents: Letters 1895–1929*. Oxford: Oxford University Press, 2011, 455.

113   **"The secret of " . . . *highly distinguished*.** Allen Tate, "Ezra Pound's Golden Ass," *Nation*, June 10, 1931, 632.

114   **In 1933 . . . national heritage."** Ezra Pound, "The Jefferson-Adams Letters as a Shrine and Monument" [1937], in *Selected Prose, 1909–1965*. New York: New Directions, 1973, 117.

114   **"If the reader will . . . *de facto*."** Pound, *Jefferson and/or Mussolini*. London: Stanley Nott, 1935, 11–12, 16, 18–19, 21, 62, 114. *Jefferson and/or Mussolini* was first published in T. S. Eliot's literary magazine, *The Criterion*.

115   **If he once required . . . "to the action."** John Kasper to Ezra Pound, February 11, 1955, Ezra Pound Papers.

115   **Hugh Kenner . . . of empty heads.** Hugh Kenner, *The Pound Era*. Berkeley: University of California Press, 1973, 509.

116   **Kasper displayed . . . LeRoi Jones.** Webb, *Rabble Rousers*, 70.

116   **In 1947 Pound . . . "dictatorship plan."** A copy of this book was found in bin Laden's Abbottabad compound.

116   **In an 1803 letter . . . "and they want."** "From Thomas Jefferson to William Henry Harrison, 27 February 1803," http://founders.archives.gov/documents/Jefferson /01-39-02-0500.

117   **For Pound the extent . . . finer things.** Ezra Pound, *Guide to Kulchur.* New York: New Directions, 1970, 27–28.

117   **Jefferson's *Notes* . . . at the medical school.** Jack Morgan, "The Legacy of Eugenics at U.Va," *Cavalier Daily*, January 17, 2022.

117   **They arrived eager . . . Integrity Act in 1924.** Alexander S. Leidholdt, "Showdown on Mr. Jefferson's Lawn: Contesting Jim Crow during the University of Virginia's Protodesegregation," *Virginia Magazine of History and Biography* 122, no. 3, 2014, 252.

118   **"Virginia Again" . . . "we have received."** "Virginia Again Leading Nation," *Daily Progress*, April 5, 1924.

118   **The director of . . . no longer existed.** Miko Endo, "'The Word "Mixed" without the "Indian" Would be Better': Virginia's Racial Integrity Act and the Destruction of the Indian Race in the Early Twentieth Century," *Native South* 7 (2014), 92–107.

118   **Virginia's use of . . . *Mein Kampf.*** Hahn, *Illiberal America*, 233, 236–37.

118   **In a May 1942 . . . "NAZI program."** Leonard W. Doob, ed., *Ezra Pound Speaking: Radio Speeches of World War II.* Westport, CT: Greenwood Press, 1978.

118   **For over half . . . hospitals and clinics.** Gregory Michael Dorr, "Assuring America's Place in the Sun: Ivey Foreman Lewis and the Teaching of Eugenics at the University of Virginia, 1915–1953," *Journal of Southern History* 66, no. 2 (2000), 257–96.

118   **Three UVA . . . purpose of study.** P. Preston Reynolds, "Eugenics, the Racial Integrity Act, Health Disparities," in Kirt von Daacke and Andrea Douglas, *After Emancipation: Racism and Resistance at the University of Virginia.* Charlottesville: University of Virginia Press, 2024, 102.

119   **Hospital buildings . . . them to UVA.** Alderman Library was renamed the Shannon Library in March 2024.

119   **Eugenics remained . . . retirement in 1953.** Bonnie Gordon, "In the Aftermath of Charlottesville," *Musicology Now*, September 8, 2017.

119   **To a friend . . . than any other.** T. S. Eliot to Emily Hale, May 16, 1933; and T. S. Eliot to Dorothy Pound, September 12, 1946, https://tseliot.com/the-eliot-hale-letters/letters/1242.

119   **His stay in Charlottesville . . . was overrun.** T. S. Eliot, *After Strange Gods: A Primer of Modern Heresy.* The Page-Barbour Lectures at the University of Virginia, 1933. London: Faber and Faber, 1934, 15–20.

120   **It was a Jew . . . from ruin.** Melvin I. Urofsky, "The Levy Family and Monticello," *Virginia Quarterly Review*, June 1, 2002, 401–7.

120   **Until the 1950s . . . UVA's faculty.** Phyllis K. Leffler, "Insiders or Outsiders: Charlottesville's Jews, White Supremacy, and Anti-Semitism," *Southern Jewish History* 21 (2018), 96.

120   **In a letter to . . . "without vulgarity."** T. S. Eliot to Emily Hale, May 16, 1933, https://tseliot.com/the-eliot-hale-letters/letters/1242.

120   **Radical Nazis . . . "German *Volk*."** James Q. Whitman, *Hitler's American Model.* Princeton, NJ: Princeton University Press, 2016, 83.

122 **The membership list . . . American Nazi Party.** Internet Archive, FBI File full text, September 2, 1956, John Kasper.

122 **According to Rockwell . . . from St. Elizabeth's.** George Lincoln Rockwell, *This Time the World*. New York: Parliament House, 1963, 146.

123 **One of Kasper's . . . time would come.** Rorty, "Hate-Monger," 536.

Part II: The Ghost in the Machine
Chapter 6: Capital of the Resistance

127 **There were any number of . . . Barnes & Noble.** Interview with Emily Gorcenski, February 4, 2020.

128 **She watched . . . sexual frustration.** Emily Gorcenski, "On Gaming and Trauma," blog post, February 2016.

128 **She might have, too . . . her work could cause.** Interview with Emily Gorcenski, February 4, 2020.

130 **In college she . . . to maneuver.** @EmilyGorcenski, October 25, 2016; Emily Gorcenski left Twitter in 2023.

130 **She asked herself . . . began to climb.** Interview with Emily Gorcenski, February 4, 2020.

130 **She mused on . . . group of protesters.** @EmilyGorcenski, February 1, 2017, and February 17, 2017.

130 **She posted a . . . foreign interests.** @EmilyGorcenski, January 26, 2017.

131 **The Democratic Party . . . all they did.** @EmilyGorcenski, June 29, 2017.

131 **Travelers with valid . . . leave the country.** Jonathan Blitzer, "When the New Travel Ban Goes into Effect Watch the Border Agents," *New Yorker*, March 7, 2017.

131 **Because of the delicacy . . . Trump administration.** Signer, *Cry Havoc*, 99–101.

131 **But Mike Signer felt . . . Public Policy.** Signer, *Cry Havoc*, 40–43; Charlottesville City Council meeting, July 17, 2017.

132 **He launched his . . . for mayor.** Lisa Provence, "Signer Elected Mayor, Bellamy Vice Mayor," *C-ville Weekly*, January 5, 2016.

132 **"lead where others had followed."** Signer, *Cry Havoc*, 11.

132 **This exasperated the city manager.** Background interview.

132 **In his January . . . fellow council members.** Charlottesville City Council, January 2, 2017; interview with Bob Fenwick, November 10, 2019.

133 **In response to . . . city hall.** Signer, *Cry Havoc*, 99–100. Interview with Kristin Szakos, August 30, 2022.

133 **In his own speech . . . Emma Lazarus.** Leffler, "Insiders or Outsiders," 67.

133 **Did this not . . . was a part of.** Signer, *Cry Havoc*, 49.

134 **After the fireworks . . . created racial divisions.** Charlottesville City Council, February 6, 2017.

135 **"rivet still closer the chains of bondage."** Winthrop D. Jordan, *White Over Black: American Attitudes toward the Negro, 1550–1812*. Chapel Hill: University of North Carolina Press, 2012, 435.

135 **In 2012 Ta-Nehisi . . . of the Constitution.** Ta-Nehisi Coates blog, "The NRA and the 'Positive Good' of Maximum Guns." Goodreads, December 21, 2012.

136 **Just as the Slave Power … "American values."** Hahn, *Illiberal America*, 330.

136 **When Trump campaigned … "or you die."** Publius Decius Mus, "The Flight 93 Election," *Claremont Review of Books*, September 5, 2015.

136 **The historian Steven Hahn … "while being wielded."** Hahn, *Illiberal America*, 173.

137 **In seminary, Pastor … of their wits.** Interview with Rev. Brenda Brown-Grooms, November 12, 2019.

138 **To keep this conversation … "not going anywhere."** Charlottesville City Council, February 7, 2017.

139 **Attendance at … the previous year.** Charlottesville Clergy Collective minutes—Chapman Grove Baptist Church, March 8, 2017.

139 **Name tags now included pronouns.** Interview with Rabbi Rachel Schmelkin, September 8, 2022.

139 **A police investigation … languished for years.** Graelyn Brashear, "Updated: Details in Sage Smith's Disappearance Come to Light," *C-ville Weekly*, December 24, 2014; Courtency Stuart, "Two Years after Sage Smith's Disappearance, Family Wants Answers over Discrepancy in Missing Person Cases," *C-ville Weekly*, November 19, 2014. Unlike the extensive manhunt, neighborhood sweeps, six-figure reward, and *People* magazine story that followed the disappearance of UVA student Hannah Graham, there had been little fanfare when Smith disappeared. It took four years before the police even declared it a homicide case, and still the main person of interest has yet to be questioned. Email from Seth Wispelwey, June 9, 2022.

139 **Grace Aheron … Sage Smith's family.** Interview with Rev. Brittany Caine-Conley, May 6, 2022.

139 **A shrine in front … "is Sage Smith?"** Email from Rev. Seth Wispelwey, June 7, 2022.

139 **After the second … Chief Al Thomas.** Solidarity Cville: A Media Outlet for the Charlottesville Community. Timeline. https://solidaritycville.wordpress.com/before-august-12th-2/.

139 **She tweeted an article … were being assaulted.** @EmilyGorcenski, June 4 and 5, 2017.

140 **As the only trans … living in Charlottesville.** Interview with Grace Aheron and Rowan Hollins, September 2, 2020.

140 **She answered personal … "lot of time crying."** Interview with Emily Gorcenski, February 4, 2019.

140 **Before her surgery … she wanted to live in.** Interview with Emily Gorcenski, February 5, 2019.

140 **"My mentions are" … to Europe.** @EmilyGorcenski, March 24, 2017.

140 **"I'm trans, I'm cute … I love being trans."** @EmilyGorcenski, May 2, 2017.

Chapter 7: We're Raising an Army, My Liege

141 **If 2016 had been … In Real Life.** IFA Exhibit #2535, Alt-Right Podcast with Richard Spencer.

141 **On March 4, 2017 … "politics is blurring."** IFA Exhibit #882, Nathan Damigo Discord Post.

141 **In mid-March Damigo . . . "I love Virginia."** IFA Exhibit #920, Nathan Damigo Discord Post.

142 **Clips of their clashes . . . drive up RAM membership.** IFA Exhibit #3761, Nathan Damigo Discord Post; IFA Exhibit #1949, Statement of Offense.

142 **A dozen Rise Above . . . to Berkeley.** ProPublica, "Unmasking California's New White Supremacists," October 19, 2017; YouTube, April 15, 2017. https://www.youtube.com/watch?v=Fpt3ImXIImY.

143 **Earlier that day . . . back on her feet.** IFA Exhibit #3808, Video recording of events at Berkeley, n.d.; and IFA Exhibit #2539.

143 **"Nathan should punch" . . . she texted back.** IFA Exhibit #487, Patrick Wolf and Samantha Froelich Discord Post.

143 **"We have entered" . . . he began.** IFA Exhibit #2539, 20.02-20.07_AltRight.com, "What Berkeley Means."

143 **Mike German . . . For hours.** A. C. Thompson, "Racist, Violent, Unpunished: A White Hate Group's Campaign of Menace," ProPublica, October 19, 2017.

143 **"The lack of policing . . . far more dangerous."** Mike German, quoted in Spencer Ackerman and Betsy Swan, "'Homeland Security' Ignores White Terror, DHS Veterans Say," Daily Beast, October 31, 2018.

143 **But the Proud Boys . . . protect the First Amendment.** Page St. John, "21 Arrested as Hundreds of Trump Supporters and Protesters Clash at Berkeley," *Los Angeles Times*, April 15, 2017.

143 **Spencer believed . . . "boomer goobers."** IFA Exhibit #2443, Posts by Richard Spencer.

144 **Spencer's message . . . "WE WILL CRUSH YOU."** IFA Exhibit #2443, Posts by Richard Spencer.

144 **Though the men . . . "Trumpian nationalism."** AltRight.com, "What Berkeley Means," YouTube. Video has been removed; excerpts available on IFA website.

144 **The *Independent* reporter . . . who Richard Spencer was.** Maya Oppenheim, "Richard Spencer: White Supremacist Leader Glitter Bombed' by Anti-fascist Protester Outside White House," *Independent*, April 10, 2017.

144 **"It has been" . . . desire to dominate.** IFA Exhibit #2517, RWW News with Richard Spencer.

145 **But Spencer's grave . . . "It's up to us."** "The Trump Betrayal," Alt-right.com, YouTube video. This video has since been removed.

145 **Not long after Berkeley . . . he suggested.** IFA Trial Transcript Direct, Richard Spencer, November 4, 2021, 66–68, 113.

145 **Richard Spencer now . . . hit a woman?** Richard Spencer, AltRight.com, "What Berkeley Means." This video has since been removed.

145 **"We don't punch women . . . treat them well."** IFA Exhibit #4028 and #4027, Text messages from Richard Spencer to Elliott Kline (Eli Mosley).

146 **A seventy-eight-page affidavit . . . demonstrating authority.** Talal Ansari, "White Nationalist Richard Spencer's Wife Says in Divorce Filings that He Physically and Emotionally Abused Her," BuzzFeed News, October 23, 2018.

146 **IGD's spokesperson told me . . . "That is shadowy."** Interview with It's Going Down, January 25, 2023.

147 **In the early 1960s . . . the Freedom Riders.** Michael E. Miller, "The Shadow of an Assassinated Nazi Commander Hangs over Charlottesville," *Washington Post*, August 21, 2017.

147 **Only the Jewish editor . . . defied the ban.** Jacob Fenston, "Arlington's Uneasy Relationship with Nazi Party Founder," *Metro Connection*, September 6, 2013.

148 **Finally, there were those . . . like fifties housewives.** Unicorn Riot, Discord voice chat recording, July 30, 2017, https://unicornriot.ninja/wp-content/uploads /2017/09/UniteTheRight-RandomChat-July30.mp3.

148 **A legendary . . . air of punk indifference.** Cf. *Alt-Right: Age of Rage*, https:// www.imdb.com/title/tt7980006/.

149 **He counsels . . . Unite the Right.** Interview with Daryle Lamont Jenkins, August 15, 2021.

149 **At nineteen, Schoep . . . in America.** SPLC, Profile of National Socialist Movement.

149 **In 1994 Schoep took . . . regalia.** SPLC, Profile of Jeff Schoep; IFA Trial Transcript, Jeff Schoep Direct, November 12, 2021, 167–68.

149 **Tenold then went . . . for a street fight.** Tenold, *Everything You Love*, 35–39.

150 **In October 2013 . . . All was soon forgiven.** SPLC, Profile of Matthew Heimbach.

150 **In the summer of 2016 . . . forming an alliance.** Vocativ, *The Man Behind the NSM, the Largest Neo-Nazi Group in America*, YouTube video.

150 **For Heimbach, the timing . . . Greek party.** Unicorn Riot Discord Leaks, MatthewHeimbach 2017-05-24 02:21:40 UTC.

151 **Heimbach liked to cite . . . "run by Jews."** Unicorn Riot Discord Leaks, MatthewHeimbach 2017-06-25 17:34:28 UTC.

151 **Heimbach would never . . . his neo-Nazi beliefs.** Unicorn Riot Discord Leaks, MatthewHeimbach 2017-04-24 03:41:26 UTC.

151 **On November 5 . . . remained unchanged.** IFA Exhibit #1481, National Socialist Movement announcement dated November 4, 2016.

152 **Instead, he drove . . . Purdue Pharma had.** Tenold, *Everything You Love*, 38–40.

152 **Because the biggest . . . Heimbach said.** Unicorn Riot Discord Leaks. MatthewHeimbach 2017-05-24 04:33:23 UTC and 2017-04-24 03:41:26 UTC.

152 **Back in December . . . sucker punch.** Tenold, *Everything You Love*, 232–33, 244.

152 **After the Battle . . . Auburn University.** IFA Exhibit #2240, Post by Matthew Heimbach.

152 **Seeing that . . . Spencer ghosted him.** Tenold, *Everything You Love*, 249, 253.

153 **Mike Enoch . . . *The Daily Shoah.*** SPLC, Profile of Mike "Enoch" Peinovich.

153 **Internecine conflict . . . stood by him.** Andrew Marantz, "Birth of a White Supremacist," *New Yorker*, October 16, 2017; "No Honor among Trolls: 'The Right Stuff' Gets Doxed by Their Own 'Movement.'" It's Going Down, January 10, 2017.

153 **Pikeville's city officials . . . no one had.** Tenold, *Everything You Love*, 249, 263, 266.

153 **The town battened . . . "we truly are."** @MMPikeville, April 28, 2017.

154 **Vandal's calling card . . . "regimented patriarchy."** Sacco Vandal, "In Defense of White Sharia," Counter Currents, June 9, 2017.

154 **In Pikeville, Sacco . . . "pothead losers."** @UR_Ninja, "White Supremacists from League of the South and Antifascists Shouting at Each Other across Police Line in Downtown #Pikeville, KY." April 29, 2017, 2:31 pm.

154 **Heimbach and Schoep's . . . Appalachian hollers.** Tenold, *Everything You Love*, 279.

154 **"I thought fascists" . . . sunglasses shouted.** T. J. Roberts, "Full Video: Nazi and Antifa Protesters Face Off in Pikeville," News2Share, April 29, 2017.

154 **On arrival, Heimbach . . . and brass knuckles.** Tenold, *Everything You Love*, 279–80.

155 **As the rallygoers . . . at a Trump rally.** @UR_Ninja, "As the Neo-Nazi Traditionalist Worker Party Left Pikeville, Their Leader Matt Heimbach Was Served w/Court Summons for a March 2016 Assault," May 1, 2017.

155 **Heimbach solicited . . . of the Nationalist Front.** Tenold, *Everything You Love*, 284–85.

155 **Hill hadn't flinched . . . swastika patches.** IFA Exhibit #2464, Photo of Michael Hill, Matthew Heimbach, and Jeff Schoep at rally in Pikeville.

155 **Not everyone . . . Odal runes.** IFA Exhibit #3842, Docket Entry 823-02, 44.

155 **Jeff Schoep promised . . . Dr. Hill told him.** IFA Exhibit #1563, Email from Michael Hill to commander.

155 **Heimbach would . . . one of the strongest.** Unicorn Riot Discord Leaks. MatthewHeimbach 2017-06-02 12:46:44 UTC.

156 **During the march . . . "Hail victory!" chants.** Unicorn Riot Discord Leaks. MatthewHeimbach 2017-05-24 02:30:50 UTC [tradworker #tradworker].

156 **He was convinced . . . to America.** Unicorn Riot Discord Leaks. MatthewHeimbach 2017-05-24 02:30:50 UTC [tradworker #tradworker].

156 **After the torches . . . "Race war now!"** Krypto Report, Episode 13—An Old Unreconstructed, May 14, 2017.

156 **For Spencer, the evening . . . she never would.** IFA Trial Transcript Direct questioning of Richard Spencer, November 4, 2021, 65; IFA Exhibit #2514; Andrew Marantz and Dorothy Wickenden, "Samantha's Journey into the Alt-Right, and Back," *New Yorker*, November 25, 2019.

156 **According to a Stormer . . . "mate selection."** IFA Exhibit #2010, "Charlottesville Ground Report—Nazi Occultists Resurrect Spirit of the Confederacy."

156 **As a local . . . wasn't worried.** IFA Exhibit #1431A, Facebook Messages Including Jason Kessler.

157 **As a young man . . . hired someone else.** *Jason Kessler v. City of Charlottesville* et al. 3:18 CV00015 Deposition of: Jason Eric Kessler June 27, 2018, 11, 25–26, 28, 159, 184.

157 **Throughout their six weeks . . . shouting incoherently.** Newsradio WINA, "Jason Kessler Participated in Occupy, Says Another Activist," n.d. 2017.

157 **Kessler ascribed his . . . revelatory tweet.** SPLC, Jason Kessler Profile page.

157 **Just before boarding . . . "I'm white!"** Jon Ronson, "How One Stupid Tweet Ruined Justine Sacco's Life," *New York Times Magazine*, February 12, 2015.

158 **Four days after . . . Charlottesville 2.0 server.** IFA Exhibit #1537, Email from
     Michael Hill.

158 **Members should . . . attend, he said.** IFA Exhibit #1551, Email from LSPres to
     Michael Tubbs.

158 **"This is gonna" . . . for his members.** Unicorn Riot Discord Leaks.
     MatthewHeimbach 2017-06-05 16:53:25 UTC.

158 **Heimbach had already . . . turned to lodging.** Unicorn Riot Discord Leaks.
     MatthewHeimbach 2017-06-09 15:18:09 UTC.

158 **The biography and profile . . . Nationalist Front website.** IFA Exhibit #0707,
     Impact Image of Matthew Heimbach and Dillon Hopper Discord Post.

158 **Vanguard America . . . from New Mexico.** Hatewatch Staff, "Meet 'Patriot
     Front': Neo-Nazi Network Aims to Blur Lines with Militiamen, Alt-Right."
     SPLC, December 12, 2017.

159 **At Pikeville he . . . combat shotgun.** Anna Merlan, "Leader of the Hate Group
     Linked to Charlottesville Attacker Was a Recruiter for the U.S. Marines." *Splinter*,
     August 14, 2017.

159 **Informed of the . . . about shields.** IFA Exhibit #1103, Impact Image of Dillon
     Hopper Discord Post 3.

159 **"We've got 90% of the real orgs . . . Heimbach replied.** IFA Exhibit #0707,
     Impact Image of Matthew Heimbach and Dillon Hopper Discord Post.

159 **"We are raising . . . comes to it."** IFA Exhibit #1455, Text messages between
     Jason Kessler and Richard Spencer.

159 **Kessler had failed . . . in Spencer's eyes.** IFA Trial Transcript Spencer Direct,
     November 4, 2021, 72.

159 **Charlottesville 2.0 . . . were coming.** IFA Trial Transcript Spencer Direct,
     November 4, 2021, 92; IFA Exhibit #1455, Text messages between Jason Kessler
     and Richard Spencer.

159 **He might not showcase . . . "to start violence."** IFA Exhibit #1410, Email from
     Jason Kessler to Jeff Schoep.

160 **"We're ready to add" . . . "and appreciate it."** IFA Exhibit #1455, Text messages
     between Jason Kessler and Richard Spencer.

160 **Megan Squire . . . Charlottesville were describing.** Interview with Megan
     Squire, November 17, 2020.

160 **As in Charlottesville . . . at the lynching site.** Carli Brosseau, "Have You Ever in
     Your Life Attended a Meeting of the Ku Klux Klan?" *News & Observer*, May 27,
     2021; Carli Brossau, "In a Small Town, a Battle for Racial Justice Confronts a
     Bloody Past and an Uncertain Future," *News & Observer*, May 19, 2021.

160 **Now the Freedom of Expression . . . "controls the future."** Megan Squire's
     "A Spotter's Guide," 9, 10, 34. The U.S. marine was named Michael Joseph
     Chesny.

161 **Meanwhile, a task force . . . Trump administration.** Peter Beinart, "Trump
     Shut Program to Counter Violent Extremism." *Atlantic*, October 29, 2018.

161 **The Department of Homeland . . . of domestic terror.** Mike German,
     "Testimony before the House Judiciary Committee, Subcommittee on Crime,
     Terrorism, and Homeland Security," February 24, 2021.

161   **Squire and her husband . . . *a big deal*.** Interview with Megan Squire, November 17, 2020.

Chapter 8: Fuck White Supremacy

163   **Lisa Draine, a local . . . for the summer.** Interview with Lisa Draine, February 24, 2024.

163   **Wes Bellamy told them . . . "end of the story."** Interview with Jenny Phillips, April 19, 2021.

164   **"This is not our system . . . working as intended."** Ta-Nehisi Coates, "Trayvon Martin and the Irony of American Justice," *Atlantic*, July 15, 2013.

164   **At the vigil . . . to defeat them.** Laura Brown email to "justice-minded folks and friends," May 15, 2017.

164   **Don Gathers spoke . . . taken it over.** Heaphy report, 29.

165   **That night . . . knocked from his hand.** Lisa Provence, "Lee Park Scene of White Nationalist Demonstration, Counterprotest," *C-ville Weekly*, May 15, 2017.

165   **Pam Starsia, a lawyer . . . dox local activists.** Lisa Provence, "Tactical Change: Not Your Grandpa's Protest," *C-ville Weekly*, May 31, 2017.

165   **Then, as the park . . . in handcuffs.** Heaphy report, 29–30; "Before August 12th." Solidarity Cville, https://solidaritycville.wordpress.com/before-august-12th-2/.

165   **"WHAT. THE. FUCK . . . Charlottesville is fucked."** @EmilyGorcenski, June 1, 2017.

165   **She followed this . . . her Fifeville home.** @EmilyGorcenski, May 15, 2017.

165   **Two weeks later . . . Flagger rally.** "Faith Leaders Vigil," Solidarity Cville, May 31, 2017.

165   **Veronica Fitzhugh . . . their friend circles.** Veronica Fitzhugh email, May 26, 2017.

166   **Local activists were . . . or phone calls.** Heaphy report, 29.

166   **Having returned from . . . Signal chat groups.** Interview with Emily Gorcenski, February 6, 2020.

166   **By the time the . . . his fellow Flaggers.** Interview with Rev. Phil Woodson, May 10, 2021.

166   **Coming two weeks after . . . feeling hopeful.** Interview with Rev. Brittany Caine-Conley, May 6, 2022.

166   **"They keep saying" . . . complained on Facebook.** IFA Exhibit #1431A, Facebook messages including Jason Kessler (as Ambien Falcon).

167   **"Shit is happening" . . . with her phone.** @EmilyGorcenski, June 1, 2017.

167   **In the spirit of . . . "in a public space."** Provence, "Tactical Change."

167   **Flyers identifying . . . Bellamy petition.** Chris Suarez, "Charlottesville on Edge as KKK Rally Approaches," *Daily Progress*, July 7, 2017.

167   **Daryle Lamont Jenkins . . . of the movement, every fall.** Documentary, *Alt-Right: Age of Rage* [30.33].

167   **For reasons . . . alcohol took effect.** "Ivy-League Racist Jared Taylor Disguised as Frenchman: Clandestinement Dans Charlottesville." It's Going Down, June 6, 2017.

168   **At the next city council . . . Black neighbors, he said.** Charlottesville City Council meeting, March 15, 2017. Public comment, Joe Starsia.

168   **Instead, Signer . . . *Washington Post*.** Mike Signer, "I'm a Progressive Mayor.

Here's Why I Voted No on Removing My City's Confederate Statue," *Washington Post*, May 24, 2017.

168   **"He's currently . . . whining to cops."** @EmilyGorcenski, June 1, 2017. Also Lisa Provence, "Miller's Time: Candidate Arrested in Mall Shutdown," *C-ville Weekly*, June 2, 2017.

168   **She didn't engage . . . "G[o]rcenski will ever see."** Anonymous Comrades Collective, "Unite the Right's 'Swastika Pin' Identified as Zachary Hudson Fisher, aka Milwaukee DJ 'Hdsn Acid,'" September 24, 2020.

169   **Kessler then complained . . . loomed over him.** Provence, "Miller's Time."

169   **"I'm not a racist" . . . a different hat.** @Emily Gorcenski, June 2, 2017.

169   **A "totalitarian Communist . . . not divide us."** Michael Hill, "League Will Be at Unite the Right Rally, 12 August, Charlottesville, Va.," June 9, 2017.

170   **"Goodnight from the side . . . slogans is bad."** @EmilyGorcenski, June 1, 2017.

170   **Most local officers . . . what a synagogue was.** Interview with Rabbi Tom Gutherz, June 18, 2022.

170   **Thus, after an evening . . . out of his pajamas.** John W. Whitehouse, founder and president of the Rutherford Institute, to Chief Al S. Thomas, June 7, 2017.

170   **Not every encounter . . . in his face.** Charlottesville City Council meeting, June 19, 2017. Public comment, Luis Ayola.

170   **Some clashes unfolded . . . and business owners.** Interview with Jalane Schmidt, September 25, 2019.

171   **"These people are trying . . . civil towards them."** Interview with Laura and Steve Brown at Casa Alma, September 13, 2020.

171   **Still, when asked to show . . . "Fuck you, Kessler."** Interview with Eric Martin, August 5, 2020.

171   **Bekah Menning had hosted . . . making trouble.** Conversation with Bekah Menning, March 11, 2024.

171   **"Instead of being empowered . . . smaller, quieter, calmer."** Marc M., "Statement to Charlottesville City Council," July 28, 2017.

171   **Technically, Smash . . . live in confirmed.** Interview with Rev. Brittany Caine-Conley, May 6, 2022.

172   **So even if members . . . all preparing themselves.** "Religion, Race and Democracy Lab," panel with Jalane Schmidt, Rev. Osagyefo Uhuru Sekou, Rabbi Rachel Schmelkin, Grace Aheron, and Don Gathers, August 12, 2020.

172   **Jason Kessler . . . "our enemies with."** Unicorn Riot Discord Leaks, Jason Kessler (MadDimension) 2017-06-07 14:44:45 UTC [Charlottesville 2.0 #general_1].

172   **Most of the action . . . after the rally?** IFA Exhibit #1433A, Jason Kessler (Ambien Falcon) post.

172   **What about burning . . . "fight this shit out."** IFA Exhibit #0552, Jason Kessler Discord Post.

172   **"Assemble every motherfucker you can."** IFA Exhibit #968, Jason Kessler Discord Post.

173   **Jalane and Don . . . "fifty years ago."** Interview with Jalane Schmidt, September 25, 2019.

173   **It had taken the director . . . her tentative takeaway.** Lisa Provence, "Still

Relevant? New NAACP President Faces Charged Civil Rights Landscape," *C-ville Weekly*, May 24, 2017.

173 **But Trump's election . . . waiting on them.** Dani McClain, "Can Black Lives Matter in the Age of Trump?" *Nation*, September 19, 2019.

174 **Raised in an intentional . . . eight years before.** Interview with Jalane Schmidt, September 25, 2019.

174 **When asked by . . . of white sympathy.** Provence, "Tactical Change."

174 **But the respectability . . . it once had.** Interview with Rev. Osagyefo Uhuru Sekou, December 15, 2022.

174 **"The tactics always" . . . would fall.** Provence, "Tactical Change."

174 **"The days when we . . . are dead and gone."** David Vaughn Straughn, "We Must Face the Klan," Medium, July 7, 2017.

174 **On June 5 . . . so did Jason Kessler.** Amanda Barker's May 24, 2017, permit application. *Daily Progress* staff, "Local KKK Group Plans July Rally in Charlottesville," *Daily Progress*, June 5, 2017.

175 **Mayor Mike Signer . . . was protected speech.** Interview with Rev. Lehman Bates, July 13, 2022.

175 **One of the first things . . . choice did he have?** Interview with Rev. Lehman Bates, July 23, 2020.

175 **Mayor Signer opened . . . send a "positive message."** Charlottesville Clergy Collective minutes, June 6, 2017.

176 **The public historian . . . last meeting she attended.** Interview with Niya Bates, July 15, 2020.

176 **To the chagrin . . . Signer's mandate.** Straughn, "We Must Face the Klan."

176 **"This rump out-of-state . . . world-class city."** Michael E. Miller, "The Ku Klux Klan Wants to Rally in Charlottesville. Now This College Town is on Edge Again," *Washington Post*, June 6, 2017.

176 **Rev. Wispelwey and Rev. Caine-Conley . . . a bridge too far.** Interview with Rev. Lehman Bates, July 23, 2020.

177 **Still, they welcomed . . . Less so her voice.** Interview with Rev. Seth Wispelwey, February 9, 2021.

177 **Rev. Bates told me . . . "level of relationship? *Fine.*"** Interview with Rev. Lehman Bates, July 13, 2022.

177 **This was Rev. Bates's . . . any different?** Interview with Rev. Lehman Bates, July 23, 2020.

177 **While Seth had hoped . . . was most needed.** Interview with Rev. Seth Wispelwey, February 2, 2021.

178 **On Rev. Edwards's return . . . "when evil arrives."** Interview with Rev. Elaine Ellis Thomas, April 15, 2021.

178 **"The people were fit . . . ready for this."** Interview with Rev. Brenda Brown-Grooms, November 12, 2019.

178 **Even if the mayor . . . killing someone.** Interview with Rev. Seth Wispelwey, February 9, 2021.

178 **"Black folks will not . . . I am dead."** Charlottesville Clergy Collective, meeting minutes, July 5, 2017.

178 **"lead the City's effort . . . to the KKK rally."** Signer, *Cry Havoc*, 144.
179 **In concert with . . . of the rally.** Interview with Niya Bates, July 15, 2020.
179 **"They are going to be . . . UNITE THE RIGHT."** Newsradio WINA report on Kessler and Proud Boys' plans.
179 **"If Antifa fucks . . . are under attack."** Unicorn Riot Discord Leaks. MadDimension 2017-06-15 20:35:30 UTC.
179 **"There's a 'Proud Boys' . . . triggered about."** Unicorn Riot Discord Leaks. MadDimension 2017-06-17 21:09:08 UTC.
179 **At a "March 4 Trump" . . . final merit badge or "degree."** @Gavin_McInnes, "Happy to announce the military division of #ProudBoys headed by @ BasedStickMan_ #AltKnights," April 22, 2017, 1:04 pm; and Bill Morlin, "New 'Fight Club' Ready for Street Violence," *SPLC*, April 25, 2017.
180 **A member of Anarchist . . . of his badge.** Charlottesville City Council meeting, June 19, 2017. Public comment, Luis Ayola.
180 **Seth went around . . . to serve Kessler.** Interview with Rev. Seth Wispelwey, February 9, 2021.
180 **Solidarity Cville . . . be present.** https://solidaritycville.wordpress.com/2017/06/17/proud-boys-in-charlottesville-with-jason-kessler/.
180 **When Kessler paid . . . "to prove, dude?"** Newsradio WINA report on Kessler and Proud Boys' plans.
180 **Denied service at . . . chased them off.** Charlottesville City Council meeting, June 19, 2017. Public comment, Luis Ayola.
180 **A local man came . . . to press charges.** Newsradio WINA report on Kessler and Proud Boys' plans.
180 **At the city council meeting . . . he replied.** Charlottesville City Council meeting, June 19, 2017. Public comment, Brandon Collins.
181 **Emily Gorcenski wasn't going . . . Kessler a permit.** Interview with Emily Gorcenski, May 22, 2020.
181 **Her second audience was . . . from a Kessler associate.** @EmilyGorcenski, July 18, 2017.

Chapter 9: Invisible Empires
183 **Rumor had it . . . Klan kept "invisible."** Andrew Nelson Lytle, *Bedford Forrest and His Critter Company*. Nashville: J. S. Sanders, 1931, 383.
183 **By 1900 one in five . . . vows of secrecy.** Dr. Kristofer Allerfeldt, "Invisible Empire: An 'Imperial' History of the KKK," July 7, 2014.
184 **Its roster included . . . Supreme Court justices.** Hahn, *Illiberal America*, 226.
184 **As a "secret" society . . . clubs and organizations.** "U. of VA. Klan No. 5," *Daily Progress*, November 6, 1922, 1.
184 **"The fiery cross . . . deepest crimson."** *Daily Progress*, June 28, 1921, 1.
185 **The state supreme court . . . of feeble-mindedness.** Pippa Holloway, *Sexuality, Politics, and Social Control in Virginia, 1920–1945*. Chapel Hill: University of North Carolina Press, 2006, 1–2, 26.
185 **Mandatory screenings for . . . its mandate read.** J. Douglas Smith, *Managing*

White Supremacy: Race, Politics, and Citizenship in Jim Crow Virginia. Chapel Hill: University of North Carolina Press, 2002, 100.

185 **Racial covenants . . . property deeds.** Jordy Yager et al., *Mapping Cville Project.* https://mappingcville.com/.

185 **All these practices . . . were reconstituted.** A classic example was the 1941 film *Virginia*, starring Fred MacMurray and Sterling Hayden. Four of the homes used in the film were designed by Thomas Jefferson. https://en.wikipedia.org /wiki/Virginia_(1941_film).

185 **"Do you believe in . . . YOUR LAST WARNING."** *Daily Progress*, July 19, 1921, 1.

185 **The robes were discovered . . . avoid after sundown.** *Daily Progress*, June 28, 1921, 1.

185 **Though the gift came . . . the donated robes.** Lisa Provence, "Skeletons in the Closet: Historical Society Displays KKK Robes, Keeps Owners Secret," *C-ville Weekly*, July 12, 2017.

185 **"It's probably some old" . . . at Jefferson's tomb.** Chris Suarez, "KKK Robes Unveiled at Historical Society, but Owners Kept Hidden," *Daily Progress*, July 6, 2017.

186 **After the appearance of . . . never again, she said.** Jalane Schmidt email August 5, 2017.

186 **In advance of . . . days of Jefferson.** Interview with Laura Goldblatt, May 4, 2021.

186 **People needed . . . for white supremacy.** Jalane Schmidt email August 5, 2017.

187 **"Stashed away in the KKKloset . . ."** @JalaneSchmidt tweet July 6, 2017.

187 **"These robes were found . . . form, or fashion."** Suarez, "KKK Robes Unveiled."

187 **Despite his professed passion . . . Timothy J. Longo, had.** Charlottesville City Council meeting, July 17, 2017. Mayor's remarks.

187 **After the Ferguson uprising . . . continuing with that.** Background interview, August 6, 2022.

187 **Richard Spencer's May 13 . . . "what they were about."** Heaphy report, 13, 30–35, 43. Email Brian Wheeler to Deborah Baker re: SPLC FOIA request, September 17, 2020.

188 **Thomas also sent . . . armed Klan members.** Heaphy report, 180; Signer, *Cry Havoc*, 147.

188 **For those unused . . . and paid taxes.** Will Parrish, "Police Targeted Antiracists in Charlottesville Ahead of 'Unite the Right' Rally, Documents Show." *Shadowproof*, March 7, 2018.

188 **"Antifa's labeling of" . . . for "Antifa" intel.** CPD intelligence assessments, "August 12th Plans" and "General Membership Numbers," n.d. FOIA.

188 **Another cited Milo . . . "Antifa" authority.** "ANTIFA—Antifascist Action," Intelligence report prepared by Det. W. Cole, Charlottesville Police Department, n.d. CVILLE-FOIA-HUFFPO-00001813.

189 **The day before . . . decided to disturb it.** *Daily Progress* editorial, "Councilor Should Speak Up Now to Calm Raging Fire," August 10, 2017.

189 **On the day of . . . first wedding anniversary.** *Daily Progress* staff, "Charlottesville Five Years Later, part 3. After the Monuments Broadcast." *Daily Progress*, August 3, 2022.

189 **"If you 'take the bait' . . . you are fair game."** Marc M., "Black Whole, Fragments of a Black Mind under (Re)Construction." http://www.black-whole .org/2017/07/10/on-not-taking-the-bait/.

189 **To Tenold . . . Mr. and Mrs. Barker.** Tenold, *Everything You Love*, 34–35.

190 **Christopher Barker's first arrest . . . their two young children.** Nate Thayer, "Unmasked: Inside America's Violent Ku Klux Klan," first published on his Substack, March 20, 2018.

190 **The terms of Barker's parole . . . Charlottesville convoy.** "Loyal White Knights of the Ku Klux Klan." *ADL*, December 7, 2018.

191 **Barker told her contact . . . she wrote.** Amanda Barker to David Shifflett, email July 1, 2017. Courtesy of Shawn Breen.

191 **A Signal thread . . . if they ran into trouble.** Erik Wikstrom, "DeBrief on July 8th," n.d.

191 **Medics and legal observers . . . from First United Methodist.** Charlottesville Clergy Collective, Steering Committee meeting minutes, June 19, 2017; interview with Jenny Phillips, April 20, 2021.

191 **On the day of . . . equipped with radios.** Heaphy report, 39, 41.

191 **By 1:00 p.m., all officers . . . their assigned zones.** Maurice Jones email to Charlottesville City Council, July 8, 2017, 1:10 p.m. Courtesy of Shawn Breen.

192 **The funneling of . . . President Bill Clinton.** Hahn, *Illiberal America*, 295.

192 **At 2:15 p.m. . . . in police reports.** Heaphy report, 181.

192 **Heyden was a familiar . . . "tax and spend carpetbaggers."** Charlottesville City Council meeting, June 5, 2017. Public comment, John Heyden.

192 **Rev. Bates spent the morning . . . local art park.** Interview with Rev. Lehman Bates, July 13, 2022. In addition, the city council contributed about $3,500 toward "Unity Day" activities. Email from Susan Kirschell to Maurice Jones, June 27, 2017.

193 **Then in her late . . . denied to her people.** Interview with Apostle Sarah Kelley, November 6, 2020.

195 **Veronica Fitzhugh . . . caught his eye.** CPD Arrest worksheet #7. Courtesy of Shawn Breen.

196 **Though he had hosted . . . "Mr. Activist."** Interview with Rev. Lehman Bates, July 13, 2022.

196 **Seth admitted they . . . ran out of songs.** Interview with Rev. Seth Wispelwey, February 9, 2021.

196 **Kay Slaughter, a former . . . were inexperienced.** Interview with Kay Slaughter, September 26, 2019.

196 **Just before 3:00 p.m. . . . trying to film.** Ézé Amos's series of photographs of July 8. My timeline and descriptions are largely based on these time-stamped photographs as well as the Showing Up for Racial Justice livestream.

196 **Elsewhere, another pastor . . . from laypeople.** Rev. Erik Wikstrom, "Debrief on July 8th," n.d.

196   **Seth became absorbed . . . realized with dismay.** Interview with Rev. Seth
       Wispelwey, February 9, 2021.

197   **To sustain the energy . . . "are under attack . . ."** Showing Up for Racial Justice
       livestream of July 8 KKK rally.

197   **A half hour after . . . taken off peaceably.** Arrest worksheets KKK rally (for-
       warded attachment) David Shifflet to Major Gary Pleasants et al., July 14, 2017.
       Courtesy of Shawn Breen.

197   **Then troopers . . . "no fascist USA, no cops."** Showing Up for Racial Justice
       Livestream of July 8 KKK rally.

197   **"I can't afford . . . can't do that."** Interview with Rev. Lehman Bates, July 13, 2022.

197   **In Charlottesville, Black men . . . half the arrests.** Radley Balko, "There's
       Overwhelming Evidence That the Criminal Justice System Is Racist. Here's the
       Proof," *Washington Post*, June 10, 2020.

198   **Her Monticello colleague . . . come with them.** Interview with Niya Bates,
       July 15, 2020.

198   **A Klansman made . . . at Black protesters.** IFA Trial Transcript, Devin Willis
       Direct Questioning, 155.

198   **The men Jack White saw . . . entirely fitting.** Interview with Jack White,
       June 17, 2020.

199   **Why had the police . . . "Who do you serve?" they chanted.** CBS Channel 6
       News, Richmond, "23 People Arrested at KKK Rally in Charlottesville."

199   **A letter signed . . . military grade equipment."** Letter from Legal Aid,
       National Lawyers Guild, ACLU, Rutherford Institute to members of city coun-
       cil, City Manager Maurice Jones, and Chief Al Thomas, July 17, 2017. Courtesy
       of Shawn Breen.

199   **"The cops are bringing . . . rally was peaceful."** @EmilyGorcenski, July 8, 2017.

199   **The first declaration . . . came at 4:40 p.m.** *@C-ville_Weekly*, July 8, 2017, 4:40 pm.

199   **Emily heard conflicting commands.** Press conference email release with at-
       tached statement by Emily Gorcenski, Unite the Right MSS16386 Series 1,
       Box 1 Folder 2, UVA Special Collections.

199   **A future city councillor . . . "watch yourself, Charlottesville."** Charlottesville
       City Council meeting, July 17, 2017. Public Comment, Michael Payne.

199   **Tear gas clouds . . . Thomas demanded.** Heaphy report, 61.

199   **Two minutes later . . . de-escalate the situation.** City Manager Maurice Jones
       to Charlottesville City Council, 5:09 p.m. Courtesy of Shawn Breen.

199   **Decades of research . . . it raises them.** Edward R. Maguire, "New Directions
       in Protest Policing." *Saint Louis University Public Law Review* 35, no. 1 (December
       2015), 75.

199   **"We've got pepper grenades . . . Emily said.** @Emily Gorcenski, July 8, 2017.

200   **A military vet saw . . . County Sheriff's officer.** Charlottesville City Council
       meeting, July 17, 2017. Public comment, Luke Harms.

200   **Women were flung to the ground.** Charlottesville City Council meeting,
       July 17, 2017. Public comment, Jalane Schmidt.

200   **A canister whizzed . . . as he was filming.** Interview with Rev. Seth Wispelwey,
       February 9, 2021.

200 **"There was no need for this."** @EmilyGorcenski, July 8, 2017.

200 **Later it was reported ... from the garage.** Arrest worksheets KKK rally (forwarded attachment) David Shifflet to Major Gary Pleasants et al., July 14, 2017. Courtesy of Shawn Breen.

200 **This ... "could go home."** Terry McAuliffe, *Beyond Charlottesville: Taking a Stand against White Nationalism.* New York: Thomas Dunne Books, 2019, 61.

200 **He later went further ... into the garage.** McAuliffe book tour, Richmond [at 44:00]. Star Peterson, Facebook video, August 1, 2019.

200 **In 1999, the police ... hours later.** Seth Ackerman, "Prattle in Seattle: WTO Coverage Misrepresented Issues, Protests," Fairness & Accuracy in Reporting, January 1, 2000.

200 **"Any violence that ... attacked peaceful protests."** Drew Dellinger, "Speaking Truth to Lies: Rev. Sekou Corrects the Record on MSNBC after Capt. Johnson Misleads Chris Hayes and All of Us," n.d.

201 **"That was an interesting realization."** Interview with Rev. Elaine Ellis Thomas, April 15, 2021.

201 **Receiving word ... "and our values."** @MikeSigner tweets, July 8, 2017.

201 **In response to ... already knew.** City Manager Maurice Jones to Charlottesville City Council, 5:47 p.m. Courtesy of Shawn Breen.

201 **Mayor Mike Signer ... claim on Facebook.** Mayor Mike Signer, Facebook statement on July 8, 2017, Klan rally.

201 **The Virginia State ... their talking points.** Corinne Geller email to Miriam Dickler, July 7, 2022, FOIA.

202 **The canisters came ... "with our training."** Interview with Rev. Brittany Caine-Conley, May 6, 2022.

202 **After submitting a report ... Clergy Collective.** Interview with Rev. Lehman Bates, July 13, 2022.

202 **Attached to his email ... "criminal minded anarchists."** Email Steven Kory Flowers of Greensboro Police Department to Capt. Wendy Lewis, Chief Al Thomas of CPD, June 22, 2017. Courtesy of Shawn Breen.

203 **It bears noting ... night in jail.** "Loyal White Knights of the Ku Klux Klan," ADL, December 7, 2018.

203 **The DHS sourced their reports ... Occidental Dissent.** Curtis Waltman, "Even amid Emerging White Supremacist Threat, Homeland Security Is Still Caught up on Leftist Groups," MuckRock, August 22, 2017.

203 **The musician who had ... woman of color.** Heaphy report, 28–29; Solidarity Cville, "Before August 12th."

203 **Apart from ... knocked to the ground.** Lisa Provence, "The Man Who Confronted White Nationalists in Lee Park," *C-ville Weekly*, May 24, 2017.

203 **Still, on the eve ... justified self-defense.** "Domestic Terrorist Violence at Lawfully Permitted White Supremacist Rallies Likely to Continue," *Homeland Intelligence Today*, August 9, 2017.

204 **That same week ... Black identity extremists.** Jana Winter and Shana Weinberger, "The FBI's New U.S. Terrorist Threat: 'Black Identity Extremists,'" *Foreign Policy*, October 6, 2017.

Chapter 10: Deep, Abiding Love

205 **"Apparently that's the term . . . with these idiots."** IFA Exhibit #349, Robert Azzmador Ray on Discord Post, July 23, 2017.

205 **"Jews have spent two . . . have ever had."** IFA Exhibit #3693, Robert Azzmador Ray Discord Post, July 16, 2017.

205 **In June Azzmador . . . Houston and Austin.** Alexander Zaitchik, "The Brawler," SPLC, August 5, 2018.

205 **Showing up . . . streets.** Molly Conger, "Burning Hate." Devil's Advocates, April 21, 2023.

205 **"The important thing . . . leave the house."** Zaitchik, "The Brawler."

205 **Being "lured into" . . . even rape.** Interview with Andy Stepanian, March 26, 2021.

206 **The blogger behind . . . come and go.** IFA Trial Transcript, Brad Griffin Transcript as Presented at Trial.

206 **A native of Eufaula . . . neo-Nazi organization.** Brad Griffin, "The Logic of Street Demonstrations," Occidental Dissent, March 25, 2014.

206 **Churning out memes . . . for young people.** Brad Griffin, "Unite the Right: Towards Alt-Right Activism," Occidental Dissent, July 10, 2017.

207 **Even Anglin was now . . . order of the day.** Allie Conti, "Neo-Nazi to Troll Army: 'We Have to Be Sexy' at the Big Alt Right Rally," Vice, August 9, 2017.

207 **No one knew . . . as the culprit.** IFA Exhibit #3766, Robert Azzmador Ray Discord Post, July 25, 2017.

207 **Supposedly, Kessler was going . . . yet to hear.** IFA Exhibit #348, Robert Azzmador Ray Discord Post, July 23, 2017.

207 **"The plan is the . . . Gas the kikes."** IFA Exhibit #0506, Robert Azzmador Ray Discord Post, July 28, 2017.

207 **Tear gas was deployed . . . for their own good.** Charlottesville City Council, July 17, 2017, City Manager Maurice Jones.

208 **Her dossier included . . . "cunt rags for good."** Emily Gorcenski, "Mike Signer Failed Charlottesville and Continues to Avoid Accountability," blog, June 14, 2022.

208 **Within a week . . . with legal counsel.** Signer, *Cry Havoc*, 162–63, 167.

208 **He couldn't ban . . . He was wrong.** Heaphy report, 157.

208 **Virginia political elites . . . discouraging public accountability.** Eric Williamson, "Is It Time for Home Rule in Virginia?" University of Virginia School of Law, March 24, 2020.

209 **After Richard Spencer's May . . . was to intimidate.** Interview with Bob Fenwick, November 10, 2019; See Code of Virginia, "Burning object on property of another or a highway or other public place with intent to intimidate," https://law.lis.virginia.gov/vacode/title18.2/chapter9/section18.2-423.01/.

209 **Unfortunately, the city prosecutor . . . didn't intimidate *him*.** A subsequent Albemarle County Commonwealth's Attorney has charged eight men, including Augustus Sol Invictus, Thomas Rousseau, and William Fears IV. Molly Conger, "Tiki Torch Roundup: Fighting the Case," Devil's Advocates, September 11, 2023.

209   **Nor could Richard . . . Resistance "press conference."** Heaphy report, 31.

210   **The legal scholar and historian . . . "those around him."** Farah Peterson, "Our Constitutionalism of Force," *Columbia Law Review* 122, no. 6, (October 2022), 1619.

210   **In advance of the . . . into the U.S. Capitol.** Jana Winter, "An Intel Analyst Tried to Prevent the Jan. 6 Attack—But DHS Failed to Act," Yahoo News, December 13, 2022.

210   **The FBI saw a post . . . "doors being kicked in."** "Capitol Attack: Federal Agencies Use of Open Source Data and Related Threat Products Prior to January 6, 2021," https://www.gao.gov/products/gao-22-105963.

210   **The intelligence wing . . . "threaten them with death."** Luke Broadwater, Maggie Haberman, Catie Edmondson, and Stephanie Lai, "Jan. 6 Transcripts Detail Failures in Surveillance and National Guard Response," *New York Times*, December 29, 2022.

210   **Yet this DHS analyst . . . "storm" the Capitol.** Winter, "An Intel Analyst Tried to Prevent the Jan. 6 Attack."

210   **According to the January 6 . . . under the Capitol.** "Red Flags Ahead of Jan. 6 Ignored, Committee Report Found," *Washington Post*, December 23, 2022.

210   **The chief of the Capitol Police . . . protesters and journalists.** Sam Levin, "White Supremacists and Militias Have Infiltrated Police across US, Report Says," *Guardian*, August 27, 2020.

211   **DC police officer . . . defend the Capitol.** Molly Ball, "What Mike Fanone Can't Forget," *Time*, August 5, 2021.

211   **At least 31 . . . active duty servicemen.** Paul D. Eaton, Antonio M. Taguba, and Steven M. Anderson, "3 Retired Generals: The Military Must Prepare Now for a 2024 Insurrection," *Washington Post*, December 17, 2021.

211   **"Homeland Security" produced no warnings . . . unused at the Capitol.** Luke Mogelson, *The Storm Is Here: An American Crucible.* New York: Penguin Random House, 2022, 259, 269.

211   **A white officer testified . . . "Black Lives Matter!"** Law Enforcement Experience on January 6, 2021. Statement of Officer Daniel Hodges, Metropolitan Police Officer, Written Statement to the Select Committee to Investigate the January 6th Attack on the U.S. Capitol 3 (n.d.).

211   **The commander of the DC . . . "vastly different response."** Broadwater et al., "Jan. 6 Transcripts Detail Failures."

211   **During the July 17 . . . Jesse Jackson.** Heaphy report, 80; Signer, *Cry Havoc*, 174.

211   **Councillor Bob Fenwick . . . like this before.** Interview with Bob Fenwick, November 10, 2019.

211   **The more pressure Signer . . . institutions were inflexible.** Signer, *Cry Havoc*, 178.

212   **They also knew . . . He had told them so.** Mark Newton, "Jones Rebuts Scathing Memo Point by Point," *Daily Progress*, August 26, 2017.

212   **Long before the trouble . . . "(needs to) go down."** Rev. Seth Wispelwey email re: new organization, n.d.

212   **Once it became . . . prayers and gospel music.** Interview with Rev. Brittany Caine-Conley, May 6, 2022.

212   **When Tracy Wispelwey . . . Could he help?** Interview with Rev. Tracy Howe, August 16, 2021.

214   **For Sekou . . . presence of love.** Interview with Rev. Osagyefo Uhuru Sekou, December 9, 2022.

214   **Love was the bulwark . . . that disarms.** Interview with Eric Martin, August 5, 2020.

214   **This was the "deep, abiding love" . . . *prepared to sacrifice?*** Martin, *Writing on the Wall*, 150.

215   **Katrina Turner and Rosia Parker . . . weren't followed.** Interview with Katrina Turner, June 17, 2021.

215   **Seth spent fruitless . . . white male clergy.** Interview with Rev. Seth Wispelwey, February 25, 2021.

215   **Members of Anarchist . . . troubled histories with them.** Interview with Rev. Brittany Caine-Conley, May 6, 2022.

215   **Pastor Brenda couldn't . . . in danger.** Interview with Rev. Brenda Brown-Grooms, November 12, 2019.

215   **Apostle Sarah had bad knees.** Interview with Apostle Sarah Kelley, November 6, 2020.

215   **One elderly Black . . . "go to the babies."** Interview with Rev. Osagyefo Uhuru Sekou, December 15, 2022.

215   **Grace Aheron was at . . . Sally Hemings puppet.** Interview with Grace Aheron and Rowan Hollins, September 2, 2020.

215   **By the end of July . . . offered backup.** Interview with Laura Goldblatt, May 4, 2021.

215   **They, in turn . . . networks for medics.** Interview with Bekah Menning, September 28, 2019.

216   **Rev. Alvin Edwards's . . . was unmistakable.** Interview with Rev. Seth Wispelwey, February 25, 2021.

216   **After describing his trainings . . . not to support them.** Interview with Rev. Osagyefo Uhuru Sekou, December 9, 2022.

216   **A Quaker who was new to . . . wasn't interested.** Cheuk, *Standing Up to Hate*, 35.

216   **On August 1 Smash . . . she would be.** Congregate Cville, "Press Conference about National Call for Clergy. #loveoverfear," Facebook, July 31, 2017.

217   **Seth raised $30,000 in twelve days.** Interviews with Rev. Seth Wispelwey, February 25, March 3, 2021.

217   **In early August . . . "civilian on civilian engagement."** "Religion, Race and Democracy Lab," panel moderated by Jalane Schmidt, August 13, 2020.

217   **Tracy Wispelwey suggested . . . Christian Peacemaker Teams.** Interview with Rev. Tracy Howe, August 16, 2021.

217   **Christian Peacemaker . . . absolute vulnerability.** Interview with Sarah Nahar Thomas, November 30, 2021.

217   **Bonnie Gordon, the UVA music . . . lasted fifteen minutes.** Bonnie Gordon email, September 22, 2020.

217   **They discussed . . . Weed also helped.** Interview with Rev. Osagyefo Uhuru Sekou, December 15, 2022.

217 **They kept returning . . . he thought to himself.** Interview with Eric Martin, August 5, 2020.

218 **Someone finally . . . "they'll succeed."** Martin, *Writing on the Wall*, 14.

218 **The official threat assessment . . . was not invited.** This July 27 briefing is not referenced in the Heaphy report. The VSP declined to respond to FOIA requests from investigators.

218 **Governor Terry McAuliffe . . . around Emancipation Park.** McAuliffe, *Beyond Charlottesville*, 62–63. McAuliffe spoke in general terms of this threat; a later Fusion Center briefing described by Mike Signer in his book said that the state troopers were far more focused on the threat to law enforcement posed by Antifa than by anyone on the far right. Signer, *Cry Havoc*, 186–87.

218 **No one recalled . . . armed neo-Nazis.** Neither city councillor Bob Fenwick nor Kristin Szakos, who had been briefed, recalled any such details.

218 **Signer made a habit . . . black bloc all summer.** Signer, *Cry Havoc*, 132–33, 203, 292.

218 **In his book . . . fasces with an ax.** Signer, *Cry Havoc*, photo section.

219 **While City Manager . . . most needed it.** Interview with Kristin Szakos, August 30, 2022.

219 **This was all in due . . . of the National Guard.** Heaphy report, 103, 106.

219 **After the Klan rally . . . police do their job.** Chris Schiano, "LEAKED: The Planning Meetings That Led Up to Neo-Nazi Terrorism in Charlottesville," Unicorn Riot, August 16, 2017. Eli Mosley to @everyone July 10, 2017.

219 **"In our communications . . . looking to do violence."** Leaked planning document: "Operation Unite the Right Charlottesville 2.0," https://unicornriot.ninja/wp-content/uploads/2017/08/OpOrd3_General.pdf.

219 **On August 2 . . . repeat of July 8.** Questions for Meeting with Law Enforcement Officials 8/2/17, Thomas Jefferson Memorial Church.

219 **After their own Fusion . . . challenge from Kessler.** Interview with Kristin Szakos, August 30, 2022.

219 **The law firm . . . at McIntire Park.** Heaphy report, 82. In the Heaphy report Chief Thomas said that McIntire Park was "marginally better," but he didn't believe the threat level met the one needed to stand up in court. This proved to be the case.

220 **He cited the estimated . . . of four hundred.** IFA Exhibit #1460D, Excerpt from Facebook conversation. "If the police ask you how many people we have coming, don't tell them. If they think we have more than 400 they might be able to help the city pull our permit"; IFA Exhibit #1396, Text from Jason Kessler to Augustus Invictus.

220 **Kessler wrote to Nathan . . . "under any circumstances."** IFA Exhibit #2098A, Posts of Jason Kessler.

220 **Damigo followed up . . . "up their ass."** IFA Exhibit #867, Nathan Damigo Discord Post.

220 **After asking Jason . . . with the Lee statue.** ACLU Virginia, "Why We Represented the Alt-Right in Charlottesville," August 29, 2017.

220 **Thomas secretly hoped . . . weaken the city's case.** Heaphy report, 84.

220 **Even the August 9 memo . . . was not included.** "Domestic Terrorist Violence at

Lawfully Permitted White Supremacist Rallies Likely to Continue," *Homeland Intelligence Today*, August 9, 2017.

221 **To preempt the far right's . . . of Balestra Media.** Interview with Rev. Osagyefo Uhuru Sekou, December 15, 2022.

221 **Stepanian had spent . . . could be heard.** Interview with Andy Stepanian, March 26, 2021.

221 **Laura Goldblatt, the grad student . . . "die this weekend."** Interview with Laura Goldblatt, May 4, 2021.

222 **Stepanian's face turned . . . press release.** Interview with Andy Stepanian, March 26, 2021.

222 **Goldblatt was also . . . want them to tell.** Interview with Laura Goldblatt, May 4, 2021.

222 **Katrina Turner, a small . . . her feelings known.** Interview with Katrina Turner, June 17, 2021.

223 **On the eve of Unite . . . "We want a war."** "Unite the Right Organizers Encourage Guns: 'We Want a War,'" It's Going Down, August 11, 2017.

223 **Under the handle . . . Daily Stormer.** Keegan Hankes, "Dylann Roof May Have Been a Regular Commenter at Neo-Nazi Website The Daily Stormer," SPLC, June 25, 2015.

223 **"I always come bare-fisted . . . nifty equipment."** IFA Exhibit #1128, Robert Azzmador Ray Discord Post, July 23, 2017. Also Zaitchik, "The Brawler."

223 **While his guys were off . . . arranging transport.** IFA Exhibit #0445, Robert Azzmador Ray on Discord Post, July 17, 2017.

223 **There was a brief hiccup . . . Waynesboro Days Inn.** IFA Exhibit #0424, Robert Azzmador Ray, August 11, 2017.

223 **The Stormer account . . . $300,000.** *The Hate Report*, "People Have Sent this Neo-Nazi over $1m in Bitcoin," SPLC, October 27, 2017.

223 **To forestall "Antifa" . . . to arrive early.** IFA Exhibit #399, Robert Azzmador Ray, July 30, 2017.

224 **He'd take on BLM . . . easier to trigger.** IFA Exhibit #449, Robert Azzmador Ray August 3, 2017.

224 **He imagined himself . . . of them all.** IFA Exhibit #0420, #6970, Robert Azzmador Ray, August 9, 2017.

224 **"GET IN LOSER WE'RE INVADING CHARLOTTESVILLE!"** IFA Exhibit #409, Robert Azzmador Ray, August 9, 2017.

Interlude: A School for Backward Southern Whites

226 **Finally, to be a Virginian . . . "of the nation were born."** Sarah Patton Boyle, editorial on Autherine Lucy's effort to desegregate University of Alabama, Sarah Patton Boyle Papers, Albert and Shirley Small Special Collections Library, University of Virginia (hereafter cited as Boyle Papers).

227 **It would be left to Patty's . . . sacrificed everything.** Sarah Patton Boyle, *The Desegregated Heart: A Virginian's Stand in Time of Transition*. New York: William Morrow, 1962, 3–10.

228 **As recently as 2021 . . . South, Dr. Michael Hill.** A list of Prof. William

Wilson's lectures for the institute can be found here: https://www.abbeville
institute.org/?s=William+Wilson.

228 **Allen Tate prized the Lindsay ... for the Lytle family.** Correspondence between Andrew Lytle, Allen Tate, and Patty Lindsay, October 1931–September
1932, Boyle Papers.

228 **Lytle's 1931 biography ... his human property.** Lytle, *Bedford Forrest*, 383.

229 **Patty decided this ... surprised at herself.** Dan Wakefield, "Charlottesville
Battle," *Nation*, September 15, 1956, 211. *Richmond Times-Dispatch*, May 8, 1951.

229 **It thus came as something ... certain social lines.** Gregory Swanson to Sibyl,
November 24, 1951, Swanson Papers, Moorland-Spingarn Research Center,
Howard University (hereafter cited as Swanson Papers); Leidholdt, "Showdown
on Mr. Jefferson's Lawn," 243.

229 **"If there really is all ... who has noticed it?"** "Dear White Southerner,"
Charlottesville Tribune, February 16, 1952, Boyle Papers.

229 **When the editors ... interfere with her housework.** T. J. Sellers to Sarah
Patton Boyle, May 24, 1958, Boyle Papers.

229 **She undertook amateur surveys ... prominent Virginians.** Letter to the Editor,
Richmond Times-Dispatch, May 8, 1951, Boyle Papers.

230 **It wasn't long ... *Richmond Times-Dispatch*.** Interview with James Morrison
Shea, August 23, 2022.

230 **She had offered to write ... did not subscribe to it.** Sarah Patton Boyle, exchange with Virginius Dabney, editor of *Richmond Times-Dispatch*, May 20,
May 25, May 26, 1951, Boyle Papers.

230 **Not one faculty member ... showed up.** Boyle, *The Desegregated Heart*, 193–96.

230 **The South was looking ... Kasper declared.** Internet Archive, FBI File full
text, September 2, 1956, John Kasper.

230 **The "red-controlled Supreme Court" ... to them directly.** Boyle, *Desegregated
Heart*, 253.

231 **Patty Boyle encountered ... on the church lawn.** *Daily Progress*, August 24,
1956.

231 **Kasper was a hollow man ... found him sinister.** Sarah Patton Boyle to Flora
Morrison, February 10, 1957, Boyle Papers.

231 **A few days later ... caught fire.** *Daily Progress*, July 24, 1956, Letter to the
Editor by Mildred Brown, 4.

231 **By the close of the ... moved north.** Sarah Patton Boyle to Flora Morrison,
February 20, 1958, Boyle Papers.

231 **The last of the four ... just attended.** *Daily Progress*, December 7, 1956, 17.

231 **Boyle chose to see her cross ... posing with it.** *Daily Progress* August 31, 1956, 2.

232 **She wrote T. J. Sellers ... she was dead.** Sarah Patton Boyle to T. J. Sellers,
January 14, 1958, Boyle Papers.

232 **Eventually she stopped ... *Southerners will rebel*.** Boyle, *Desegregated Heart*, 238.

233 **She'd once considered ... left her cold.** Boyle, *Desegregated Heart*, 292, 297.

233 **"What a different picture ... Black law student.** Sarah Patton Boyle to Gregory
Swanson December 1, 1961, Swanson Papers.

233 **Before that year was out ... close confederates.** Webb, *Rabble Rousers*, 60.

233 **"We got it Gramp . . . are on Alabam."** John Kasper to Ezra Pound n.d. [1956], Ezra Pound Papers.

234 **Mirroring the spate . . . after Confederate officers.** Corey Mitchell, "The Schools Named After Confederate Figures," *Education Week*, June 17, 2020.

Part III: Unite the Right
Chapter 11: Nameless Field

239 **The morning before . . . "may be the catalyst."** @EmilyGorcenski, 7:29 a.m., 7:48 a.m., 8:31 a.m., 10:21 a.m.

239 **Two days before . . . night torch march.** Heaphy report, 111.

239 **Her instinct told her . . . awaiting confirmation.** Interview with Emily Gorcenski, February 5, 2020.

240 **Her DMs filled with death threats.** @EmilyGorcenski, 11:27 a.m. "The dozens of death threats I've been getting mostly. 'I will murder you. I will find where you live and I will cut your throat' 'I will follow you home and crush your skull.'"

240 **In an August 4 email . . . "help their cause."** "An Important Message from Teresa A. Sullivan Regarding August 12th," August 4, 2017.

240 **To act according . . . act of complicity.** Willis Jenkins, "Ethics Under Pressure," in Nelson and Harold, *Charlottesville 2017*, 167.

240 **A law professor . . . like children.** Anne M. Coughlin email, August 5, 2017.

240 **Jalane Schmidt tried . . . institutional blinkers.** Interview with Laura Goldblatt, May 4, 2021.

240 **In a draft of . . . "helped to construct."** Jalane Schmidt email, August 5, 2017.

240 **Instead, Sullivan invited . . . local history.** "Full Message from University of Virginia President Teresa A. Sullivan to the University Community," *Daily Progress*, July 13, 2017.

241 **Where the League of the South's . . . movie night at Scott Stadium.** Hunter Wallace, "Unite the Right: Towards Alt-Right Activism," Occidental Dissent, July 10, 2017.

241 **Emily scoffed at . . . "faces in photos."** Emily Gorcenski, "No, the White Supremacists Aren't Looking for Attention," blog, June 25, 2017.

241 **Ignoring Nazis . . . *World of Warcraft*.** Interview with Emily Gorcenski, February 5, 2020.

242 **Cantwell had become . . . parking lot on 29 North.** IFA Exhibit #188, Email from Christopher Cantwell to Jason Kessler, August 10, 2017.

242 **Emily got in . . . and set off.** Interview with Emily Gorcenski, February 5, 2020.

242 **Tyler Magill was . . . the Jefferson statue.** Interview with Tyler Magill, August 2, 2021.

243 **Someone told me . . . playing *Pokémon Go*.** Interview with Rev. Dr. Jeffrey Pugh, September 13, 2020.

243 **Goad had an ongoing . . . Friday night torch march.** Interview with Kristopher Goad, July 18, 2021.

244 **Four days after . . . statue on UVA Grounds).** Heaphy report, 110; IFA Exhibit #1306B, Text message between Elliott Kline and Jason Kessler.

244   **Governor Terry McAuliffe ... the torch march.** McAuliffe, *Beyond Charlottesville*, 78.

244   **Goad was told to keep ... to the Jefferson statue.** Interview with Kristopher Goad, July 18, 2021.

244   **Work started early ... to provide specifics.** Heaphy report, 111, 188.

245   **He'd been trying ... "I must focus."** IFA Exhibit #3317, Cantwell produced text messages with various codefendants and third parties.

245   **Spencer was spied ... Peirce joined them.** IFA Trial Transcript, Direct Questioning Richard Spencer, November 4, 2021, 134; Interview with Ann Marie Smith, September 17, 2020.

245   **Despite misdemeanor ... chatting to law enforcement.** Affidavit in Support of Applications for Search Warrants, Case No. 20-mj-31-01d-AJ, January 21, 2020.

245   **Emily tweeted ... and knew everything.** @EmilyGorcenski, August 11, 2017.

245   **Spooked, Spencer sent ... McIntire Park.** IFA Exhibit #1455, Text messages between Jason Kessler and Richard Spencer.

246   **She had reassured ... "and Lawn," she wrote.** Nora Neus, *24 Hours in Charlottesville*. Boston: Beacon Press, 2023, 65.

246   **Seth Wispelwey believed ... by Friday morning.** Interview with Rev. Seth Wispelwey, March 2, 2021; Heaphy report, 111.

246   **By the time the university ... open flames on Grounds.** Jack Stripling, "Inside the U. of Virginia's Response to a Chaotic White-Supremacist Rally," *Chronicle of Higher Education*, November 20, 2017.

246   **Supposing the University ... "Lady of Charlottesville."** Stripling, "Inside the U. of Virginia's Response."

246   **Blout alerted ... university spokesperson.** Vice Provost for Administration and Chief of Staff Anda L. Webb's email to Chief Mike Gibson, Marjorie L. Sidebottom, Director of Emergency Preparedness, and Spokesman, Anthony Paul deBruyn, cc Louis P. Nelson, Provost, August 11, 2017, 3:23 pm.

247   **Blout also left word ... Thomas's assistant.** Closed session of the Charlottesville City Council on the "review of performance and discipline of an elected official," August 30, 2017.

247   **Another "confidential source" ... outside city limits.** Heaphy report, 109–10, 123; Joe Heim, "Recounting a Day of Rage, Hate, Violence and Death," *Washington Post*, August 14, 2017.

247   **Pastor Brenda ... prefer the lie.** Interview with Rev. Brenda Brown-Grooms, November 12, 2019.

247   **At a 4:30 press conference ... never reached him.** Signer, *Cry Havoc*, 203.

247   **Cantwell wanted him ... "with torches," someone said.** IFA Trial Transcript Direct Questioning, Christopher Cantwell, November 16, 2021, 137.

247   **Cantwell told Sgt. Wendy ... an actual location.** Here the UPD timeline conflicts with the time stamps from the *Sines v. Kessler* phone records, so I've depended on the latter. Also, Kessler would probably have known that Nameless Field was a real place. Cantwell made the call to CPD, imagining he wasn't giving anything away.

248   **At 7:41 p.m., the University ... had retweeted it.** @EmilyGorcenski, 6:49 p.m. EG retweets IGD announcement.

248 **At 7:47 p.m. . . . "news to me," she replied.** Neus, *24 Hours in Charlottesville*, 73.

249 **A later investigation . . . "deliberately misleading."** "The University's Response to August 11, 2017: Observations and Improvements." University of Virginia August 11 and 12, 2017: Recovery and Response web archive. Albert and Shirley Small Special Collections, https://archive-it.org/collections/20680.

249 **President Sullivan had . . . signed as UVA students.** Neus, *24 Hours in Charlottesville*, 74.

249 **At 8:00 p.m., Richard . . . "people in Charlottesville."** IFA Trial Transcript Direct Questioning, Richard Spencer, November 4, 2021, 139–40.

249 **"I think we are good . . . "this plays out."** Stripling, "Inside the U. of Virginia's Response."

250 **The John Brown Gun Club . . . security was unarmed.** Interview with Andy Stepanian, March 26, 2021.

250 **Jenkins thought some . . . their bags searched.** Interview with Willis Jenkins, March 15, 2017.

250 **Jalane Schmidt, Rev. Phil Woodson . . . "I come running."** Sojourners, "Charlottesville's Mass Prayer Service. Dr. Cornel West and Rev. Traci Blackmon speaking to #CvilleClergyCall," Facebook, August 12, 2017.

251 **Rev. Traci Blackmon . . . well she'd manage.** Interview with Rev. Seth Wispelwey, March 2, 2021.

251 **In March 1965 . . . the history books.** Cornelia F. Sexauer, "A Well-Behaved Woman: Sister Mary Antona's Journey to Selma," *American Catholic Studies* 3, no. 4 (Winter 2004), 37–38.

251 **Even the Wispelweys' seven-year-old felt it.** Interview with Rev. Seth Wispelwey, March 2, 2021.

251 **And just as Selma . . . Rev. Traci Blackmon.** Interview with Rev. Elaine Ellis Thomas, April 15, 2021.

251 **Mayor Mike Signer . . . "and James Monroe."** Signer, *Cry Havoc*, 202–3.

252 **An hour or so into the service . . . and the ACLU.** Heaphy report, 189; Signer, *Cry Havoc*, 203–4.

252 **The Virginia chapter . . . "an unforgiving tutor."** ACLU Virginia, "Why We Represented the Alt-Right in Charlottesville," August 29, 2017.

252 **The national . . . demonstrate with guns.** "Charlottesville Violence Prompts ACLU to Change Policy on Hate Groups Protesting with Guns," PBS, August 18, 2017.

252 **Signer was too dismayed . . . got up and left.** The *Washington Post* has Signer leaving near the start of the service; Signer claimed he was there at the time Spencer's tweet was posted [8:45] but at home when the church went on lockdown [8:43]. He was still home when the torch march got underway [9:45].

252 **He texted Richard Spencer . . . "hundreds and torches."** IFA Trial Transcript, Direct Questioning Richard Spencer, November 16, 2021, 60–61.

252 **When Signer reached . . . "just give in?"** @RichardBSpencer tweet, August 11, 2017, 8:45 pm.

252 **In the sanctuary . . . livestream the service.** Interview with Rev. Seth Wispelwey, March 2, 2021.

253 **No one knew . . . angle of the photograph.** Interview with Jordan Leahy, September 24, 2020.

253 **Everyone in . . . panic people unnecessarily.** Interview with Rev. Brittany Caine-Conley, May 6, 2022.

253 **Willis Jenkins . . . no word of either threat.** Interview with Willis Jenkins, March 15, 2023.

253 **Tyler Magill, the part-time . . . above Nameless Field.** Interview with Tyler Magill, August 2, 2021.

253 **About thirty members . . . at a nearby table.** Heim, "Recounting a Day of Rage, Hate, Violence and Death."

253 **Rev. Blackmon described . . . "hand of the Lord?"** Sojourners, "Charlottesville's Mass Prayer Service. Dr. Cornel West and Rev. Traci Blackmon Speaking to #CvilleClergyCall," Facebook, August 12, 2017.

254 **Andy Stepanian was in . . . "to engage, sir," he said.** Interview with Andy Stepanian, March 26, 2021.

255 **Goliath didn't just come . . . off Goliath's head.** Sojourners, "Charlottesville's Mass Prayer Service."

255 **Every so often . . . Goliath's head.** Interview with Rev. Seth Wispelwey, March 2, 2021.

255 **Rev. Blackmon acknowledged . . . "in my mind's eye."** Sojourners, "Charlottesville's Mass Prayer Service."

256 **Students in a green Toyota . . . "please come in."** Interview with Andy Stepanian, March 26, 2021.

257 **"They are coming back . . . DAMN HEAD OFF!"** Sojourners, "Charlottesville's Mass Prayer Service."

257 **An altar call hadn't been . . . the singing going.** Interview with Rev. Brittany Caine-Conley, May 6, 2022.

258 **Kay Slaughter, a former mayor . . . more standing.** Interview with Kay Slaughter, September 26, 2019.

258 **For a long time . . . white nationalism together.** Interview with Rabbi Tom Gutherz, June 18, 2021.

258 **Like Rabbi Gutherz . . . "Blood and soil."** Bonnie Gordon phone texts, August 11, 2017.

259 **"I knew we shouldn't . . . church on Shabbat."** Bonnie Gordon, "On Listening," in Nelson and Harold, *Charlottesville 2017*, 146.

259 **Thomas recalled the . . . safety and shelter.** Interview with Rev. Elaine Ellis Thomas, April 15, 2021.

259 **While they were on . . . they needed help.** Interview with Willis Jenkins, March 15, 2023.

259 **Smash told her to wait . . . "fill up water jugs."** Interview with Rev. Brittany Caine-Conley, May 6, 2022.

259 **It was Rev. Sekou who . . . go back inside.** Interview with Rev. Osagyefo Uhuru Sekou, December 15, 2022.

260 **Willis Jenkins called it . . . *you been listening?*** Interview with Willis Jenkins, March 15, 2023.

260 **Smash would deeply regret . . . peace with it.** Interview with Rev. Brittany Caine-Conley, May 6, 2022.

260 **Spared the details . . . thought all was well.** John Edwin Mason, "History, Mine and Ours," in Nelson and Harold, *Charlottesville 2017*, 22.

260 **"They are coming for the church . . . marching with torches!"** Joe Heim, "A Stark Contrast: Inside and Outside a Charlottesville Church during the Torch March," *Washington Post*, August 19, 2017.

Chapter 12: The Torch March

261 **A neo-Nazi . . . his Proud Boys crew.** Anonymous Comrades Collective, "White Art Collective Musician 'James Jayan' Revealed: Jamie Ryan Troutman of Harpers Ferry, WV"; @AnonCommieStan, April 3, 2023.

262 **He told Ziegler . . . security went out.** Jon Ziegler, RebZ.tv, Periscope, August 11, 2017, 47:00.

262 **A French journalist . . . "just like we are."** Ford Fischer, "Fight and One Arrest as Protesters with Torches March Through UVa," News2Share, August 11, 2017.

263 **Emily Gorcenski had . . . barking orders.** Emily Gorcenski, "Nazis Marching: #Defend Cville," Periscope, August 11, 2017.

263 **The torch march and rally . . . long dreamed of.** IFA Trial Transcript, Samantha Froelich Deposition, 33.

263 **Though Samantha Froelich . . . shut it down.** IFA Trial Transcript, Samantha Froelich Deposition, 30–31, 35.

263 **His team of men . . . following his commands.** Heim, "Recounting a Day of Rage, Hate, Violence and Death."

263 **"I run this as a . . . in the army."** Alexis Gravely, Tim Dodson, and Daniel Hoerauf, "Torch-Wielding White Nationalists March at U.Va.," *Cavalier Daily*, August 12, 2017.

263 **Their numbers were now well into the hundreds.** A. C. Thompson, "A New Generation of White Supremacists Emerges in Charlottesville," ProPublica, August 13, 2017.

263 **"Listen up, everyone" . . . on his megaphone.** Gorcenski, "Nazis Marching."

264 **"As of today, the Constitution" . . . the assembled cameras.** Fischer, "Fight and One Arrest."

264 **Chris Schiano of Unicorn . . . from his hand.** Press Freedom Tracker, "Unicorn Riot Journalist Attacked While Reporting in Charlottesville," August 11, 2017.

264 **President Sullivan, standing . . . heard them too.** Stripling, "Inside the U. of Virginia's Response."

265 **"All right, we have got" . . . his polo player.** Anonymous Comrades Collective, "Unite the Right's 'Swastika Pin' Identified as Zachary Hudson Fisher, aka Milwaukee DJ 'Hdsn Acid,'" September 24, 2020. He was also a member of a Bowl Patrol chatgroup.

265 **Swastika Pin was accompanied . . . and brawling gloves.** IgnitetheRight.net calls Brawling Gloves #NeckLaceGoateeUTR. He has not been identified.

265 **Cowlick was later identified . . . as a Tampa Realtor.** His name was Andrew Coleman. @MIAagainstFash, August 13, 2022.

265 **Emily subsequently identified Checked . . . an Amtrak train.** This was Taylor Michael Wilson. Andy Campbell, "Neo-Nazi Convicted of Domestic Terrorism Was among 'Very Fine People' at Unite the Right." *Huffington Post*, November 9, 2018.

265 **Anti-fascists would later . . . a Milwaukee DJ.** This was Zachary Hudson Fisher. https://accollective.noblogs.org/post/2020/09/24/unite-the-rights-swastika-pin-identified-as-zachary-hudson-fisher-aka-milwaukee-dj-hdsn-acid/.

265 **Emily ignored him . . . snarky and unimpressed.** Gorcenski, "Nazis Marching."

266 **Tyler Magill thought . . . the Jefferson statue.** Interview with Tyler Magill, August 2, 2021.

266 **Instead, the march turned . . . "I got a gap."** Ziegler, RebZ.tv.

266 **Magill decided . . . their Lawn rooms.** Interview with Tyler Magill, August 2, 2021.

266 **Emily noted that . . . short for Heil Hitler.** Gorcenski, "Nazis Marching."

267 **The torches passed . . . another said no.** Ziegler, RebZ.tv.

267 **The last exchange . . . all was going well.** Stripling, "Inside the U. of Virginia's Response."

267 **Then a single voice . . . "Into the Ovens!"** Fischer, "Fight and One Arrest."

267 **"You are eminently" . . . a single police officer.** Gorcenski, "Nazis Marching."

268 **At 9:56 p.m. . . . relayed this to Dean Groves.** Stripling, "Inside the U. of Virginia's Response."

268 **Nineteen minutes into . . . were still coming.** Gorcenski, "Nazis Marching." Tim Heaphy, the former prosecutor who directed the official inquiry into the events of August 12, had the march taking a different route, one that did not take the marchers past the Clark Engineering Building. He was mistaken.

268 **President Sullivan updated . . . "are at the amphitheater."** Stripling, "Inside the U. of Virginia's Response."

268 **Tyler Magill saw . . . lights of Cabell Hall.** Interview with Tyler Magill, August 2, 2021.

268 **The yips started up . . . got too close.** Fischer, "Fight and One Arrest."

268 **Though Emily tried . . . Spencer's destination.** Interview with Emily Gorcenski, February 6, 2020.

269 **On Ziegler's livestream . . . "'Cause this shit ain't gonna stop."** Jon Ziegler, RebZ.tv, "Charlottesville: Hundreds of White Nationalists March with Torches," YouTube, August 11, 2017.

269 **Deciding to get out in front . . . "your domestic terrorists."** Gorcenski, "Nazis Marching."

269 **Wendy Baucom, the wife . . . to the church.** Interview with Wendy Baucom, April 11, 2023.

269 **"Even Leftists have to" . . . Jefferson statue stood.** Gorcenski, "Nazis Marching."

270 **At around the same moment . . . And so angry.** Interview with Kristopher Goad, July 18, 2021.

270 **When Emily arrived . . . filmed the students' feet.** Gorcenski, "Nazis Marching."

271 **Above their heads . . . Allah, Zeus, and Ra.** Lauren Jones, "Let Freedom

Ring: U.Va. Professor Discovers Sacred Story Behind Jefferson Statue," UVA Today, July 2, 2014.

271 **The surrounding plaza appeared . . . "against what is coming."** Gorcenski, "Nazis Marching."

271 **Tyler Magill sat down . . . "was gonna die," he said.** Interview with Tyler Magill, August 2, 2021.

271 **"The situation is very tense" . . . "replace *them*," he shouted.** Ziegler, RebZ.tv, "Charlottesville."

271 **Emily's phone captured . . . chanting quickened.** Gorcenski, "Nazis Marching."

272 **Tyler Magill arrived . . . to encircle them.** Interview with Tyler Magill, August 2, 2021.

272 **As he approached . . . pointed at him in alarm.** Democracy Now! "Terror in Charlottesville, Part II." Tyler Magill appears 0:52 seconds into this broadcast.

272 **Magill lifted both his hands . . . student in a wheelchair.** Interview with Tyler Magill, August 2, 2021.

272 **BLM activists . . . had also shown up.** Interview with Rev. Osagyefo Uhuru Sekou, December 9, 2022.

272 **Richard Spencer, who had been . . . transfixed by the view.** IFA Trial Transcript, Elizabeth Sines Testimony, November 12, 2021, 58–60.

272 **Jake Westly Anderson . . . he later related.** Jake Westly Anderson, "Insane New Footage from Charlottesville," YouTube, August 11, 2017.

272 **That the police . . . he found shocking and suspect.** Jon Ziegler, RebZ.tv interview with Jake Westly Anderson, Periscope, August 11, 2017.

272 **"And then, you know . . . We were surrounded."** Interview with Tyler Magill, August 2, 2021.

272 **Her friend Devin Willis . . . during the rally.** IFA Trial Transcript, Devin Willis Testimony, October 29, 2021, 159. The group was People's Action for Racial Justice or PARJ.

273 **They had hoped to finish . . . joined by others.** Erin O'Hare, "Standing Together," *C-ville Weekly*, August 23, 2017.

273 **As a diverse group . . . Jason Kessler and Richard Spencer.** Letter to President Sullivan from members of UVA faculty and students regarding her use of Jefferson as a moral compass.

273 **A member of their group . . . in a wheelchair.** Sylvan Miller, "Charlottesville: A Weekend of Terror," *Argot Magazine*, August 18, 2017.

273 **They didn't see any Nazis . . . people to show up.** IFA Trial Transcript, Devin Willis Testimony, October 29, 2021, 163–69.

273 **Natalie wished . . . felt exposed.** IFA Trial Transcript, Natalie Romero Testimony, October 29, 2021, 21–31.

273 **At first the roar came . . . as soon as he heard it.** IFA Trial Transcript, Devin Willis Testimony, October 29, 2021, 165–88.

273 **Natalie looked . . . dense, suffocating.** IFA Trial Transcript, Natalie Romero Testimony, October 29, 2021, 21–31.

274 **"If you want to know" . . . Walt Heinecke walking by.** Gorcenski, "Nazis Marching."

275 **He had been on his way . . . he pulled away.** O'Hare, "Standing Together."

275 **Dean Groves also intervened . . . was sliced open.** IFA Trial Transcript, Devin Willis Testimony, October 29, 2021, 165–88.

275 **Swastika Pin opened his mouth . . . punch at someone.** Gorcenski, "Nazis Marching."

275 **Ford Fischer of News2Share . . . and their protectors.** @FordFischer, October 8, 2018, 2:05 p.m.

275 **Azzmador had caught . . . still suffering partial blindness.** Interview with Tyler Magill, August 2, 2021.

275 **While fists flew . . . bobbing up and down.** "Fight and One Arrest as Protesters with Torches March Through UVa," News2Share, August 11, 2017.

275 **He saw a bald man . . . in everyone's eyes.** Interview with Kristopher Goad, July 18, 2021.

275 **Unicorn Riot captured the moment.** Conger, "Burning Hate"; see also Democracy Now! "Terror in Charlottesville, Part 2."

275 **Goad had never been maced . . . had maced himself.** Interview with Kristopher Goad, July 18, 2021.

276 **When a torch landed . . . kept hitting her.** IFA Trial Transcript, Natalie Romero Testimony, October 29, 2021, 21–31.

276 **To her left, a fourth-year . . . "they were," she said later.** O'Hare, "Standing Together."

276 **Devin kept his head . . . grabbed and pepper sprayed.** IFA Trial Transcript, Devin Willis Testimony, November 17, 2021, 72.

276 **A law student named Elizabeth . . . on Facebook Live.** IFA Exhibit #3204A-D, excerpts of video of August 11, 2017.

276 **Her roommate, standing next . . . moving on to the next one.** IFA Trial Transcript, Elizabeth Sines Testimony, November 12, 2021, 58–60.

276 **Conferring with the others . . . Devin said no.** IFA Trial Transcript, Devin Willis Testimony, October 29, 2021, 165–88; and November 17, 2021, 72–73.

276 **One livestream showed . . . she was hyperventilating.** "Torch Bearing Nationalists March at University of Virginia," August 11, 2017. Getty Images.

277 **Natalie couldn't recall . . . by an anti-fascist.** O'Hare, "Standing Together."

277 **At 10:15, Kessler . . . "come out front."** IFA Exhibit #1455, Text messages between Jason Kessler and Richard Spencer.

277 **Someone gave Spencer . . . like a returning conqueror.** IFA Trial Transcript, Elizabeth Sines Testimony, November 12, 2021, 58–60.

277 **"We own these streets . . . your brawn," he told them.** Conger, "Burning Hate."

277 **Lisa Draine, the arts . . . "I bet you Sophie's here."** Interview with Lisa Draine, April 2, 2023.

278 **They found her . . . holding the banner.** Lisa Draine talk at Center, September 17, 2021.

278 **Caroline Bray had been . . . make it out alive.** Interview with Lisa Draine, April 2, 2023.

278 **City police officers . . . until 10:16 p.m.** Heaphy report, Timeline, 190.

278 **Emily Gorcenski . . . berating them all.** Heaphy report, 119.

278 **When Seth Wispelwey . . . happened at the statue.** Interview with Rev. Seth Wispelwey, March 2, 2021.

279 **Everyone understood . . . the following day.** Interview with Rev. Elaine Ellis Thomas, April 15, 2021.

279 **Andy Stepanian went out . . . had to learn.** Interview with Rev. Seth Wispelwey, March 2, 2021.

279 **President Sullivan . . . speech and assembly.** "President Sullivan Condemns Demonstration Violence," UVA Today, August 12, 2017.

279 **"Don't expect us to be reading . . . responsibility here, too."** Solidarity Cville, "Charlottesville, Six Months Later."

279 **UPD chief Mike Gibson . . . didn't last long.** University Police Department Timeline: August 11, 2017. Posted September 11, 2017. Tim Heaphy wrote that Chief Gibson "downplayed the incident, noting that it lasted for less than an hour and did not result in any serious injuries," Heaphy report, 119–20. Solidarity Cville, "Charlottesville Six Months Later."

279 **When Caroline persisted . . . "deserve our attention."** "August 11th Survivors Demand Justice," UVa Students United, Facebook, May 21, 2018.

279 **Waiting for a car . . . *All bets are off.*** Interview with Rev. Brenda Brown-Grooms, November 12, 2019.

Chapter 13: Emancipation Park

281 **When Brian Moran . . . how tiny it was.** McAuliffe, *Beyond Charlottesville*, 78.

282 **Chief Thomas's operational plan . . . also be barricaded.** Heaphy report, 95–97.

283 **As a member of the . . . to the Jewish community.** Interview with Rabbi Tom Gutherz, June 18, 2021.

283 **For the first time ever . . . during the Holocaust.** Interview with Rabbi Tom Gutherz, in Jackson Landers's documentary *Charlottesville: Our Streets* [18:51].

283 **A conversation picked up . . . "and vent them to Water Street."** Heaphy report, 125.

284 **The white nationalists had . . . as a "niggerhood."** Interview with Don Gathers, March 10, 2020.

284 **"Fucking amateur hour at CPD."** @EmilyGorcenski, August 10, 2017.

284 **The service had emboldened . . . face the devil himself.** Interview with Katrina Turner, June 17, 2021.

284 **Katie Couric left the church . . . follow the clergy.** Interview with Rev. Seth Wispelwey, March 2, 2021.

284 **Rev. Elaine Thomas . . . the community march.** Defend Cville livestream on YouTube and Periscope, August 12, 2017.

285 **Lisa Draine showed up alone . . . answering her texts.** Interview with Lisa Draine, December 18, 2022.

285 **The procession set off . . . "This is *our* town."** Jordan Leahy, Congregate Cville livestream, Facebook, August 12, 2017.

285   **The large Sally Hemings puppet . . . look like in the future.** Jordan Leahy interview with Grace Aheron in Congregate Cville livestream, August 12, 2017 [02:30].

286   **Megan Squire, the computer . . . as her children.** Interview with Megan Squire, November 17, 2020.

286   **Before he left . . . "have to be careful."** Conger, "Burning Hate."

286   **When he stopped . . . Ézé snapped again.** Conversation with Ézé Amos, October 5, 2022. Ézé Amos's thousands of photographs of August 12, all of which were time-stamped, were indispensable in establishing an August 12 timeline. I am grateful to him for sharing them. I cross-checked them with Twitter posts, also time-stamped, to establish what was going on and where. Fields appears in several of them.

286   **After the doors . . . left with Don Gathers.** Interview with Rev. Elaine Ellis Thomas, April 15, 2021.

287   **Among the fifty or so . . . as a Christian act.** Interview with Brandy Daniels, July 20, 2020; interview with Eric Martin, August 5, 2020.

287   **A queer minister . . . happen unopposed.** Interview with Rev. Seth Wispelwey, March 2, 2021.

287   **Smash realized . . . were on the same page.** Interview with Rev. Brittany Caine-Conley, May 6, 2022.

287   **Yet, whether they joined . . . bloc—that showed up.** Email from Tony Crider, February 23, 2024.

287   **Rev. Traci Blackmon . . . fight another day.** Interview with Willis Jenkins, March 15, 2023.

288   **Cornel West . . . to run his mouth.** Landers, *Charlottesville* [06:20].

288   **A white ordained . . . streets doomed them.** Interview with Dr. Jeffrey Pugh, September 13, 2020.

288   **Bekah Menning, the reluctant . . . faithful nonviolence.** Interview with Bekah Menning, September 28, 2019.

288   **Smith was the mother . . . to civil disobedience.** Interview with Ann Marie Smith, September 17, 2020.

288   **Raised as a Christian evangelical . . . theology at UVA.** Interview with Brandy Daniels, July 20, 2020.

289   **Eric Martin, the Catholic Worker . . . going to be there.** Interview with Eric Martin, August 5, 2020.

289   **Bee Lambert was a local atheist . . . to be arrested.** Interview with Bee Lambert, August 23, 2022.

289   **As they left First Baptist . . . "Violence and injury likely."** @JeffreyPugh, August 12, 2017, 7:37 a.m.

289   **Wes Bellamy, escorted from . . . were still needed.** Bellamy, *Monumental*, 159, 162, 167.

289   **They exchanged jokes . . . but Seth shushed them.** Interview with Eric Martin, August 5, 2020.

290   *Holy shit . . . saw the militias.* Interview with Dr. Jeff Pugh, September 13, 2020.

290   **They had been . . . the militias.** Interview with Eric Martin, August 5, 2020.

290   **Beth Foster from Chattanooga . . . "city," she said.** Interview with Beth Foster, August 4, 2023.

290   **Even the Virginia State Police . . . "armed than we are."** Heaphy report, 123.

290   **Thirty-two members . . . Charlottesville Police Department.** @JoeHeim August 12, 2017, 9:58 a.m.

290   **When questioned, they said . . . keep the peace.** @JoeHeim, August 12, 2017, 9:31 a.m.

290   **Rev. Sekou cut the tension . . . "supremacy in ourselves."** Sojourners Facebook video, "Clergy Marching in Silent Protest Through Charlottesville."

290   **"Is this every lesbian" . . . they were legitimate.** Defend Cville Livestream Periscope, August 12, 2017.

290   **Brandy Daniels was used to . . . joined them in song.** Interview with Brandy Daniels, July 20, 2020.

291   **Rev. Sekou would periodically . . . her heart pounding.** Interview with Rev. Brittany Caine-Conley, May 6, 2022.

292   **Every shuttle van . . . need for a police escort.** IFA Michael Chesny Deposition, 9.

292   **Like other warnings . . . of upper management.** Heaphy report, 88.

292   **Sgt. Newberry . . . purposely misled him.** Heaphy report, 124.

292   **Rousseau was the eighteen-year-old . . . Rousseau-engineered coup.** Merlan, "Leader of the Hate Group." ADL Patriot Front page, June 23, 2022.

293   **Among the events planned . . . the Jackson statue.** People's Action for Racial Justice handout.

293   **Kristopher Goad saw . . . the wrong park.** Interview with Kristopher Goad, July 19, 2021.

293   **The Vanguard America lines . . . started chanting.** IFA Exhibit #1985A, Video of Vanguard America and Elliott Kline marching; @_CraigStanley August 12, 2017, 9:38 a.m.

294   **Peterson had been at . . . out of people's eyes.** Neus, *24 Hours in Charlottesville*, 114.

294   **Reaching the southwest side . . . facing the clergy line.** Sojourners Facebook video, "Clergy Marching."

294   **Fields would soon . . . Texas entourage.** ADL Background "Patriot Front," December 15, 2017.

294   **Tarrio had first strolled . . . an air horn.** Tony Crider Facebook video, August 12, 2017, 9:47 a.m.; Tricorne Hat was later identified as Andrew Dodson. Patch O'Furr, "Charlottesville Marcher Linked to Furry Fandom and Neo-Nazi Organizing," March 20, 2018.

294   **In the clergy line . . . before going in.** Interview with Brandy Daniels, July 20, 2020.

294   **Just before 10:00 a.m., Tanesha . . . "them from happening."** Heaphy report, 125–26; interview with Tanesha Hudson, November 9, 2020.

295   **They were led by a willowy . . . viral Berkeley video.** Four of the nine were later identified by A. C. Thompson of ProPublica as Benjamin Daley (24), Michael Miselis (27), Cole Evan White (23), and Thomas Gillen (33). Brett Barrouquere, "Four Members of Rise Above Movement Indicted in Charlottesville, One Went

to Europe to Meet with White Supremacist Groups Before 'Unite the Right,'" October 11, 2018, SPLC.

295 **Near the First United Methodist . . . "that generated them."** Landers, *Charlottesville* [19:00].

295 **The Revolution Now . . . with a bloodied head.** Ézé Amos photograph, August 12, 2017, 10:18 a.m.

295 **The man's girlfriend . . . with a head butt.** Cole Evan White pled guilty to this at his trial.

295 **Both had . . . committed to nonviolence.** Interview with Beth Foster, August 4, 2023.

296 **Volunteers in the church . . . was set upon.** Ézé Amos photograph, August 12, 2017, 10:14 a.m.

296 **The unarmed forensic . . . stop to the attack.** Heaphy report, 127.

296 **Mosley retreated . . . to keep moving.** Ézé Amos's photographs of the attack at the FUMC parking lot are my source for this description. Tony Crider filmed their return to the park. Facebook, August 12, 2017, 10:17 a.m.

296 **"The Nazis just continued" . . . required twelve stitches.** Alana LaFlore, "Chattanooga Activists Say Charlottesville Rally Was 'the Worst Evil' They've Seen." ABC News, Channel 9, August 14, 2017.

296 **When a fifty-eight-year-old . . . liked the rallygoers.** Interview with Tim Messer, April 13, 2021.

296 **Five minutes after . . . "save their energy."** Heaphy report, 125, 128. Two years later, after being exposed by A. C. Thompson of ProPublica, the four men pled guilty to pushing, punching, kicking, choking, and headbutting as part of the riot charges against them. Their plea deal required them to admit that none of their actions could be defended by a claim of self-defense. A. C. Thompson, "Racist, Violent, Unpunished: A White Hate Group's Campaign of Menace," ProPublica, October 19, 2017; "Three Members of California-Based White Supremacist Group Sentenced on Riots Charges Related to August 2017 'Unite the Right' Rally in Charlottesville," press release, U.S. Attorney's Office, Western District of Virginia, July 19, 2019.

297 **Grace and the Puppetistas . . . "They were, like, 'wait . . . *what?*'"** Ézé Amos's photograph, August 12, 2017, 10:20 a.m.; interview with Grace Aheron and Rowan Hollins, September 9, 2020.

297 **Then, at 10:21 a.m. . . . . Carolina Anti-Racists.** Internet Archive, "A Cheer Goes Up along the Road from Unite the Right. The Anti-fascists Have Arrived, Unmasked, Chanting 'Alerta, alerta, antifascista!'"; Ford Fischer, "Streetwar: Charlottesville, a News2Share documentary," YouTube, August 12, 2017.

297 **Megan Squire marched . . . Committee.** Megan Squire Facebook post, August 14, 2017, 10:36 a.m.

297 **Among them . . . arriving rallygoers.** @Letsgomathias, August 12, 2017, 10:22 a.m.

297 **A multiracial . . . with the anti-fascists.** Interview with Kristopher Goad, July 19, 2021.

297 **Enrique Tarrio, standing ... "what I am."** Getty Images, "Proud Boys CEO Enrique Tarrio in Charlottesville Unite the Right Rally," August 12, 2017.

298 **When Rev. Sekou decided ... the public entrance.** Interview with Rev. Osagyefo Uhuru Sekou, December 15, 2022.

298 **Word came down ... to enter the park.** Interview with Rev. Brittany Caine-Conley, May 6, 2022.

298 **Such an action ... at the southwest entrance.** Interview with Rev. Seth Wispelwey, March 2, 2021.

298 **After confirming with ... at the jail.** Interview with Ann Marie Smith, September 17, 2020.

298 **But when the zone ... engaging with rallygoers.** Heaphy report, 129.

299 **Another carried the tube ... control of America.** IFA Exhibit #0542, Robert Azzmador Ray Discord Post. IFA Exhibit #0403, Robert Azzmador Ray Discord Post.

299 **Reaching Rev. Sekou ... front of the steps open.** Interview with Tony Crider and his Facebook comment. Interview with Ann Marie Smith, September 17, 2020, and Brandy Daniels, July 20, 2020.

300 **A Hispanic man ... taunting the anti-fascists.** Tony Crider Facebook video, August 12, 2017, 10:36 a.m.

300 **"You dress like a whore ... biding his time.** @C-villeWeekly, August 12, 2017, 10:43 a.m.

300 **Behind them all ... one hundred men.** Interview with Rev. Brittany Caine-Conley, May 6, 2022.

300 **Eric Martin's father ... go south quickly.** Interview with Eric Martin, August 5, 2020.

300 **"Forward march!" ... Azzmador behind them.** Tony Crider Facebook video, August 12, 2017, 10:36 a.m.

301 **Someone shouted, "Kill the faggot priest!"** Interview with Dr. Jeffrey Pugh, September 13, 2020; interview with Rev. Seth Wispelwey, March 2, 2021.

301 **Seth, facing the park ... struggled to his feet.** Interview with Rev. Seth Wispelwey, March 2, 2021.

301 **The clergy "opened" ... "for the rope."** IFA Exhibit #3805, Video of August 12, 2017; Robert Ray aka Azzmador August 12 livestream; @EmilyGorcenski, August 12, 2017.

301 **Beth Foster found ... men as "brother."** Interview with Beth Foster, August 4, 2023.

301 **While they were still ... she said crossly.** Interview with Rev. Brittany Caine-Conley, May 6, 2022.

301 **Bekah and Annie Marie ... "next time, right?"** Interview with Brandy Daniels, July 20, 2020.

301 **Smash wasn't so ... failed the community.** Interview with Rev. Brittany Caine-Conley, May 6, 2022.

301 **Later, she and Seth ... marchers through.** Interview with Rev. Seth Wispelwey, March 2, 2021; interview with Beth Foster, August 4, 2023.

301 **After the last of the . . . view of the street.** Interview with Brandy Daniels, July 20, 2020.

301 **But now the Wobblies . . . "Protect. Us. Instead."** @C-villeWeekly, August 12, 2017, 10:50 a.m.; Landers, *Charlottesville* [23:15]; Richmond Counterculture RVA YouTube, August 12, 2017, 10:30 a.m.

302 **"What are you doing? . . . letting them in."** Interview with Dr. Jeffrey Pugh, September 13, 2020; interview with Rev. Brittany Caine-Conley, May 6, 2022.

302 **Sekou told them . . . accepted their protection.** Interview with Rev. Osagyefo Uhuru Sekou, December 15, 2022; interview with Rev. Seth Wispelwey, March 2, 2021.

302 **Daryle Lamont Jenkins greeted . . . He ignored him.** Landers, *Charlottesville* [23:00].

302 **Eli Mosley . . . snuck in after him.** @letsgomathias, August 12, 2017, 10:46 a.m.

302 **"I love the smell of mace" . . . Spencer shouted.** Naternot, "I Love the Smell of Mace in the Morning," YouTube video, August 12, 2017.

302 **"Hail Spencer" . . . "burning poison ivy."** Red Mage, "Behind the Scenes Footage of 'Unite the Right' White Nationalist Rally in Charlottesville, VA," Part 10, YouTube.

303 **Matthew Heimbach of the . . . never got back to him.** Vegas Tenold, "The Cops Dropped the Ball in Charlottesville," *New Republic*, August 16, 2017.

303 **They all assembled . . . to take the park.** IFA Trial Transcript, Michael Tubbs testimony, November 8, 2021, 33.

304 **Tubbs, on the other hand . . . Jacksonville, Florida.** Kevin Knodell, "A Convicted Domestic Terrorist Was at the Charlottesville Nazi March," War Is Boring, August 15, 2017.

304 **A giant of a man . . . South shield wall.** @letsgomathias, August 12, 2017, 10:57 a.m.

304 **The League leadership appeared . . . TWP logo in white.** IFA Exhibit #587, Matthew Heimbach Discord Post.

305 **I counted over . . . Nationalist Front lines.** I am grateful to Shawn Breen for sharing "Unite the Right Rally Riot," August 12, 2017, and his collection of FOIA docs.

305 **David Duke . . . livestreamed on Periscope.** Hunter Wallace, "The Road to Charlottesville: Hunter Wallace edition," Occidental Dissent, August 31, 2017.

305 **No one noticed Emily . . . Southern anarchists.** Interview with Emily Gorcenski, February 5, 2020.

305 **After filing assault . . . following her on Periscope.** Emily Gorcenski, Periscope, August 12, 2017.

305 **At 10:50 a.m. Rev. Traci . . . on the steps.** MSNBC, "Pastor Pulled to Safety at Charlottesville's White Nationalist March," August 12, 2017, 10:52 a.m.

305 **"All right. Here comes . . . "We need more people!"** Tony Crider Facebook video, August 12, 2017, 10:51 a.m.

305 **The Seven Hill Autonomous . . . filled the air.** @letsgomathias, August 12, 2017, 10:57 a.m.

305 **Two and a half minutes . . . "gotta go."** MSNBC, "Pastor Pulled to Safety," August 12, 2017, 10:52 a.m.

306 **Bekah Menning would never . . . all that was evil.** Interview with Bekah Menning, December 5, 2019.

306 **Ann Marie Smith . . . had been a delusion.** Interview with Ann Marie Smith, September 17, 2020.

306 **Brandy Daniels's first thought . . . "Okay, here goes."** Interview with Brandy Daniels, July 20, 2020.

306 **The theologian Jeff . . . "get these guys."** Interview with Dr. Jeffrey Pugh, September 13, 2020.

306 **Tubbs hadn't hesitated . . . sent him sprawling.** @_CraigStanley, August 12, 2017, 10:56 a.m. "Clashes have started."

306 **Jeff Pugh heard . . . "Everyone disperse."** Interview with Dr. Jeffrey Pugh, September 13, 2020; interview with Brandy Daniels, July 20, 2020.

306 **The four Wobblies . . . up in front of them.** MSNBC, "Pastor Pulled to Safety."

306 **A second wave . . . whaling on each other.** Interview with Dr. Jeffrey Pugh, September 13, 2020.

306 **Counterprotesters launched . . . with blue paint.** Heim, "Recounting a Day of Rage, Hate, Violence and Death."

306 **Tony Crider, still . . . "cops have left."** Tony Crider Facebook video, August 12, 2017, 10:51 a.m.

306 **After a brief cutaway . . . he narrated.** MSNBC, "Pastor Pulled to Safety."

307 **Cornel West later credited . . . "like cockroaches."** "Antifa Rising: The Aftermath of Charlottesville." It's Going Down, August 25, 2017.

307 **During the first two minutes . . . his viral moment.** @xshulax, August 12, 2017, 11:12 a.m.

307 **She leaned away . . . out of her grip.** Internet Archive, "One of the First Fights at the Counterprotest vs. Nazi Rally in Charlottesville," August 12, 2017.

307 **She pursued him . . . she was surrounded.** Ézé Amos photographs, 10:52 a.m.

307 **More men set upon her . . . sticks and fists.** Jon Ziegler RebZ.tv Facebook video, August 12, 2017.

307 **One grabbed her hair . . . did she retreat.** IgnitetheRightUTR identified him as Jason Hunter from Jacksonville; Ford Fischer, "Raw Footage of the Violence on August 12, 2017, in Charlottesville," News2Share, August 12, 2017.

307 **Tony Crider later . . . calmly scrolling.** Tony Crider Facebook video, August 12, 2017, 11:00 a.m. [1:41].

308 **The Wobblies were pushed . . . forced off the steps.** Megan Squire Facebook post, August 14, 2017. Interview with Megan Squire, November 20, 2020. Megan Patten, "Charlottesville Didn't Want This." Times News, August 14, 2017.

308 **By 11:03 a.m. . . . sweep of the southeast steps.** Ézé Amos photographs and Tony Crider Facebook video, August 11, 2017, 11:00 a.m.

308 **For eleven minutes . . . without fighting back.** Patten, "Charlottesville Didn't Want This."

308 **A woman standing . . . "fuck are you doing?"** Heaphy report, 131.

309 **An MSNBC reporter . . . "in the distance."** MSNBC, "Pastor Pulled to Safety."

Chapter 14: A State of Emergency

311 **While listening to various . . . Bridge Arts Initiative.** Interview with Lisa Draine, December 18, 2022.

311 **Despite the beating . . . the porta potties.** IFA Trial Transcript, Devin Willis Testimony, October 29, 2021, 192–95.

311 **After her daughters . . . and noisemakers.** Interview with Lisa Draine, December 18, 2021.

312 **Some had been . . . instruments to carry.** IFA Trial Transcript, Devin Willis Testimony, October 29, 2021, 165–88; and November 17, 2021, 195.

312 **Then her daughters saw . . . as Sophie's mom.** Interview with Lisa Draine, December 18, 2021.

312 **Natalie Romero . . . where she came from.** IFA Trial Transcript, Natalie Romero Testimony, October 29, 2021, 33, 41–42.

312 **Just as the students . . . no officers inside it.** Heaphy report, 132–33.

313 **With the police gone . . . "Hold the line!"** Avery, "Charlottesville, VA, Unite the Right Rally," August 12, 2017 [1:43].

313 **In the bushes . . . "The fight begins."** Tony Crider Facebook video, August 12, 2017, 11:00 a.m.

313 **"It is getting more . . . more like it."** MSNBC, "Pastor Pulled to Safety."

314 **At 11:25 a.m. . . . Lisa followed him.** Tony Crider Facebook video, August 12, 2017, 11:24 a.m.

314 **Just as the Hiwaymen . . . sailed back.** Heaphy report, 133.

314 **As smoke clouds . . . "will be arrested."** Tony Crider Facebook video, August 12, 2017, 11:30 a.m.

314 **Jon Ziegler of . . . "Lives Matter," he added.** Jon Ziegler, RebZ.tv Facebook video, August 12, 2017.

314 **Lisa Draine didn't hear . . . over their mouths.** Interview with Lisa Draine, December 18, 2021; Tony Crider Facebook video, 11:30 a.m.

315 **Once the pepper . . . the ground.** IFA Trial Transcript, Devin Willis Testimony, October 29, 2021, 208.

315 **Lisa eventually found . . . lost her daughters.** Lisa Draine email, August 14, 2023.

315 **Before too long she got . . . on her own.** Interview with Lisa Draine, December 18, 2022.

315 **At twenty-three . . . woman at knifepoint.** Hatewatch, "White Supremacist William Fears to Get Five Years in Prison," SPLC, October 11, 2019.

316 **"Careful, careful" . . . of the shield wall.** Red Mage, "Behind the Scenes Footage of 'Unite the Right' White Nationalist Rally," Part 13, YouTube, August 12, 2017.

316 **Pepper spray cleared . . . "I'll shoot you."** Fischer, "Street War" [10:24].

317 **A man with a . . . "Fuck Fascism" banner.** Red Mage, "Behind the Scenes Footage of 'Unite the Right' White Nationalist rally," Part 15, YouTube, August 12, 2017.

317 **"Get out of our city!" . . . in their way.** Jon Ziegler, RebZ.tv Facebook video [53:15, 57:00]; Duerst the Wuerst, "#Antifa Vs. #AltRight," August 12, 2017 [8:09].

317   **The first man Tubbs . . . by counterprotesters.** IFA Trial Transcript, Michael Tubbs testimony, November 8, 2021, 40.

317   **The *C-ville Weekly* . . . as a prize.** Landers, *Charlottesville* [32:33].

317   **Imperial Wizard . . . "these fucking faggots."** Avery, "Charlottesville, VA Unite the Right Rally/Bottles Flying," August 12, 2017 [1:41]; Red Mage, "Behind the Scenes Footage of 'Unite the Right' White Nationalist Rally," Part 16. YouTube, August 12, 2017; Landers, *Charlottesville* [41:25].

317   **Bee Lambert retreated . . . "powerful shit."** Jon Ziegler, RebZ.tv, Periscope, August 12, 2017.

317   **Daryle Lamont Jenkins . . . foot of the steps.** Duerst the Wuerst, "#Charlottesville #UniteTheRight Stream #2," YouTube, August 12, 2017.

317   **Jenkins later . . . of the violence.** Interview with Daryle Lamont Jenkins, August 15, 2021.

317   **The militias had mysteriously . . . the southeast steps.** Avery, "Charlottesville, VA, Unite the Right Rally," YouTube, August 12, 2017; Landers, *Charlottesville* [39:05].

318   **Apart from the four- . . . their adversaries were.** Interview with Daryle Lamont Jenkins, August 15, 2021.

318   **A heavily armored man . . . by Texas anti-fascists.** Reply to @letsgomathias, August 12, 2017, 9:45 a.m.; @seeshoItz August 12, 2017, 4:01 p.m. Identified as Christopher Ritchie from Austin, Texas, by IgnitetheRightUTR.net.

318   **As he lay sprawled . . . "I promise you that."** @JackSmithIV, August 12, 2017. Twitter account since removed.

318   **After showing a clip . . . "not going anywhere."** @RichardBSpencer, August 12, 2017, 11:37 a.m.

319   **Eli Mosley was darting . . . already left.** IFA Exhibit #2538, Video of August 12, 2017, 2:34–3:29; Evan Nesterak, "Before Police Clear Emancipation Park in Charlottesville," YouTube, August 12, 2017; Heaphy report, 191.

319   **Thomas Rousseau . . . association with Fields.** ADL Background "Patriot Front," December 15, 2017.

319   **Close behind Rousseau . . . on their heels.** Ézé Amos photographs, 11:41 a.m.; 11:43 a.m.; 11:44 a.m.; 11:48 a.m.; 11:51 a.m.

320   **During the standoff . . . unflappable self-assurance.** Ford Fischer, "Street War" [12:11].

320   **"This is where" . . . written on it.** Daniel Borden, https://www.cnn.com/2019/01/08/us/charlottesville-racial-beating-sentencing/index.html.

320   **One megaphone bleated . . . of the race war.** Blake Montgomery @BuzzFeedNews Periscope [12:40].

320   **The Tactical Field Force . . . "I'm scared!"** Red Mage, "Behind the Scenes Footage of 'Unite the right' White Nationalist Rally," Part 16 [07:26–09:08]; Landers, *Charlottesville* [41:25].

321   **"You are pushing" . . . to the police.** Heaphy report, 135.

321   **At 11:52 a.m. . . . He looked lost.** Yesha Callahan, "How Corey Long Fought White Supremacy with Fire," The Root, August 14, 2017.

321   **As a Virginia Klansman . . . the paint can.** IgnitetheRightUTR identified him

as Scott "Woodsy" Woods from Glasgow, Virginia. Murfreesboro Anti-Fascist Action, "Akia Woods: A Confederate 'White Knight,'" September 29, 2019.

321 **Preston, who had circled . . . into the ground.** IBTimes UK, "Video Shows Man Firing in to Crowd in Charlottesville," YouTube, August 12, 2017.

321 **A former Charlottesville . . . to arrest him.** Interview with Frank Buck, November 11, 2019; Frances Robles, "As White Nationalist in Charlottesville Fired, Police 'Never Moved,'" *New York Times*, August 25, 2017.

321 **In a criminal complaint . . . "Kill that nigger."** Criminal complaint filed August 12, 2017, by former mayor Frank Buck.

322 **The BuzzFeed News . . . "highly unusual."** Blake Montgomery, "Here's What Really Happened in Charlottesville," BuzzFeed News, August 13, 2017.

322 **"You wanna know what . . . right?" Couric asked.** Jon Ziegler, RebZ.tv, August 12, 2017 [1:11–1:29].

323 **Meanwhile, the men in . . . down the steps.** Red Mage, "Behind the Scenes Footage of 'Unite the Right' White Nationalist Rally," Part 15; Landers, *Charlottesville* [50:45, 53:19].

323 **The departing fascists . . . with raised fists.** @JackSmithIV, August 12, 2017 [:30]. Twitter video since removed.

324 **Another Black man . . . intended for children.** @JDeanSeal, August 12, 2017, 11:58 a.m.

324 **"We're Charlottesville . . . out of our town."** Caris Adel, "Charlottesville: An Experience in Five Parts."

324 **Clare Ruday, in a purple . . . kicked it back.** Interview with Clare Ruday, December 9, 2021; Landers, *Charlottesville* [55:21].

324 **Grace Aheron . . . and came back.** Interview with Grace Aheron and Rowan Hollins, September 2, 2020.

325 **Suddenly, there was . . . rushed past.** Montgomery, "Here's What Really Happened in Charlottesville," BuzzFeed News, August 14, 2017.

325 **Instead, he used . . . straight past them up Market.** Red Mage, "Behind the Scenes Footage of 'Unite the Right' White Nationalist Rally," Part 16 [19:32].

326 **The "Kill. All. Nazis." black bloc woman . . . man in chains.** Styrofoam inthesea Turtles, "Charlottesville Unite the Right Rally Charlottesville VA," YouTube, August 12, 2017.

326 **The sight of the rallygoers . . . and ended there.** Ford Fischer, "Street War" [14:10].

326 **At the top of the southeast . . . never did manage to get arrested.** Red Mage, "Behind the Scenes Footage of 'Unite the Right' White Nationalist Rally," Part 16; interview with Bee Lambert, August 23, 2022.

326 **Lining the sidewalk . . . "do something."** Duerst the Worst #BLM Vs #AltRight Parking Garage Battle (BRUTAL!) #Charlottesville #UniteTheRight [4:13; 5:04].

326 **After leaving the steps . . . "We fucked up."** Interview with Eric Martin, August 5, 2020.

326 **They went to a . . . call to make.** Interview with Rev. Osagyefo Uhuru Sekou, December 15, 2022.

327 **After venting her feelings . . . Smash was in charge.** Interview with Eric Martin, August 5, 2020.

327 **They left the café . . . break up one fight.** Interview with Rev. Seth Wispelwey, March 2, 2021.

327 **"I think people" . . . Smash said simply.** Interview with Rev. Brittany Caine-Conley, May 6, 2022.

327 **The clergy lined up . . . to McIntire Road.** @JackSmithIV. Tweet has since been deleted.

327 **Then, when a line . . . to McGuffey Park.** Jack Smith IV, "We're Live Reporting from the 'Unite the Right' Rally in Charlottesville, VA, Where a Local State of Emergency Has Just been Declared," Facebook video, August 12, 2017 [02:00]; Styrofoam inthesea Turtles, "Charlottesville Unite the Right Rally."

327 **On Fourth Street NE . . . to stand down.** Heaphy report, 162.

327 **Passing her . . . rising dramatic action.** Red Mage, "Behind the Scenes" Part 19, YouTube [16:02–22:26].

328 **DeAndre Harris . . . up Market.** Red Mage, "Behind the Scenes Footage of 'Unite the Right' White Nationalist Rally," Part 19 [16:02–21:26]; David S. Cloud, "Hip-hop Artist Recalls His Beating in Charlottesville: 'They were trying to kill me out there,'" *Los Angeles Times*, August 13, 2017.

328 **Upon reaching . . . over the flag ensued.** Hawes Spencer and Matt Stevens, "Charlottesville Counterprotester Who Ignited Spray Can Is Charged," *New York Times*, October 16, 2017. The name of the League of the South family lawyer is Harold Ray Crews. Also, Blake Montgomery, "The KKK, neo-Nazis, and Other Hate Groups Are in Charlottesville for the Unite the Right Rally," BuzzFeed News, Periscope, August 12, 2017 [28:51].

328 **The *New York Daily News* journalist . . . tried to stop it.** @ChuckModi1, August 12, 2017, 12:35 p.m.

328 **One hit him . . . with a wooden tire thumper.** This was Tyler Watkins Davis. Samantha Baars, "Last Man in August 12th Parking Garage Beating Pleads Guilty." *C-ville Weekly*, February 12, 2019; also Brett Barrouquere, "League of the South Member Tyler Watkins Davis Arrested in Florida, Charged with Charlottesville Beating," SPLC, January 26, 2018.

328 **The Proud Boys were . . . Order of Alt-Knights.** This was Alex Michael Ramos. Brett Barrouquere, "Jacob Scott Goodwin, Alex Michael Ramos Sentenced to State Prison in Beating of DeAndre Harris," SPLC, August 24, 2018.

329 **The teenager in . . . high school classmates.** This was Daniel Borden, from Huber Heights, Ohio.

329 **Another, yet to be . . . in the standoff.** Molly Conger @socialistdogmom covered the trials of DeAndre Harris's attackers and is still on the hunt for the final two attackers. @socialistdogmom, February 14, 2023; @splcenter, April 9, 2018.

329 **The seventh man . . . four years later.** This was Ted Nukem, identified by Molly Conger. Timothy Bella, "Unite the Right Marcher Captured in Viral Photo Dies by Suicide before Trial," *Washington Post*, February 15, 2023.

329 **A city sheriff witnessed . . . taken shelter.** Heaphy report, 138.

329   **While the Harris attack . . . in front of the police station.** Montgomery, "The KKK, neo-Nazis, and Other Hate Groups"; Landers, *Charlottesville* [1:02.14]; Molly Conger identified this man as Emerson Randolph Williams, a former teacher who creates historically suspect instructional videos for homeschooled children and anti-Semitic memes.

329   **Crews . . . by DeAndre Harris.** Spencer and Stevens, "Charlottesville Counterprotester Who Ignited Spray Can Is Charged," *New York Times*, October 16, 2017.

329   **While Tubbs and his men . . . "get to the front!"** Red Mage, "Behind the Scenes," Part 15.

330   **Blake Montgomery, a reporter . . . go unchallenged.** Montgomery, "The KKK, neo-Nazis, and Other Hate Groups" [54:55].

330   **At 1:08 p.m . . . shared at McGuffey.** WTJU, August 12, 2017, 1:08 p.m. Update from McGuffey Park. Courtesy of Nathan Moore.

330   **There was a sense . . . the activists had won.** Interview with Lisa Draine, December 18, 2022.

331   **Seth Wispelwey . . . peanut butter sandwich.** Interview with Rev. Seth Wispelwey, March 2, 2021.

331   **The DJ was playing reggae . . . coming on.** WTJU, August 12, 2017, 1:08 p.m.

331   **Elizabeth Sines, the law . . . "at the end of the world."** Maggie Mallon, "Elizabeth Sines and Leanne Chia Were in Charlottesville When White Supremacists Descended," *Glamour*, August 18, 2017.

331   **Emily introduced herself . . . later press charges.** Interview with Kristopher Goad, July 19, 2021.

331   **The governor's declaration . . . "there, are you?"** Interview with Clare Ruday, December 9, 2021.

331   **Natalie Romero . . . on the swings.** IFA Trial Transcript, Cross of Natalie Romero, 136.

331   **When Lisa went . . . she was tired.** Interview with Lisa Draine, December 18, 2021.

331   **Unbeknownst to any . . . "put that radio down."** McAuliffe, *Beyond Charlottesville*, 93; Landers, *Charlottesville* [45:00].

332   **Before the VIP after-party . . . "heads are going to spin."** IFA Exhibit #2527, Video Richard Spencer, August 12, 2017.

Chapter 15: The Dodge Challenger

333   **Heather's mother was . . . with that name.** McAuliffe, *Beyond Charlottesville*, 100.

333   **Twenty minutes after . . . the car attack.** Katy Brandt and William Clarke, FUMC Storycorps.org, February 16, 2018 [08:39].

333   **Though Rev. Phil Woodson . . . turned it in.** Interview with Rev. Phil Woodson, May 10, 2021. Susan Bro said the person who answered the phone said it had been found on the sidewalk.

334   **Like a metal baseball . . . Elizabeth Sines said.** IFA Trial Transcript, Elizabeth Sines Testimony, November 12, 2021, 66.

334   **It wasn't a crash . . . in front of it.** Interview with Emily Gorcenski, February 6, 2020.

334   **Because so many . . . sound of a helicopter.** IFA Trial Transcript, April Muniz Testimony, November 11, 2021, 226–27.

334   **The smell of citronella or burnt rubber.** Emily Gorcenski, "The Relentlessness of Trauma," blog, December 30, 2021.

334   **The incantatory rhythm . . . "Replace Us!"** IFA Trial Transcript, Natalie Romero Testimony, October 29, 2021, 23.

334   **A witness to . . . eventually let go.** IFA Trial Transcript, April Muniz Testimony, November 11, 2021, 231.

334   **There are the outbursts . . . again and again.** IFA Trial Transcript, Marcus Martin Testimony, November 10, 2021, 27.

334   **The incandescent fury . . . of complicity.** Gorcenski, "The Relentlessness of Trauma."

334   **For church members . . . on the streets.** Brandt and Clarke, FUMC Storycorps .org.

335   **Heather explained . . . but solidarity.** Gail Sheehy, "What Heather Heyer Knew," The Cut, *New York*, August 31, 2017; McAuliffe, *Beyond Charlottesville*, 80–81.

335   **An hour before . . . toward their cars.** Styrofoam inthesea Turtles, "Charlottesville Unite the Right Rally."

336   **In their words . . . "being infringed upon."** Heaphy report, 140. Heaphy calls this militia American Revolutionary Warrior. They have since disbanded.

336   **Several Threepers . . . January 6 insurrection.** Mark Hosenball and Jan Wolfe, "Three Percenters Charged in Capitol Attack," Reuters, June 10, 2021.

336   **After crossing over . . . They didn't stop.** Heaphy report, 141. Relying on the militia's own livestream, the Heaphy report held that the militia did not realize they had stopped near an African American housing complex. In this video they were told numerous times where they were headed. Styrofoam inthesea Turtles, "Charlottesville Unite the Right Rally."

336   **Back at McGuffey . . . for more details.** Interview with Emily Gorcenski, February 6, 2020.

336   **Star Peterson wanted . . . right away.** Neus, *24 Hours in Charlottesville*, 209.

336   **Kristopher Goad felt . . . needed numbers.** Interview with Kristopher Goad, July 19, 2021.

337   **With a neat auburn . . . back to their cars.** Styrofoam inthesea Turtles, "Charlottesville Unite the Right Rally" [05:28].

337   **Reaching the parking . . . "a good argument."** Sheehy, "What Heather Heyer Knew." Courtney Commander's August 12 footage was included in the Investigation Discovery documentary *Impact of Hate: Charlottesville.*

337   **An older woman . . . on South First Street.** Fischer, "Street War" [14:29].

337   **Marcus was on . . . of trouble.** IFA Trial Transcript, Marissa Blair Testimony, November 8, 2021, 64–65.

338   **Word of rocks . . . very hot, he said.** Interview with Rev. Seth Wispelwey, March 2, 2021.

338 **Heather returned . . . and disappeared.** Skyclad drone footage.

338 **Nikuyah Walker . . . "We will leave."** Ford Fischer, News2Share, "Militiamen Administer First Aid in Charlottesville, Try to Separate Opposing Sides," YouTube, August 12, 2017 [03:10].

338 **Even after Walker . . . as he left.** Heaphy report, 142; @JDeanSeal, August 12, 2017, 12:29 p.m.

338 **To Emily Gorcenski's chagrin . . . counterprotesters.** Interview with Emily Gorcenski, February 6, 2020.

339 **Continuing his livestream . . . traffic light.** Ford Fischer, "Street War" [16:00].

339 **"So this is the scene . . . counterprotesters and media."** Jon Ziegler, RebZ.tv Periscope, August 12, 2017 [03:07–07:00].

339 **At 1:20 p.m. . . . with the same intention.** Heaphy report, 192.

339 **Seeing the McGuffey Park . . . for her job.** IFA Trial Transcript, Marissa Blair testimony, November 8, 2021, 68.

340 **Squire was just following . . . wherever they took her.** Megan Squire Facebook post, August 14, 2017.

340 **For Emily . . . "Everything was fine."** Interview with Emily Gorcenski, February 6, 2020.

340 **"Looks like a large" . . . "wants to drink a beer!"** Jon Ziegler, RebZ.tv Periscope, August 12, 2017 [03:07-07:00].

340 **Katrina Turner . . . so she relented.** Interview with Katrina Turner, June 17, 2021.

340 **Niya Bates . . . livestream went crazy.** Interview with Niya Bates, July 15, 2020.

341 **James Alex Fields . . . back to Market.** This is speculation on my part; Tenth Street is the first turnaround point.

341 **Fields drove down Fourth Street SE . . . which way to go.** Based on the surveillance video of Red Pump Kitchen and "Fields Water Street—4th St View from Slightly Elevated Position 'Black Lives Matter' and Car Impact." Courtesy of Shawn Breen. Exhibit at James Alex Field's trial.

341 **Marcus Martin, whose . . . in front of Courtney.** Full Marissa Blair video, "Fields Street View Heather Heyer's Back, 'Marcus!'" Courtesy of Shawn Breen. IFA Exhibit #0297, clip of video recording of Marissa Blair video.

342 **Tiny Natalie Romero . . . when she was hit.** IFA Trial Transcript, Natalie Romero Testimony, October 29, 2021, 50.

342 **Then he was hit . . . ankle shattered.** IFA Trial Transcript, Marcus Martin testimony, November 10, 2021, 19.

342 **A frame in the series . . . front of Marcus.** IFA Exhibit #287, Photo of August 12, 2017. Some of the stills are also in the video link in Madison Park, "Couple Who Survived Charlottesville Car Attack Get Married," cnn.com, May 15, 2018.

342 **Rebecca saw the car . . . behind the Toyota truck.** Interview with Lisa Draine, December 18, 2021. "Fields 4th St Crash from Side, Slowed Down Marcus on Ground Screaming." Courtesy of Shawn Breen.

342 **The activist and medic . . . back broken.** Farah Stockman, "In Charlottesville Murder Trial, Courtroom Relives Trauma of a Violent Day," *New York Times*, December 5, 2018.

343   **That was . . . people as possible.** IFA Trial Transcript, Elizabeth Sines testimony, November 12, 2021, 66.

343   **Had Natalie not . . . run over her.** IFA Trial Transcript, Natalie Romero Testimony, October 29, 2021, 50.

343   **Sophie narrowly escaped that fate.** Interview with Lisa Draine, December 18, 2021.

343   **A Richmond activist . . . knocking her unconscious.** Erin Cramer, *Impact of Hate: Charlottesville*, documentary; Neus, *24 Hours in Charlottesville*, 222.

343   **When Fields's reversing . . . he was gone.** IFA Exhibit #0236, Photo of August 12, 2017.

343   **Marissa's hands were . . . where Heather was.** IFA Trial Transcript, Marissa Blair Testimony, November 8, 2021, 71–73.

343   **Natalie Romero was . . . in the ambulance.** IFA Trial Transcript, Natalie Romero Testimony, October 29, 2021, 51.

343   **Someone pushed Katrina . . . Rosia and Timmy.** Interview with Katrina Turner, June 17, 2021.

344   **Clare Ruday was . . . some painkillers.** Interview with Clare Ruday, December 9, 2021.

344   **Emily Gorcenski had been . . . "what to do."** Interview with Emily Gorcenski, February 6, 2020.

344   **When Rebecca found . . . a gun at them.** Interview with Lisa Draine, December 18, 2021.

344   **Clare saw a Black . . . she was okay.** Interview with Clare Ruday, December 9, 2021.

345   **The early toll . . . another ten.** Spencer, *Summer of Hate*, 8.

345   **Later this was . . . to come forward.** Fields hearing, based on medical records at UVA and Martha Jefferson hospitals. Paul Duggan, "Charge Upgraded to First-Degree Murder for Driver Accused of Ramming Charlottesville Crowd," *Washington Post*, December 14, 2017.

345   **Katrina's son . . . what happened.** Interview with Katrina Turner, June 17, 2021.

345   **"They just literally . . . revive somebody."** Vice News, "Charlottesville: Race and Terror" [12:40].

346   **When the clergy got back . . . siren going.** Interview with Andy Stepanian, March 26, 2021; interview with Rev. Seth Wispelwey, March 2, 2021.

346   **The first thing Andy . . . has never returned.** Interview with Andy Stepanian, March 26, 2021.

347   **Just as Seth . . . in her arms.** Interview with Rev. Seth Wispelwey, March 2, 2021.

347   **Clare hadn't been . . . saw Heather's face.** Interview with Clare Ruday, December 9, 2021; Neus, *24 Hours in Charlottesville*, 232.

347   **Beth Foster from . . . "Stuff like that. Yeah."** Interview with Beth Foster, August 4, 2023.

348   **Lisa Draine hadn't been . . . to her daughters.** Interview with Lisa Draine, December 18, 2021.

349 **Pastor Brenda . . . online threats.** Interview with Rev. Phil Woodson, May 10, 2021.

349 **In Fellowship Hall . . . they were safe.** Interview with Jenny Phillips, April 19, 2021.

349 **Those stationed in . . . the car attack.** Interview with Rev. Phil Woodson, May 10, 2021.

349 **Apostle Sarah was glad . . . like that.** Interview with Apostle Sarah Kelley, November 11, 2021.

349 **Certified trauma . . . began howling.** IFA Trial Transcript, April Muniz Testimony, November 11, 2021, 224.

350 **To this day . . . the woman's grief.** Interview with Apostle Sarah Kelley, November 11, 2021.

350 **Pickup trucks . . . "Lockdown!"** FUMC Storycorps.org, Katy Brandt and William Clarke, February 16, 2018.

350 **Kristopher Goad remembers . . . sprinting with them.** Interview with Kristopher Goad, July 19, 2021.

350 **Rabbi Tom Gutherz . . . shawl and kippah.** Interview with Rev. Phil Woodson, May 10, 2021.

350 **From the portico . . . his synagogue.** Interview with Rabbi Tom Gutherz, June 18, 2021.

351 **Tyler Magill stalked . . . through the bushes.** Interview with Tyler Magill, August 2, 2021.

351 **On September 30 . . . Brandon, Florida.** Email from Rev. Steve Johnson, June 7, 2022.

351 **The phone at First . . . white people in.** Interview with Rev. Phil Woodson, May 10, 2021.

351 **Someone on a far-right . . . "or a boxcar?"** Interview with Rabbi Tom Gutherz, June 18, 2021.

351 **All this made it . . . drive them around.** Interview with Rev. Phil Woodson, May 10, 2021.

352 **The two white . . . in the dark.** @RichardBSpencer, "Back in Charlottesville," Periscope, October 7, 2017.

352 **Some went over . . . weren't alone.** Interview with Rabbi Tom Gutherz, June 18, 2021.

352 **"We came, we triggered . . . the *Times* crew.** Cott and Ellis, "How an Alt Right Leader Lied."

352 **At 8:11 p.m. . . . on Twitter.** @RichardBSpencer, October 7, 2017, 8:11 p.m.

353 **Before the end . . . as a private citizen.** Laura Bassett, "Richard Spencer Listed Himself on Bumble as Politically 'Moderate.'" Jezebel, June 14, 2022.

353 **He dismissed the events . . . as "yesteryear."** "Responding to a Non-Story in the New York Times," Odysee, September 5, 2021.

353 **Then, toward the end . . . as a child.** @RichardBSpencer tweet, November 7, 2018.

353 **In a podcast . . . anti-Jewish sentiment.** @RichardBSpencer, "My Interview with Nicholas Fuentes, with @MarkBrahmin and Others," November 30, 2023.

353   **Jason Kessler . . . Peinovich were all-in.** Judy Maltz, "How White Supremacists from Charlottesville Rally Are Finding Common Cause with Hamas," *Haaretz*, December 21, 2023.

353   **On August 12, 2017 . . . "the fucking world works."** Jane Coaston, "Audio Tape Reveals Richard Spencer Is, as Everyone Knew, a Racist," Vox, November 4, 2019.

Epilogue

355   **His conclusions were . . . after the rally.** Heaphy report, 10, 16, 112–15, 157. Heaphy stated that Gibson's response was "fragmented and disorganized." Virginia state agencies' responses to Heaphy's FOIA requests were limited. I tried for a long time to gain access to the archive Heaphy amassed in the course of his work for the City of Charlottesville. The city's FOIA officer first told me he did not have it or know where it was. When I located the archive housed in an electronic storage company (for which the city paid a monthly rental fee), I was told that to access it, store it, and redact it would cost me over $20,000. So I created my own archive.

355   **Instead, McAuliffe . . . Klan rally wrong.** McAuliffe, *Beyond Charlottesville*, 65, 142.

356   **For those activists . . . come from the activists.** Heaphy report, 81.

356   **During the trial . . . "motherfuckers."** Interview with Lisa Draine, December 18, 2021.

356   **A photograph of thousands . . . thrown to the wolves.** O'Hare, "Standing Together."

356   **When Wendy Baucom . . . on August 11.** Interview with Wendy Baucom, April 11, 2023.

356   **No one in UVA's . . . how she was.** "August 11 survivors demand justice." Facebook, May 21, 2018.

356   **For a period . . . drop-kicked her.** A. C. Thompson, "A New Generation of White Supremacists Emerges in Charlottesville," ProPublica, August 13, 2017.

357   **After a Twitter . . . she was swatted.** Sam Levin, "The Data Scientist Exposing US White Supremacists: 'This Is How You Fight Nazis,'" *Guardian*, October 1, 2020.

357   **She eventually . . . in his sights.** "Neo-Nazi Group 'Atomwaffen Division' Spreads Fear in Germany," *Der Spiegel*, November 13, 2019.

357   **Conger sat through . . . found him.** @socialistdogmom, February 14, 2023.

357   **In December 2023 . . . groups in Europe.** Ellie Quinlan Houghtaling, "Missouri GOP Candidate: It's OK, I'm Only an 'Honorary' KKK Member," *New Republic*, February 29, 2014; @socialistdogmom, December 2, 2023.

358   **Self-taught . . . "you can do this."** Aaron Gell, "Anti-fascists Are Waging a Cyber War—and They're Winning," Medium, September 9, 2019; Conger isn't the only local undertaking this work. A week after August 12, Rev. Steven Johnson came across two men flying Confederate flags by the side of the road outside Ruckersville, just north of Charlottesville. He stopped his car and told them

that Heather Heyer's family lived nearby, and their display was in poor taste. They didn't see it that way. After January 6 Johnson, a white Southern Baptist, became a "sedition hunter," working off FBI lists, photographs, and video streams to identify January 6 insurrectionists.

358   **"Life is trying . . . an ivory tower."** Notes from phone conversation with Megan Squire, November 17, 2020; email follow-up, December 18, 2020.

358   **Squire is now . . . million distributed.** Hatewatch, "Extremists Crypto and Finance."

358   **"I keep hoping . . . Everywhere is Charlottesville."** Interview with Dr. Jeffrey Pugh, September 13, 2020.

359   **A Black photographer . . . they were that day.** Cheuk, *Standing Up to Hate*, 38–39.

359   **Covering the protests . . . Richmond jail.** U.S. Press Freedom Tracker, July 26, 2020.

359   **Kristopher Goad . . . several times.** Will Gonzalez, "The Great Gatsby," RVA Mag, December 10, 2020.

360   **Tweeting a photograph . . . open the view.** @socialistdogmom, July 10, 2021.

360   **That fall . . . they want to see.** Jefferson School African American Heritage Center, "Confederate Statues Offer: Robert E. Lee Statue."

360   **Like the 2016 vote . . . ole boy diehards.** Website, *The Monument Fund: Preserving and Defending Our Historic Monuments and Memorials*.

360   **When Jalane Schmidt . . . sued for defamation.** Hannah Natanson, "A Newspaper Reported That a Man's Ancestors Were Slaveholders. He's Suing for Defamation," *Washington Post*, September 25, 2019.

360   **On October 21 . . . Lisa Draine.** Teo Armus and Hadley Green, "Charlottesville's Lee Statue Meets Its End, in a 2,250-Degree Furnace," *Washington Post*, October 26, 2023.

361   **A tiny pro-Palestine . . . a bitter moment.** Jonathan M. Katz, "When the Hammer Came Down at UVA," Theracketnews.com, May 7, 2024.

362   **The mainstream media . . . will ever happen.** Interview with Kristopher Goad, July 19, 2021.

INDEX

DEBORAH BAKER's books have been finalists for the Pulitzer Prize in Biography and the National Book Award in Nonfiction. She has been the recipient of a Guggenheim fellowship and a Whiting Creative Nonfiction Grant, and she is a former Fellow at the Cullman Center for Scholars and Writers at the New York Public Library. Her previous book, *The Last Englishmen: Love, War, and the End of Empire*, is set in London, Calcutta, and the Himalaya and takes place in the years leading up to Indian Independence. She lives in Brooklyn and Charlottesville.

Graywolf Press publishes risk-taking, visionary writers who transform culture through literature. As a nonprofit organization, Graywolf relies on the generous support of its donors to bring books like this one into the world.

This publication is made possible, in part, by the voters of Minnesota through a Minnesota State Arts Board Operating Support grant, thanks to a legislative appropriation from the arts and cultural heritage fund. Significant support has also been provided by the National Endowment for the Arts and other generous contributions from foundations, corporations, and individuals. To these supporters we offer our heartfelt thanks.

To learn more about Graywolf's books
and authors or make a tax-deductible donation,
please visit www.graywolfpress.org.

The text of *Charlottesville* is set in Adobe Caslon Pro.
Book design by Rachel Holscher.
Composition by Bookmobile Design & Digital
Publisher Services, Minneapolis, Minnesota.
Manufactured by Friesens on acid-free,
100 percent postconsumer wastepaper.